MUSEUM EXHIBITION PLANNING AND DESIGN

MUSEUM EXHIBITION PLANNING AND DESIGN

Elizabeth Bogle

A Division of Rowman & Littlefield Publishers, Inc.
Lanham • New York • Toronto • Plymouth, UK

Published by AltaMira Press
A division of Rowman & Littlefield Publishers, Inc.
A wholly owned subsidiary of The Rowman & Littlefield Publishing Group, Inc.
4501 Forbes Boulevard, Suite 200, Lanham, Maryland 20706
www.rowman.com

10 Thornbury Road, Plymouth PL6 7PP, United Kingdom

British Library Cataloguing in Publication Information Available

Library of Congress Cataloging-in-Publication Data

Bogle, Elizabeth.
Museum exhibition planning and design / Elizabeth Bogle.
pages cm
Includes index.
ISBN 978-0-7591-2229-1 (cloth : alk. paper) — ISBN 978-0-7591-2230-7 (pbk. : alk. paper) — ISBN 978-0-7591-2231-4 (ebook)
1. Museum exhibits—Planning. 2. Museum buildings--Designs and plans. I. Title.
AM151.B64 2013
069'.5—dc23

2013005586

∞™ The paper used in this publication meets the minimum requirements of American National Standard for Information Sciences—Permanence of Paper for Printed Library Materials, ANSI/NISO Z39.48-1992.

Printed in the United States of America

John F. Larkin

Contents

List of Figures

Foreword

The task of developing and designing an exhibition is fraught with potential traps and pitfalls, and even the experienced professional may fall into them while completing the complex, demanding task. The planning/designing of exhibitions resembles many other disciplines in the arts and draws from them. An architect, a product designer, a graphic designer, a fine artist, and an engineer (and, possibly, a contract lawyer) all play roles, and frequently all these roles must be played by one person, the exhibition planner/designer.

Elizabeth Bogle has had a long and distinguished career as an exhibition planner/designer, and as a professor of graduate studies in the University of the Arts' graduate program in Museum Exhibition Planning and Design. Each chapter in this book could serve as a primer for its area of professional practice, distilling and clarifying a bewildering range of necessary information. Bogle successfully and succinctly addresses the conceptual, intellectual, aesthetic, and technical aspects of exhibition development as it is now practiced.

For the solo practitioner perhaps working with limited or no staff in a relatively small institution, *Museum Exhibition Planning and Design* offers guideposts to every task that will be faced as the project develops. For the staff member of a larger institution or firm, this book will serve as a checklist, reinforcing the instruction that comes from peers and previous experience.

In the period when Bogle and I prepared for a career in planning and designing exhibitions, no specialized training was available, and the professional had to rely on personal experience (with a liberal dose of common sense) to succeed. This forced upon us careful analytical thought as we proceeded through the process. Many current professionals have a similar absence of training in the necessary skills, and even the trained exhibition planner / designer frequently needs reminders of "best practice" rules when facing a new challenge.

I can only thank Bogle for producing this very useful labor of love and recommend that anyone addressing the task of developing and designing an exhibition utilize her wisdom.

Jane Bedno
founding director, graduate program in
Museum Exhibition Planning and Design;
cofounding chair, Graduate Museum Studies; and
professor emerita, University of the Arts

Acknowledgments

In writing this book I have been fortunate in having the help of many talented people. In particular I want to thank John Larkin whose knowledge and professionalism provided me with the valuable advice and support that I needed; without his help this book would not have been possible. I send a special thanks to Eileen Wisman who was relentless in finding me the elusive images that I so needed. I also want to thank William J. Barker Jr., Jane and Ed Bedno, Stacey Costantino, David M. Egner, Dennis Gerhart, Mitch Gilbert, Aaron Goldblatt, Micki Kind, Michael Meister, Lydia Romero, Alex Navissi, and Brian and Laura Wisman.

Introduction

> Functional designs can emerge either from nature or from the minds of people, but visual designs, strictly speaking, are considered to be the deliberate creative acts of men and women.
>
> —*Design through Discovery*, Marjorie Elliott Bevlin

It is a widely held belief that the act of planning/designing exhibits for a museum is a simple and intuitive process. It is not! Rather, it is a complicated and multifaceted procedure based on well-founded technical knowledge and an awareness of good design theories and principles.

When writing *Museum Exhibition Planning and Design* I focused on providing the information that museums or other institutions would need to produce well-designed, quality exhibits. This book discusses all aspects of the planning/designing, production, and contractual issues that a professional designer encounters and solves during the concept-to-reality exhibit process, including the following:

- Procedures that are required to ensure a project will run smoothly and be on time and on budget
- Tasks and issues encountered during each phase of the work and their resolution
- Elements involved in producing a well-designed, visually harmonious exhibit
- Criteria used to evaluate an exhibit and measure its success
- Design and development project phases used by professional planners/designers
- Principles of good design as they pertain to color, light, shape, form, space, line, balance, accent, rhythm, proportion, and scale

- Visitors' psychological and physiological reactions to the exhibition and its environment
- Types of contractual agreements
- Aspects of the bidding process

Who Is the Reader?

Although most who read this book will have had some knowledge or experience in planning/ designing exhibits, I felt that it was best when writing this manual to be mindful of a reader who, while smart and educated, might lack the planning/designing tools needed to produce a professional-class exhibit. It is for this reason that I explain in great detail the phase-by-phase, logical progression that is used when planning, designing, and developing an exhibit, and discuss all the nitty-gritty issues that have to be addressed and the ways to resolve them. All of the tasks and issues involved in assisting a reader to bring an exhibit to reality are discussed in great detail.

Who Is the Planner/Designer?

One cannot plan an exhibition without designing it or design without planning it. These two tasks are conjoined, and during the exhibit design process, they are so interrelated that they cannot be separated. For that reason, when referring to exhibit designer or exhibit design, I have used the terms planner/designer or plan/design throughout this book.

Is an Exhibit an Artistic Endeavor?

Producing exhibits that are well designed is not a choice; it is a must. When anyone takes on the mantle of exhibit planner/designer, he or she must accept its mandate to create harmonious, well-designed, attractive exhibits. Frankly, it doesn't matter whether an exhibit is large or small, well or meagerly funded, rural or urban located, or historically or scientifically based; there are no excuses for visually bland, badly proportioned exhibits that lack basic, good design principles.

Similar to an architect, a sculptor, or any other artist, an exhibit planner/designer must strive to produce aesthetically pleasing results by being well versed in the principles of design when creating an exhibition. Theories that are based on good design are not elusive; they are easy to comprehend and are addressed throughout this book.

What Does This Book Contain?

The book explains in detail the numerous tasks, issues, and responsibilities involved in the exhibit process. It is composed of five chapters:

Chapter 1: Phases

This chapter details the same phase-by-phase method that professional museum exhibit planners/designers employ when they develop their projects. A brief overview and a work schedule of each phase are presented.

Chapter 2: Tasks and Issues

The tasks and issues listed on the work schedules in chapter 1 are discussed and explained in great detail in this section.

Chapter 3: Color and Light

The theories that serve as the basis for the selection of a successful exhibit color scheme and its lighting, and the methods and considerations employed by designers when preparing a color palette, are a few of the items addressed in this chapter. The visitors' physiological and psychological reactions to various colors are also discussed.

Chapter 4: Shape, Form, and Space

This section details design theories involving these three elements and their impact on the aesthetic success of a concept. It also discusses how they can affect a visitor and influence the exhibit's theme and ambience.

Chapter 5: Materials

Basic exhibit materials as well as "green" materials are discussed in this section. Their advantages and disadvantages are addressed.

Will Technology Change the Design Process?

While process and artistry have always been the two main factors in producing an exhibition, technology today has become a major part of the exhibit planning/designing process. Will technology change the methods and the theories that are used to achieve good exhibition design? I don't think so. I still remember using a "low-tech," T-square, linen drawing paper and a drafting board to design exhibits. They are now long gone, and today, via the computer, I can produce computer-aided design (CAD) drawings and dispatch them electronically thousands of miles away, where seconds later they can be reproduced or be viewed electronically. Yet, no matter how the technology has evolved, and continues to evolve, the basic design principles and the methods used to produce an exhibition and to achieve a visually credible exhibit will always be valid.

Why Did I Write This Book?

Writing this book has been a long journey that started years ago when I received a National Endowments for the Arts grant to compile its research. Later I realized the need for this type of manual when I taught "Museum Exhibition Planning and Design" and "Exhibit Materials and Construction Technique" to graduate students at the University of the Arts in Philadelphia.

Actually, long before receiving the grant and teaching, the need for this type of book first became apparent the moment I realized how ill prepared and scared I was when, as a fledgling American industrial designer working for the Consortium Oil Companies in Tehran, I was designated to create, produce, and install the organization's first exhibition. It was scheduled to open in three months at a museum the government was building to showcase its industries.

To be responsible for a project that represented not only the National Iranian Oil Company but also all of the other major international oil companies was overwhelming, especially when I discovered that the industry had been assigned the largest, most prestigious, and prominent space in the new building. Even though I had never designed an exhibit for a museum, being given this assignment was not surprising. While working for the consortium I had regularly been assigned any project that was remotely artistic, since all my colleagues had either business or engineering degrees, and I seemed to be the only one with a degree in design. However, I did have one advantage: nobody was aware of how little I knew about museum exhibitions. As I set about to plan, design, and oversee this project, my inexperience became my daily nightmare.

I still remember negotiating with local carpenters while standing in an unpaved courtyard and knowing that all exhibit fabrication would be done outdoors in that space. Hoping that it wouldn't rain, I had to forget about dust-free finishes. When I heard that a professional photographer traveling through the Middle East was in Tehran, I persuaded him to take a side trip to Abadan to photograph the refineries. I also recollect pleading with a very reluctant coworker who was going to London on vacation to take my camera-ready art with him, have transparencies made there, and bring them back to be installed in the exhibition. When opening day arrived, the Shah with his entourage of government officials and oil company executives was in attendance. Everyone was delighted with what they saw and showered the exhibit with praise. It was at that moment that I fell in love with the profession of museum exhibition planning/designing, and I never wanted another.

On returning to the States, I established Limn Studios, a museum exhibition planning/designing consulting firm, taught the subject to graduate students, worked with many museum professionals, and teamed with construction firms that built museum exhibitions. For me this profession has always been a wonderful experience, and I want it to be the same for anyone desiring to enter or to be involved in museum exhibit design.

Just because I was scared and alone when I designed my first museum exhibit doesn't mean that has to happen to you, which brings me again to my reasons for writing this book, and why I feel compelled to pass on what I have learned. During my years as a planner/designer, many wonderful museum professionals advised and helped me along the way, and now it is my turn to pass on that knowledge. I also believe that my years of teaching and the joy that it gave me have added motivation. I do hope this book will help you and that you will not be as unprepared as I was when first venturing into this profession.

What Words Are Constantly Used throughout This Book?

Key words are defined and discussed when first presented, and for general usage a "Museum Terms" section is also located in the back matter. However, the following words are constantly used, and for that reason, they are defined here:

deliverables. Copies or photographs of sketches, drawings, models, and other documents prepared during a particular phase and delivered to the exhibit committee for review.

display. A group of items having a commonality; part of an exhibit. Several displays can make up an exhibit.

display object or display item. Any two- or three-dimensional exhibit object, such as an artifact, a painting, an illustration, or a specimen.

exhibit. A subdivision of an exhibition that has a common theme and usually contains several displays.

exhibition. The total area devoted to presenting exhibits and displays that have a common theme.

exhibit planner/designer. A person who plans and designs displays, exhibits, and exhibitions and produces the construction drawings and specifications.

exhibit team. A group of people involved in the development of an exhibition or an exhibit.

museum or institution. A building open to the public with a mandate to collect, safeguard, store, and display objects of educational value. Throughout this book these words are used interchangeably.

plan/design. The process that conceives and produces displays, exhibits, and exhibitions. In the exhibition realm there is no way a person can plan an exhibit without designing it, or design one without planning it. For this reason these two words are used together throughout the book.

Notes!

- Sometimes the same design theory can apply to an exhibit, display, and exhibition, and for that reason at times these three terms will be used interchangeably.
- The information in this book is based on my experience and the knowledge that I have acquired as a museum exhibition planner/designer. It is only a guide, and at times you may disagree with it and take a different tack. Frankly, that is what you should do; the exhibit that you design has to be uniquely yours.
- When planning/designing an exhibition there is always a sea of tasks that must be quickly understood and resolved, and a lack of time usually becomes the enemy. It is for those reasons that this book was laid out so that all the information pertaining to a particular task could be instantly retrieved. In so doing, you will find that there are a few instances where the same information is required to augment more than one task.

1

Phases

> Functional designs can emerge either from nature or from the minds of people, but visual designs, strictly speaking, are considered to be the deliberate creative acts of men and women.
>
> —Marjorie Elliott Bevlin, *Design through Discovery*

Exhibit planning/designing is a phase-by-phase process that always involves a great deal of multitasking and problem solving. No matter how simple or complex a project is, it has to be well organized so that it can proceed in a systematic and logical manner from start to finish.

When commencing an exhibit, a work schedule for each phase must be prepared. These plans serve as the backbones of the project for they address all the tasks and issues imposed by the project's size and complexity. Work schedules are essential for they organize and control a museum's exhibition project and the numerous tasks and issues that are involved with it.

However, not all phases require the same amount of time for completion, and I have found that the number of hours required can vary widely. For me the preliminary and intermediate phases always take a great deal of time, while the final design phase usually requires the least amount to complete, and the documentation phase can be a breeze or it can seem endless.

This chapter is divided into the following phases. A typical work schedule and a brief description of the effort needed to complete a particular phase are discussed. Every task or issue listed in a work schedule is explained in greater detail in chapters 2, 3, and 4.

Preexhibit Planning/Designing
- Master Plan Phase
- Feasibility Study Phase

Exhibit Planning/Designing
- Schematic Phase
- Preliminary Phase
- Intermediate Phase
- Final Phase
- Documentation Phase
- Bidding Phase

Post-Exhibit Planning/Designing
- Construction Phase
- Installation Phase
- Post-Opening Phase

Preexhibit Planning/Designing

Master Plan Phase

The master plan (MP) is a comprehensive study that involves all aspects of the institution involved. It usually results in a long-range plan that determines the institution's raison d'être, and establishes the direction for development of the building, its grounds, and future exhibitions.

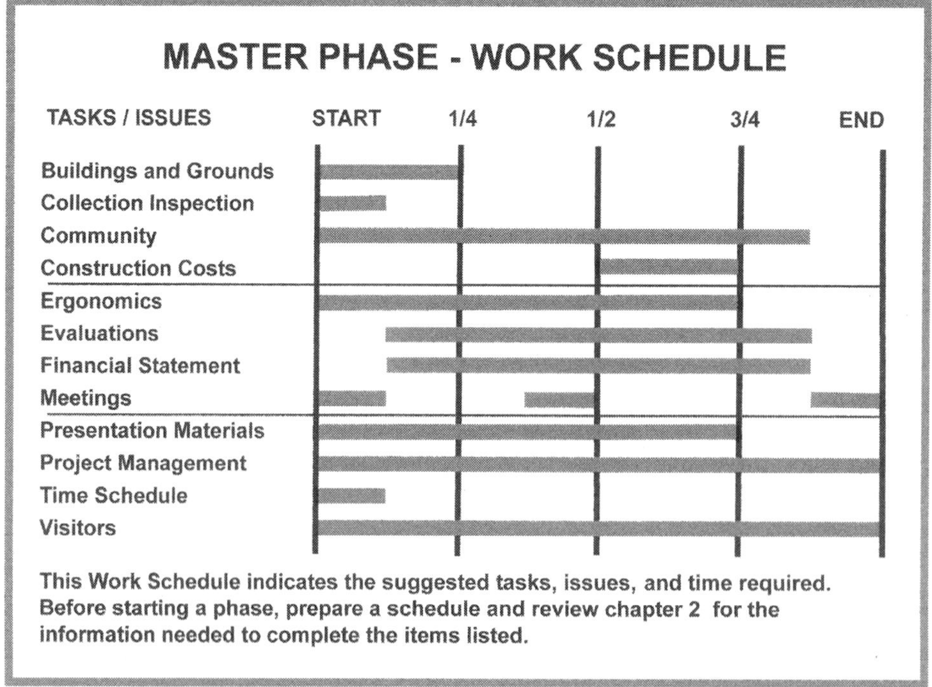

Figure 1.1. Master phase work schedule.

Widely focused, the MP evaluates every major and even minor aspect of a museum and the community it serves. It is an institution's road map that informs its directors where they should be going and the paths they should use to get there. Normally it covers a ten-year time frame.

The MP is multipurpose. It can establish new concepts for the institution; make recommendations for its growth; suggest changes to the existing building, grounds, exhibits, and workspaces; and recommend future exhibitions for consideration. It also details a time schedule and the costs involved in completing any proposed work.

This multifaceted study invariably requires a team of staff members and consultants that could include business advisors, architects, consultants, conservators, curators, educators, engineers, exhibit planners/designers, graphic designers, landscape architects, managers, scholars, and specialists. When building renovations or new construction is anticipated, an architectural firm usually heads up the project, and they, in turn, may either retain or have on staff the required specialists. During master planning, team members will address every aspect of the institution in order to develop a model for the types and the quality of experiences that the museum should offer.

This phase usually concludes with a master plan report, drawings, and sketches. An MP is an important document, and the planner/designer should always review it prior to preparing any new exhibits or upgrading existing ones, for it will invariably contain important information and mandates that could impact an exhibition design project.

Feasibility Study Phase

Is it feasible? This is the pivotal question that must be addressed before any exhibition planning/design project begins. A feasibility study determines if a proposed exhibition or even a simple exhibit or display could be successful and financially viable.

The feasibility study ascertains whether or not a proposed exhibition will, in all probability, attain its goals and have a reasonable chance for success, or if it will fail and become a black hole into which time and money disappear. Regardless of its anticipated size or subject, every project should start with this study.

Normally, members of the museum staff produce this study. If the proposed exhibition area is small, a few staff members may suffice. However, the larger the project, the more extensive and diversified the investigation and the team will have to be, and it could include administrators, curators, educators, exhibit planners/designers, marketing and public relations people, and visitor services personnel.

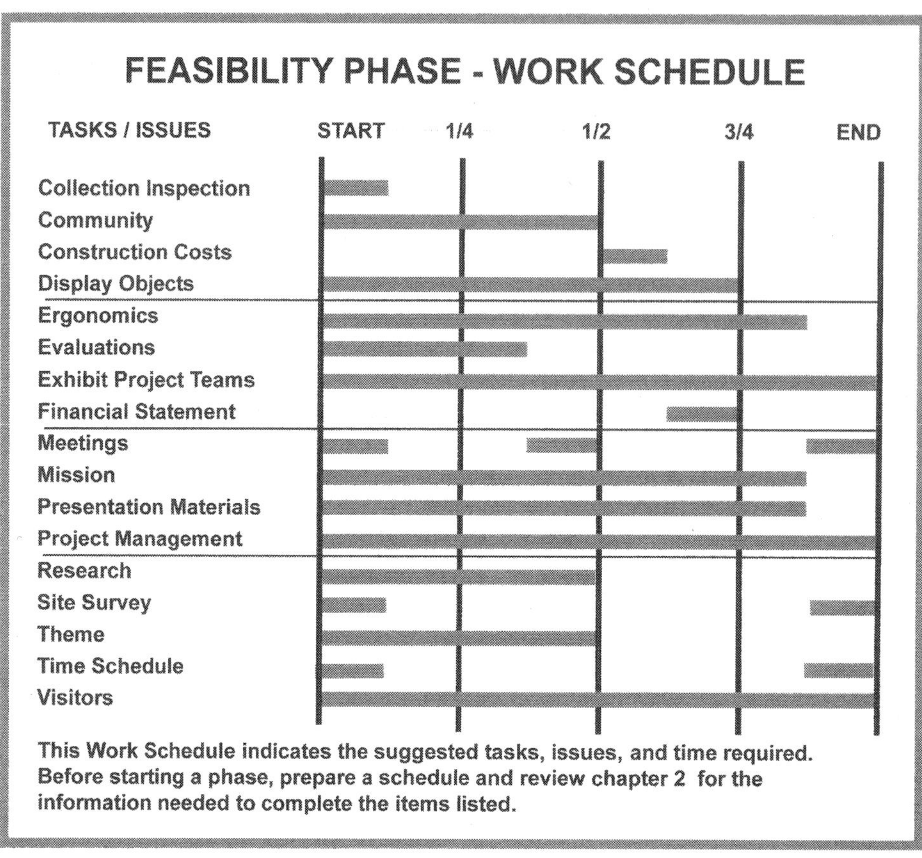

Figure 1.2. Feasibility phase work schedule.

At the start of this study, the mission of the exhibition should be addressed and a list of concerns prepared. The following is a sample of some of the questions that might be considered:

- Will it be beneficial for the visitor and for the institution?
- Can the building accommodate the proposed exhibits and the increase in visitation?
- Will it attract the targeted audience?
- What are the special displays and items to be shown?
- What is the estimated cost of the project's planning/designing, construction, and installation?
- Can the project be funded?
- What are the pivotal education goals and special programs?
- What lectures, outreach programs, and guided tours should be considered?

- Are there people available to prepare and to staff the exhibits and their ancillary programs?
- Will part or all of the work be constructed in-house or contracted out?
- Can the exhibit materials and display items be protected during unloading and installation?
- Can the exhibit structures be reused?

Even when these questions have been successfully answered, the two major items that must always be addressed are talent and time (T&T), for they are always needed to plan/design, build, staff, and provide for the exhibition's tours, lectures, events, funding, public relations, advertising, security, maintenance, and so forth. Without the positive T&T results, the success of a project is doubtful.

At the conclusion of a feasibility study all anticipated concerns and goals relating to a proposed exhibition should have been addressed. If the responses to the questions raised were not positive, then careful consideration must be given before a go-ahead is agreed upon. Unfortunately, no one can be 100 percent certain that any proposed exhibition will succeed. However, a feasibility study should provide the information needed to make an educated decision.

Exhibit Planning/Designing

Schematic Phase

The schematic phase is just what its title implies: during this time, several design schemes are prepared for the proposed exhibition, culminating in one concept being selected for further development.

Each scheme must meet the established goals and have the potential to become the final exhibit design. A concept should be developed only to the degree that reviewers can understand it and visualize its layout and structures. Before the planning/designing can commence with this phase, it is paramount that the mission statement be completed (see chapter 2). The schematic stage is frequently referred to as the conceptual phase.

Each scheme should comply with the policies and guidelines established in the master plan (MP) and the feasibility study (FS). Since they could have an impact on the exhibit concepts, the MP and FS should be reviewed in detail prior to commencing this phase. However, if such studies do not exist, those items discussed in the MP and FS that are pertinent to developing the exhibition design should be addressed by the planner/designer.

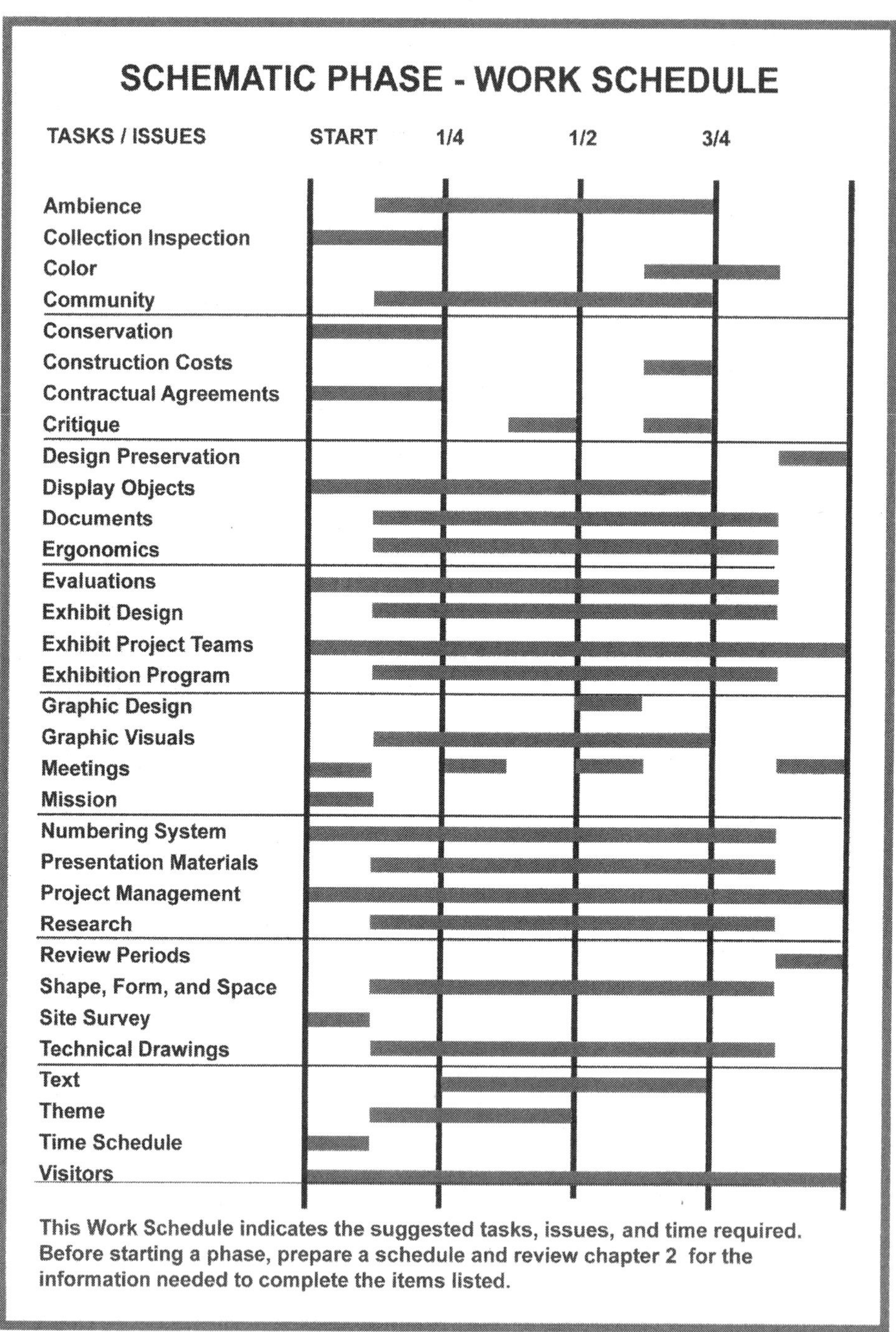
SCHEMATIC PHASE - WORK SCHEDULE
TASKS / ISSUES
START
1/4
1/2
3/4
Ambience
Collection Inspection
Color
Community
Conservation
Construction Costs
Contractual Agreements
Critique
Design Preservation
Display Objects
Documents
Ergonomics
Evaluations
Exhibit Design
Exhibit Project Teams
Exhibition Program
Graphic Design
Graphic Visuals
Meetings
Mission
Numbering System
Presentation Materials
Project Management
Research
Review Periods
Shape, Form, and Space
Site Survey
Technical Drawings
Text
Theme
Time Schedule
Visitors
This Work Schedule indicates the suggested tasks, issues, and time required. Before starting a phase, prepare a schedule and review chapter 2 for the information needed to complete the items listed.

Figure 1.3. Schematic phase work schedule.

For the planner/designer the schematic phase is usually the most creative and exciting stage. Although it is the time to establish the foundation for a memorable exhibition, this phase can also be grounded in apprehension and trepidation. The very thought of producing several designs when, at the beginning, you couldn't even think of one, is challenging enough. Then, asking others to review the designs and to assist you in selecting a single scheme to be developed can produce a deep dread, especially when there is the possibility that your favorite concept might be rejected. Fear not! Maybe I have been fortunate, but I have always been able to produce several credible designs, and the selection committee has invariably selected the one that I favored. It has happened to me, and it can happen to you.

While this phase has its challenges, there are many benefits to be derived from it. The comments and suggestions made by reviewers during the selection process are always extremely helpful and beneficial, and they almost invariably guide and improve the design. Another advantage is that since all members associated with the project are given an opportunity to express their ideas, everyone develops a vested interest in it, and they always seem willing to work for its successful outcome.

Preliminary Phase

This is the seminal phase where the selected exhibition design takes form and evolves from a concept to a reality. Most of the important planning/designing decisions are made in this phase.

The purpose of the preliminary phase is to develop the selected design concept so that it can mature into a successful exhibition. At the beginning of this phase the chosen exhibition scheme always seems to be fluid and disorganized, and the issues and concerns posed by members of the review committee are critical and must be resolved.

Before this phase can commence, the selected scheme must be approved for development and signed off by the person or committee in charge. It is also important for the planner/designer to know at this time the type of construction contract and construction delivery method that the institution anticipates employing, since this information will definitely influence the kind, depth, and development of the documents required.

I have always felt that of all the project phases, this one was the most critical, since it is at this time that the exhibition's final direction is formed and most of the major decisions are made. Unfortunately, what happens in the preliminary phase always seems to be "written in stone" and can rarely be changed, so it is important to take the time to be careful and to make decisions wisely. At the conclusion of this phase, the exhibition concepts will have been firmly established.

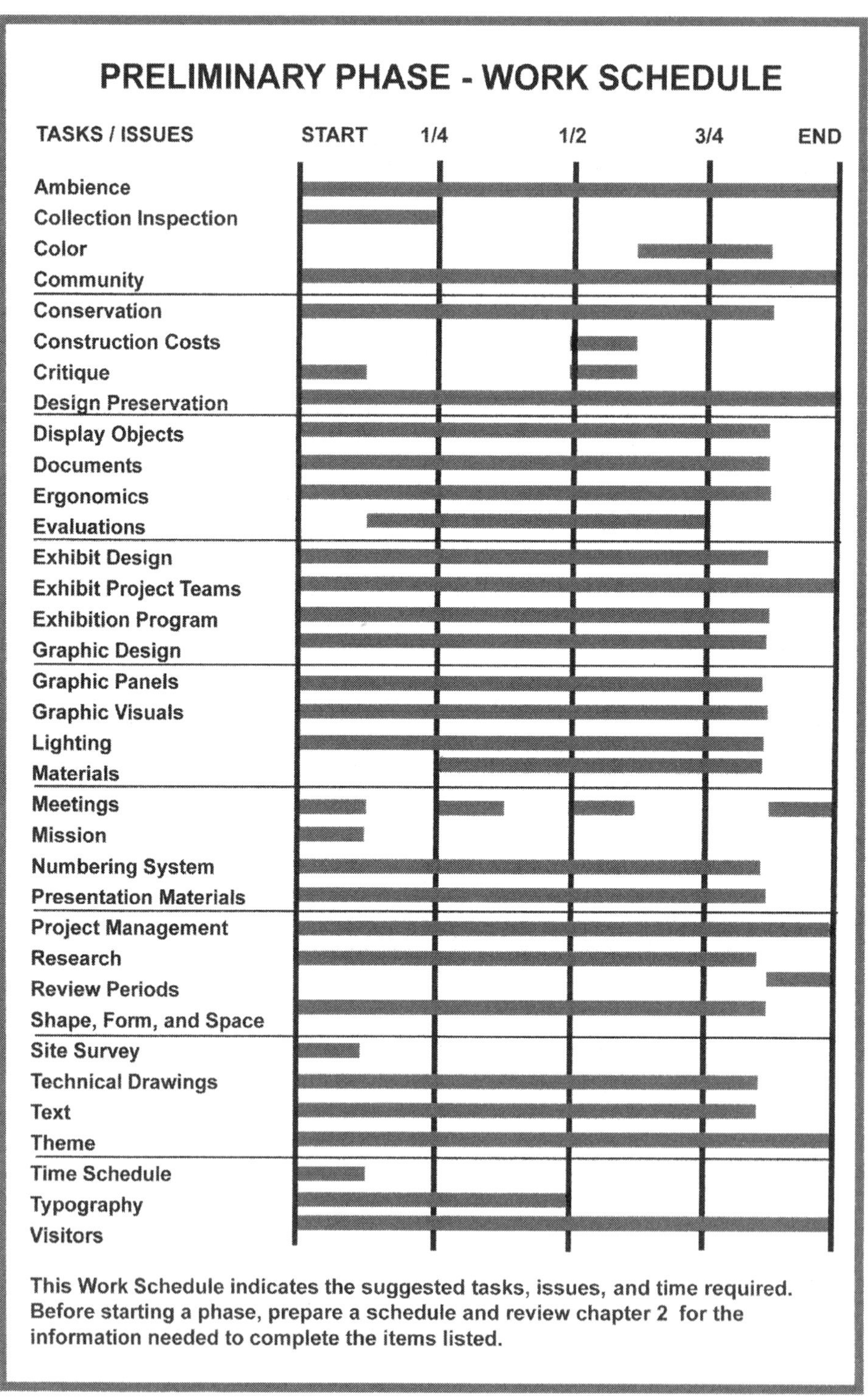

Figure 1.4. Preliminary phase work schedule.

Intermediate Phase

During this phase every exhibit element is studied and refined, and made ready for the next phase. Every element to be included in the exhibition must be studied, matured, and refined during this phase. The concerns posed by the exhibition committee, which has had the opportunity to review the previous phase's work, need to be addressed, and the enormous number of issues pertaining to the exhibition must be planned/designed, researched, and resolved.

Frankly, I have always felt that the intermediate phase was essential, since it allowed me the opportunity to step back and study every aspect of the exhibition in-depth and to make sure that all its elements are compatible. Although sometimes this phase is deleted, I have rarely done so. Once, in order to reduce the planning/design fee, I unwisely succumbed to a client's wishes and eliminated this phase, only to realize later that it was really needed; so that the exhibit would not suffer, I did it gratuitously.

At the end of this phase every major planning and design issue should have been resolved and the exhibition committee should have a cohesive and mature exhibition to review.

Final Phase

Final means just that! During this phase, every item and issue that pertains to the exhibition design has to be resolved.

At the start of this phase the design will have been firmly established. The planner/designer now has the opportunity to research and resolve all the details and issues that pertain to the design of the exhibition, to question and check all its aspects, and to ensure the following:

- artifacts will be properly protected and conserved;
- the needs of the visually, physically, and mentally challenged are met;
- construction materials and design details are adequately addressed; and
- visitors will have an enjoyable and informative experience.

During this phase the exhibition design and the graphic layouts are finalized and research conducted to ensure that all fixtures, materials, hardware, and electrical, mechanical, or computer devices are appropriate. Elevations, floor plans, and all the display objects are located on the drawings. The bid package and its technical drawings are started, and details and information are added as they become available.

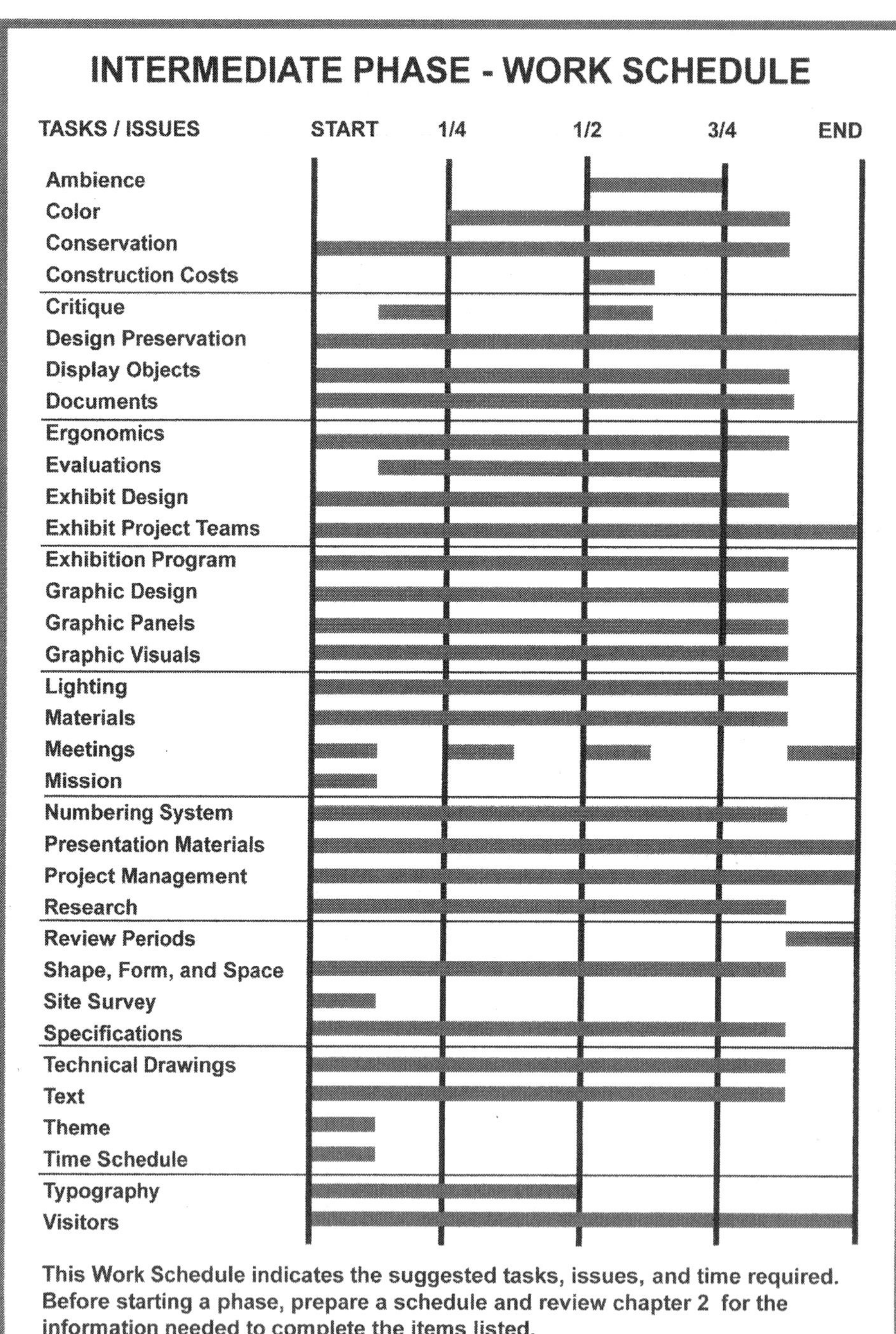

Figure 1.5. Intermediate phase work schedule.

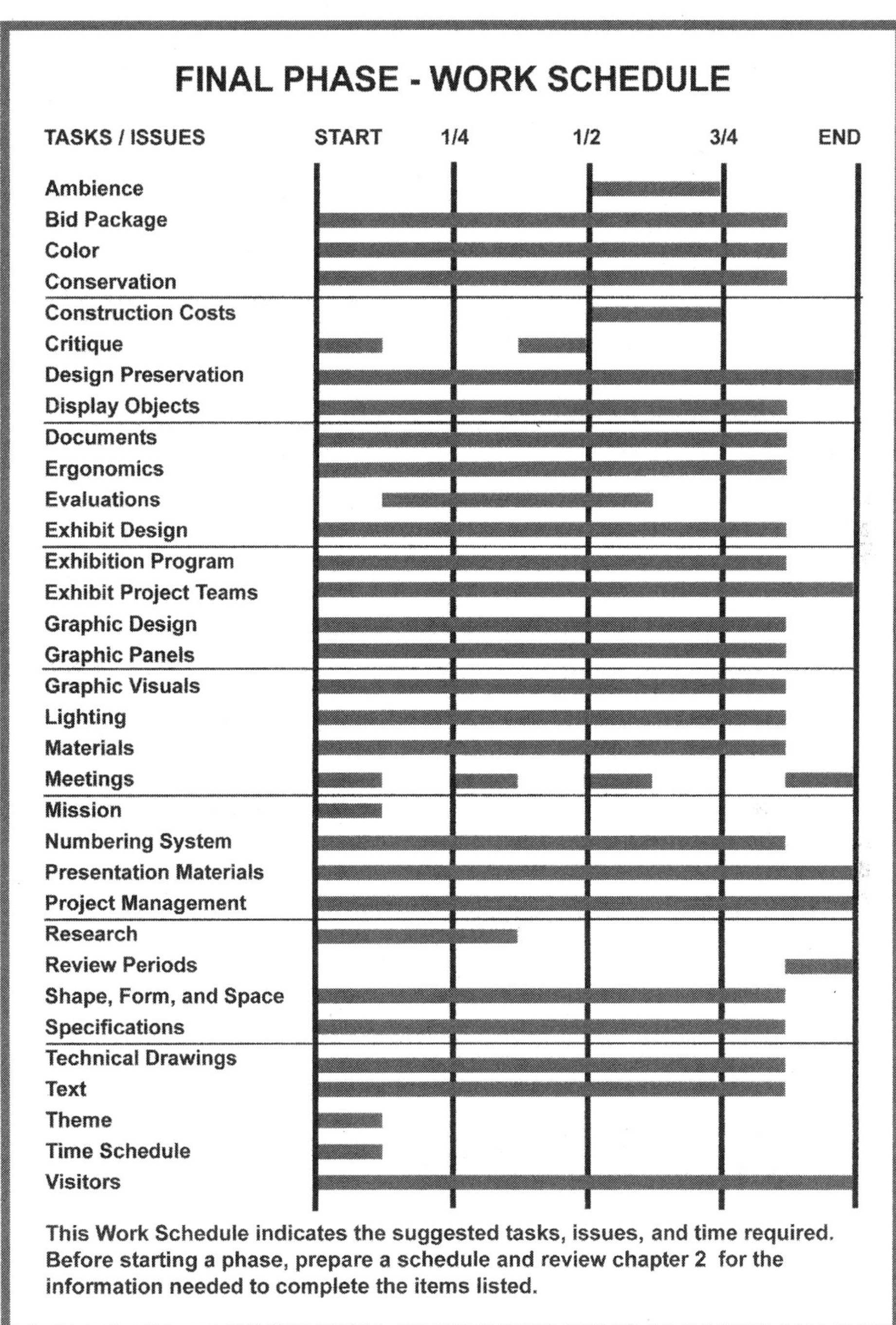

Figure 1.6. Final phase work schedule.

At the termination of this phase, the design must be finalized, and no changes or surprises should occur. The exhibition program, graphic layouts, and the technical drawings are now ready for the museum staff to review.

Documentation Phase

All the documentation needed for contractors to bid on construction and installation of the exhibits is produced in this phase.

During all of the previous phases, the exhibition was developed with the visitor in mind and was judged on its content, educational value, and

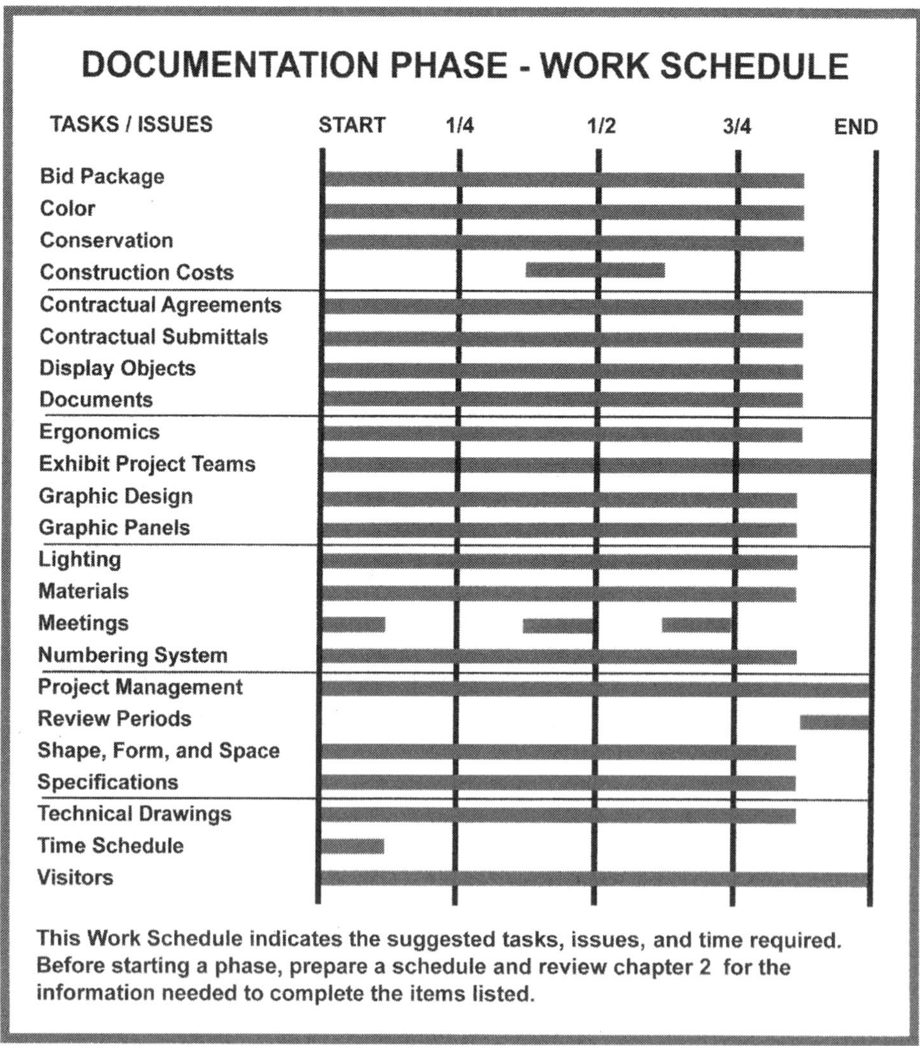

Figure 1.7. Documentation phase work schedule.

visual appearance. Now, when preparing the documentation needed for bidding and constructing the exhibition structures and materials, the planners/designers must view their work through the lens of the contractors who will be competing for the exhibit work and who will scrutinize every item in minute detail. The documentation produced in this phase is judged for its precision and clarity. Anything omitted from the drawings and the specifications will not be quoted on and could lead to an "extra" later on.

Prior to commencing this phase, the type of construction contract that will be awarded should be reviewed once more so that the required documentation and any other information needed for bidding will be compatible with it.

During this phase the technical drawings and the project manual are completed. Care must be taken to maintain the integrity of the exhibition's established goals, design, and display objects. At its conclusion the exhibit team will deliver to the museum committee the work prepared in this phase for their review and approval.

Bidding Phase

The bidding process and the construction and installation contract signing take place during this phase. This period normally requires three to six or more weeks depending upon the scope and complexity of the project.

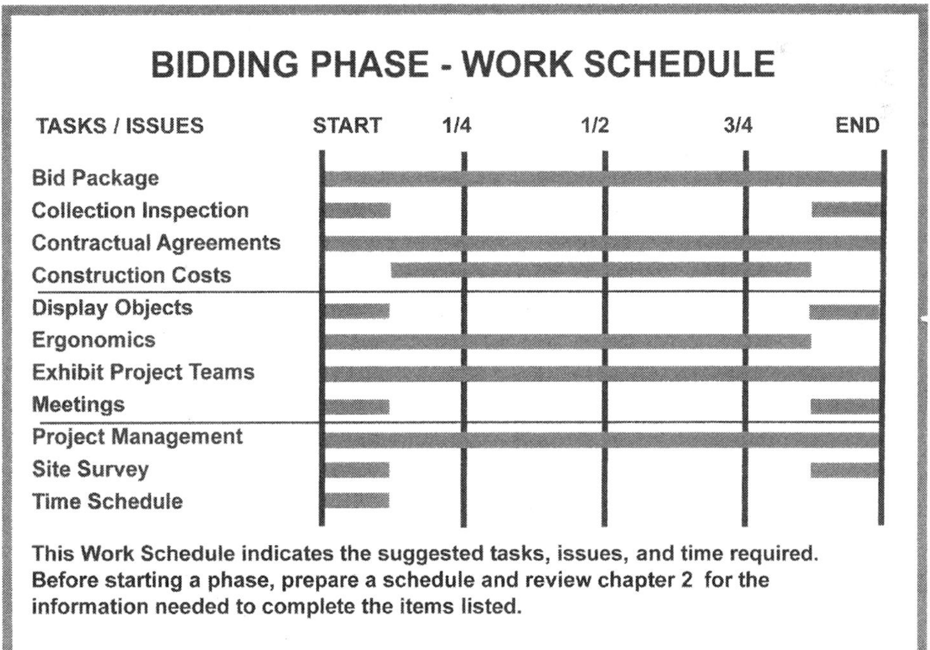

Figure 1.8. Bidding phase work schedule.

This phase should not present any problems or surprises if the bid package contains competent drawings, instructions, and specifications. The institution sends out the package to a reasonable number of interested construction firms to bid on fabricating and installing the exhibit structures. Publicly owned institutions are usually required to advertise their projects. The bidder's submissions are reviewed, and a contract for the job is signed with the successful builder.

Most of the work for the planners/designers is now over. During this phase, the exhibit team assists the institution when requested; they usually attend the prebid and bid-opening meetings and are available to answer any questions affecting the work.

Post-Exhibit Planning/Designing

Construction Phase

Once the contract to build the exhibits has been signed, construction begins and the successful firm is now responsible for producing the work as detailed in the bid package.

This phase is always critical for exhibit team members: they have to be constantly vigilant to ensure that the exhibit designs are not changed or compromised during construction and that the scope of work as detailed in the signed contract is maintained.

Although planners/designers represent the institution, and must always work on their behalf, they also have to be sensitive to the contractor's needs by keeping their submittal review time to a minimum, providing any information requested by the construction firm in a timely fashion, and resolving any contractual disputes in a fair and impartial manner.

This phase includes construction and shipping, and ends when the exhibition materials arrive on the museum loading dock.

Installation Phase

This phase starts when the exhibit materials and structures are delivered to the museum site. It ends when all the materials are successfully installed and the institution has approved and assumed responsibility for the work.

During this phase the construction contractor installs all the exhibits and completes all the items detailed in the agreement with the institution.

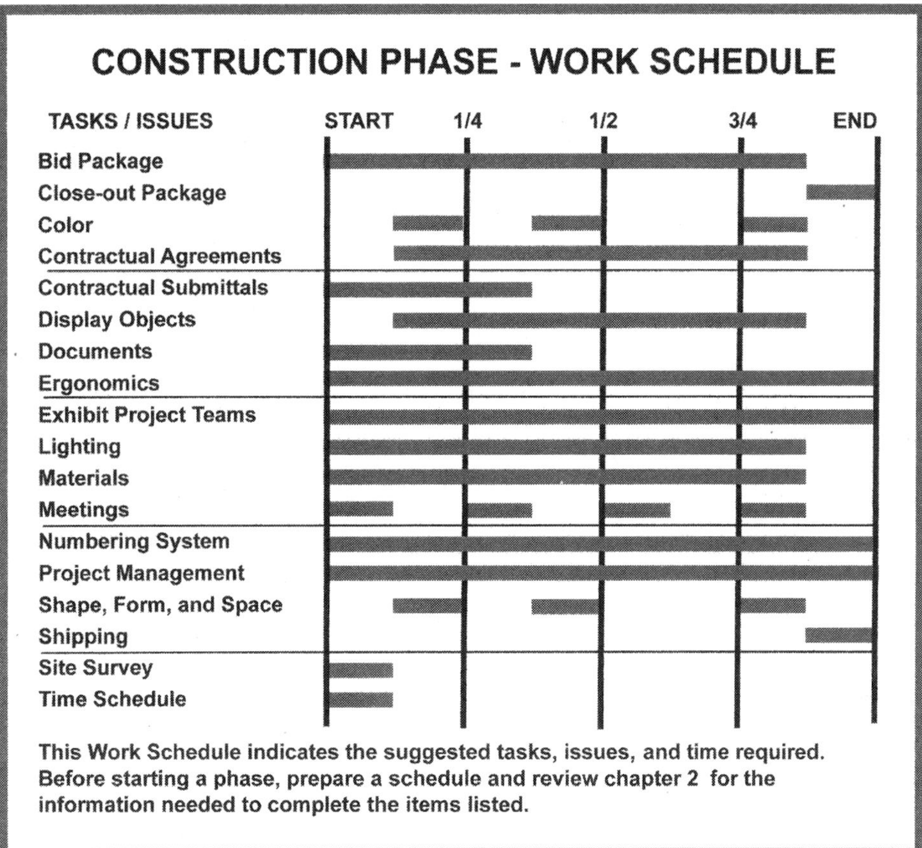

Figure 1.9. Construction phase work schedule.

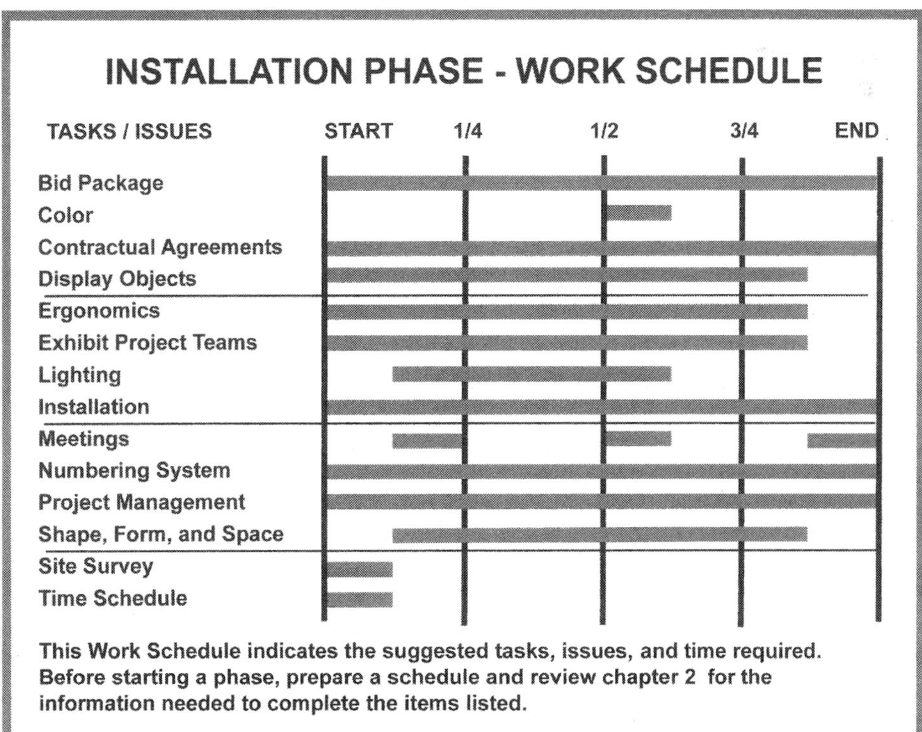

Figure 1.10. Installation phase work schedule.

All planning and designing discussions and decisions are now finished; the exhibition is coming to life and will soon be a reality. Installation always seems to be an exciting time. The atmosphere appears to be charged, and the exhibit project team members and the installers usually work together in a busy, friendly, supportive manner.

For the planners/designers, it is exhilarating to watch the display structures come to life on the floor, yet at the same time, it is always nerve racking waiting for that imaginary disaster to strike. But, thanks to intensive planning and good design, Chicken Little's sky rarely falls, and the exhibits and displays usually slide comfortably into their permanent homes.

Post-Opening Phase

The exhibition now enters one of its most important and prolonged phases. Opening day has come and gone, and visitors now have the opportunity to leisurely experience the finished displays.

Shortly after opening day the wrap-up period begins. All documentation pertaining to the exhibits must be revised to reflect the changes, if any, that were made. An evaluation should be performed. Just to cut the

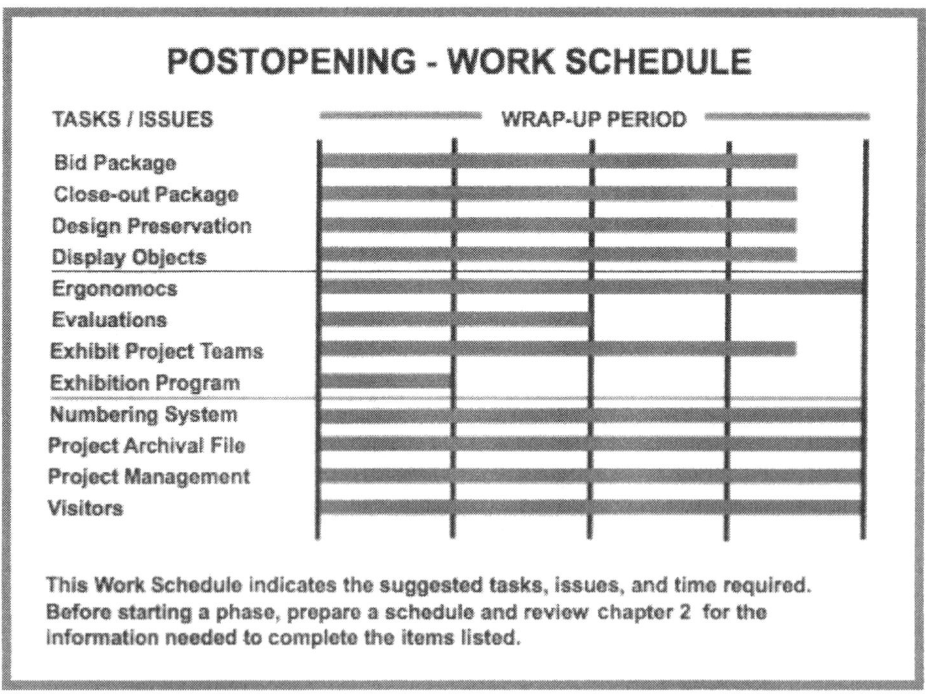

Figure 1.11. Post-opening phase work schedule.

ribbon and run ensures that an exhibition will slowly and sadly destruct and die. Displays must be kept relevant and should be periodically evaluated and updated when needed so that they address current needs of the community, the visitors, and the institution. Not only do exhibits have to be upgraded regularly, but also they must always be maintained properly and kept dust and dirt free.

How long will the exhibition be an exciting and important entity in a museum? It all depends on how long it remains relevant. If the visitors find the displays enjoyable and meaningful, chances are that the exhibition will have a long and happy life.

2

Tasks and Issues

Design is the organization of parts into a coherent whole.

—Marjorie Elliott Bevlin, *Design through Discovery*

Museum exhibit planning/designing is a multifaceted endeavor that combines artistic, intellectual, and practical techniques and theories. It demands that planners/designers have an in-depth knowledge of the tasks and issues involved, an understanding of basic design principles, and an awareness of construction procedures. When these factors are understood and used properly, a cohesive, well-planned, well-designed exhibit should be the result.

Unfortunately not every task or issue is quickly resolved, and some must be nurtured and matured throughout several phases before they are completed. Again, it is how well the planner/designer understands and manages the multitude of related items that will ultimately determine how well organized and successful an exhibition will be.

Each task or issue listed in chapter 1 "Work Schedules" is explained and detailed in this chapter and will appear in alphabetical order.

Ambience

Walking through an exhibition with a wonderful ambience can be akin to being surrounded by a fine piece of sculpture where every element is in sync and nothing is in disarray. Ambience is the invisible fog that envelops an exhibition and magically affects the visitor both intellectually and emotionally.

Ambience Phases: Special Considerations

Schematic Phase
  Suggest ambience for each exhibit.
Preliminary Phase
  Finalize the ambience.
  Prepare and place a written description of the proposed ambience in the exhibition program.
  Obtain approval from exhibition committee members.
Intermediate and Final Phases
  Review to ensure that the agreed-upon ambience has been maintained and that deviations have not occurred.

Value and Importance

Before visitors view the text or the photographs, a well-defined ambience can inform them about the exhibition's theme, time, and place. Depending on the design of an area, it can create either a positive or a negative impression that will have a major influence on the viewer's experience.

Regardless of the type of exhibit (scientific, art, environmental, historic, etc.), ambience is always a major design consideration and has to be carefully studied. Throughout all phases, planners/designers must be vigilant and select the appropriate colors, forms, lighting, textures, and spaces that will promote the exhibit's aim and mission and create an environment that is appropriate to the theme of the exhibition.

Ambience versus Gestalt

These two terms address the psychological and the physiological experiences of a visitor; however, they are not interchangeable, and great care should be exercised in considering their impact.

Ambience is the total experience of what we see and how we feel at a particular moment, and can be so inclusive that it seeps into our minds and our being. Ambience involves all our sensual experiences including light, color, form, sound, touch, and smell. These are the reasons that I prefer using the word "ambience" when describing a museum's environment.

Gestalt is based on the theory that people tend to organize items into groups that have common characteristics. Therefore, the visually stronger a grouping is, the more powerful a person's perception of it will be. This theory centers on an exhibit's form, line, and color.

Bid Package

The bid package (BP) provides all the information, specifications, graphic layouts, and drawings that are required for construction firms to estimate on the building, shipping, and installation costs of exhibits. It establishes the project's standards of quality, workmanship, grades of materials, construction details, types of finishes, and so forth, and addresses the museum, exhibit, and construction team's relationships and responsibilities. The BP is a major part of the contractor/institution contract and is a legal document that can be and is used in settling disputes. It also serves as the basis for preparing the contractor's shop drawings and purchasing materials.

When preparing a BP, exhibit team members must constantly analyze their work through the eyes and the mind of the contractor, and they must check to make sure that no item or detail—even the smallest—has been overlooked. This document must be accurate, provide complete information, be easy to comprehend, and be laid out in a logical manner. Since the BP will become part of a legal contract, it is important to clarify all terms that could be misconstrued.

Bid Package Phases: Special Considerations

Final Phase
  Assemble BP to include all available information.
Documentation Phase
  Produce all the work needed to complete the BP.
  Have museum committee members review and approve BP.
Bidding Phase
  Send BP to construction firms for bidding.
Construction Phase
  BP can be used as the source to prepare shop drawings and as the basis for all exhibit graphics and construction.
Installation Phase
  BP can be used to settle any disputes.
Post-Opening Phase
  Incorporate BP into the project archival file.

Responsibilities

I have always found that preparing a BP can be tedious and time consuming, and it is an exacting chore that requires a great deal of patience—

BID PACKAGE - RESPONSIBILITIES

	Administrator	Planner/Designer
General Conditions	P	
Project Manual	R	P
Bidding Drawings	R	P

KEY:
P = Prepares the document
R = Reviews and approves the document and drawings

Figure 2.1. Bid package responsibilities.

not one of my strong points. Years ago, because of the serious nature of the BP, I felt it important to prepare a paper titled "The Bid Package" for the American Alliance of Museums' annual meeting. Figure 2.1 is a chart that I prepared for that presentation.

General Conditions

Prepared by the museum team and sometimes in conjunction with the exhibit team, the general conditions (GC) section is also known as the boilerplate or special conditions. This GC focuses on the relationship between the institution and the contractor, and contains all relevant information not included in the project manual or the other bidding documents. The following is a brief sample of some items that are usually included in the GC.

Procedures for Bid Submission

This section establishes the procedures and documents that contractors must address when submitting their bids. If they are not adhered to, the contractor can be disqualified. It usually includes the following:

- Prebid meeting: time, place, and date
- Bid form to be used
- Number of copies needed for bid submission
- Date, time, and location for bids to be received
- Bonding requirements, if any

Project's Special Conditions

This section informs both the contractor and the client of any project conditions and restrictions that might impact the work. The information could include the following:

- Project's time and payment schedules
- Hours and days the institution will be open for installation
- Responsibilities of institution and contractor
- Craftsmanship and materials guarantees. This usually covers a period of one to three years.
- Details for handling, protecting, and installing the artifacts and display items
- Requirement that the contractor must provide a maintenance manual (see later in this chapter) and close-out package (see later in this chapter).
- Requirement that the contractor must adhere to all pertinent building codes

Legal Aspects

The following legal documents are usually included in the general conditions section:

- A sample of the construction contract
- Contractor's required insurance coverage for the exhibit materials during construction, shipping, and installation
- Insurance coverage for all workers employed or contracted for by the construction firm

Contractor's General Information

The following is the information that is usually needed to inform the museum personnel that the contractor is qualified to complete the work required:

- Construction facilities description
- Issues that could impede or influence the construction firm's performance or affect its costs
- Project management procedures
- Project organization chart
- Contractor's qualifications (request for qualifications [RFQ])
- Subcontractors' qualifications and facilities

Project Manual

The project manual and the bidding documents are companion pieces and contain all the information needed to construct the exhibit and to maintain quality control. The project manual is divided into three parts:

- Construction conditions
- Construction specifications (see "Specifications" section in this chapter)
- Graphic specifications (see "Specifications" section in this chapter)

Construction Conditions

This section on construction conditions addresses the conditions that will influence or have an impact on the construction of the exhibition. The following is just a sampling of a few such conditions that are normally included:

- Cleanup: Contractor is responsible for cleaning up during the course of the job and prior to turning over the work to the institution.
- Conflicts: Specifications may often state that in the case of a conflict between the drawings and the specifications, the specifications govern.
- Electrical power: The institution usually provides the power to each exhibit or display; the contractor connects the exhibits to the power source.
- Permits: The contractor is responsible for obtaining all permits.
- Quality control: "All work must be of museum quality." This statement is usually included and helps to establish a standard, even though it is too broad and can be legally questionable.
- Samples: The planner/designer usually requires samples of an item when it is not feasible to adequately specify or describe a particular finish, special joint, hardware, or material. When making this request, it should be stated that the "work cannot proceed until the sample has been approved." Since the cost to produce samples is always included in the bid, I prefer to keep these requests to a minimum and, whenever possible, state in the BP that the item will be returned to the contractor and can be used in the exhibit, thus saving the client the cost of the sample.
- Shop drawings: All shop drawings must be prepared by the contractor and approved by the institution or its designer before construction of that item can begin. These drawings show the materials,

shape, and size of each unit and contain the information needed for the contractor to build it.
- Site inspection: Contractors are usually required to visit the exhibition site prior to bidding and construction. The successful bidder must measure and inspect all existing conditions and be responsible for the accuracy of any measurements that could impact the construction and installation of the exhibit materials.
- Site protection: Contractors are generally required to provide a statement that details the methods that they will use to protect the institution's facilities during the installation period.

Bidding Drawings

The bidding drawings (BD) are the completed technical drawings that contain the information needed to bid on the project. They are included in the bid package and are keyed to the specifications.

Resource Materials

Bid packages are complex documents, and preparing them could be called an acquired art; frankly, I call it a copied art. I have read many documents from well-established exhibit design firms and have found that the exact same paragraphs have stood the test of time and are commonly used.

Most designers have a library of bid packages that they use for reference. Where do they get these documents? Construction firms that quote on museum projects and museums themselves generally have shelves full of obsolete BPs. Usually they will be glad to give you a few bid packages, and often BPs can be found on the Internet.

The Need for Accuracy

The success of an exhibition ultimately hinges on the information provided in the bid package; this is an unforgiving document and allows no room for mistakes. Once a project has been bid on and a contract signed, the specifications and drawings that comprise the BP cannot be altered without a written change order signed by the client and the contractor.

Always remember that if an item is not included in the bidding documents, it will not be quoted on, and if added at a later date, the item will undoubtedly be more expensive. There is an old adage in the construction business: "Put them in by orchards, and take them out by apples," meaning that any additions to the original contract will be very expensive, and any deletions to it will be calculated at a modest cost.

Producing a BP is not an easy task; it requires a tremendous amount of work, and there are hundreds (sometimes thousands) of details and items that must be addressed. All have to be accurately indicated. In the end there is only one question that has to be answered: can the contractor estimate, build, and install the exhibit structures from the information that you have provided in the bid package? The answer must be YES!

Building and Grounds

Any building that stores and displays objects should present and protect them under ideal conditions and accommodate visitors and staff members in a comfortable and productive environment. A general inspection of the building should be made periodically to ascertain that the building, grounds, and facilities are suitable for the people and the exhibitions.

Even though the science and technology of managing a museum and caring for and displaying its holdings have advanced dramatically in recent years, unfortunately there are still many museums housed in structures that are relics of the past. When a museum's building and grounds are in need of major renovations, a "master plan" is usually prepared.

Maintaining the Iconic Image

In striving to keep up with the times, many museums are creating master plans that call for major upgrades and extensive renovations. However, in establishing the criteria for these changes, they should be careful not to throw out the baby with the bathwater. Institutions must ensure that renovations do not ruin a building that has a well-known, iconic persona.

The Philadelphia Museum of Art was fully aware of its image when preparing for the expansion and renovation of its landmark neoclassical building that dominates and overlooks the Benjamin Franklin Parkway. The criteria that they established for their renovations stated,

> The 10-year master plan includes creating dynamic new spaces for art and visitors, modernizing the aging infrastructure and building systems, and reclaiming existing spaces for public use. The iconic building will be expanded without disturbing its classic exterior, while existing interior spaces will be renovated to enable a broader and richer display of the Museum's renowned holdings and accommodate collections growth. (http://www.philamuseum.org/)

Exterior and Surroundings

Yes, first impressions do count; a museum building's exterior and its grounds do reflect its collection and exhibits. If they are run down, badly maintained, and uninviting, the public will assume that its interior, artifacts, and exhibits are in the same deplorable condition and could be deterred from entering.

Planners when inspecting the site must always "view" the building facade and its grounds through the eyes of visitors. They must critique the entrance, exterior signage, grounds, driveways, parking lot(s), loading docks, maintenance facilities, and so on, and determine whether the museum conveys the proper impact and image, and if the entrances and exits to the building and its parking lots are readily accessible and easy to comprehend.

Public Spaces

These spaces consist of all the areas that are open to the public: for example, exhibition spaces, entrance areas, corridors, libraries, museum shops, restrooms, and lecture halls. These spaces have to be investigated to make sure they have safe and barrier-free access, foster the image of the institution, function well, and are compatible with the surrounding areas.

Staff Areas

Out of public view the museum is a beehive of activities and relies on its staff and volunteers for administrative, research, and curatorial efforts, and to care and plan for its exhibitions, visitors' activities, special educational programs, fund-raising endeavors, and so forth. To successfully maintain all these activities, an institution should have up-to-date and efficient equipment, facilities, laboratories, storage areas, offices, work areas, loading docks, and corridors.

Likened to "spring cleaning," every aspect of the private areas should be scrutinized and evaluated. To determine if the facilities, equipment, and spaces are adequate, function well, are properly located, and meet the required needs, planners interview staff members and volunteers and, when necessary, make recommendations for changes and upgrades.

Building Systems

Usually built into the building's walls, ceilings, and floors are the systems that provide a comfortable and protective environment for the staff, visitors, and collections. Architects and/or engineers may be required to inspect the electrical, water, heating, air-conditioning, ventilation, humidity control, and fire and security systems to ensure they are in compliance with building codes and in proper working condition. Exhibit planners/designers should make sure that electrical outlets and control panels do not interfere with the exhibits and that their locations are convenient and accessible. Floor loading may be of importance depending on the placement and weight of the exhibits.

Many times, planners/designers find it difficult to employ current and innovative exhibit trends and technology because of a building's obsolescence.

Building-Use Plan

After the building and grounds investigations have been completed, the master planning team usually prepares a report that addresses all of the above items and, where necessary, recommends changes. They also establish a cost estimate and a time schedule necessary for implementing any suggested upgrades. This document usually consists of the following reports:

- Building report: an assessment of the building's structure, suggested renovations, and expansion possibilities
- Analysis: a study of pedestrian and vehicular traffic patterns and their circulation and density. An assessment of the hallways, ramps, and stairs is made to determine if they are well illuminated, hazard free, and secure.
- Directional signage report: an analysis of the effectiveness of the interior and exterior signage and their graphics, illustrations, texts, and locations
- Interior spaces review: a statement addressing the function and effectiveness of all spaces, including physically and visually challenged requirements
- Equipment and furniture report: a review of the effectiveness of furniture, computers, equipment, and so forth, and recommended upgrades
- Infrastructure study: report on the condition of the security, fire, HVAC, and lighting systems, and so on, and recommended upgrades

Close-Out Package

Before an exhibition can be considered finished, the construction firm must prepare and deliver to the museum a close-out package. This document contains all the information and instructions needed to assist the institution in maintaining and upgrading their exhibits. It is prepared and delivered at the beginning of the post-opening phase, and normally it will contain the following items.

Maintenance Manual

This document is meant to assist the museum in maintaining and repairing the exhibits. Usually it will include the following:

- Guarantees covering equipment and devices
- Names, addresses, telephone numbers, and websites of all suppliers and vendors
- Materials and finishes specifications and their maintenance instructions
- Graphic specifications, layouts, electronic file(s), and so forth
- Supplies and guarantees needed for repairs and replacements

As-Built Drawings

Also called record drawings, as-built drawings are the contract and shop drawings that have been marked up by the builder to reflect final changes made during the construction and installation process.

Touch-up Kit and Keys

The touch-up kit and the keys usually consist of

- A small amount of paint for each color used in the exhibition
- Extra keys for each lock installed by the contractor.

Collection Inspection

Artifacts, documents, specimens, library holdings, and the like, define a museum's purpose and importance, and these items should be compatible with an institution's mission and the image that it desires to project.

Collection Inspection Phases: Special Considerations

Collections inspections are important and usually occur during the following phases:

Master Plan
  Summative Collection Inspection
Feasibility Study and Schematic, Preliminary, and Bidding Phases
  Thematic Collection Inspection
Construction Phase
  The construction firm will inspect the pertinent display objects and make suggestions that could influence the detailing and the construction of the exhibit structures.

Summative Collection Inspection

The summative collection inspection is an institution's complete inspection of its total collection. Usually performed during the master plan or when the total collection needs to be evaluated, this inspection determines if the artifacts are properly exhibited and stored. A few of the questions that need to be resolved during this phase are as follows:

- What is the extent, importance, and focus of the holdings?
- What artifacts should be displayed in the permanent exhibit?
- How can the artifacts, specimens, books, and so forth, be preserved, maintained, and protected?
- What items should be accessioned or deaccessioned?

This inspection culminates in a collections management report that contains acquisition and deacquisition policy reports, a list of suggested exhibits and exhibitions to be developed, an itemized artifact condition report, the conservation policy, and a storage condition report.

Thematic Collection Inspection

This review is selective and only pertains to the objects that inspection suggests would or could be displayed for a particular exhibition. It culminates in a display object report that lists the objects and the information needed to properly display and protect them.

Warehouses Are Not Always State of the Art

Unfortunately, inspecting a collection is not always an orderly process where you are shown stacks of neatly kept artifacts. Many times I have viewed artifacts that were beautifully preserved, stored, and recorded. Yet, at other times, I have visited barns with the museum's holdings scattered across the floor. Once I even visited a group of hot, dusty, wooden shacks and garages filled with piles of valuable yet grimy artifacts and documents, many stored in supermarket paper bags. Frankly, I am convinced that there are untold numbers of collections being kept in this manner, and I know that I can't be the only planner/designer who has experienced such terrible conditions. The people who are responsible for warehousing always seem to be dedicated and committed to the collection; they mean well and certainly are doing their level best. Frequently, they simply lack the funds to manage their artifacts properly, yet they always seem hopeful that help will come. Sometimes just a report that addresses the terrible storage conditions can result in saving valuable artifacts, and for me, that can be a priceless outcome.

Color

> Color is crucial in painting, but it is very hard to talk about. There is almost nothing you can say that holds up as a generalization, because it depends on too many factors: size, modulation, the rest of the field, a certain consistency that color has with forms, and the statement you're trying to make.
>
> —Roy Lichtenstein, artist

Refer to chapter 3, "Color and Light," for information about this subject.

Community

Today most museums understand that one of their major roles is to serve the community. To fulfill this function, many have adjusted hours, established exhibits, and prepared programs to meet local needs.

Over the years, the size and concept of the community have changed; with automobiles and public transportation so readily available, it is now common for a museum to draw from a distance of a hundred miles or more. Today, planners/designers must consider both an institution's local and its extended communities.

Community Phases: Special Considerations

Master Plan
- Defines and identifies the needs of the communities that the institution serves

Feasibility, Schematic, and Preliminary Phases
- Develops exhibits and programs that are community oriented

Community Assessment Study

When analyzing an institution's role in the community, planners usually tour the surrounding areas and interview and work with local educators and civic and cultural leaders. If possible, they also review the community's long-range plan. The following are a few questions that are usually addressed:

- What are the communities and the regions that the institution serves, and how can they be best provided for?
- Can the institution be a catalyst for community / regional economic development? If so, how?
- What are the economic, social, and cultural needs of the people, and, via the museum, how can they be best addressed?

Community Assessment Report

The community assessment report consists of a profile and a historic overview of the community, and, if they are available, a long-term growth report and an economic development plan. This report culminates in suggesting outreach programs, partnering endeavors with local organizations, and special community-related activities and programs.

Conservation

"When in doubt, check it out," is always a prudent motto to use when handling and exhibiting any artifact or display item.

Planners / designers are mandated to preserve and protect the artifacts that have been entrusted to them. When designing and refurbishing display cases or structures, they must be constantly vigilant to make sure that the finishes, materials, lighting, and so on, will not damage the items on display. During all phases, conservation of the display objects must be considered.

Conservation Phases: Special Considerations

Schematic Phase

Conservation considerations and techniques should be recorded for each selected display item.

Preliminary, Intermediate, Final, and Documentation Phases

Research, design, and detail the structures and their environment to ensure that the display objects will not deteriorate or be damaged.

Professional Advice

It is important to have a curator or a conservator available to render advice during the development of an exhibition design for they know the best methods to preserve and protect the artifacts that will be displayed. In the event that such experts are not available to offer advice as to the proper lighting and humidity levels and the mounting techniques to employ, then it becomes the responsibility of the planner/designer to make sure that every item on display will not be damaged.

CASE HISTORY: "BETSY'S SIGNATURE"

I am convinced that, of all museum professionals, the conservator has to have the most courage. Once I was assigned to design a display case for the purpose of preserving and protecting the only document that is known to exist containing Betsy Ross's signature. Discovered in a dusty closet in Philadelphia's City Hall, this document had been neglected for centuries; it was torn and taped and in very bad condition. To "protect it," it had been heat-sealed between two sheets of plastic. These were the same sheets that are used to laminate cheap menus. The conservator had to remove the plastic and the tape, and clean centuries of grit from the surface of the paper. For me it seemed like a Herculean job compared to my task of just designing a display case for this irreplaceable signature.

There are times when designers do not have professional assistance and must rely on reference materials concerning the display and protection of artifacts. The following is just a brief overview of the information on which I have relied.

Offgassing

This is the release of a gas from a material under normal temperature and pressure conditions in a confined, unventilated case or space. As materials, finishes, and artifacts age, they break down and produce gases that can harm visitors and damage artifacts. Materials such as stone are inert.

Artifacts themselves can also be very destructive. When enclosed in a sealed case, an artifact can outgas and damage itself and the other artifacts enclosed with it. For example, a wooden mask could outgas and destroy a silk cloth that is attached to or positioned nearby the mask.

Wood, a commonly used exhibit material, is a perfect example of a wonderful product that has a destructive nature and can be a silent and invisible destroyer of artifacts. All woods outgas and can emit volatile, corrosive compounds that, when confined to an enclosed space, can cause damage.

Gases emitted from wood can corrode metal and destroy clothing, paper, and other organic materials. The worst woods for offgassing are white pine, oak, chestnut, and beech. Offgassing damage can also occur when artifacts come into direct contact with wooden shelves, display mounts, and stands. Any species of wood can be used in exhibit construction, as long as it does not touch the artifact and its gases are allowed to dissipate.

When a museum has gas-emitting wooden display cabinets it is best to completely seal the interior area of the case with a wood finish that will cover the wood surfaces, joints, screws, and screw holes. In addition, the cabinet should be frequently aired out.

CASE HISTORY: "THE RED OAK DILEMMA"

Once I was called in to plan/design exhibits for a museum, and I discovered that they had just installed beautiful, red oak display cases to house their collection of fragile, hand-painted artifacts. Faced with the fact that the cases were permanent and would never be redone, I recommended that the red oak interior surfaces and the hardware be sealed with a wood finish. On the chance that cracks or scratches could release red oak gases, I also advised the museum director to open the doors of the cases once a week to allow any trapped pollutants to dissipate.

Offgassing and Outgassing

These two terms refer to the emission of a gas from a material. Offgassing indicates that the gas is being released in an enclosed space. Outgassing refers to a gas that is released in a large area or an exterior space. Both terms are used interchangeably.

Light

Usually it is counterproductive to display an item in a darkened environment where its details and colors cannot be appreciated. Yet the more visible an artifact is, the higher the probability that damage from natural or artificial lighting will occur. It is the total length of time that an artifact is exposed to a light source that damages it; therefore, the longer and brighter the exposure, the more irreversible the damage will be.

The two main culprits that can fade and cause an artifact to deteriorate are light (ultraviolet and infrared) and the heat from that light. Light intensity can be measured using a meter calibrated in lux or foot candles. To determine the level, a light meter should be held next to the artifact. Figure 2.2 provides a good guide to use.

LIGHT LEVELS and MATERIALS

Maximum Light Level	Materials
200 lux (20 foot candles)	Most ceramics, glass, metals
150 to 200 lux (15- 20 foot candles)	Oil and tempera paintings, undyed leather, lacquer, wood, horn, bone, ivory, stone
50 lux (5 foot candles) or less	Watercolor paintings, manuscripts, prints, drawings, vulnerable textiles, photographs

Figure 2.2. Light levels and materials.

To reduce or control exposure to damaging light, the Philadelphia Museum of Art recommends the following:

- Timer switches in galleries or inside exhibition cases
- Computer-controlled systems to turn lights off when the museum is closed
- Curtains or light-diffusing materials placed on windows
- Ultraviolet filtering plastic sleeves or tubes placed over artificial light sources (http: / / www.philamuseum.org /)

CASE HISTORY: "A GENERAL'S SILK BREECHES"

For years a very small but important historic society displayed in front of a sun-drenched window a priceless pair of silk breeches worn by a famous Revolutionary War general. Of course, over time the sun's ultraviolet rays played havoc with this garment to the point that the society had to spend a considerable amount of money to have it conserved. After the breeches were repaired and returned to the society, the powers to be, in spite of my "ultraviolet sun damage" warning, returned the breeches to the same display case in front of the same window, only to ensure that the destructive process would start again.

Migration

An artifact's dyes or paints can be transferred to another artifact if they are placed together and are allowed to touch for any length of time. Migration can happen when items are on display as well as when they are in storage.

Temperature and Humidity

The amount of water vapor in the air is referred to as humidity, and it fluctuates as the temperature changes. Hot air absorbs water; cold air expels water. As a result, any moisture that is expelled clings to or is absorbed by nearby materials. This action causes metal artifacts to rust and wooden ones to swell.

As the temperature fluctuates, materials, adhesives, and even joints used in construction will contract and expand at different rates as they absorb and expel moisture. It is extremely important to keep a microclimate constant, especially when an artifact is a composite of various materials. The following are general guidelines for displaying and preserving objects on exhibit:

Temperature
  60 to 70 degrees F (15.5 to 21 degrees C)
Relative humidity
  Should deviate no more than 3 percent
  Most materials should be maintained at 40 to 60 percent
  Metals should be held below 40 percent

The American Institute for Conservation of Historic and Artistic Works in "Caring for Your Treasures," *Journal of the American Institute for Conservation* 44, no. 3 (2005), article 8, made this very important statement: "Locate sensitive objects in the most stable locations. Do not place moisture-sensitive collections in the path of direct sunlight, near heating or air-conditioning ducts, against external walls, or in damp locations such as basements. Avoid putting cases and framed works along exterior walls."

Construction Costs

Fabrication, shipping, and installation are the three main tasks included in exhibit construction costs, but there are times when ancillary expenses may also be included. So, before commencing a project, it is essential to know exactly the items that the institution desires to include in its exhibition construction contract. The term "time and materials" is the same as "labor and materials."

Construction Costs Phases: Special Considerations

Feasibility Study
  Establish a budget.
Schematic Phase
  Compile a ballpark estimate.
Preliminary Phase
  Prepare a time and materials estimate.
Intermediate Phase
  Review and revise the time and materials estimate as necessary.
Final Phase
  Review and revise in detail the time and materials estimate. This estimate has to be very precise.
Documentation Phase
  Revise the time and materials estimate to reflect any changes that occurred during this phase.
Bidding Phase
  Contractor's construction costs are submitted by firms bidding on the project.

The following are two commonly used methods to calculate costs; each has a different meaning and purpose, and they are not interchangeable.

Budget

A budget is established during the feasibility phase; it is somewhat inexact and is just a reasonably intelligent guess meant as a guide to establish the costs of a proposed project. Since the exhibit is only a concept and does not yet exist, a professional cost estimator usually is not needed. Rather, with the input from a few experienced colleagues, an institution can arrive at a credible budget by analyzing the project's density, complexity, and types of displays proposed. Traditionally, there are two types of budgets.

Linear Budget

This budget is employed when the proposed displays, usually pictures and graphics, will be hung (gallery fashion) on the walls.

Length of wall(s) × dollar amount per running foot = linear budget

Area Budget

Sometimes called a square-foot budget, this is used when an exhibit area is involved and the displays and structures are placed throughout the floor.

Square feet of space × dollar amount per square foot = area budget

Estimate

Based on labor and materials costs of the actual design, an estimate is employed during the preliminary, intermediate, final, and documentation phases. As the project advances, and more detailed information becomes available, the cost analysis will change and become more precise.

There is no point in presenting a wonderful exhibit design that exceeds the construction budget. So, even before starting a presentation sketch, it is important to review your concepts with a professional estimator. Such a consultant is well worth the fee and can save you the time and expense that you might spend detailing items, which, if over the budget, will certainly be eliminated. Another advantage of consulting with an estimator is that the exhibit's materials and construction techniques can be reviewed and discussed in detail. There are two types of estimates usually employed.

Ballpark Estimate

This type of quotation is usually compiled for each schematic design that is presented, or when a rough idea of cost is required. Basically, it is a guesstimate, and therefore rather inexact. Without spending much time, an experienced estimator can produce a reasonably competent ballpark estimate. In addition, a contingency factor of 5 to 15 percent for unknown items is worth considering at this time.

Time and Materials Estimate

Starting during the preliminary phase, and updated throughout the remainder of the project, this type of estimate addresses the exact cost of the project. It requires that a dollar amount be applied to all the labor, materials, shipping, and installation costs.

Construction Delivery Methods

The purpose of a construction delivery methods (CDM) contract is to establish a working relationship between the institution, the exhibit team, and the construction firm. It is not a contract. After the institution has established the CDM they desire, a proposal is initiated, and a contract signed.

At the beginning of the design process, the exhibit team's project manager must be informed as to the type of CDM that the institution intends to employ so that the team, tasks, and documentation can be adjusted to meet the requirements of a particular delivery method. There are three basic contract types.

Negotiated

Under this system, the construction firm is chosen, joins the team at the beginning of the project, and works closely with the exhibit and the museum's teams to provide technical information and cost analysis. The construction firm will also construct and install the exhibits. This type of relationship has advantages and disadvantages.

Advantages

If it is a minor project, such as a small exhibit area or a few display cases that need refurbishing or require a few changes, the planner/designer can produce a simple concept or even a written description of the required work. The selected contractor then submits an estimate and, if the institution agrees, proceeds with the work.

When an institution's staff is not well versed in construction details and methods, and needs technical advice and cost estimates during the design process, a negotiated contract with a builder may be appropriate. The contractor will act in an advisory role during the plan/design process and will usually build the exhibits.

If a project has a tight, drop-dead time frame, the contractor can fast-track the work by preordering materials and constructing the items piecemeal as the designs are being produced.

Disadvantages

The costs are usually higher because the projects are not normally competitively bid.

Design-Bid-Build

This is the traditional method used to plan/design and construct exhibitions. It is composed of the following three separate phases of work:

- Design: Exhibit team conceives the exhibits and produces the bid drawings and specifications.
- Bid: Institution oversees and is responsible for the bidding procedures with the assistance of the designer.
- Build: Successful construction firm builds the exhibits.

This type of contract relies on a realistic time frame and on planners/designers who can produce accurate and complete bidding documents. It has definite advantages: the design staff is probably professionally trained, and the quality of design invariably is very good. In addition, the ability to obtain competitive quotes generally results in lower construction costs.

Design-Build

This method is employed when the museum contracts with a construction firm to plan/design and build the exhibits. To hand over the project

THE ROAD TO THE EXHIBITION VIA DESIGN-BID-BUILD

Step 1	Exhibit Team	Plans and designs the exhibits Produces the: Project Manual & Bidding Drawings
Step 2	Museum Team	Prepares the: General Conditions & Contract Assembles the RFP Sends RFP to construction firms
Step 3	Construction Team	Estimates the project Prepares a RRFP Submits RRFP to Institution
Step 4	Museum Team	Receives and reviews the RRFP Selects the construction firm
Step 5	Museum Team	Prepares the contract
Step 6	Museum & Construction Firm	Representatives sign the contract
Step 7	Construction Team Museum & Exhibit Teams	Builds and installs the exhibits Observe construction and installation

Figure 2.3. The road to the exhibition via design-bid-build.

to a construction firm can be reassuring for a museum, since they can generally be confident that the exhibits will be produced on time and on budget. The major reason for employing the design-build method is when a museum has an impossible deadline or lacks the trained personnel to carry out the work.

It is vitally important to select a construction firm that will employ trained museum planners/designers and can produce a quality product. The major disadvantage of this method is that most exhibit construction firms specialize in trade show exhibits. They design glitzy exhibits, and their designers are not trained in the principles involved in museum exhibition planning/designing. Further, since many of the design and construction decisions are made at the construction shop, when the client is not present, the museum can lose some control of the project.

Construction Contracts

This is the legal agreement between the museum and the contractor for the exhibition's construction. There are many different types of contracts, the most commonly employed being lump sum, unit price, and time and materials contracts.

Lump Sum

In a lump sum contract, the contractor agrees to construct, deliver, and install all the exhibit materials described and detailed in the request for proposal (RFP) for a fixed price. This is the most common type of contract employed by institutions.

Unit Price

A unit price contract is used when a project is divided into segments, and each supplier is asked to provide and install a particular exhibit. Usually, it is for a display or a unit that can stand alone and requires a certain skill to produce, such as a diorama, a replica, a participatory element, or a wall or floor covering.

The advantage of dealing directly with individual suppliers is that the institution can eliminate the normal markups (usually 25 to 50 percent) on all "outside" purchases that the contractor with a lump sum contract must apply. The disadvantage of unit pricing is that the institution becomes its own general contractor and must hire, schedule, and supervise all the subcontractors and suppliers. This is a skill that many do not possess, and a responsibility that most do not want.

Another reason for requesting unit pricing occurs when a project is suspected of being over budget and a few of its displays might have to be eliminated. In this case, the general contractor is asked to price all or some of the displays separately. Knowing the cost of each unit helps the institution to determine which exhibits could be eliminated. These costs are generally submitted as "alternates to the contract" in the contractor's "response to the request for proposal" (RRFP) submittal.

Time and Materials

Also called cost plus, a time and materials contract is based on the contractor's estimating each piece of material and every hour of labor separately, and adding an agreed-upon profit. It is mostly used when time is tight and the planning/designing and construction phases must overlap. This method is usually more costly because all the work is done on a unit basis, and it requires more time to estimate and administer the project.

Bonding

A bond is basically an insurance policy that guarantees that the contractor awarded the project will submit a serious bid and will successfully complete the project. It is often requested by museums, especially on a large project.

Bonds are expensive, and contractors legitimately include the bonding fees (sometimes hidden) in the construction costs of the project. A museum has to determine if they want to pay for this fee or spend that money on a much-needed display. According to the needs of the project, bonds can differ greatly; the following is an overview of the two basic types.

Bid Bond

A bid bond guarantees that the contractor, if awarded the contract, will honor his or her bid and sign the contract. If the contractor refuses to do the work, the museum will usually be reimbursed for the additional cost required to rebid the project.

Performance Bond

Many institutions request that construction firms when submitting a bid include a performance bond. This bond is, in reality, an insurance policy that guarantees the museum that the construction firm will complete the contract, and if the contractor defaults on the project, the work as detailed in the contract will be completed by others.

Guarantee

Contractors are usually required to guarantee their work and materials for a certain period of time. This guarantee is included in the contract and is usually for a year.

Change Order

A change order document is used when work is added to or deleted from the original contract. It usually involves a change to the scope of work, project cost, and completion date. Once a change order is submitted and approved by both the museum and the contractor, it effectively alters the original contract.

The construction firm or the institution initiates the change by describing the new work to be added or deleted. The work involved should not proceed until all parties are in agreement as to its cost and schedule implications, and the change order is signed. In the case where the cost of the work involved does not change, a no-cost change order is issued.

At the beginning of construction and installation, I recommend that the museum team members involved in the project discuss the change order form and its procedure, and that they should be alerted to the fact that changes, most of the time, will increase the costs of the project.

Bid Review

The museum, most times, with the assistance of the exhibit team's project manager, reviews all the submitted quotations. The museum then selects the construction firm and awards the contract. Before the contract is signed, however, the institution usually meets with the selected contractor to review the work involved and to make sure that everyone understands its scope.

Before signing a contract, it goes without saying that it is of paramount importance for the museum's staff to read and understand everything that is in the contractor's bid submission, since there could be a change from the bidding documents (response to the request for proposal [RRFP]). Once agreed to and signed, the contract always supersedes the institution's request for proposal (RFP). In other words, the contractor has the last word, since what is in his or her RRFP is incorporated into the construction contract and that is what gets built.

Contractor's Submittals

The contractor has to provide the museum's representatives, usually the planner/designer, with any submittals listed in the bid package and where they were made part of the construction contract. Each submittal must be reviewed and approved before the construction of that item can take place.

Submittals are not free; their costs are included in the construction costs, so it is important to ask just for the ones you really need. If a dispute occurs, a submittal or an actual sample can serve as legal evidence. The following are the typical required submittals and the approval method.

Shop Drawings

Based on the technical drawings and specifications produced by the planner/designer, the contractor prepares shop drawings (SD) showing exactly how an item will be built and installed. These drawings bridge the gap between the designer's technical documents and the construction process. Shop drawings are used by the construction firm and installers to fabricate and install the exhibits.

CASE HISTORY: "TECHNICAL DRAWINGS ARE NOT SHOP DRAWINGS"

Once, a contractor sent his shop drawings to me for approval. I looked at them, and they seemed quite familiar. And they were! They were my drawings with his title block replacing mine. I rejected them immediately. The designer's technical drawings are meant to tell the contractor exactly what the structure should look like and how it should work, not how he is expected to build it in his shop. I rejected the drawings because not only did they not indicate the construction methods that he would be using but also it wasn't fair to the other construction firms that had competed for the project and had estimated on producing their own shop drawings. He complained, saying that he would not have a problem building from my drawings; the museum agreed with him, and I was left feeling that I had swallowed a "nasty" pill that day. After much discussion, the contractor was finally forced to produce the required shop drawings. I think he got some high school kid to create them, for they were so bad that I had to reject many of them at least five times. So much for the low bidder!

Samples

The designer requests samples for review when drawings or specifications cannot precisely ensure quality control. Plastic laminates, woods, fabrics, floor tiles, paint, acrylic joints, replicas, finishes, and graphic reproductions are just a few of the items normally requested and serve as a reference file during construction.

Product Data

When an off-the-shelf product is called for, such as an electronic or mechanical device, hardware, or a light fixture, the contractor submits documentation that illustrates the quality and performance of the product. The product data can vary and may include illustrations, performance charts, instructions, brochures, and diagrams.

Approved/Rejected Procedure

Shop drawings are usually electronically received, and they must be approved or rejected and returned to the contractor. Drawings can be either stamped or signed off. Anything that you write on a drawing can be questioned in court. So it is best not to be too casual about this process. For that reason, I am suggesting figure 2.4 to use for the approval/rejection stamp.

NO EXCEPTION __________

REVISE & RESUBMIT __________

FINISH AS MARKED __________

REJECTED __________

Comments made on the shop drawings and/or submittals during review are not intended to and do not relieve contractor from compliance with all requirements of the drawings and specifications. Review is solely for the benefit of Owner and may not be relied upon by Contractor and/or Supplier as basis to change requirements of contract documents. Review is limited to general compliance with contract documents and is not detailed for dimensions or for configuration. Contractor remains responsible for determining quantities, dimensions, fabrication processes, techniques and schedule of construction, coordination with all trades and performing his work safely and satisfactorily.

Firm's or Museum's Name Here

By_______________ **Date** ______

Figure 2.4. Approval/rejection stamp for shop drawings.

Case Study 2.1: What Is the Process Used to Bid and Build an Exhibit?

I met with David M. Egner, the director of project management of the Museum Division at Art Guild (AG), an exhibit fabrication firm, to discuss the process that AG uses to produce and install their museum exhibitions. He felt that the Golisano Children's Museum of Naples exhibition that they had just completed could be used to explain their operating procedures. Although this museum was large in scale, he explained that the procedure involved is the same regardless of the size of the project.

The Golisano Children's Museum is a newly minted museum in Naples, Florida. Its mission is to "provide an exciting, inspiring environment where children and their families play, learn and dream together" (http://www.cmon.org/). It contains thirty thousand square feet comprising twelve galleries of exhibits filled with state-of-the-art interactive displays that AG constructed and installed.

I felt that this museum was certainly worth discussing, and I asked David what information the designer gave them, especially for the computerized and the electromechanical exhibits. How did they program, engineer, and construct all these high-tech exhibits? And what procedures did AG use to expedite this project, especially when the museum was located in Florida, the exhibit designer, Jack Rouse Associates (JRA), was based in Ohio, and the construction firm was in New Jersey?

David obligingly answered my questions and showed me photographs of the exhibits. I learned that the designer and educator had worked closely together to create exhibits that would assist children in their learning and physical development. Also, they were very mindful that most Florida visitors rarely experienced ice and snow, so when developing the winter exhibit they designed an igloo display that contained a sheet of real ice so the children could touch and feel its slippery and icy surface, a frosted window to write on, and a full-sized faux snowman to play with.

For Art Guild, the Golisano Children's Museum project actually started five years earlier when they responded to the museum's RFQ. Since they had completed numerous exhibits for museums, their response was extensive and included photographs and case histories of completed projects, resumes of key personnel who would be involved in the project, and the organization chart shown in figure 2.6.

Several firms submitted their RFQs, and after an intensive review, the museum selected Art Guild and a few other firms to bid on their project. Via the designer's file transfer protocol (FTP) site, AG received a

Figure 2.5. Igloo exhibit, Golisano Children's Museum of Naples, Florida. Courtesy of JRA; Exhibit Design and Project Management.

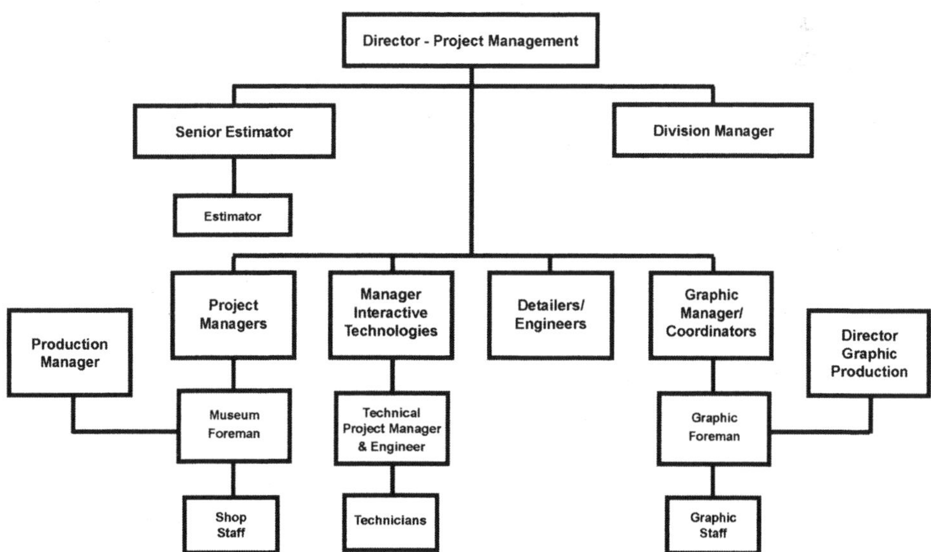

Figure 2.6. Organization chart, Art Guild. Courtesy of Golisano Children's Museum of Naples, Art Guild, Inc., West Deptford, New York.

request for proposal (RFP) that included technical drawings, representative graphics and type, specifications, sketches, and a brief description of all exhibit components.

Giving Art Guild a short time to review the documentation, the museum scheduled a conference call interview. Representatives from the museum and the design firm then visited an AG project that was being installed at the Liberty Science Center in Jersey City, New Jersey. Here they inspected the quality of AG's work, met the senior project manager who was designated to run the Golisano, and had a question-and-answer session. Based on the information obtained from the RFP, the conference call, and the meeting, AG was able to estimate on the construction and installation of the exhibits.

AG's response was certainly impressive, for it addressed every exhibit; described the materials, equipment, and finishes; listed each graphic; and detailed every electromechanical device and hardware and software that would be needed. Constant use, ease of maintenance, and longevity of the exhibits were also major considerations in preparing their response. Their response served several purposes:

- It informed the museum personnel of the cost of the project and assured them that AG understood it and all the work involved.
- The information in the response would allow AG, during construction, to schedule the project, order materials, and coordinate approximately three hundred individual graphics.
- The "interactive scope summary" was also part of Art Guild's response and described the operating procedures and the mechanisms required for each participatory exhibit. This summary enabled AG to order materials immediately and prepare the shop drawing once the contract was signed.

"The Trolley," shown in figure 2.7, is one of the many exhibits that AG estimated on that was described in the interactive scope summary. AG not only built the exhibit but also provided the engineering and computer programming services and equipment. This exhibit allowed children to select a destination on an interactive map of the museum and watch the trolley navigate the path they had selected.

During the estimating period, Art Guild provided value engineering services that included recommending to the museum when an item could be purchased directly from a source, thus avoiding their normal markup. A large, stand-alone exhibit, the thirty-feet-tall and forty-five-feet-wide "Banyan Tree" was just such a purchase, and AG helped to coordinate the effort. The banyan is shown in figure 2.8.

Figure 2.7. "The Trolley Exhibit, Golisano Children's Museum of Naples," Naples, Florida. Courtesy of JRA; Exhibit Design and Project Management.

A project as large as this one is rarely awarded without a visit to the construction facility by the client and the designer, and I am sure they were as impressed as I was when I toured AG's shop. Art Guild has a huge, well-organized facility consisting of a carpentry shop containing state-of-the art equipment, including a router that is the size of a truck and several huge spray-paint rooms that can dry a display's paint finishes within fifteen to twenty minutes. They also have a very impressive graphic production facility with many inkjet printers, plus one that can print on any substrate, including two-inch-thick boards. AG even maintains a fully equipped silk-screen facility for designers who still like that look or desire to screen directly on a wall surface.

Once the museum's representatives had inspected AG's facility, they knew, as I did, that the firm could handle any museum exhibit construction project, no matter how large or complicated it might be. Based on Art Guild's response to the RFP and the inspection visit to their plant, museum personnel were assured that the exhibits would be well built of quality materials and that the integrity of the exhibit design would be maintained. As a result, AG was awarded the assignment to build and install all the exhibits for the museum.

Once the construction contract was signed, work at Art Guild began. A start-up meeting was scheduled at their shop to discuss all pertinent

Figure 2.8. "The Banyan Tree Exhibit, Golisano Children's Museum of Naples," Naples, Florida. Courtesy of JRA; Exhibit Design and Project Management. Photo by Heather Witt. See MEPD 2.7 CRA Spec.

details with the Golisano and the designer's personnel, review the time schedule, and allow the members who would be involved in the project to get acquainted. AG was able to start immediately to prepare shop drawings and samples such as finishes and construction joints. The colors and materials board and the graphic layouts prepared by JRA gave AG the information they needed to assemble their own board, which consisted of two-inch-square swatches of the colors specified in the RFP (there were over a hundred such swatches). Twelve-inch-square, graphic reproductions of selected layouts were also provided by AG. As soon as these items were completed, they were forwarded to the designer for review and approval. Construction never began on an item until approval was obtained.

Since most of the exhibits had curvilinear forms and angular joints, AG's computer-driven router was in constant use during construction. And the "World Café" exhibit with its circular artifact cases and headers composed of angular joints and intersections was no exception. The purpose of this particular exhibit is to introduce the visitors, both young and old, to the various cultures that exist throughout the world (see figure 2.9). Visitors hear a region's music, view a menu showing its cuisine, and see a counter filled with replicas of local dishes. Artifacts and items from that culture are displayed throughout the room and in display cases. Every three to six months, a different region is highlighted.

Many times, participatory exhibits need to be mocked up and tested before final construction can begin, so during the preparation of these exhibits, AG constructed several mockups of electromechanical and computer-driven displays. Children were then invited to test them and to give their response.

During the construction period, Golisano and the designer were kept fully informed by means of Art Guild's weekly progress reports and visits to the construction facility. Before the project left the shop, the client made the mandatory final inspection, and the exhibits were then wrapped and shipped to the museum. AG sent their carpenters to the site to install the project, and in order to maintain the schedule they augmented their staff with local journeymen carpenters. When artifacts need to be installed, AG always retains professional artifact mount makers and installers. However,

Figure 2.9. "The World Café Exhibit, Golisano Children's Museum of Naples," Naples, Florida. Courtesy of JRA, Exhibit Design and Project Management.

in this case, Golisano museum personnel installed the few artifacts that were required. Before the job was finished, AG completed the items that were on the "punch list," cleaned all the exhibits, and made the exhibit areas "broom clean." The entire installation went smoothly, and thanks to JRA's professionalism in producing a complete set of drawings and specifications, and reviewing all shop drawings and samples and returning them speedily, all the work was completed on time and ready for opening day.

Upon returning to their New Jersey facility, AG prepared a close-out package and sent it to the client. AG guarantees their work for a year, and of course they are always available during the life of the exhibits to assist with upgrades.

Contractual Agreements

Planners/designers are not trained as lawyers, yet they have to generate the documentation that will become part of the institution's contract with the builder. Since the bidding documents are often used to settle any legal disputes that may arise, it is critical that planners/designers have a basic knowledge of contractual procedures and terminology.

Contractual procedures can vary greatly because they are influenced by the kind of institution, the administration, the legal advice available, and the type and size of the project.

Contractual Agreements Phases: Special Considerations

Schematic Phase

The institution informs the exhibit team as to the type of construction delivery method it requires.

Documentation Phase

The planner/designer produces the documentation that will become part of the agreement.

Construction and Installation Phases

The planner/design observes the work to ensure that the contractual requirements are fulfilled.

Request and Responses

Briefly stated, institutions request and construction firms respond. The following are the traditional types of requests and responses involved in an institution's selection of a bidder or one with whom a contract will be negotiated. The request issued by an institution will normally consist of a request for proposal (RFP), a request for qualifications (RFQ), or both

(RFP/RFQ). The typical contractor's response is a response to the request for proposal (RRFP), a response to the request for qualifications (RRFQ), or both (RRFP/RRFQ).

RFP: Request for Proposal

Prepared by the institution and the designer, the RFP is usually sent to several contractors asking them to submit bids for the construction of a specified exhibit. For most projects, the RFP is the bid package.

RFQ: Request for Qualifications

This type of request occurs when the institution solicits information about a construction firm's personnel, situation, facilities, and experience. They want to be assured that the firm can successfully complete their project, has a competent workforce, and is financially solvent. Cost considerations are not part of the RFQ. After a construction firm has been selected, a negotiated contract between the institution and the contractor based on a bid package may be initiated and signed. At other times an approved firm will be included in a list of bidders, sometimes called a short list. Most times, an RFQ is used when a project is technically complicated, very large, or requires a high level of craftsmanship.

RFP/RFQ: Request for Proposal and Request for Qualifications

As indicated by its title, this is a combination of the above requests. The RFP/RFQ is the most commonly used method to choose a construction firm, since it allows the institution to select a qualified firm and, at the same time, obtain competitive construction bids.

RRFP (Bid): Response to the Request for Proposal

This response details the construction firm's cost to construct, ship, and install the exhibits.

RRFQ: Response to the Request for Qualifications

This response provides the qualifications of a construction firm.

RRFP/RRFQ

This is a combination of the above two responses and requires that the contractors submit both their qualifications and their bids to do the work.

Critique

Critique, meaning to review and discuss a project, is an informal appraisal of the exhibition design and is performed frequently throughout all exhibit planning/designing phases. These get-togethers mainly involve members of the planning/design team but sometimes include other members who are directly involved in the exhibition project. A critique is not an evaluation (see later in this chapter).

It is always important that the planners/designers frequently stop, step back, and analyze all aspects of the exhibition design. When working on a project, tunnel vision can and usually does occur, and critiques help to ensure that the project will not deviate from its intended goals and that the integrity of the design is maintained. They should check that the design is "on track," that it hasn't deviated from the exhibit program and the requirements that were established, and that the exhibit structures are properly placed and their forms and shapes well designed. Most important, they should think about the visitors and make sure that all their needs are met.

> In order to understand someone it is necessary to walk in his shoes.

Mindful of this old adage during the early design development phases, it is always beneficial to critique the concept by mentally "walking" through the exhibition from entrance to exit and visualizing and imagining the visitor's experience. During many of these journeys, the mentality of each age group and the level of interest of the anticipated audience should be addressed. These walks invariably result in changes that always improve the design and the visitor's experience.

Other times it is beneficial to have a question-and-answer session. The following is just a sampling of some of the pertinent questions that could be addressed:

- Are the goals of the mission statement and exhibition program being met?
- Are the displays compatible with the exhibition's theme and its ambience?
- Is the exhibition visually exciting and well designed?
- Are the graphics, exhibit areas, displays, and artifacts logically placed?
- Are the visitors' ages and interests successfully addressed?
- Is information being presented in a clear and concise manner?
- Will the exhibits be an exciting and fulfilling experience for all visitors?

Design Preservation

During its life span, a successful, permanent exhibition has to evolve and mature. This development is especially critical for small museums, historic sites, and environmental venues where return visitation and community support are their lifeblood.

Producing exhibits that can change over time while maintaining the integrity of the original design is always a challenge, and this is especially important if the planner/designer is not on hand to supervise the modifications and maintain the fundamental design principles that served as the initial basis for the exhibit. During all the design phases and the post-opening phase, there are methods that planners/designers can employ to inform future caretakers as to the principles inherent in a design.

Tutorials

At every occasion during the exhibit development phases, particularly during presentations and meetings, exhibit team members should take every opportunity to explain to the museum's personnel the design principles that dictated the selection of colors, shapes, forms, textures, illumination, and so forth, and the reasons for the placement of the display items and structures.

CASE HISTORY: "THE TUTORIALS"

When designing exhibits for a newly formed, small firefighting museum, I knew that upon completion of the exhibits the responsibility to upgrade the displays would be left in the hands of the firemen. Therefore, it was very important that they had the confidence and the knowledge to enable them to successfully upgrade the exhibits without my help.

Throughout the design process the firemen had patiently given me a tutorial on fire-related subjects, and I returned the favor by giving them an Exhibit 101 plan/design course. As I presented my design, I subtly touched upon all relevant design theories and issues. I explained why I had selected particular forms, shapes, colors, illumination, ambience, and so on, and I also discussed future changes that could be made to the exhibits and the various themes that might be explored.

Did my design theory tutorial work? Yes! Some time after completion, I stopped by the museum and was delighted to find that they had installed many newly acquired artifacts, developed several temporary exhibits, and successfully added to the permanent exhibits that I had designed. All the changes that were made incorporated the design concepts that I had discussed in the presentation meetings, and happily, the changes improved and did not destroy the integrity of the design.

Plan/Design Report

Verbalization is only effective as long as the people you are talking to continue to be involved with the project. For that reason, planners/designers should prepare a written report that discusses all the topics and design theories that were employed to plan/design the exhibition. This report should be made part of the project archival file and referred to during any future refurbishing.

Display Objects

Art is the accumulation of knowledge.

—Toni Morrision, author

Planners/designers are mandated not only to provide visitors with the opportunity to view display objects in a suitable manner but also to conserve and protect the objects.

Display Objects Phases: Special Considerations

Feasibility Study
- Pivotal display objects are suggested.

Schematic Phase
- Prepare an "exhibition inventory form."
- Major display objects are selected and documented, and exhibit locations are suggested.

Preliminary Phase
- All prime display objects are selected and inventoried.
- Commence to select and inventory secondary objects.
- Assign an exhibit location for all selected display items.

Intermediate Phase
- Select and inventory most secondary display objects.
- Continue to assign exhibit locations for the selected display items.
- Address conservation and protection techniques.
- Commence to design artifact supports and mounts.

Final Phase
- Review conservation and protection techniques.
- All display items should have been selected and inventoried, and their exhibit locations finalized.
- Continue to design or specify the artifact supports and mounts.

Documentation Phase
Locate display items on the technical drawings.
Specify the display mounting devices.
Bidding Phase
Pertinent display objects are reviewed.
Construction Phase
Construct or provide mounting devices.
Installation Phase
Install the artifacts.
Post-Opening Phase
Include the exhibition inventory forms in the project archival file.

Handling

Handle each display item with extreme care! Always treat it as if it were a newborn baby; make sure that it is not too hot, not too cold, and in a safe environment, and above all, don't drop it. Always wear gloves, make sure that a camera flash is not detrimental, and when touching, moving, or installing any display item, plan ahead and take all proper precautions.

Inventorying

Inventorying can be a formidable task, and even a relatively small exhibition can include hundreds of objects. During the exhibit development, construction, and installation phases, the exhibit team members must keep track of each display item. When inventorying, it is important for the planners/designers to work with the museum personnel who are usually very knowledgeable about each artifact and always seem to have wonderful bits of information that could be used in the exhibit to make a seemingly mundane item come alive.

No one wants to be responsible for designing an exhibit case that is too small for the artifact or a pedestal that collapses under the weight of an object. When inventorying, accuracy and consistency are extremely important. The traditional order used to record an object is length × width × height (L × W × H), and since flat art is framed or mounted on a substrate, it also has depth. Generally a scale is not available during inventorying, and the weight of an artifact is usually approximated, but when the weight of a display item is critical, a scale is a must.

Usually, after inspecting an artifact, it is returned to storage and becomes inaccessible during the exhibit development phases. Therefore, throughout the inventorying process, a form is used to record the important information about each item. In lieu of the artifacts, these forms are used during development of the exhibition design and the construction and installation phases.

Figure 2.10 is a typical inventory form; please feel free to use it, critique it, change it, and if you care to, make it yours. The italicized statements that appear in the form are for clarification only and are not intended to be part of it.

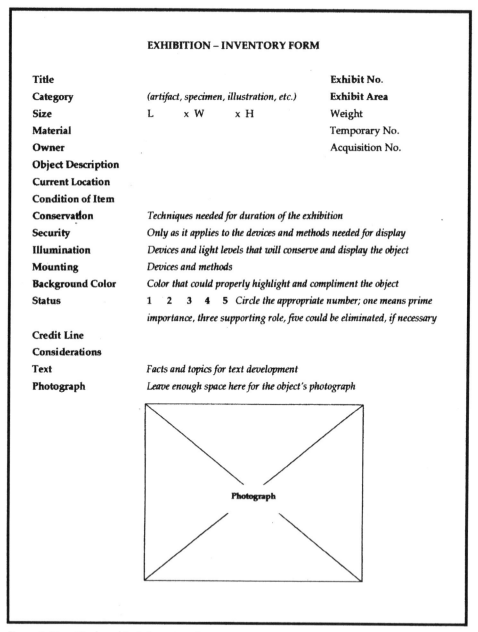

EXHIBITION – INVENTORY FORM

Title		**Exhibit No.**
Category	*(artifact, specimen, illustration, etc.)*	**Exhibit Area**
Size	L x W x H	Weight
Material		Temporary No.
Owner		Acquisition No.
Object Description		
Current Location		
Condition of Item		
Conservation	*Techniques needed for duration of the exhibition*	
Security	*Only as it applies to the devices and methods needed for display*	
Illumination	*Devices and light levels that will conserve and display the object*	
Mounting	*Devices and methods*	
Background Color	*Color that could properly highlight and compliment the object*	
Status	**1 2 3 4 5** *Circle the appropriate number; one means prime importance, three supporting role, five could be eliminated, if necessary*	
Credit Line		
Considerations		
Text	*Facts and topics for text development*	
Photograph	*Leave enough space here for the object's photograph*	

Photograph

Figure 2.10. Display object: Inventory form.

Identification Numbers

The inventory form in figure 2.10 has three different identification numbers; each is important in locating, identifying, and controlling a display item.

Exhibit Number

This is the exhibit identification number for each display item. It is assigned only after the design concept is firm and the display object is allocated to a particular exhibit. This number is keyed to its assigned exhibit so that its location can be easily identified during the design, construction, and installation periods.

Temporary Number

At the storage area, when display objects are being selected for an exhibition, artifacts are viewed on a first-come basis. At this time they are given a temporary number until their location in the exhibition has been determined and their exhibit number can be assigned.

Acquisition Number

The acquisition number is one that has been assigned to an artifact by the institution. It is used only for reference purposes.

Photography

When inventorying it is critical that a picture of each display object be taken and that it becomes part of the inventory form. During the exhibit planning/designing phases, when most objects are in storage, these photographs become a valuable visual reference.

Documents

Preparation of documents commences in the schematic phase and is changed, matured, and advanced throughout all phases until they are utilized in the bidding documents. For that reason it is prudent at the very beginning of the project to design and lay out your work so that it can be upgraded easily. A good rule to follow is to always build on and never redo a document. In other words, "forget the eraser." Whenever I had to make a major, time-consuming change to a document, it usually meant that I didn't get it right the first time.

Development of Documentation

Phases	Exhibition Program	Graphics	Drawings	Specifications
Schematic Design	Startup Program		Schematic Drawings	
Preliminary Design	Transitional Program	Rough Layouts	Design Development Drawings	
Intermediate Design	Advanced Program	Advanced Layouts	Design Develpment Drawings	Outline Specifications
Final Design	Completed Program	Completed Layouts	Design Control Drawings	Advanced Specifications
Documentation		Electronic Files or Graphic Layouts	Bidding Drawings	Bidding Specifications
Construction			Shop Drawings	

Note: Designer produces all the documentation except the shop drawings; they are prepared by the construction firm.

Figure 2.11. Documented development.

The chart in figure 2.11 shows the development of the various documents and their progression through the planning/designing and construction phases.

There is a variety of existing documents and reports that informs and assists the planner/designer during development of an exhibition. Two of these documents are the feasibility study report and the master plan report.

Feasibility Study Report

At the end of the feasibility phase a report that pertains to a particular exhibition is normally prepared and includes the following:

- mission and theme statements
- building facilities report
- exhibition construction ballpark estimate
- display objects report; only pivotal items are listed
- education goals analysis
- human resources report

Master Plan Report

The master plan phase concludes with a report that is usually prepared by the architect and any other specialists involved in the planning process. The master plan report could include the following:

- accessibility report
- architectural sketches
- building-use plan
- business plan
- collections management study
- community assessment report
- estimated construction cost
- existing conditions study
- floor and site plans
- historic overview
- institution analysis report
- long-range plan
- time schedule
- visitor evaluation report

Ergonomics

Trying to learn while standing up in a crowded room surrounded by strangers is not the best way to absorb information, and, at times, it can become abusive. Yet, this is the typical museum environment. During all design phases of a project, planners / designers must be vigilant to ensure that all ergonomic requirements are met and that the visitor's comfort and safety are assured. This is not an easy task, since people vary in size, shape, and physical ability. To address this subject the following topics must be considered.

Standard Dimensions

During the schematic and preliminary phases, to save time and not get bogged down in details that might never develop, I rely on the standard ergonomic dimensions that are available in publications, catalogs, and on the Internet. It is only during the intermediate, final, and documentation phases when the design is firm that I research, check, and adjust all dimensions and conditions to make sure that the ergonomic factors are correct. When in doubt, a full-size mockup of an exhibit structure is a valuable tool to employ, especially for children's exhibits.

Physically Challenged

> There are approximately 43 million disabled persons in the United States; it is estimated that one in five Americans have one or more impairments.
>
> — American Alliance of Museums, *The Accessible Museum*

Some people have obvious disabilities, while many others effectively conceal theirs. Yet we can readily spot the visitors with physical problems for they are the ones that frequently use the benches, decline the walks in the woods, use the ramps, and avoid the steps.

When planning/designing an exhibition, it is always prudent to make it physically and visually easy for everyone to enjoy by providing plenty of benches for resting, doors that are easy to operate, and displays that are physically effortless to use. Be considerate: tell the visitors before they venture forth that it is a long and rough walk to the pond, or that the stairs are steep and difficult to climb. Have the information readily visible regarding the accessible facilities that an institution provides. Above all, plan/design exhibits so that all visitors will have a comfortable experience.

Making an exhibition accessible to all visitors is a mandate to which we should adhere to the best of our abilities and circumstances. Yet there are always questions as to who is challenged, how many, and to what extent. For example, considerations should be given to the following impairments:

- Visual: Color-blind, low vision, and the totally blind
- Audio: Hearing impaired and the deaf
- Physical: Paraplegic and motor-skill damaged
- Cognitive: Brain damaged, dyslexic, and learning disabled

Fortunately we have guidelines and publications available to help us; the Americans with Disabilities Act (ADA) of 1990 established the criteria for exhibit design, and every planner/designer should comply with it. In addition, there are other excellent publications available to assist us such as *The Accessible Museum* produced by the American Alliance of Museums, and *Accessible Exhibitions: Testing the Reality* and *Equal Access* prepared by the Smithsonian Institution.

The subject concerning the physically challenged is an evolving issue with new studies and theories regularly being brought forth. For that reason, the following information has been restricted to the general requirements that apply to all museums. For the visually challenged specifically, refer to the Graphic Design, Visually Accessible Guidelines, section later in this chapter.

The ADA has not only assisted the physically challenged but also helped all of us to better enjoy the museum experience. For me, I now ignore staircases and use ramps, and I am happy that aisles are wider and people aren't constantly elbowing past me. I have also felt that in recent years, due to the ADA guidelines, the elderly, many with walking problems, and mothers with small children in strollers seem to be attending museums in greater numbers.

As planners / designers, we must strive to make our exhibits accessible; it's only fair and decent. Yet, at times, adhering to these standards can present a conundrum: how do you design accessible areas for environmental and historic sites without destroying the sites? Sometimes in concert with architects, we have to find solutions that will satisfy most needs. Yet there are some historic buildings, archaeological sites, and the like, that would be ruined if ramps, elevators, and handicapped restrooms were installed. In cases where it is not possible to provide such facilities, a special audio-visual presentation of the inaccessible areas could be a solution.

Wheelchair Accessible

The dimensions of wheelchairs can vary according to a person's size and whether electrically or manually operated. Figure 2.12 is a composite of illustrations and information from the ADA Standards for Accessible Design.

Ramps

It can be very dangerous to place exhibits and overhead signs on ramps because visitors can become so engrossed in the exhibit that they forget they are standing on an incline and trip as they step to the next display. The physically challenged could also have a difficult time when they attempt to maneuver their wheelchairs, walkers, or crutches on a ramp to view a wall hung display.

Figure 2.14 shows the recommended ADA dimensions required for a maximum slope (rise) of a ramp. When a longer ramp is needed, it should be interrupted with a level landing. ADA recommends that the maximum slope of a wheelchair ramp should be one inch of rise for each twelve-inch section of run.

WHEELCHAIR SPACE AND REACH GUILDELINES

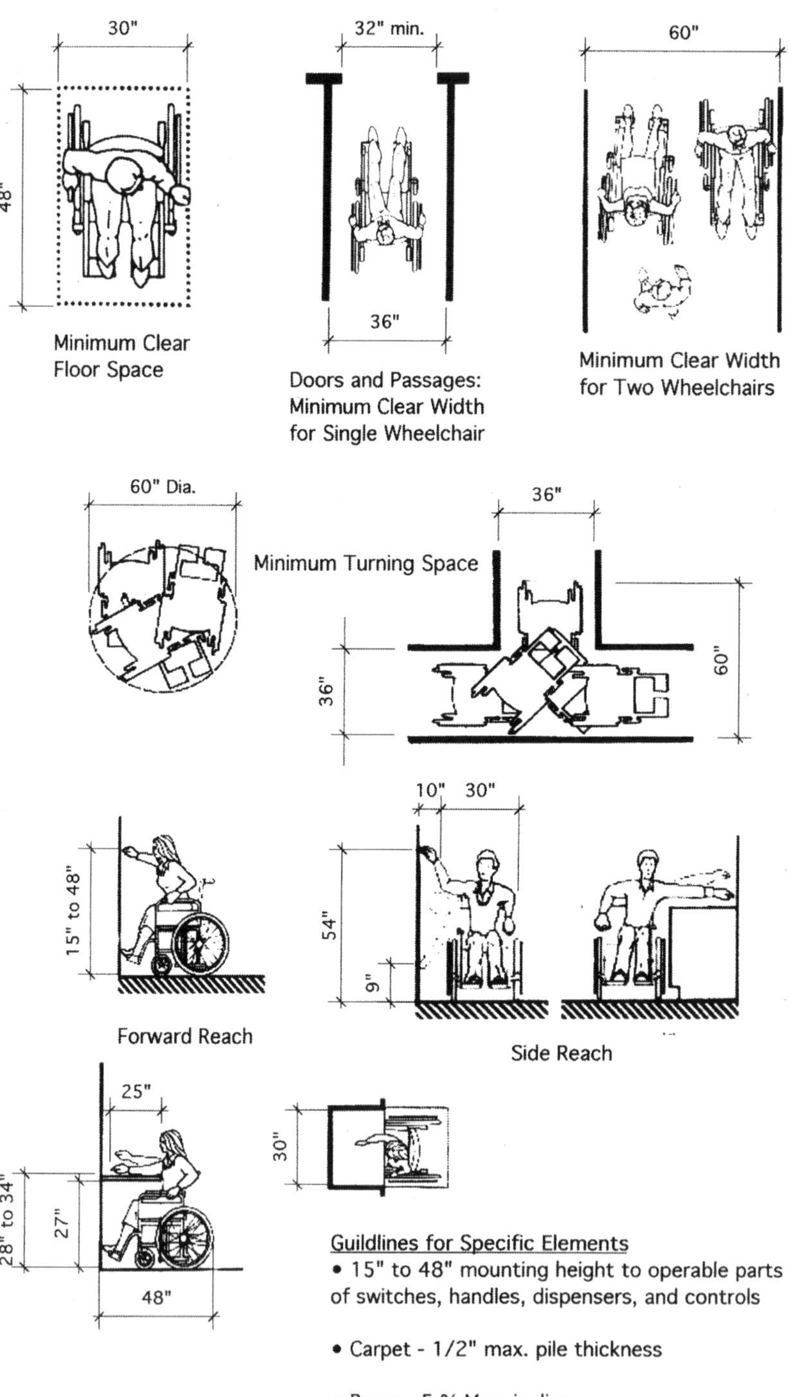

Figure 2.12. Wheelchair space and research guidelines. Courtesy of the U.S. Department of Justice.

CASE HISTORY: "WHO SHOULD STAND UP?"

It always amazes me that there is still resistance when adjusting an exhibit design to meet the needs of the disabled. The height at which a graphic panel is placed always seems to be especially controversial. Once when presenting an exhibit design, I mentioned that I would be using a fifty-inch-high eye level for the labels, which would be comfortable for people in wheelchairs. One very tall man objected and said that he did not want to have to stoop over to read the text. Shocked, I "jokingly" responded that it was easier for him to stoop over than to ask a person in a wheelchair to stand up. He agreed. We moved on.

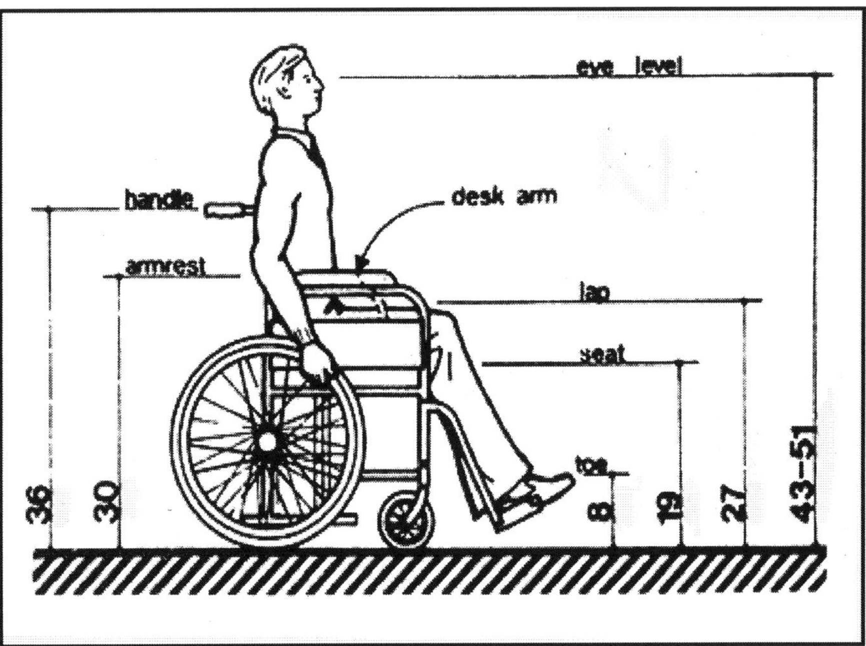

Figure 2.13. ADA, person in a wheelchair dimensions. Courtesy of the U.S. Department of Justice.

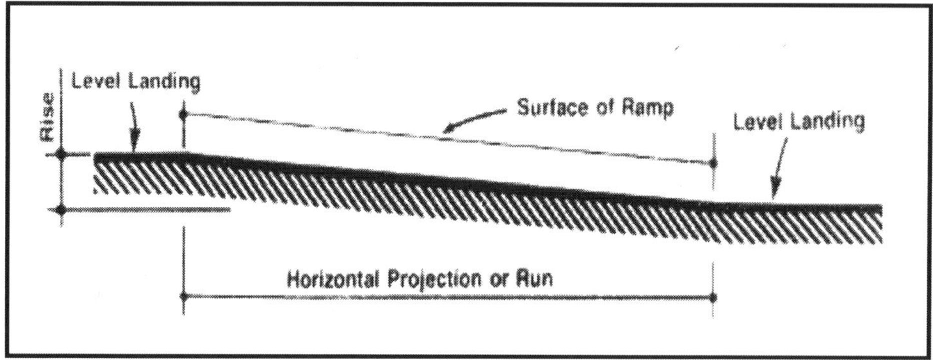

Figure 2.14. Riser and length. Courtesy of the U.S. Department of Justice.

Evaluations

> What constitutes an effective exhibition will depend on the viewpoint, be it of the museum or the visitor, and what it achieves for them.
>
> — Michael Belcher, *Exhibitions in Museums*

An evaluation is the act of examining something in order to judge its value and importance, and it is a major form of communication between the exhibition's planners and their proposed audience. These studies address the needs, desires, and interests of the visitor and assist in the validation and effectiveness of an exhibition.

Observations, questionnaires, and interviews are all techniques that can provide important information when developing or revising an exhibit. Studies should be pretested to ensure that they are acceptable to the person being interviewed. I have participated in several such interviews concerning exhibitions and felt that they invariably took up too much time, and I always felt trapped. In addition, some of the questions were very intrusive: one interviewer (a perfect stranger) actually asked me my annual income.

When selecting evaluation techniques, evaluators usually employ personnel observations, questions, and interviews. It can also be helpful to augment these techniques with props such as floor plans, sketches, models, scaled and full-size graphic layouts, and mockups of displays and interactive exhibits. Evaluations are usually finalized in a report that addresses the success of an exhibition's purpose, requirements, and conclusions.

Evaluations Phases: Reports

Master Plan and when conducting a general institutional review
  Comprehensive Evaluation

Feasibility Study and Schematic Phase
  Front-end Evaluation
Preliminary, Intermediate, and Final Phases
  Formative Evaluation
Post-Opening Phase
  Summative Evaluation

Comprehensive Evaluation

"Getting to know you, getting to know more about you" is an old and familiar lyric that sums up the museum's needs to understand its visitors. Performed during the master planning phase, the objective of this evaluation is to comprehend how visitors might use and enjoy the exhibits and the display objects, and how they perceive the entire museum building, surroundings, exhibition areas, and learning facilities. It behooves exhibit team members during this investigative process to wear their Sherlock Holmes' hats and to ask pertinent questions:

- Who are the visitors? Why do they come, and what do they require?
- What are their interests, and how do they learn?
- How many others come with them?
- How often do they come?
- What are their expectations and perceptions of the museum?
- How is their behavior during their visit? How can they best be served?

Ultimately, a comprehensive evaluation should define a museum's purpose and its market.

Front-end Evaluation

This evaluation is always prudent for it will help to determine whether the proposed exhibition has validity and assess its probability of success. In addition, it can also provide valuable information about the visitors' interest in and knowledge of the subject, and questions whether they will understand the exhibition's objectives, information, and its relationship to the visual materials.

A front-end evaluation can also assist the museum and the exhibit team to understand what the visitor will hope to see, learn, and experience, and to establish the exhibition's goals so that they will be compatible with the visitor, the institution, and the proposed exhibition. This assessment also provides insight into and information about potential visitors by evaluating the visitors:

- Will the exhibits be age appropriate?
- Will the exhibition evoke good or bad memories?
- Will they come?

Unfortunately, there are times when, due to a lack of available funds, a professional evaluator cannot be hired, and by default, museum staff or exhibit team members have to perform this task.

Before starting, it is best to perform certain tasks:

- List the information that is needed.
- Interview the staff, especially those who work with visitors. Many times the input received from cashiers and docents is invaluable and can greatly impact the design.
- Compose a brief statement about the aims of the exhibition that can be used when interviewing visitors and give them enough background information about the proposed exhibit so that their comments will be more incisive.
- Prepare a list of insightful questions for visitors to answer.

Formative Evaluation

The formative evaluation occurs during the planning/designing stages of the project. Its purpose is to determine whether the exhibition design, graphics, and displays will successfully communicate their messages and fulfill their intended purpose. A formative evaluation is very important for the success of an exhibition since it is relatively easy to make design revisions during the formative phases, and almost impossible to do so once the exhibits have been constructed and the money spent. It should be conducted several times during the planning/designing process. A model of a display or a mockup of a graphic are props that can be use for this evaluation.

The formative evaluation can question every aspect of the exhibition and in so doing ensure that the exhibits, displays, and graphics are physically and mentally appropriate for the targeted audience. Of course, every exhibition has its unique concerns that need to be addressed. The following is just a sample of questions that could be asked:

- Are the exhibit areas appropriately placed?
- Does the information flow logically?
- Will the interactive exhibits be visitor friendly?
- Have the visitor's exhibit needs been met?
- Is the text understandable, logically placed, and visitor appropriate?
- Are the proposed colors, graphics, and structures compatible with the theme?

Summative Evaluation

The die is cast, and your exhibition has opened. With exhibits and displays in place, the time has come to learn whether it is a success. It is also the opportunity to evaluate every part of the exhibition and, if needed, to fine-tune displays and text.

After opening day and during the life span of an exhibition, many evaluations should be made to determine if the visitors understand and enjoy the displays and graphics, and to assess whether revisions and upgrades are required. Since each design is unique and elicits its own concerns, here are just a few considerations:

- Does the exhibition have a favorable impact?
- Do the visitors understand how to proceed through the exhibit areas?
- Have the learning goals been met?
- Are the visitors enjoying their experience?
- Are the exhibits and displays visitor friendly?
- What is the percentage of return visitation?
- Do visitors understand the text, and do they read the labels?
- Are the docents and staff effective?

For a planner/designer, a summative evaluation can be very difficult to do, for it is the nearest thing to telling a mother that her "beautiful" baby is actually ugly. However, if the information you received from the front-end and formative evaluations was incisive and perceptive, then in all probability this evaluation will be favorable. Now it's time to listen to the visitors, since they are the ones who really count.

Exhibit Design

> The designer brings two important ingredients to any creative work: the inspiration that gives birth to a particular design, and the originality that sets it apart from other designs.
>
> — Marjorie Elliott Bevlin, *Design through Discovery*

I believe that the planning/designing process is the hardest part of any project. After all the surveys, planning, research, and meetings have taken place, it is the planner/designer who designs the exhibition and the one who must open the exhibition program and face an empty floor plan.

For me, the design process is not like walking, where you place one foot in front of the other; rather, it is like jumping off a cliff and figuring out on the way down how to land. Unfortunately, since every project is different, there can never be one prescribed way to begin it or to end it. Yet over the years, I have developed a series of actions that I avoid doing. I will

- never visit another museum or exhibit that has similar subject matter before my exhibit concepts have been formulated, since I have found that predesign visits only hamper my creativity. I do visit similar institutions or exhibits after the exhibit design is firm, and at that time, I am interested in studying the information and the display techniques that others have used.
- never start the design before the research phase is well under way. Prior to developing schemes, I need to be actively involved in the research, the selection of the display objects, and the preparation of the exhibition program. Performing these activities always seems to trigger a particular design approach and suggests the ambience that might be feasible. Another benefit to be derived from compiling research is that it will later assist in selecting the materials, colors, typeface, and so forth, that will be used.
- never reject even the craziest and most far-out suggestion; often, they are the ones that turn out to be the germs of very creative solutions.

Planning/designing takes courage; it is not for the faint of heart. While writing this book, I tried to present the subject in a simple and straightforward manner, and provide the information and tools that are part of every museum exhibition planner/designer's repertoire. Yet it is hard to put into words the two most important elements that are needed to produce an outstanding design: creativity and inspiration.

Creativity and Inspiration

Although these terms can seem illusive, you can take comfort in the fact that you are usually surrounded with talented people who are willing to critique you work and give you excellent advice.

Once, when laboring over a painting, my instructor told me that "it takes two people to make a painting: one to paint and one to say stop." This is also true when planning/designing an exhibit; you have to be able to sense how far you can go and to know or to be told when the process is over. Another time I overheard the same instructor tell a student who was complaining about the paint, "It's not the paint, son; it's the painter." When planning/designing an exhibit, it is important for all involved to understand what constitutes the basic theories of good design and how to create a well-designed end product.

You also have to take chances, or else your design can become commonplace and boring. Yet if you stretch too far, you can fall and fail, and picking up the pieces after the exhibition has opened is a feat that even

Humpty Dumpty couldn't resolve. On the one hand, you have to be practical, and on the other you have to be creative and exciting. Both can work together, but it is only your professionalism as a planner/designer that can make them succeed. Before proceeding to plan/design, it is important that you read both chapter 3, "Color and Light," and chapter 4, "Shape, Form, and Space," in this book.

Creativity

Creativity is the act of conceiving new ideas or relationships. To apply the term "creative juices" to a planner/designer indicates that he or she has demonstrated the ability to develop original concepts. Producing innovative and creative exhibits does not mean that caution can be thrown to the wind. Any imaginative scheme has to be based on good design theories and must be compatible with the visitors, the institution, and the display items.

Granted, it is not easy to be creative; it's a lonely process. Only one person can sit at the "drafting board" and make that empty floor plan come alive, and that person is the planner/designer. The best thing to do is to relax and remember that you have the ability and talent to produce an innovative exhibition.

Inspiration

> With all the currents sweeping through the design world, however, certain ideas remain constant. First, design is an all-pervasive activity that governs every area of human endeavor, from the visual arts through industry, communications, and transportation. Second, the human designer can find endless inspiration in the ingenious and beautiful designs created by nature.
>
> —Marjorie Elliott Bevlin, *Design through Discovery*

Inspiration is the stimulation that you derive from other sources. So just look around; it's everywhere. You just have to take what you see, sense and feel, and when appropriate, integrate it into your exhibit design.

When the profession of museum exhibit planning/designing was being established, the pioneers of that period did not have the advantage of viewing expertly designed exhibitions. So, for their inspiration they studied art, architecture, drama, expositions, literature, and nature. Today, planners/designers still derive their major inspiration from those same sources, but now they can also view and critique professionally executed exhibits.

All types of design are worth studying, for often a two-dimensional concept can successfully be applied to a three-dimensional solution and vice versa. Many times I have been able to use the principles that I discovered in a painting, applying them successfully to a three-dimensional display.

Thanks to advances in communications, for example, television, the Internet, and numerous publications, we are constantly exposed to all the latest trends and developments that are taking place throughout the art world, and when appropriate we can apply them to our designs. The following are just a few of the inspirational forms that we should study.

Architecture and Space Planning

> The complexity of architecture means that, unlike any other art form, it has to be judged in the context of the era in which it was built. Not only have the surrounding vernacular buildings to be considered, but the sociopolitical climate at the time of the structure's conception through to its completion. Architecture, in other words, does not travel, unlike a painting or a sculpture that are rarely specific to one place.
>
> —James Neal, *Architecture: A Visual History*

Architectural structures used in an exhibit can create a certain ambience and inform the visitor as to the exhibit's who, when, where, and why. Since both architecture and exhibition design deal with structure, illumination, space, and materials, it is essential for the exhibit planner/designer to examine the principles of design, creativity, and ideology that are part of building structures. It is advantageous to study not only ancient and traditional architectural monuments but also the exciting, and yes, trendy, works that are now being created by so many talented architects including Rafael Vinoly, Richard Meier, Frank Gehry, Cesar Pelli, I. M. Pei, and the most exciting architect that I feel exists today, Santiago Calatrava (see figures 4.9 and 4.10, Milwaukee Art Museum addition, designed Calatrava).

Commercials and Advertisements

Whether it is an artifact that we are displaying or a theme that we are presenting, exhibit planners/designers are in essence "selling" these itemvs and concepts to the public. Commercial producers, whether on television or in print, have mastered the art of quickly presenting their products, and for us it is certainly worth studying their techniques. Observe how they can focus our attention, subtly get their messages across, and even successfully tweak our senses.

High-end Trade Shows and Theme Parks

These venues produce state-of-the-art displays coupled with exciting environments and strong, powerful themes. Here is where prestige is on the line, and copious amounts of money are spent on displays. Given that these venues usually have relatively short life spans and lucrative exhibit construction budgets, their designers can employ the latest materials, innovative lighting, audiovisuals, computerization, and audio techniques. Such venues allow the exhibit planner/designer the opportunity to observe how well state-of-the-art materials can withstand visitor abuse and to study crowd-control techniques. These are premier showcases for innovative displays and presentations and a fertile learning ground for us.

Fine Arts

From classical to contemporary, Eastern to Western cultural influences, and two- to three-dimensional creations, there is such a wide variety of art forms available that it is hard to generalize. However, by studying just one painting or piece of sculpture, planners/designers can derive an endless number of ideas. They can understand how and why an artist successfully used illumination, shapes, forms, colors, and textures to balance and create a well-designed work of art.

Often a variety of exhibit design ideals can be derived from just a single work of art. Jan Vermeer's *Woman Holding a Balance* shown in figure 2.15 is one of my favorites and has frequently inspired me when designing dioramas and historic settings.

In just one painting and without words, observe how much information Vermeer gives us about the lady. She is obviously not poor; her dress indicates that she enjoys an upscale, seventeenth-century Dutch lifestyle. Her form tells us that she seems to be with child, and by grouping her pregnant body with the painting of the *Last Judgment* hanging on the wall, the artist suggested birth and rebirth.

Vermeer is also asking us to decide on a materialistic or a spiritualistic life. A table covered with jewelry represents material possessions and is the opposite of the empty scale that the lady is balancing, thus suggesting that she might be contemplating a more spiritual way of life. Vermeer further contrasts her situation with the "cosmic scale" shown in the *Last Judgment*, where we are all to be evaluated on the basis of good or evil behavior.

This painting is also a study in balance. First, light and dark divisions occur when a diagonal "line" from the upper left to the lower right of the canvas divides the painting equally into two areas of different value. Second, a further division occurs and indicates how the painting is separated into two equal horizontal segments: the lower half contains earthly possessions, and the upper is spiritual in nature.

It is just a small canvas, but it contains a huge story.

Figure 2.15. Jan Vermeer's Woman Holding a Balance. *Courtesy of the National Gallery of Art, Washington, D.C.*

Literature

Books are a wonderful source of research information and can also be of valuable assistance in laying out an exhibition. "I can't put the book down" is a comment that we have all heard and said. The techniques that authors use to present information and tie it together should also be studied. Many authors have used the "Hansel and Gretel" approach to entice readers; only, rather than breadcrumbs, they drop bits of tantalizing information to lead readers through the book. In so doing, they introduce and prepare readers for a major happening and spark their interest in a subject that would be addressed later on. By implanting bits of information early in an exhibition, the planners/designers can introduce facts and heighten the visitors' interest in a topic that will be addressed later on.

Many times a book's format can be so well organized that the reader is readily able to envision the author's outline. By closely adhering to an exhibit outline, planners/designers can lay out exhibits, displays, and artifacts in an understandable, clear, and concise manner.

Motion Pictures and Television Programs

There are many excellent, artistically designed motion pictures and television shows that can be of benefit to your exhibit schemes. Observe how these productions suggest a particular time, place, or economic situation by employing the appropriate types of structures, materials, costumes, lighting, space, color, and form. Also study the techniques and the methods used to group and frame the props, present the performers, and unfold the story line.

Natural Environments

The colors and forms found in nature always seem to produce a vast palette that has guided artists, architects, and designers throughout the centuries, and they can be an endless source of inspiration to you as well. Observe how the color of the sky and of the vegetation changes with the seasons and yet how they remain in harmony with each other. Note how the dense, powerful form of a tree in summer can become a delicate structure with beautiful spaces formed by its denuded branches in winter. It is amazing how many dull, drab exhibits have been created when all that had to be done to liven them up was to observe and be inspired by the wonderful visual gifts that nature has provided.

Opera and Theatrical Productions

To create a particular ambiance or dramatic effect, a stage designer balances and blends performers, materials, colors, illumination, and special effects to produce a wonderful theatrical experience for the viewer. Of all the art forms, the opera and the theater have influenced me the greatest when designing exhibits. An operatic performance always seems like a wonderful painting that is constantly moving and changing but never loses its balance or its focus.

Of course, only a few are fortunate enough to live next door to a major opera house and to be able to benefit from its productions. However, with operas presenting simulcast broadcasts of their live productions worldwide in numerous theaters, we now have a greater opportunity to experience this delightful art form. Also through videos, computer images, and photographs, opera and theatrical productions are becoming more readily available to be studied and enjoyed.

Originality versus Copying

I believe it is possible to work successfully with these two opposing considerations. Remember that your designs and the ambiance that you

Figure 2.16. "Aida, The Triumphal Scene." Source: Ignor Bulgarin/Shutterstock.com.

create have to be original, different, and exciting with a fresh, new look. That is the planner/designer's job, but don't forget that the wheel has already been invented, and that many good, basic concepts are in constant use. Most of us have successfully created exhibits using smell boxes, Pepper's Ghost,* and question-and-answer displays, even though each of these techniques was originally someone else's brainchild. Yet, it is foolish to avoid using a tried and true exhibit technique when it is a perfect fit.

Design Process

When it comes to exhibit planning/designing, each of us has developed a unique process. For what it is worth, here is mine. I always start with the exhibition program and an empty, scaled floor plan of the exhibition area. I then sketch in display structures, pivotal objects, and pertinent notes. By repeating this process over and over, a stack of designs emerges. From that pile of sketches, several schemes that seem to have potential begin to develop. With each concept, I do several mental walk-throughs, and during these strolls I assume a visitor's mantle: young, old, astute, or casual. I try to imagine what each visitor will emotionally, physically, and intellectually experience. After many such journeys, I

*Pepper's Ghost is an illusionary display that consists of clear glass, mirrors, and special lighting techniques. As the light changes, objects that were very visible seem to blend together and disappear.

> **CASE HISTORY: "NUMBER OF DESIGNS"**
>
> Most times I have been able to develop three totally different schemes that reflect varying visitors' experiences, themes, and ambiance. However, this has not always been the case. For a permanent exhibit commissioned by the regional office of the National Archives and Records Administration (NARA), located in a historic section of Philadelphia, a "Fourth of July" concept seemed like such a perfect fit that all three schemes that I developed were based on that theme. I suggested different floor plans, exhibits, and displays for each one.
>
> Another time, I felt that a single exhibit design that I had developed for a client was such a perfect solution that I presented only that scheme. The client was just as enthusiastic and excited about the design as was I. However, I was aware that when I dared to submit only one exhibit scheme, there was the distinct possibility that it would be rejected and I would be very embarrassed.

usually select a few exhibit schemes that appear to have possibilities that may emerge, and these are the ones that I prepare for the schematic phase presentation. During the preliminary phase, one of these designs will be chosen and more fully developed.

Exhibits Program

The exhibition program (EP) contains the exhibit outline and the information needed to develop the exhibition. The EP precedes the exhibit planning/design phase and is revised and matured as the artifacts are selected, the content is agreed upon, and the design is refined. This is an important document for it is

- the vehicle that informs the institution about aspects of the exhibit design that can or cannot be addressed in the presentation sketches;
- the method used to keep all participants current and in agreement with the design during its development; and
- the document used to assist in fund-raising and to gain community support.

The exhibition program serves as the basis for developing the exhibit project. This document always contains important information that is so valuable to the success of the project that any exhibit team that does not prepare such a program is imprudent. The planning/designing process should not start until this program is at least 60 percent developed.

Exhibition Program Phases: Special Considerations

Schematic Phase
- Prepare the exhibition program (EP).
- Add all available information.
- Complete the exhibit brief.
- Prepare a description or a walk-through for each scheme.

Preliminary Phase
- Revise and continue to add information to the EP.
- Prepare the selected scheme's exhibit description or walk-through.

Intermediate Phase
- Revise and advance the EP.
- Update the description or a walk-through for the chosen scheme.
- Include the scheme's theme and ambiance.
- Describe display items and learning objects.

Final Phase
- Revise and complete the EP.

Post-Opening Phase
- Include EP in the project archival file.

The exhibition program is divided into two parts: the exhibit brief and the exhibit design description.

Exhibit Brief

The purpose of the exhibit brief (EB) is to clarify all the conditions and ramifications that will impact the exhibition, and to list every item that is necessary for its development. It should aid the planner/designer to create a design concept but never dictate the design itself.

Usually the members of the exhibit team prepare the brief. However, there will be many times when, due to a lack of available personnel, a planner/designer must produce the brief without assistance.

Prior to the schematic's start-up meeting, the planner/designer prepares an outline for the brief that includes all available information. During this meeting the brief is discussed and reviewed, and information is added. This document should be completed and approved before the preliminary phase begins. The following is a sample of an EB outline:

Institution
- Official address
- Mission statement
- Universal design requirements

Exhibition
- Working title
- Location
- Mission statement
- Theme
- Purpose
- Longevity and reuse
- Learning objectives
- Budget for exhibit development, construction, and installation
- Staff and docents
- Personnel required during public viewing hours
- Level of training needed
- Time schedule
- Programs
- Fund-raising
- Outreach and educational issues
- Public relations
- Special and ancillary events
- Pivotal display items
- Conservation issues

Visitors
- Profile
- Why they come
- Learning objectives
- Level of knowledge
- Language
- Physically and visually challenged concerns and provisions

Building
- Restrictions
- Truck access and unloading
- Hallway dimensions and elevator capacity
- Fire and security considerations

Exhibit space
- Size
- Restrictions

Exhibition Design Description

The exhibition design description is a written document that explains all the details and ramifications of each schematic design. Where appropriate, reference is made to the design's sketches, floor plans, and visuals. Below is a sample of some of the items that should be addressed:

Title or working title
Exhibition concept statement
Learning objectives
- Main theme
- Ambiance
- Exhibit area
- Area title
- Aims and objectives
- Theme
- Description
- Displays (each display must be listed and the following information provided)
  - Display techniques
  - Learning outcome
  - Graphic panels (this task starts with the preliminary design phase)
    - Label hierarchy
    - Content outline
    - Visuals (if applicable)
  - Display objects
- Typeface
- Written voice
- Walk-through description
- Conclusion and learning outcome
- Construction budget

Exhibit Project Teams

> If I dream alone, it's only a dream. If we dream together, it's the beginning of reality.
>
> —Brazilian proverb, Montréal Science Centre

From concept to reality it usually takes several teams to produce an exhibition or even a simple exhibit. The following teams are formed at the beginning of the various phases.

Phases: Exhibit Project Teams

Feasibility Study
- Museum Team

Schematic Phase
- Exhibit Team

Construction Phase
- Construction Team

Anatomy of a Project

Just as three ballerinas are able to dance in perfect harmony, the museum, exhibit, and construction teams must be in sync with each other. Each has particular duties and responsibilities and will at various times assume major responsibility and effort.

In order for a project to run smoothly, it is important that everyone involved in an exhibition understands how the teams interface and who plays the dominant role. The chart in figure 2.17 is a typical overview showing the responsibilities of the various teams.

ANATOMY OF A PROJECT

	Museum	Exhibit	Construction
Feasibility Phase	M	e	
Schematic Phase	m	E	
Preliminary Phase	m	E	
Intermediate Phase	m	E	
Final Phase	m	E	
Documentation Phase	m	E	
Bidding Phase	M	e	C
Construction Phase	m	e	C
Shipping			C
Installation Phase	m	e	C
Artifacts Installation	M		
Post-Opening Phase	m	E	

KEY:

M = Museum Team
E = Exhibit Team
C = Construction Team

NOTES:

Upper case letter indicates major role
Lower case letter indicates minor role

Figure 2.17. Anatomy of a project.

Museum Team

These are the true visionaries for they are the ones who originate the concept and usually perform the feasibility study to determine the need for the exhibition. Usually their aims are to produce an exciting and successful event that will foster the exhibition's missions and goals; increase the institution's image, visitation, and prestige; and be financially rewarding. The museum team oversees every aspect of the project and is ultimately responsible for its success. They work closely with the exhibit and construction teams, and their team usually includes administrators, accountants, lawyers, and fund-raisers.

Exhibit Team

When a project is large and involved, an exhibit team usually consists of many professionals who are experienced in developing museum exhibitions. Invariably, each person brings his or her unique expertise to the project and contributes to its success. For a project to run smoothly, every team member should be creative, with the ability to visualize suggested design concepts, capable of working with all the other team members, and committed to maintaining the agreed-upon exhibition program.

There are times, however, when a project or an institution is so small or underfunded that all the work becomes the responsibility of a lone planner/designer. When forced to go solo, it is essential to study and to understand the various roles performed by the following professionals who normally would constitute an exhibit team.

Content Developer

The content developer is responsible for developing the story line and writing the text. The content developer is usually involved in research, selecting artifacts, obtaining copyrights, and developing the exhibit's outreach and education programs.

Curator

As overseer and manager of the museum's collection, the curator possesses the unique knowledge needed to select the display items for the exhibition. The curator is responsible for conserving, protecting, and caring for the artifacts and normally assists in the research, content development, and placement of the items on display.

Educator

The main responsibility of the educator is to ensure that the visitors will receive the best possible educational experience. Educators are involved in research, developing content and text, preparing special and outreach programs, and suggesting educationally based displays.

Graphic Designer

The graphic designer designs and lays out the graphics and assists in selecting any visuals.

Planner/Designer

The planner/designer plans, designs, and documents the exhibition's structures and spaces, and oversees the visitor's experience. The planner/designer is also involved in the research, selection, and placement of the display items and images, and in the graphics and text development. In addition, this person usually assists with bidding and provides advice during the construction and the installation phases.

Project Managers

See "Project Management" section later in this chapter.

Researcher

The researcher locates documents, images, and display items, and assists in developing the text.

Specialists

Depending on the exhibition's topic, there are times when specialists such as archaeologists, geologists, historians, and naturalists are added to, and become valuable members of, the exhibit team.

Construction Team

During the construction and installation phases of an exhibition, the construction team's prime responsibility is to prepare shop drawings and to construct, ship, and install the exhibits.

Case Study 2.2: What Does an Exhibit Team Do?

I tried to find an answer to that question when I met with Michael Meister, director of exhibition design, and Lydia Romero, exhibit designer, at the American Museum of Natural History (AMNH) to discuss the *Traveling the Silk Road* exhibition with them. I had viewed this exhibition, which was produced and first shown at the AMNH in New York City, and found that it brimmed with a variety of interesting displays. I felt that for any designer who needs to produce an exhibition with a complex subject that all visitors can enjoy and understand, this one was certainly well worth studying.

This exhibit was meant to portray the journey involved as commercial goods traveled the 4,600 miles of ancient trade routes from Asia to Europe. In telling this complex story of deserts, mountains, and sea routes; ships, cities, and oases; and the furs, spices, and gems that were transported along this network, the result could easily have been a highly esoteric exhibition. Yet the exhibit team succeeded in creating a wonderful exhibition filled with excellent information, visual excitement, and meaningful participatory displays that seemed to captivate and fascinate visitors of all ages and interests.

My "travel" began when, upon entering the exhibition, I was confronted by three life-size replicas of camels, each laden with sacks of "exotic" goods. Behind them was a hand-painted mural of a vast endless desert that was at least 120 feet long.

Figure 2.18. "Camel Caravan" exhibit. Photograph by Denis Finnin. © American Museum of Natural History.

I was then given a "Silk Road Passport," which was stamped when I entered the "cities" of Xi'an, Turfan, Samarkand, and Baghdad. Via their displays, the exhibit team was able to convey each city's uniqueness and importance to the trade route. For example, in Xi'an, at that time the capital of China, visitors saw live silkworms spinning cocoons, viewed a seventeen-foot, life-size replica of a Tang-era silk loom, and listened to Chinese musical instruments.

Arriving next at Turfan, a Central Asian oasis, visitors experienced a variety of exotic sights, smells, and sounds while walking through a replica of a bazaar filled with an array of luxurious fabrics, furs, gems, and spices. Several participatory displays including a "Market Smell" interactive exhibit were encountered.

At Samarkand, once a cosmopolitan city of merchants, visitors saw and heard a computer-animated book that related ancient tales, came upon two life-size replicas of Bactrian camels, and viewed fine papermaking, luxury metalwork, rare books, and coins.

In Baghdad, the heart of the Islamic world, a family-friendly interactive exhibit allowed visitors to determine the time of day by marking the position of the stars using a working model of an ancient astronomical instrument. Decorative glass cups, bottles, and pitchers of the period were also beautifully displayed.

Visitors were surprised to learn that ships played a major role in the silk road commerce. Near the end of the exhibition they were invited to walk through a forty-one-foot-long portion of a full-sized replica of a seventy-one-foot-long Arab dhow that had been split in half to reveal its cargo of ceramics and elaborate metalwork (see figure 2.19). The *Traveling the Silk Road* exhibition concluded with a written epilogue that connected the Silk Road to today's global economy.

As I exited the exhibition I felt that most exhibit designers would never have the financial and professional support that was available at the AMNH. Yet in other venues when faced with limited resources, designers are obliged to provide visitors with an original, exciting, and intellectually rewarding exhibit experience. For that reason, it is beneficial for anyone involved in the planning/designing process to understand the procedures that AMNH used to tell this huge, complicated story of a lengthy trade route and the multicultural merchants who traveled it.

I therefore asked Michael and Lydia to explain the journey that they had taken to produce the *Traveling the Silk Road* exhibition. From their comments, I quickly realized that at AMNH the exhibit designer was part of a highly trained, professional team that included a curator, a researcher, an evaluator, an educator, a graphic designer, a writer, multimedia personnel, a conservator, a subject specialist, a consultant, and a project man-

Figure 2.19. "Arab Dhow Showing Its Cargo of Ceramics" exhibit. Photograph by Roderick Mickens. © American Museum of Natural History.

ager. AMNH also has its own group of artisans, called preparators, who sculpted the camels and built the replica of the dhow, and a staff of paleontologists who made sure that the animals were anatomically correct. How totally envious I was, since when specifying replicas of animals, I always had to make sure that a veterinarian inspected the piece and verified that it was anatomically correct before I could approve it.

At AMNH the designers explained that the genesis for this exhibition began with a feasibility study or, as they called it, the incubation period. That was when an AMNH curator, an educator, an evaluator, and selected consultants scrutinized ten or more possible exhibition themes. After many marketing analyses, visitor interviews, and numerous evaluations, one theme, in this case the "Silk Road," was selected.

Once an exhibit theme had been approved for development, the schematic phase began. The curator verbally presented the exhibit concepts that had been developed during the feasibility phase to selected members of the exhibit team. They then prepared the exhibit brief (AMNH refers to this as an exhibit outline). Once the brief had been approved, these members, the curator, and the rest of the exhibit team leaders worked together to develop the exhibition program. This paper informed everyone involved in the Silk Road project about its concept, theme, mission, and ambiance. It listed the key exhibits to be developed, the major artifacts to be displayed, and the exhibit hall to be used. Based on this report, the project manager prepared a time schedule for each exhibit area.

Another major consideration that is always a given when designing an exhibition at AMNH was that their exhibits are meant to be traveling exhibitions and have to be designed for international venues for a period of ten years. To accommodate various sites, AMNH has established a set of standards that must be addressed when designing any exhibition. The exhibits must fit in an area of about eight thousand square feet and not exceed an eleven-foot-high ceiling. To help regulate the humidity and to protect the artifacts, all display cases must have joints that are tightly sealed and contain silica gel, and the exhibits have to break down to fit through standard-size double doors and into standard-size shipping crates. Although electrical power can vary widely throughout the world, AMNH designs its exhibits to meet the U.S. electrical code. Each venue is responsible to provide local power and the proper connections. The AMNH graphic panels are always designed with English texts, and the graphic files and layouts are sent to each foreign venue where, if necessary, English would be replaced with the local language, and new graphic panels made and installed at the site. AMNH oversized their text blocks so that they could accommodate local translations that normally required a larger text block area.

During the schematic design phase, the exhibition concepts were very fluid and changed as research and ideas developed. This phase began as the exhibit designer, curator, researcher, and other team members collected the images and information needed to prepare the text, graphics, educational materials, special programs, multimedia displays, participatory exhibits, and the like.

Although *Traveling the Silk Road* would prove to be a delightful adventure for visitors, it was a formidable task for everyone involved in its design and production. Most of the exhibit team worked in close proximity to each other, thus allowing for many informal meetings and a continuous exchange of information and ideas; for that reason, the work on the exhibition always seemed to flow quickly. Thanks to the project manager who scheduled and oversaw the project, it remained on schedule.

During the planning/design phases, Michael had to divide his time among other projects all in various stages of development, while Lydia worked exclusively on the *Silk Road*. For guidance and inspiration, she taped to the studio walls images of caravans, bazaars, and so forth, that were found during the research effort. A floor plan of the exhibition area was prepared. Guided by the exhibition program, the designer sketched footprints of exhibits on the floor plan, located the major exhibit areas,

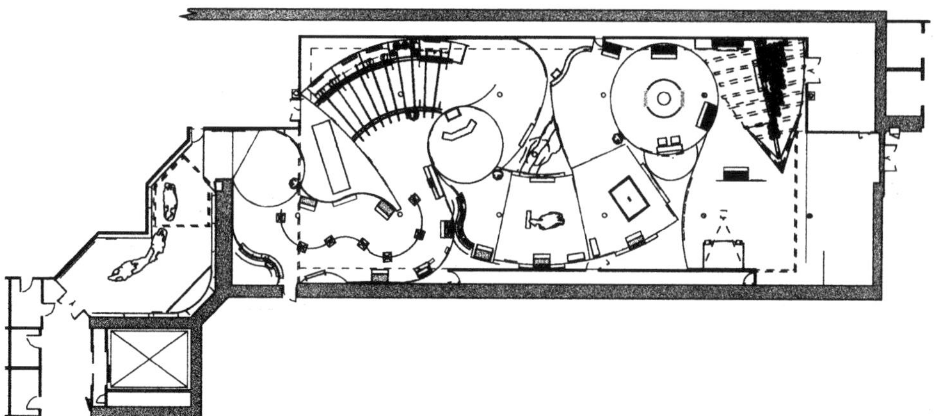

Figure 2.20. "Traveling the Silk Road" floor plan. Drawn by Lydia Romera. Courtesy American Museum of Natural History.

and sometimes even indicated pertinent objects and artifacts. After several changes, the schematic design phase concluded when selected AMNH personnel and exhibit team members met to discuss all the work prepared in this phase and to approve the scheme for further development.

During the ensuing preliminary design phase, the team members focused on developing their parts of the *Traveling the Silk Road* exhibition. The exhibit designer advanced the floor plan to include the location of the major exhibits, displays, artifacts, and graphic panels. Pertinent elevations and sketches were produced, and a model and a construction cost estimate were prepared. In the meantime, the other exhibit team members continued their research, prepared a layout for each typical graphic panel, acquired artifacts and display items, addressed conservation techniques and requirements, developed the text, located images, suggested educational programs, designed multimedia and participatory displays, and conducted various evaluations. At the end of this phase, the exhibition design and its major components had basically been resolved.

After the preliminary design had been approved, the exhibit team continued to work together to complete the intermediate and final phases, and to bring the *Traveling the Silk Road* exhibition to fruition. At this time, all structures and the displays had been designed and precisely located by the exhibit designer, who also prepared the color scheme; produced a color model; drew the pertinent plans, elevations, and technical drawings; researched construction materials and techniques; and reviewed the construction cost budget. Other team members finalized the text, produced the graphic layouts, and prepared the multimedia and participatory displays. They also acquired artifacts and display items from the AMNH collection and other sources.

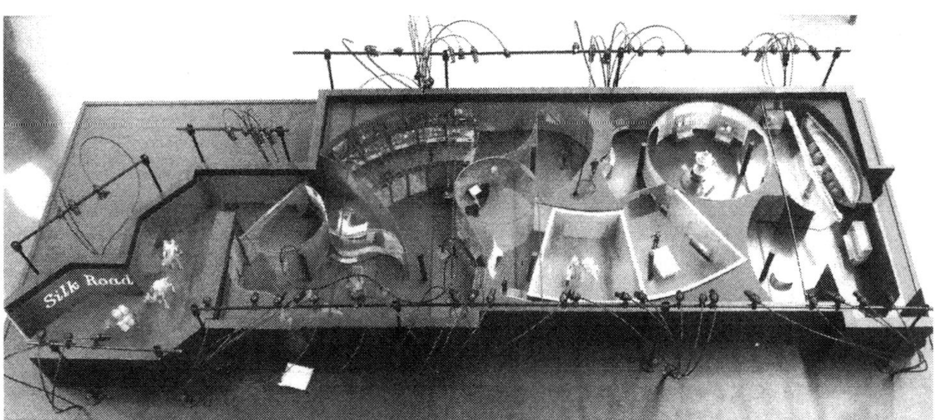

Figure 2.21. "Traveling the Silk Road" model. Photograph by Denis Finnin. © American Museum of Natural History.

During the next or documentation phase, the exhibit designer prepared all the drawings and specifications needed to bid and construct the exhibits, while other members of the team documented their work, and the project manager constantly checked to make sure that everything was on schedule and on budget. This was a good team that worked well together.

For the displays that needed plenty of lead time, such as the camel replicas, the ship, and the hand-painted mural, work on these items started at the AMNH facilities as soon as the details were finalized. However, most of the construction was outsourced to exhibit fabricators and had to wait for the bid/build process to take place. Some of these items included "The Night Market at Turfan" exhibit, the Samarkand and Baghdad galleries, and the fabric backwalls. AMNH specified this type of backwall because it is lightweight, readily rolled for shipping, and less expensive than the traditional wood-framed, Masonite construction.

During the construction phase, Michael and Lydia visited the fabrication shops regularly to inspect the work in progress. Lydia also had to check the shop drawings produced by the fabricators and would mark them up as approved or rejected. When checking these drawings, she and most designers like to work on twenty-two-by-thirty-four-inch paper copies and then reduce or "shrink" the drawings to eleven-by-seventeen inch so they can be scanned and e-mailed to the construction facilities. At the same time, the other team members were overseeing the testing and construction of their multimedia and participatory exhibits, and checking the graphic reproductions.

During installation, Lydia and other members of the team were constantly at the exhibition site to answer any questions that might arise. Another designer was also on site to photograph the installation so that

Figure 2.22. "The Night Market at Turfan" exhibit. Photograph by Roderick Mickens. © American Museum of Natural History.

instructions and photographs could be sent to the various foreign venues for their reference.

After the *Silk Road* exhibition opened at AMNH, members of the exhibit team had the year that it would be shown at the museum to study visitor reactions and to inspect the exhibits to make sure that they could withstand their rigorous travel schedule. When necessary, exhibits were revised or refurbished.

Undoubtedly, AMNH is fortunate to have such a professional, diversified staff to design and produce its high-quality exhibitions. Yet even members of small, understaffed museums, historic sites, environmental centers, and so on, must design and produce professional quality exhibitions. Many times they are able to retain consultants, but when funds are not available, they have to design the exhibits in-house. Fortunately, a great deal of information is available to help them in publications produced by the American Association of State and Local History (AASLH), the National Association of Museum Exhibitions (NAME), and the American Alliance of Museums (AAM).

Financial Statement (Project Budget)

Liza Minnelli and Joel Grey sang the duet "Money, Money, Money" in the musical *Cabaret*, and this fact is also true for the people planning an exhibition. It is the money that makes an exhibition possible, for without financial backing it will never take place.

How will the project be financed, and when will the money be needed? These are two important questions that must be addressed. When preparing a statement detailing funding sources, the endowments, grants, contributions, and ticket sales are usually listed. It should also contain the major expenses that will occur prior to opening day, for example, professional fees, construction costs, advertising, and PR costs.

The financial statement is prepared during the master planning and feasibility phases. It has to be realistic and include every expense that the exhibition will engender: building renovations, professional fees, construction, shipping and installation costs, insurance, publicity, and staffing are just a sampling. There are times when a museum will be able to absorb utility and maintenance costs, and possibly even the salary of the staff members, so before calculating the estimated total project outlay, it is wise to resolve what should and should not be included.

Graphic Design

Composed mostly of text and illustrations, graphics are the glue that holds an exhibition together, and the quality of their design is of utmost importance. Graphics convey a great deal of important information: they explain the purpose of the exhibition or of a display and assist in providing continuity. Attractive, compelling graphics can draw in visitors who are at a distance and persuade them to approach the exhibition or to view a special display. Before you start to design graphics, it is important to review chapters 3 and 4.

Graphic Design Phases: Special Considerations

Schematic Phase

- Prepare a graphic design only if it is needed to convey the concept of an exhibit scheme.

Preliminary Phase

- Design a master graphic grid.
- Design a typical graphic layout for each type of panel; indicate its size and shape.

Intermediate Phase

- Produce layouts for all graphics. These should also identify and designate the space on the layout for any proposed text or images that are being developed or located.
- Produce mockups.

Final Phase
Complete all graphic layouts.
Documentation Phase
Prepare an e-file that includes all fonts and graphic layouts.
Produce colored reproductions of each layout. Copy can be scaled down.
Prepare a specification that includes all information needed for reproduction.

Terminology

A rose by any other name would smell as sweet.

—William Shakespeare

William Shakespeare felt that importance of an item lay in what something really was and not what it was called. However, with graphic terminology it is easier and less confusing if we use the commonly accepted graphic vocabulary as defined in the dictionary. This approach can also assist people where English is their second language. Simply put,

- Graphic designers design graphics.
- Graphic producers produce graphics.
- Carpenters build graphic panels.
- Installers install graphic panels.

While most people agree with Shakespeare, the fact that exhibit planners/designers may use different terms to describe the same thing is not just whimsical; it is historically based. As the profession was evolving, it lacked a universal graphic vocabulary, and to fill this void many planners/designers developed their own terminology based on their education, experience, and geographical location. At that time I was also faced with the same dilemma; because I had always been closely associated with the graphics and the exhibit construction industries, I adopted their vocabulary since it was commonly used and readily understood. Based on the considerations listed above, the graphic terms that I use have to meet three goals:

- Keep the terms simple; don't confuse.
- Employ common expressions that are prevalent in the graphics and construction industries.
- Make sure that the terms are compatible with usage found in the dictionary.

E. **Bedno**	**E. Bogle**	**B. Serrell**
Entrance Title	Title Panel	Title Labels
Exhibition Introduction	Entrance Panel	Introductory or Orientation Label
	Orientation Panel	
Section Opening	Exhibit Panel	Section or Group Label
Topic Description	Display Panel	
Object Description	Label Panel	Caption and Specific Label
	Exit Panel	

Figure 2.23. Graphic terminology.

However, I have not been alone in my struggle to come to grips with graphic terms. Ed Bedno and Beverly Serrell are two fine professionals who also have had to address this need. Since Bedno and I taught exhibition planning and design courses to a wide array of students, and Serrell has written several books on the subject, each of our graphic vocabularies is far reaching and their dissimilarities can result in confusion. For that reason, I have prepared the chart in figure 2.23. Please feel free to select the graphic design terms that you find most comfortable.

Graphic Layouts

A graphic layout is a scaled or full-size layout that represents a proposed graphic.

Graphic Mockups

A mockup is used to evaluate a particular graphic design. Normally it is a full-size, computer-generated reproduction of a proposed graphic, and it should replicate the exact typefaces, colors, and visuals. It ought to be viewed and critiqued using the same illumination and viewing distance that the visitor will experience. From a group of similarly designed graphic layouts, usually only one needs to be mocked up.

Graphic Panel Hierarchy

All graphic panels are not of equal value; some are more important than others. The size, shape, and layout of a particular panel, therefore, should instantly inform the visitor as to its hierarchical position within the context of the exhibition.

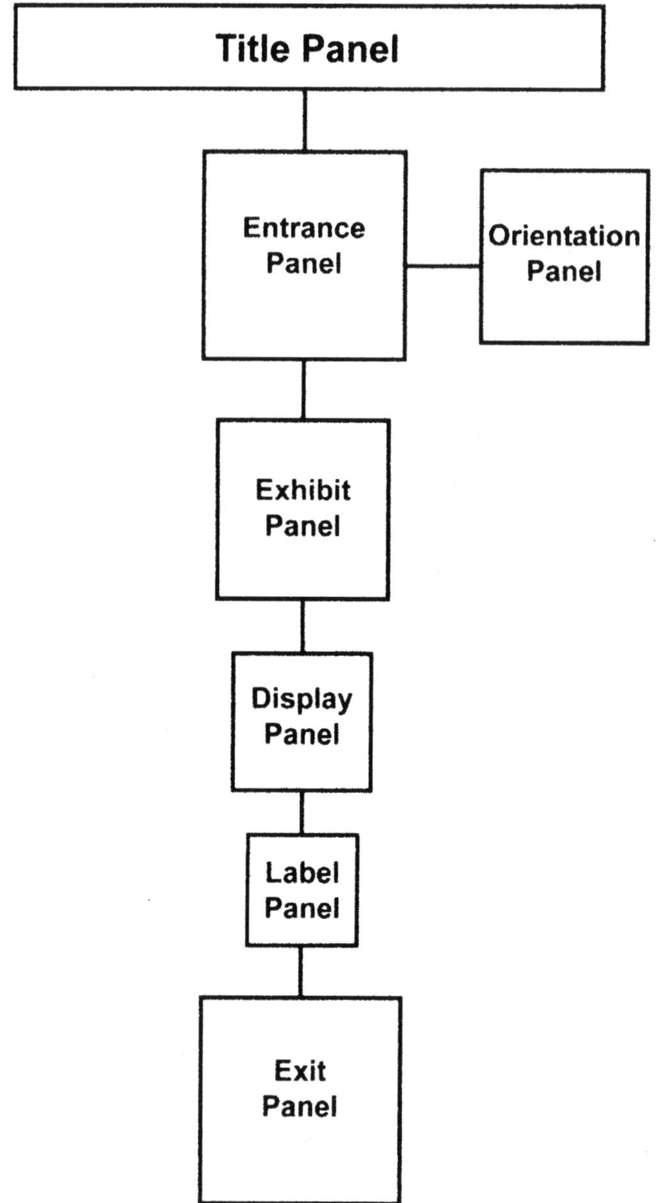

Figure 2.24. Graphic panel hierarchy chart.

Figure 2.25. Graphic panel displays. Drawing by Denis Gerhart.

Levels of Information

The following information is a general guideline for developing the entrance, orientation, exhibit, and exit panels. It is based on black letters on a white background.

Headline or Title

Purpose: Identifies and outlines the subject matter and is the lure that stops and draws visitors to the panel
Text: Should be short and compelling
Typeface: Large, usually bold, and easy to read
Number of words: Approximately one to five
Letter height: 140 to 200 points
Viewing distance: Should be readily seen from a distance

Subheadline or Subtitle

Purpose: Supports the headline by adding information
Number of words: Seven to fifteen
Letter height: 120 to 170 points; typeface should be a smaller than the headline

Viewing distance: About three to five feet. Also refer to the data in figure 2.27.

Introduction

Purpose: This is the introductory portion of the graphic panel. It presents a brief overview and a general understanding of the subject matter. Further, it entices the viewer to stay and read all the information it contains. An introduction is sometimes composed of a major and a minor paragraph.
Number of words: twenty to one hundred
Letter height: 50 to 72 points; smaller than the subheadline but larger than the body of the text
Viewing distance: Refer to the data in figure 2.27.

Text

Purpose: To explain a secondary topic. It usually consists of a title and a body of text.
Number of words: fifty to one hundred
Letter height: 18 to 30 points
Viewing distance: Refer to the data in figure 2.27.

Caption

Purpose: Describes or explains an image
Number of words: five to fifty
Letter height: 14 to 24 points
Viewing distance: Refer to the data in figure 2.27.

Credit Line

Purpose: To acknowledge the ownership of a visual
Number of words: three to ten
Letter height: 8 to 10 points

Sidebar

Purpose: To present additional information that is not directly included as part of the main text. Sidebar texts could contain comments, observations, and even contrasting information. It is similar to the sidebars on your computer screen and is often boxed and isolated from the main graphic area.
Letter height: 20 to 30 points
Viewing distance: Refer to the data in figure 2.27.

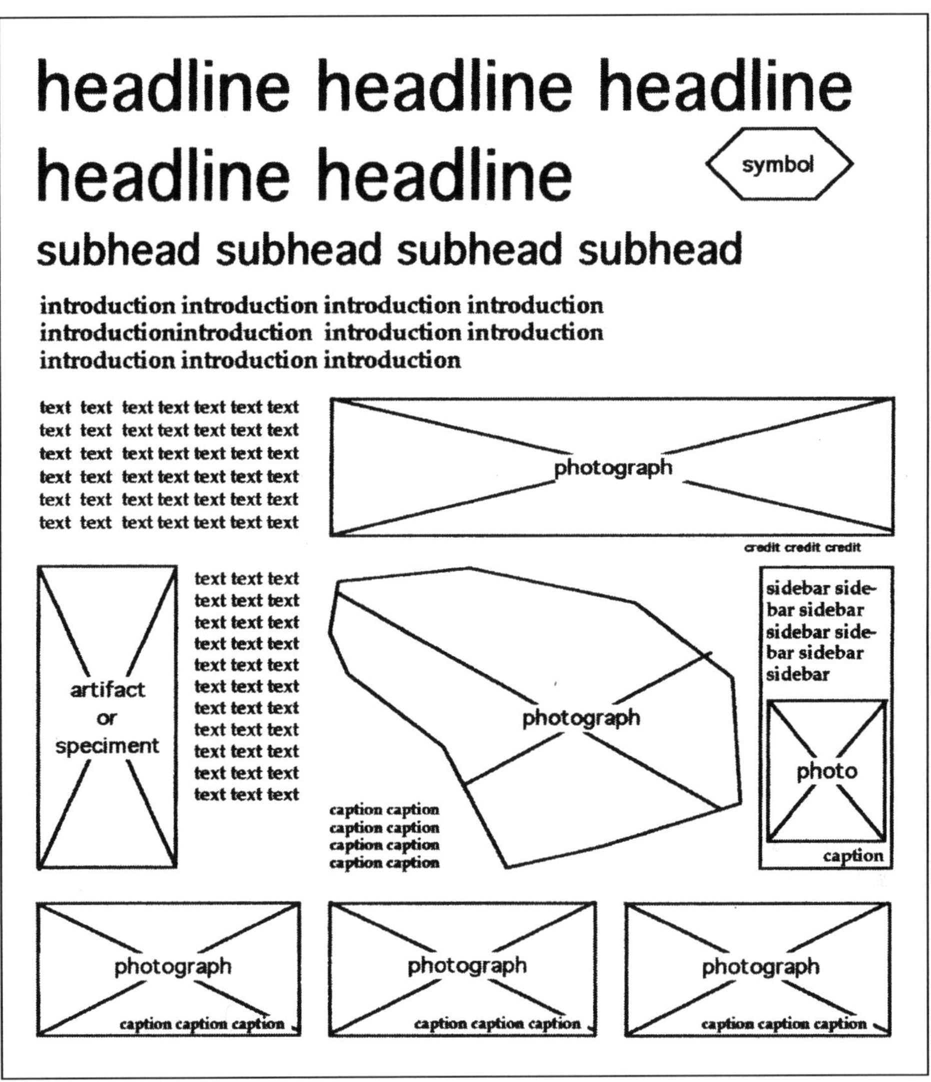

Figure 2.26. Levels of information superimposed on a grid.

Visually Accessible Guidelines

Unfortunately, not everyone has twenty–twenty eyesight, and as planners / designers, we should strive to make sure that the vast majority of visitors can see the text. The following is a brief composite of some of the recommendations in the "Smithsonian Guidelines for Accessible Exhibition Design" and the "Canadian Park System Guidelines for Media Accessibility."

Titles: San Serif, large letters, few words as possible
Text blocks: Avoid italic, script, condensed, extended, and uppercase letters
Point size: Refer to the "Levels of Information" section
Color: High-constrast colors between typeface and background
Graphic surface: Matte or nonglare
Approachable distance: Within three inches of the surface of any graphic panel
Alternative forms: Braille, audio, or a folder containing the graphic panels, illustrations, and text

Viewing Distance and Letter Height

Without reservation, the viewing distances established for the visually challenged should be the gold standard for every planner/designer. Honestly, having to adjust our designs to accommodate the visually impaired has helped us all, and as a result font sizes are now larger and easier to read. Thanks to the increase in letter size, the quantity of copy has been dramatically reduced, is now briefer and more concise, and has virtually eliminated those boring "books" on the wall.

The chart in figure 2.27 details the height and the point sizes of letters. It is based on the data published in the "Smithsonian Guidelines for Accessible Exhibition Design" and the "Canadian Park System Guidelines for Media Accessibility." The viewing dimensions and capital heights are in inches, and the chart is based on Helvetica Regular, black type, white background, and daylight illumination. The point and letter sizes are minimum heights, and it indicates the maximum viewing distance.

Graphic Grid

A grid is a two-dimensional network of invisible lines that is used by designers to lay out and unite a wide variety of graphic panels that have different shapes and sizes. It is common to all graphic panels, regardless of their size, shape, or hierarchy. A grid adds consistency and creates a harmonious, family look to all panels.

Master Grid

A master grid serves as the basis for all the graphic layouts, regardless of the amount of text and the size and shape of the images. Designing a grid that can be used successfully for a wide variety of panel sizes and density of text and images for an exhibition can be a challenge. The following procedure has helped me in preparing a grid and it might help you:

1. Establish the size and shape of each type of graphic panel. Construction materials such as plywood and Masonite normally come in four-by-eight-foot sheets, so it is always economical to consider this basic dimension as a guide when determining the sizes of the panels.
2. Design one grid that can be adjusted to the various sizes, shapes, and types of panels, such as introduction, orientation, exhibit, display, and object.
3. Evaluate the grid to make sure that it can accommodate the exhibit's densities of characters and text:

   Check the title with the most characters and the title with the fewest. Assess the graphic panel with the greatest quantity of text, images, and so on, against the one with the least amount.

Viewing Distance and Letter Height

Viewing Distance	Point Size	Capital Height
3	24 pt	
39	48 pt	
78	100 pt	
118	148 pt	
158		2-1/2
197		3
236		3-3/4
276		4-1/4
315		5
354		5-1/2
394		6-1/8

Figure 2.27. Viewing distance and letter height.

As a general rule, images and text blocks are aligned with the upper left-hand corner of a grid block. Usually a grid is composed of rectangular shapes and columns; however, sometimes free forms are employed. The illustrations in figures 2.28 and 2.29 show a master graphic grid and how it can be adjusted to different sizes and types of panels.

It is important to note that a graphic grid is only a guide, and it should never become a straitjacket that restricts or inhibits the information being presented. There will be times when the text or the visuals won't exactly fit the format imposed by the grid, so slight adjustments must and should be made. A graphic grid is just a layout tool and, as such, should never be made visible.

Figure 2.28. Master grid.

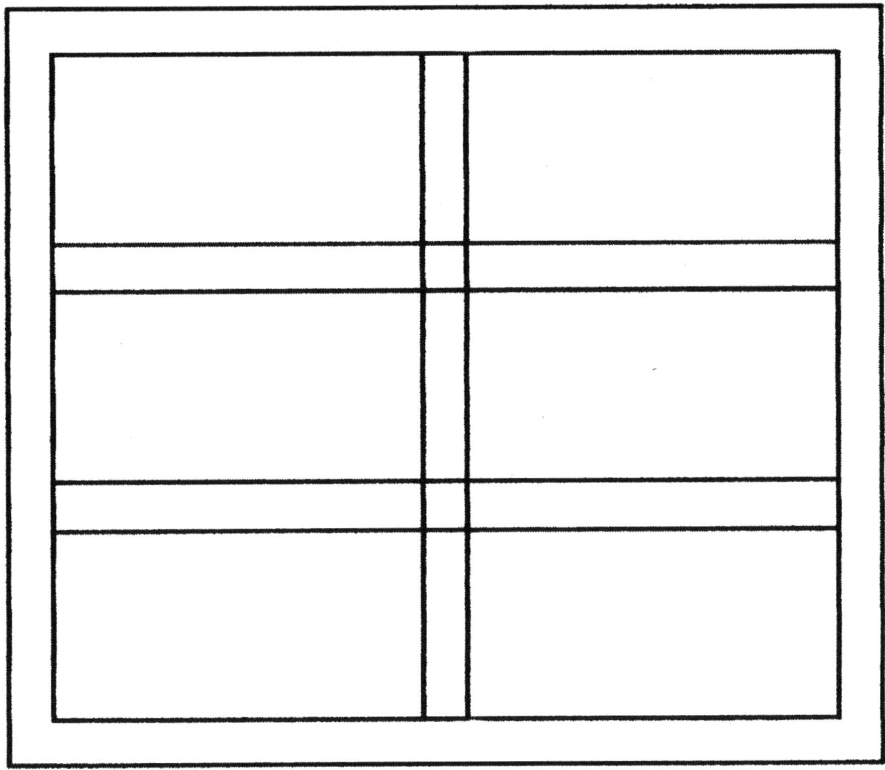

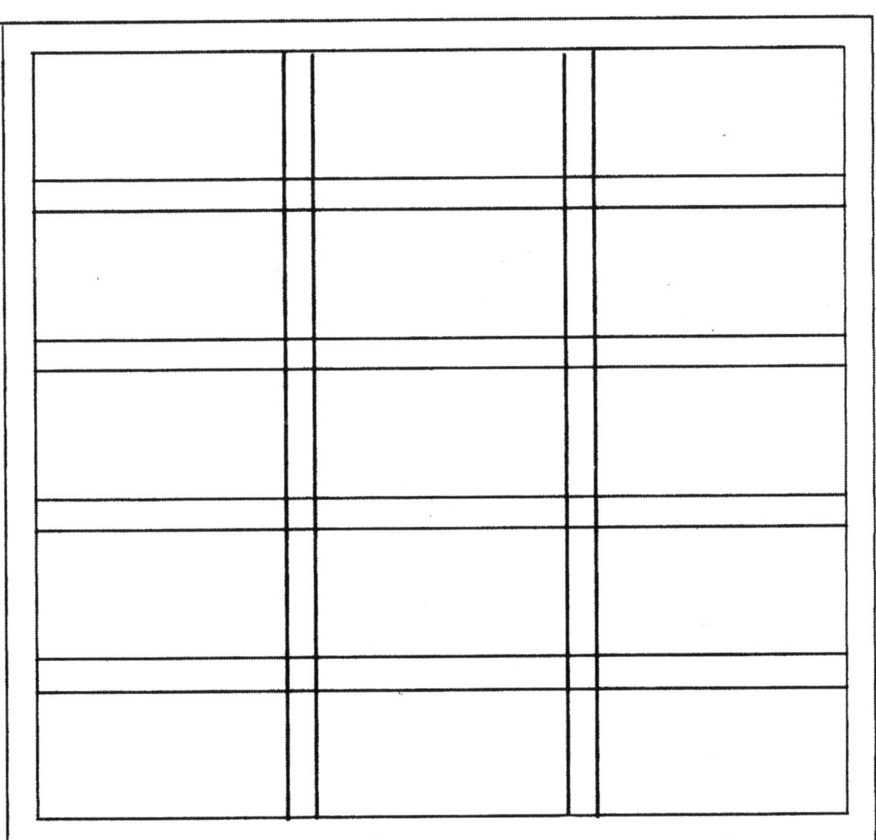

Figure 2.29. Grid adjusted to three different size panels. *(continued)*

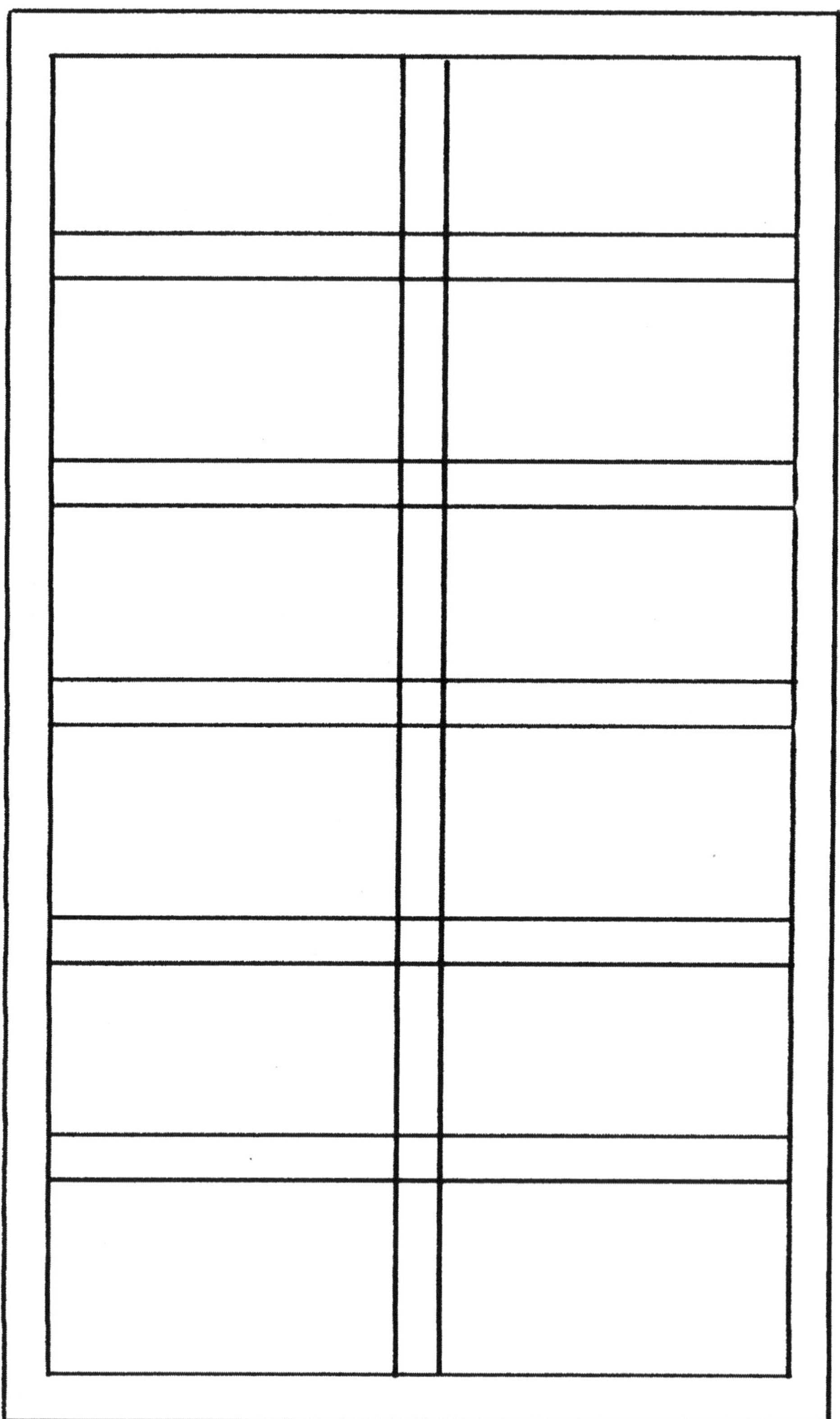

Figure 2.29. (continued)

Column Width

A graphic grid usually depends on the width of a column of print. Generally, a twenty-degree swath is considered to be a comfortable viewing zone, for it allows visitors to read a line of text at one glance without having to move their bodies or heads. The chart in figure 2.30 illustrates column widths and distances.

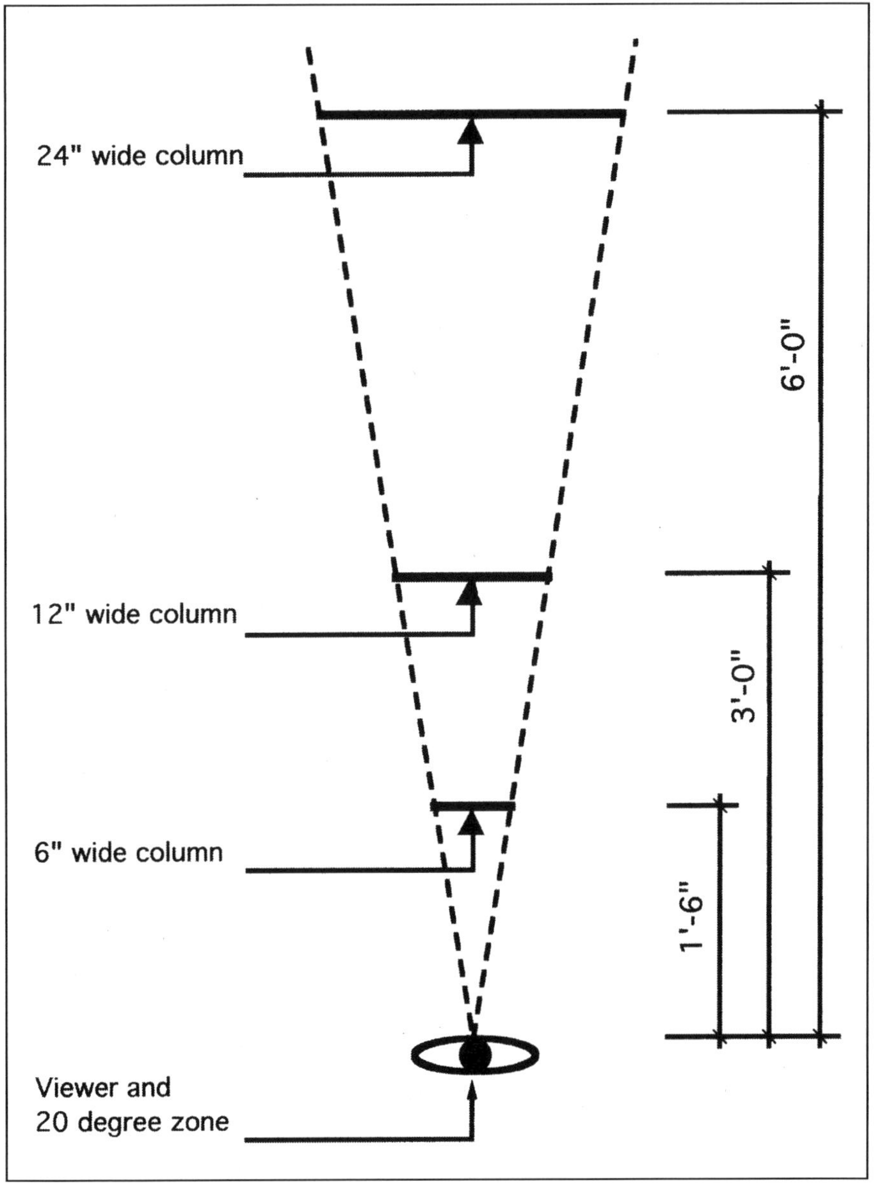

Figure 2.30. Text column width.

Column Grid

Each graphic grid is unique because it is designed for and serves the needs of a particular exhibition. Figures 2.31 to 2.35 show a grid based on a typical newspaper column layout and the graphic layout on which it was based. Even though there is an overwhelming amount of text that could be very boring, the grid used for all the panels was designed to create a unified look, add variety, and organize a diversified collection of images and information.

Figure 2.31. Unity and variety.

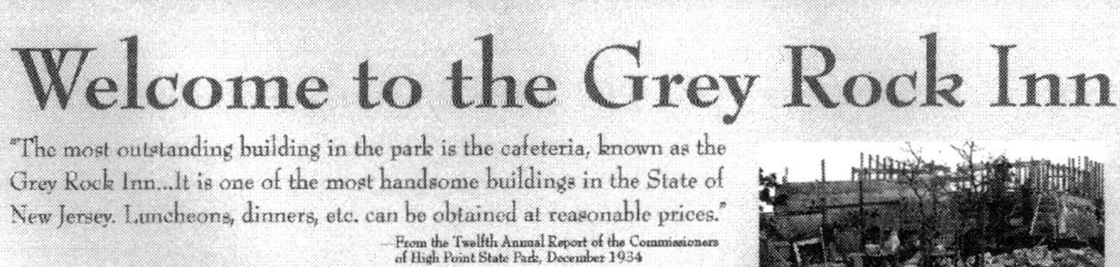

Welcome to the Grey Rock Inn

"The most outstanding building in the park is the cafeteria, known as the Grey Rock Inn...It is one of the most handsome buildings in the State of New Jersey. Luncheons, dinners, etc. can be obtained at reasonable prices."

—From the Twelfth Annual Report of the Commissioners of High Point State Park, December 1934

The entrance hall you're standing in, pictured during the early years of the restaurant's operation.

The kitchen is now a classroom, located at the northern end of the building.

The Restaurant/Cafeteria

This building, constructed in 1930-31, was a restaurant that operated during the summer months until 1959. Colonel Anthony Kuser, who maintained an active interest in his former estate, selected the site prior to his death in 1929. Wyeth and King, the architectural firm that designed the High Point Monument, also drew the plans for the Grey Rock Inn.

The Restaurant/Cafeteria

This building, constructed in 1930-31, was a restaurant that operated during the summer months until 1959. Colonel Anthony Kuser, who maintained an active interest in his former estate, selected the site prior to his death in 1929. Wyeth and King, the architectural firm that designed the High Point Monument, also drew the plans for the Grey Rock Inn.

A Part of the Landscape

The Grey Rock Inn is an excellent example of the architectural style common to park buildings in the early 1900s, sometimes called "park-itecture." Buildings were constructed using local materials in a way that complemented the surrounding landscape. The Grey Rock Inn, like many other park structures at that time, was built from red-tinged rock quarried within the park.

Looking towards the southern end of the building, ornamental embellishments added in the '40s can be seen.

The Civilian Conservation Corps was particularly known for this style architecture, but this building was constructed under the direction of the High Point Park Commission just prior to the CCC's arrival.

William H. Broadwell
Park Photographer

A Broadwell photograph of the Grey Rock Inn shortly after construction was completed in 1931.

Many of the photographs and postcards on display in this building are the work of William Broadwell, a commercial photographer based in Newark, New Jersey, who photographed High Point in the 1920s and 30s and operated a souvenir stand within the park for several years.

This postcard shows the small studio Broadwell maintained nearby to process and print his film.

Figure 2.32. Newspaper variation no. 1. Designed by Judy Elchin.

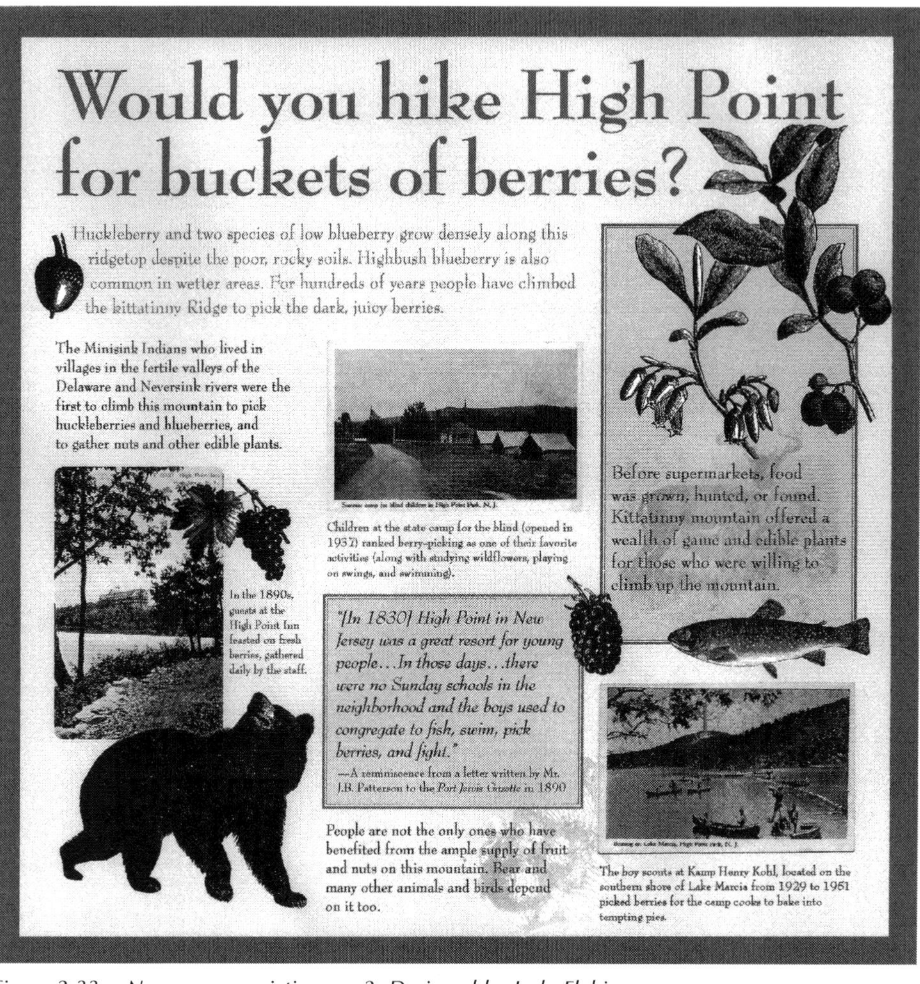

Would you hike High Point for buckets of berries?
Huckleberry and two species of low blueberry grow densely along this ridgetop despite the poor, rocky soils. Highbush blueberry is also common in wetter areas. For hundreds of years people have climbed the kittatinny Ridge to pick the dark, juicy berries.
The Minisink Indians who lived in villages in the fertile valleys of the Delaware and Neversink rivers were the first to climb this mountain to pick huckleberries and blueberries, and to gather nuts and other edible plants.
Children at the state camp for the blind (opened in 1937) ranked berry-picking as one of their favorite activities (along with studying wildflowers, playing on swings, and swimming).
Before supermarkets, food was grown, hunted, or found. Kittatinny mountain offered a wealth of game and edible plants for those who were willing to climb up the mountain.
In the 1890s, guests at the High Point Inn feasted on fresh berries, gathered daily by the staff.
"[In 1830] High Point in New Jersey was a great resort for young people…In those days…there were no Sunday schools in the neighborhood and the boys used to congregate to fish, swim, pick berries, and fight."
—A reminiscence from a letter written by Mr. J.B. Patterson to the Port Jervis Gazette in 1890
People are not the only ones who have benefited from the ample supply of fruit and nuts on this mountain. Bear and many other animals and birds depend on it too.
The boy scouts at Kamp Henry Kohl, located on the southern shore of Lake Marcia from 1929 to 1951 picked berries for the camp cooks to bake into tempting pies.

Figure 2.33. Newspaper variation no. 2. Designed by Judy Elchin.

"High Point is a spot of beauty and a joy forever."

—*The Sussex Independent, July 11, 1890*

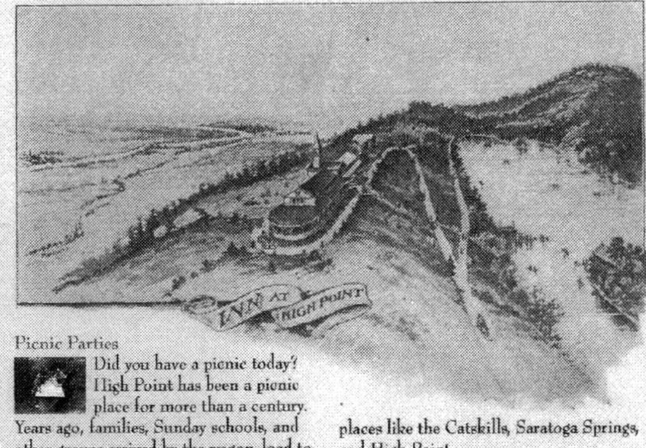

Picnic Parties

Did you have a picnic today? High Point has been a picnic place for more than a century. Years ago, families, Sunday schools, and other groups arrived by the wagon-load to have "picnic parties" and "beefsteak feeds" alongside Lake Marcia. When High Point became a park, it was not unusual for thousands of people to be picnicking on sunny Sunday afternoons.

The Rise of the Mountain Resort

As cities grew and filled with factories in the 1800s, they became more and more polluted. The industrial advances also created "free time"—something that was hard to come by for people living in rural areas working the land. Those who had the money and the time escaped the cities in summer, but not by returning to the farms. They traveled by train or steamboat to scenic, "healthy" mountain resorts—places like the Catskills, Saratoga Springs, and High Point.

The High Point Inn – A Grand Hotel

To capitalize on the scenic locale and the new market of people looking to return to nature (albeit temporarily), Charles St. John, an entrepreneur from Port Jervis, New York, built the High Point Inn on the bluff overlooking Lake Marcia in 1890. In doing so, he turned what had been a popular picnic spot into a destination for wealthy vacationers. The Inn operated during the summer months for nineteen years.

Post Card

Naming High Point and Lake Marcia

Dr. William Kitchell completed the first topographic survey of Sussex County in 1855. In doing so, he discovered that the summit of Kittatinny Mountain was the highest elevation in the state, and on his map he marked the spot with a point and the word "high." It's been called High Point ever since.

Bill Kitchell's Romantic Gesture

One summer day, Kitchell traveled with friends to Sussex for a picnic party on the banks of the lake at high point. As the sun set he talked to the group about the geology of the lake, and then he read a poem he had written, Rose Leaf and Lavender, in which he named the beautiful lake after his sweetheart, Marcia Smith. It was the only poem he ever wrote, and he and Miss Smith married one year later.

Rose Leaf & Lavender

Listen, ye hills and fragrant groves;
Ye glades, all made for angel's loves;
Ye mountain tops the kiss the sky,
Ye fields that with Elysium vie!

Assembled on this silvery wave'
Immortal honors we would crave –
The beauty, virtue, truth arrayed
All in one solitary maid;

Permit us by the Muse's fountains,
Permit us by the Grace's mountains,
Permit us by the modern Garcia,
Henceforth to call this lake –
Lake Marcia!

Figure 2.34. Newspaper variation no. 3. Designed by Judy Elchin.

Welcome to the Neighborhood
High Point's Habitats are Home
Field
Cedar Bog
Lake
Vernal Pond
Rock Outcrop
Rocky Ridge
Forest
Beaver Marsh
Stream
As you hike the trails, drive the roads, or take in the views, you'll see many different habitats at High Point. Each habitat is a unique community of plants and animals living together, relying on one another for survival.
While some animals, like deer, can find what they need to survive in a variety of habitats, others have specific requirements. Spotted salamanders return to the same vernal ponds every year to breed. If the pond isn't there, the salamanders don't reproduce.
Atlantic White Cedar Bog
The most unique habitat at High Point is the Cedar Bog. This type of forested wetland is typically found at low elevations. At 1,500 feet above sea level, this one is believed to be the highest cedar bog there is.
A unique combination northern and southern species of plants can be found growing there and the dense foliage shelters many animals including deer, bobcat, coyote, bear, and porcupine. The bog is also a haven for many birds including the threatened barred owl.

Figure 2.35. Newspaper variation no. 4. Designed by Judy Elchin.

Graphic Panels

Graphics are applied to panels, so a layout should not be started until the size, shape, and type of panel have been determined. The size and shape of a graphic panel informs the visitors as to the type and level of information that they will be viewing.

Graphic Panels Phases: Special Considerations

Preliminary Phase
- Assign the type of panel to be used to each graphic layout.
- List and locate each panel; designate its hierarchical position.
- Produce a layout for each type of panel; indicate size and shape.

Intermediate and Final Phases
- Each panel should be assigned a particular graphic layout.
- Locate all graphic panels on the technical drawings, plans, and elevations.

Documentation Phase
- Document in detail each type of panel.

Types of Graphic Panels

Size and cost are the major considerations when determining the type and materials of graphic panels. Obviously, the cost rises as the size of the panel increases, since it will require more construction hours and material to accomplish.

Construction materials are always a major consideration when designing a panel. Sintra, Masonite, and plywood are the standard substrates used. Sintra is a lightweight, rigid polyvinyl chloride (PVC) composite material, and it and Masonite are excellent materials for graphics, since they have smooth, finished surfaces, and their edges require just a light sanding and minimum finishing. Plywood, used mostly when constructing very large panels, is a strong, heavy material and requires a smooth, grade A surface; exposed edges have to be sanded and finished, framed, or edge banded with solid wood strips. Refer to chapter 5, "Materials," for more information.

Today, a graphic printout that covers the surface of a panel is the popular method used to display images and text. However, silk-screened texts and applied photographs are still employed. Three-dimensional items, artifacts, computer monitors, and the like, can also be applied to a graphic panel.

Appliqué Panel

An appliqué panel is simple and inexpensive to construct and is used mainly for small panels and for temporary installations. Because they are not framed, appliqué panels can be of a variety of shapes including geometric or free forms. I have even seen appliqué panels in the form of silhouettes and logos. In addition to the traditional materials, they can also be constructed from lightweight art boards.

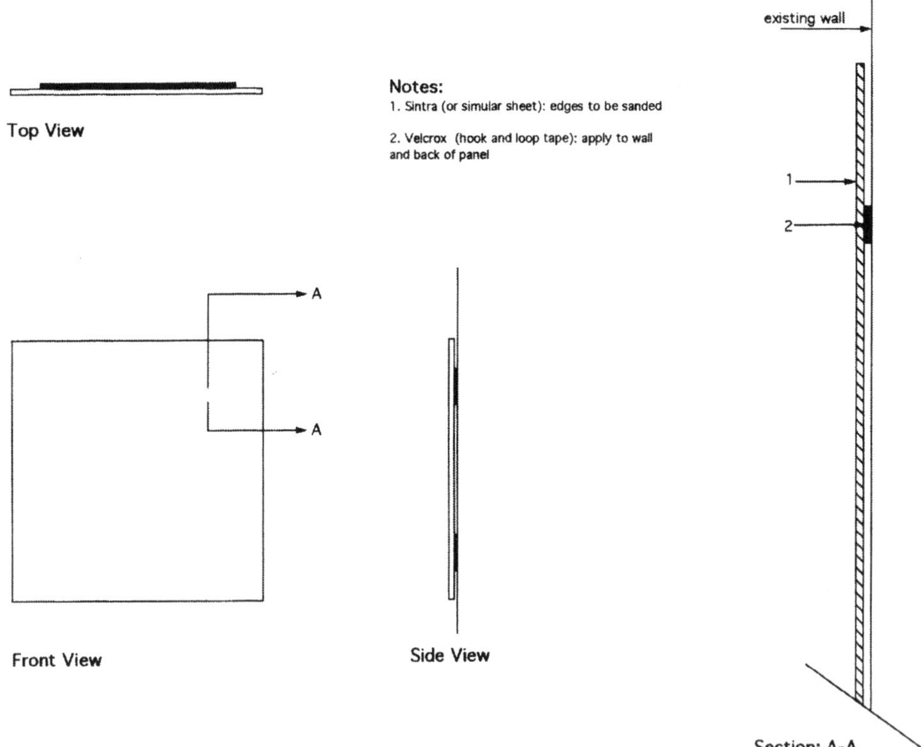

Figure 2.36. Graphic panel: Appliqué.

Boxed Panel

A boxed panel is the workhorse of museum graphic panels. It is visually and physically strong and can be used wherever a large graphic is required. Because the sides are visible, they have to be sanded and finished. This panel is relatively expensive.

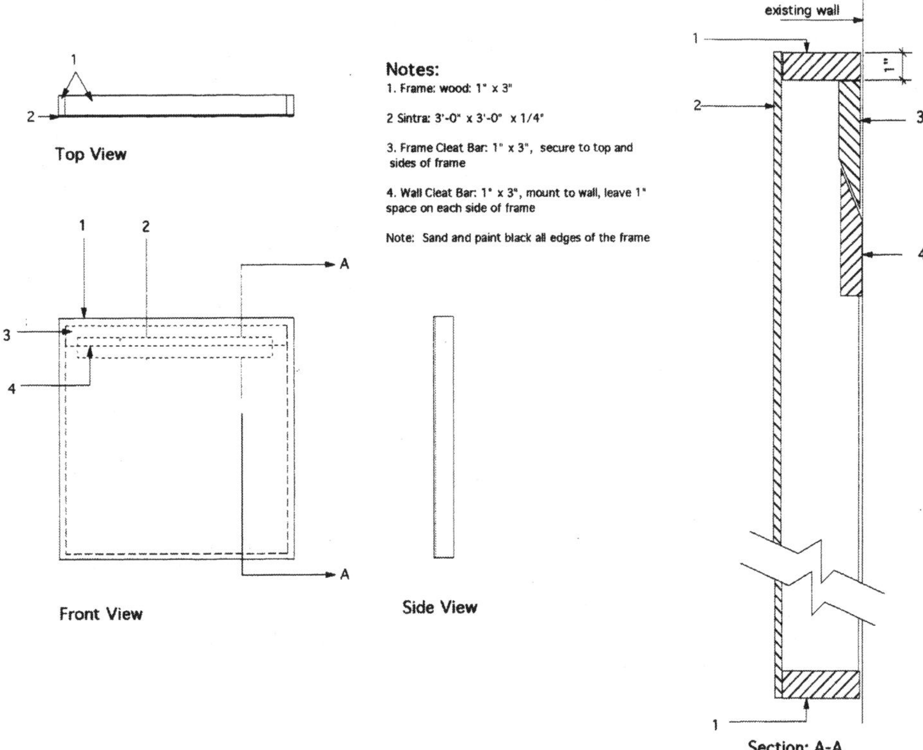

Figure 2.37. Graphic panel: Boxed.

Floating Panel

Usually specified when small- and medium-size graphics are required, a floating panel seems to float free of the wall and has a lightweight appearance. Its frame does not have to be finely finished, since it is recessed and not visible. For that reason, it is easier and less expensive to construct than a boxed or framed panel. Another advantage for using this panel is that it does not have to be limited to the traditional square or rectangular shape, and as with the appliqué panel, it can have rounded edges and free-form shapes.

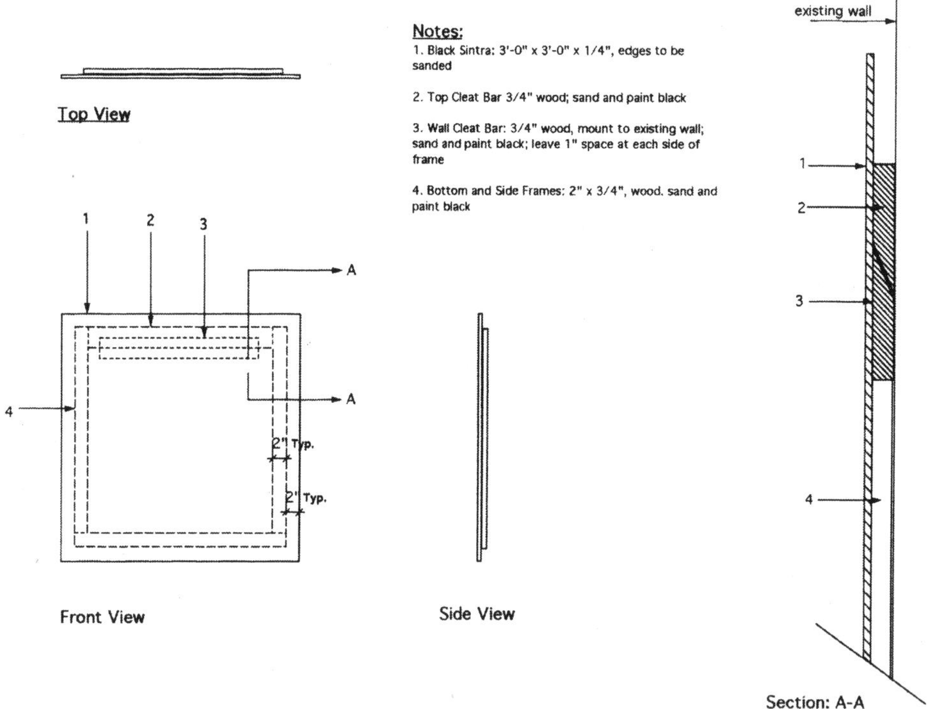

Figure 2.38. Graphic panel: Floating.

Framed Panel

Based on a picture frame design, a framed panel usually employs mitered joints and has a nice, traditional, elegant look. Depending on the thickness of the frame, it can be structurally strong and used for large graphics. Since it requires the most labor to construct, this panel is the most expensive of all those shown here.

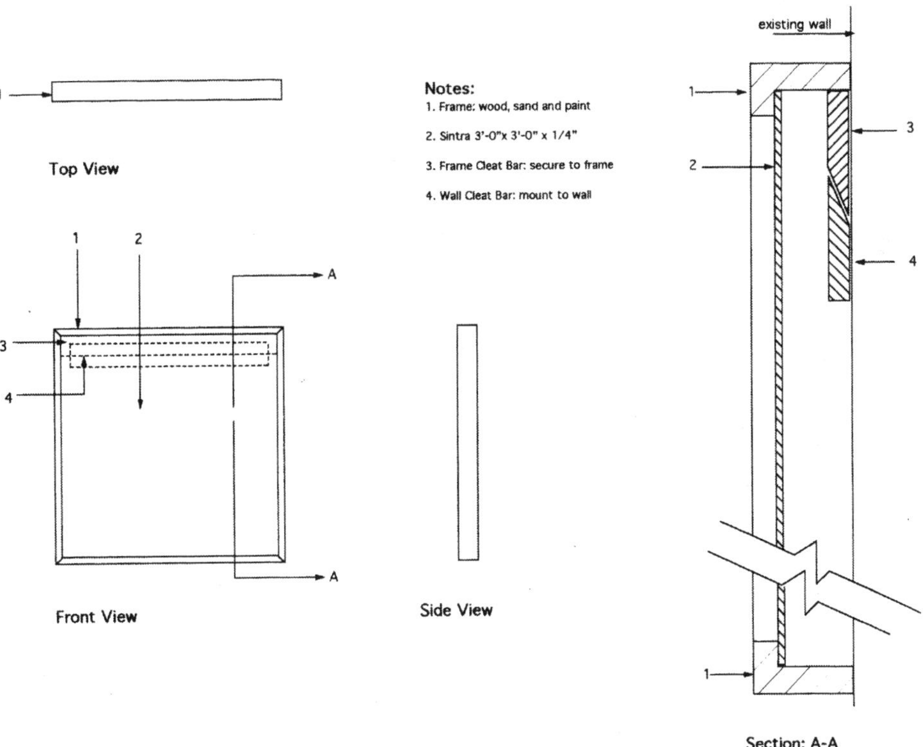

Figure 2.39. Graphic panel: Framed.

Graphic Visuals

Two-dimensional items such as pictures, drawings, and illustrations can contribute greatly to the success of an exhibition for they can attract attention, impart a significant amount of information, and leave a lasting impression. Care should be taken to make sure that they are appropriate and reflect the exhibition's goals, ambiance, and content, and that copyright approvals, if needed, are obtained. When an image is used as background or as a space filler, it should be selected or toned down and not visually overpower the exhibit text and the images presented.

Graphic Visuals Phases: Special Considerations

Schematic Phase
  Choose and list pertinent images required in the exhibition program.
Preliminary Phase
  Continue to select images.
  Commence to place visuals in the graphic layouts.
Intermediate Phase
  Continue to select and place visuals in the layouts.
  Commence obtaining copyrights and permissions.
Final Phase
  Place all visuals in the final graphic layouts.
  Obtain all copyright approvals and permissions.

Professional Sources

Artists, photographers, and illustrators can be contracted with to produce images that are not readily accessible or that don't yet exist. However, when selecting someone to do the work, a thorough investigation is always needed to make sure that the person can successfully fulfill the assignment. The following is a brief list of considerations to use when making your choice. Can the professional

- create the visual that is needed?
- produce a professional, high-quality product?
- deliver the work on time?
- adhere to the established guidelines?
- accept the fact that his or her work will be critiqued and might need to be revised?

Since many of the exhibitions that I have designed have been located in remote areas, I have always relied on local talent to produce the art that was needed. Maybe I have been lucky, but these artists have been very talented and professional, and always wonderful and enjoyable to work with. They unfailingly seem to be excited and committed to the project and take special pride in their work, and because they are local, they always seem to possess a unique knowledge of and commitment to the area.

CASE HISTORY: "NEVER UNDERESTIMATE LOCAL TALENT"

At the Lake Shelbyville Visitor Center in Illinois, a large eight-by-twelve-foot mural depicting the native prairie grass landscape as it was in the nineteenth century was required. A hand-painted mural was necessary since that type of landscape has long since disappeared. Asking around, I heard that a local farmer's wife, Janet Roney, was a "prairie artist" and was known for her paintings on this subject. After seeing several examples of her work, and feeling that she had the talent that was needed, I recommended that she be awarded the commission. Later I heard that because the mural was so huge she had to paint it in her husband's barn. Did she do a great job? Did she install it on time? And was everyone extremely happy with the results? The answer was a resounding "Yes." Several years later, I received a letter from her thanking me for giving her the opportunity; painting that mural provided her with the kick start that she needed and deserved, and today she is a full-fledged prairie artist with numerous commissions.

Figure 2.40. Mural: Illinois Grand Prairie. Painted by Janet Roney.

Illustrations and Photographs

"A picture is worth a thousand words." We've all heard it, and although I find the expression to be a bit hackneyed, it is so true! Visuals can quickly relay a great deal of information and eliminate a vast amount of text.

Yet their selection has to be well thought out, for if the photograph or illustration is not compatible with the other visuals being displayed, the exhibition could lack unity. However, when an illustrator or a photographer produces a series of visuals to be used throughout the project, it can result in a cohesive exhibition.

CASE HISTORY: "WHEN YOU CAN'T EXPERIENCE THE REAL THING"

When designing the exhibits for the Valley of Fire Visitor Center in Nevada, I felt that the park was so vast and physically challenging that many visitors would not be able to experience the numerous complex habitats that prevailed in its desert and mountain regions. In addition, much of the flora and fauna was to be found only in remote, inaccessible areas and bloomed for just brief periods. To make matters worse, most desert animals are nocturnal and are not seen by visitors during the daytime. Although this huge park seemed empty, it was full of exciting life, but explaining it proved highly challenging. The complex story of the valley was resolved when a local artist, Jan Gunlock, and a photographer, Gail Bandini, were retained to produce a series of illustrations and photographs. Both did amazing jobs and were wonderful to work with.

The photograph shown in figure 2.41 is of wall-mounted photo murals, wall-mounted graphic panels, and kiosks. The two murals were photographed

Figure 2.41. "Life in the Desert" exhibit.

(continued)

CASE HISTORY: "WHEN YOU CAN'T EXPERIENCE THE REAL THING" (*continued*)

from the exact same spot and were meant to illustrate the valley's two contrasting, harsh environments. The mural on the left shows the desert during daylight hours when the temperature can soar to 120 degrees. On the right, the photograph was taken in the early evening and depicts the desert at nighttime when it can sometimes fall below freezing.

Wall-Mounted Graphic Panels

Using photographs, text, and illustrations, the two panels mounted below the murals detail how plants and animals adjust to the harsh changes in the desert climate. In the center of each panel are illustrations of plants and their root structures that allow them to survive the dry environment. Desert animals are also illustrated showing how they exist underground during the heat of the day and above ground at night.

Kiosks

In the foreground are several three-sided kiosks, with each face devoted to a specific habitat that exists in the Valley of Fire. Graphic panels consisting of an illustration of a habitat's signature plant and photographs and text that detail its unique flora and fauna are included. Each plant illustration also indicates its root structure.

Figure 2.42. Habitat: Plant illustration. Drawn by Jan Gunlock.

Charts

With only a minimum of words, charts can visually convey complex and statistical information in a manner that is easy to comprehend and remember. They generally come in an array of formats, including line, bar, and pictorial.

Charles Minard's 1869 chart presents the tragedy of Napoleon's 1812 Russian Campaign (see figure 2.43). It shows in an unforgettable, easy-to-understand illustration: his army's movements, time frame, survival rates, and the temperatures encountered.

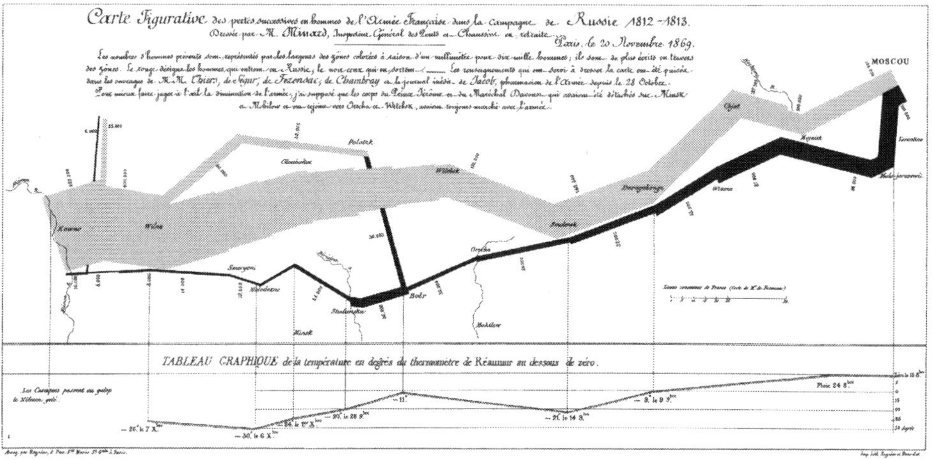

Figure 2.43. Napolean 1812 Russian campaign chart.

Three-dimensional Items

Many times just seeing the real thing can be a powerful experience. Artifacts, specimens, and the like (hopefully small), mounted on graphic panels can be immensely helpful when explaining scientific theories and historic events.

CASE HISTORY: "SPECIMENS CAN BE MOUNTED"

When designing an exhibition for a natural history museum, a graphic panel entitled "Frogs Got a Free Ride with Continental Drift" was part of the exhibit. To demonstrate this prehistoric event, a Jurassic-period frog (fossilized in a stone block) and a contemporary Pacific Northwestern frog (preserved in a jar) were mounted on the same panel. By integrating these two similar specimens with the text and the illustrations, this rather esoteric subject became uncomplicated and understandable.

Installation

The museum personnel oversee the exhibit installation, and prior to the arrival of the display structures at the site, they should ensure there are no obstacles that could damage the exhibits or impede their movement from the van to the exhibition site. It is also important that the unloading and staging areas be secure and weather protected. In order to resolve issues that might develop, it is prudent to have copies of the bid package, contract, and shop drawings available at the site. At the point of installation, a member of the exhibit team should be present to

- inspect all materials and structures;
- maintain quality control;
- assist in resolving any issues or questions that might develop;
- observe that everything is installed properly;
- ensure that the terms of the contractual agreement are fulfilled; and
- assist with preparation of the punch list.

Most times museum staff members install the artifacts, and the construction firm installs the exhibit structures. When needed, professional artifact installers can be retained. During installation, the "china shop" syndrome ("If you break it, you buy it") can be enforced. For that reason, there are certain boundaries that should never be transgressed. The golden rule is "leave the work to the experts who were assigned the task; never interfere, and don't try to be too helpful."

During installation, the planner/designer is in an advisory role, and it is for that reason that I always wear a suit, never jeans or work clothes. I want everyone to understand that I have been retained only to observe the installation and to help mediate any conflicts that might occur. I have not been authorized to assist in installing the exhibits or to handle the artifacts, and frankly the professionals who do that work are much better at that job than I am.

Before the construction firm can complete its work and have a museum representative sign it off, the firm must

- participate in a punch-list inspection and provide or repair all the items listed;
- clean and polish all structures, remove debris, and broom sweep the exhibition area;
- train the museum staff on the operation and maintenance of the special exhibits; and
- deliver the close-out package to the institution.

Lighting

For information pertaining to this subject, refer to chapter 3, "Color and Light."

Materials

For information pertaining to this subject, refer to chapter 5, "Materials."

Meetings

Meetings are excellent vehicles for keeping everyone informed, for reviewing issues, and for receiving valuable comments. The subjects discussed and the frequency of meetings will depend upon the people who are involved and the scope of work that will be performed.

Meetings Phases: Types of Meetings

- Master Plan, Feasibility Study, and Schematic Phase
  - Start-up Meeting
  - Job Meeting
  - Presentation Meeting
- Preliminary Phase
  - Job Meeting
  - Start-up Meeting
  - Presentation Meeting
- Intermediate, Final, and Documentation Phases
  - Job Meeting
  - Project Meeting
- Bidding Phase
  - Prebid Meeting
  - Bid-Opening Meeting
- Construction Phase
  - Start-up Meeting
  - Inspections
- Installation Phase
  - On-Site Clarifications
  - Punch-List Inspection

Bid-Opening Meeting

At the bid-opening meeting, each bid for construction of the exhibits is unsealed, and its cost read out. Even though there will be only one successful bidder, it is always prudent for the institution to invite all the construction firms who have submitted bids to attend this meeting. Since all the bidders will leave knowing that the process was fair, they will probably be willing to bid on future work.

During this meeting, planners/designers should be somewhat apprehensive, because they could leave with "egg on their face." When the bids are opened, the contractors' costs should all be relatively close. Granted that sometimes a few companies might be desperate for work, and shave their prices, but when there is too large a variation in bids, it is always a strong indicator that the exhibit team has produced a sloppy bid package. For the institution, that should raise a red flag that the project could be in trouble.

Inspections

On a regular basis during the construction of the exhibition, selected members from the museum team and the exhibit team ought to visit the fabrication shop. The contractor conducts these meetings and is responsible for writing and distributing minutes. The purpose of these visits is to

- review and discuss the project;
- ensure that the specifications and the detail drawings are being adhered to;
- inspect the display materials that are under construction or already completed to maintain quality control; and
- authorize payment for finished work.

The first shop inspection should occur very early during the construction period, when there are only a few displays nearing completion. This visit is extremely important, for it will be the only opportunity the planner/designer has to establish the level of craftsmanship that is desired. Obviously, once the exhibits are fabricated and ready to ship, it's too late to address the quality of the workmanship. During this first inspection, be very picky but also pleasant and fair. Tight-fitting joints, scratch-free surfaces, dust-free finishes, and quality graphics are the obvious items to review. Once the construction firm knows that only the highest level of craftsmanship will be accepted, the firm will usually assign its best and most experienced personnel to the project, and needless to say, the work will probably run smoothly and be very professional.

The number of meetings at the carpentry shop will depend on the size and complexity of the project and the travel time and expense required. There are occasions when the institution's budget cannot cover the travel costs and lodging expenses needed for a visit. In such cases, the number of inspections may have to be reduced, and progress photographs of the completed or partially completed elements substituted.

The final inspection should occur approximately ten days prior to shipping, when about 95 percent of the exhibits will have been completed, assembled, and ready for your "white glove" review. Check for scratches and defects; test the electrical and mechanical devices to make sure that they are in working order. Inspect everything, for once the exhibits are shipped, it is almost impossible to make changes, and frankly, it is really too late to complain.

CASE HISTORIES: "INSPECTIONS ARE IMPORTANT"

I once was commissioned to supervise construction of an exhibition that I had planned/designed. It was a government project, and of course the work was awarded to the lowest bidder. On my first inspection at the fabrication shop, there were many construction details that confused me, until the president of the firm told me that he hated to read. Unbelievable! My heart almost stopped when he further informed me that he had estimated the project without reading my specifications and that he based his bid solely on my technical drawings. I knew immediately why he was the low bidder, that I was in for a rough ride, and that this project would require close supervision. What happened? Fortunately, through close coordination the result was more than satisfactory.

Another time on a different project, I made a surprise visit to the shop that was building a replica, only to discover that the thirty-five-foot reproduction of a rock outcropping was sitting outside in the parking lot. The contractor explained that he lacked the needed indoor storage space, and he even had the nerve to tell me that he didn't think it would rain. I persuaded him to cover the replica with a waterproof tarp and arrange for its immediate delivery to the project site.

Job Meetings

Usually held once a week, job meetings are generally limited to members of the exhibit team; their purpose is to discuss all aspects of the project, review the work that is remaining or has been accomplished, establish upcoming assignments and directions, and review the time schedule and the construction budget.

Minutes of a Meeting

At each meeting someone should be assigned to record the results and to distribute copies of the minutes to all present and absentee members. This document is the project's official record of all issues that were discussed during the meeting and is of critical importance because it

- clarifies what was and was not resolved, and
- establishes what actions need to be taken, when, and by whom.

Written records of a meeting are obviously important; they keep all participants on the same page and lessen the chance for disagreement. Since they may be ultimately used to resolve legal misunderstandings, minutes have to be accurate. They should be as brief and concise as possible; each topic discussed is listed with its resolution or nonresolution, and every item should be numbered for easy reference.

Minutes all seem to have one basic format. They state the date, time, location, attendees, absentees, items discussed, actions taken or to be taken and by whom, distribution list, person who prepared the minutes, and the date, time, and place of the next meeting. They usually conclude with this type of statement: "We believe that these minutes accurately reflect what transpired at this meeting. Unless notified in writing to the contrary within ten days after receipt, we will assume that you concur with the accuracy of this transcription."

CASE HISTORY: "MINUTES ARE IMPORTANT"

Once when discussing with a colleague a meeting that we had attended, I discovered that we had two completely different ideas as to what had been agreed upon. Perusal of the official minutes resolved the issue promptly.

On-Site Clarifications

During installation of an exhibit there are always a few issues that need to be settled, and informal discussions usually resolve them. When additional work or materials are agreed upon during one of these meetings, change orders must be written and approved before the work can proceed.

Prebid Meeting

Members from the museum and the exhibit team meet with the bidders to discuss design and construction details, and administrative and bidding procedures. This meeting is held before the bidders start to estimate the project and is meant to address their concerns and answer their questions. It usually ends with a visit to the exhibition site. The institution initiates and conducts this meeting and follows up by distributing minutes to all attendees.

Presentation Meeting

Exhibit concepts are presented to the museum team members for review and approval in the presentation meeting. For the planner/designer, this meeting can be a critical time because here you are "selling" your ideas and the design concept that you believe in. Many times having your designs approved depends on how well you prepare for the meeting and your presentation. This meeting usually culminates with mini-copies of the presentation materials being distributed to the museum team members for their review.

For me, no matter how many times I have presented an exhibition design, my shy genie always uncorks, and as I look out at that sea of eyes in front of me, I always wish that I could ride a flying carpet and be whisked away. But that never happens, so I am left standing with just one remnant of inner comfort: the knowledge that I know the subject, I believe in the design concepts, and I am prepared.

Preparation

No matter how good the exhibit design ideas and schemes are, if the presentation meeting is handled badly, it will impact negatively on the project. The presenters for this meeting must be fully prepared, be knowledgeable, and leave nothing to chance. In advance of the meeting they should do the following:

- Prepare an agenda with a copy for each attendee.
- Reserve the meeting room, checking that it is adequate for their needs.
- Ensure that the HVAC system is working.
- Review the location and capacity of the electrical outlets.
- Check that the furniture is sufficient and properly placed.

Presentation Delivery Methods

When presenting a design concept, there are two basic methods used.

Conclusive Approach The conclusive approach is when the sketches of the exhibition are presented first, followed by the floor plans, additional sketches depicting special displays, circulation diagrams, and lastly selected research materials. I prefer this approach because I believe that everyone is highly anxious to know, "What will the exhibit look like?" at the beginning of the meeting. Once that question has been answered, the audience always seems to relax, and since they have gained insight into the design concept, they seem better able to comprehend the issues and details. I usually leave the exhibition concept sketch and the floor plan on view during the presentation, so that the audience can readily refer to them.

Gradual Approach When initially presenting their concepts, most planners/designers use the gradual approach. Here, by starting with the floor plan and ending with the exhibition concept sketches, the visuals are presented in a logical progression. I feel that with this approach the audience can become highly impatient as they are forced to wait to see the final exhibition design. This method is also referred to as the build-up approach.

Project Meetings

The purpose of project meetings is to keep the museum team informed of the progress of the exhibition and of any changes that were made. Attended by selected members of the museum and the exhibit teams, the exhibition design is reviewed and pertinent details are discussed. This meeting should conclude with everyone in agreement.

Protocol

During the construction and installation phases, there are certain unwritten courtesies and protocols that should be followed. The most important is when a problem or a question arises. In this case, the plan-

CASE HISTORY: "DESIGN/BUILD"

I have only dropped protocols a few times, and it always occurred when the project's time frame required that the planning/designing and construction phases take place simultaneously. In those cases, the builders asked me to plan/design and to supervise the construction for them. Before proceeding, and knowing that shop drawings would be deleted and that many design decisions would have to be made at the construction site, I insisted that the managers of the construction firm inform the client and the carpenters in writing that I would be overseeing construction. Everyone agreed; we all worked together, and the exhibits opened on time.

ner/designer should only discuss the matter with the on-site construction supervisor and never, never, never with any of the supervisor's subordinates, workers, or other contractors.

Yet, as every designer knows, there are always projects where the time schedule is just too tight. It is at these moments that the traditional protocols become the first causalities. We all have our stories; the "Design/Build" case history is mine.

Punch-List Inspection

Once a client asked me, "Why do you call it a punch list?" Well, to be frank, even though we would never have to step into a ring with boxing gloves on, there are times when it can be just about as brutal. This final inspection of the exhibits occurs after all the displays are installed but prior to opening day and is usually preformed by representatives of the exhibit and museum teams and the construction firm. During this "walk-through," all the exhibit materials built and installed by the contractor are reviewed, and a punch list is prepared that itemizes any missing or damaged items. Before the builder is paid in full, every item on the punch list must be completed or credit given to the owners if they have to finish the work themselves.

Start-up Meetings

At this time all participants involved in the project are introduced and have an opportunity to

- discuss each person's responsibilities and
- discuss the proposed design and any other issues pertaining to the project.

Schematic Phase

This start-up meeting occurs at the beginning of schematics; it includes members of the museum and exhibit teams. At this time all the exhibition's parameters are discussed and agreed upon, and the information needed for the designs to commence and for the project to run smoothly is obtained. An exhibit team member initiates this meeting and prepares and distributes the minutes.

Since any exhibition's planning/designing must be compatible with the institution's master plan, feasibility study, or fund-raising materials, these documents should be made available to the exhibit team, so that they can be reviewed in advance and, if necessary, discussed at the meeting. Before commencing any work it is essential to do the following:

- Establish the time schedule and budget for the project.
- Know who will be attending the meetings, their expertise, and their project responsibilities.
- Request copies of the latest architectural and engineering drawings of the exhibition areas. These drawings are excellent reference materials and can be most helpful during the planning/designing phases.
- Assign a person to record and distribute the minutes of the meeting.
- Prepare an outline of the exhibition program's exhibit brief so that each item can be reviewed.
- Assemble a list of questions that could impact the project:
    - What is the reason for and the importance of the exhibition?
    - What are the exhibit team members' assignments and responsibilities?
    - What are the lines of communication, and who will receive copies of minutes and correspondents?
    - Will fund-raising efforts impact the design and the time schedule, and will special presentation materials such as models or renderings be required?

At this meeting I always ask a lot of questions. Some that may seem irrelevant can often produce surprising answers that can impact the exhibit design, as shown in the case histories "Never Rewrite History" and "It Didn't Matter Who Came First."

CASE HISTORY: "NEVER REWRITE HISTORY"

When designing an exhibit that highlighted America's Revolutionary War leaders, I asked at the start-up meeting what appeared to be a stupid question, "Why did the museum directors want this exhibition?" Needless to say I was shocked when they replied that our founding fathers had been divinely ordained and that "fact" must be the focus of the exhibition. Since rewriting history is not what I do, I declined the project.

CASE HISTORY: "IT DIDN'T MATTER WHO CAME FIRST"

Another time when preparing an exhibition that focused on local manufacturing firms that existed near the beginning of the Industrial Revolution, I asked the question, "Who is funding this project?" I was told that the main sponsor was a local firm that had been established in the nineteenth century, that its executives wanted an exhibit that highlighted their company, and that they wished to have their display prominently placed at the entrance. Their request was easy for me to comply with, and it did not adversely affect the exhibit. Knowing that piece of information before I started to lay out the floor plan saved me several redesigns.

Preliminary Phase

At the beginning of this phase, a meeting is held to discuss in-depth the exhibition concept that has been selected for development. This meeting includes museum and exhibit team members, and it must conclude with everyone in agreement and a consensus to move ahead with the exhibition. Without such approval, further exhibit planning/designing should not start.

This meeting has its perils, since normally there are parts of the rejected schematic schemes that some attendees would like to incorporate into the chosen concept. Although it may be acceptable to pick and choose when selecting from a Chinese menu, applying that procedure to an exhibition design can be detrimental. However, there are times when an idea from a rejected scheme can become part of and actually improve the chosen design. Yet no matter how appealing a concept may be, if it doesn't relate to the selected design, it could destroy it. For that reason it is important for the presenter to always maintain a clear vision of the chosen exhibit concept and never allow it to be compromised.

Construction Phase

The purpose of this meeting is to launch the construction phase of the project. Usually held at the fabrication site, this meeting includes representatives of the museum and the exhibit and construction teams. At this time, the pertinent administrative, construction, and installation issues are discussed. The construction firm initiates this meeting and prepares and distributes the minutes.

Mission

The mission statement addresses the "why" and "what" of the visitor's interpretive experience and is the constant that binds together and influences every aspect of an exhibition.

Mission Statement Phases: Special Considerations

Feasibility Study or Schematic Phase
 Discussed and prepared
Preliminary Phase
 Reviewed, approved, and signed off
Intermediate and Final Phases
 Reviewed exhibit designs to ensure that the mission has not been compromised

Exhibit team members should never forget the mission statement of the exhibition, for it is the basis for its planning/designing and the criterion for judging its success. This statement should be succinct and confined to a brief paragraph. Since it is critical to the outcome of the exhibition, it is wise never to start the planning/designing process before its mission statement is finalized and agreed upon by all participants.

The mission of the exhibition is the star that guides the "ship." To ensure that the project will not deviate from it during the exhibit development phases, it is always helpful to display a copy of the statement prominently for all members of the exhibit team to see.

Even though an exhibition mission statement is singular, in reality I do believe that there really are two missions: the official mission and the tacit mission.

Official Mission

Many times the mission statement is established and finalized before the planner/designer is retained. This was true in the case of the Pennsylvania National Fire Museum (PNFM), a newly established museum, located in a recently renovated, late nineteenth-century firehouse in Harrisburg, Pennsylvania. The following were the statements they had prepared for me. I found them to be adequate and ones with which I could work.

- "To preserve, collect, record, and exhibit the history of the fire, rescue, and emergency medical services with emphasis on the City of Harrisburg and the Greater Harrisburg Area and the Commonwealth of Pennsylvania."

- "To interpret the sociological, economic, cultural, and technological influences on the fire and the emergency services throughout their development."
- "To serve as a memorial to the paid and the volunteer firefighters who dedicated their lives to fire and emergency services."
- "To discuss the evolution of the cultural and other facets of the fire and emergency services."

Tacit Mission

Planners / designers should take a fresh look at the needs of the institution and the purpose of its exhibition before starting a project. In the case of the PNFM, after touring the neighborhood, asking questions, and listening to comments made by the staff, I prepared a tacit mission statement (for my eyes only) that proved to be extremely critical for the success of the project. I felt that the exhibition should also

- achieve community acceptance;
- promote donations of artifacts;
- protect the visual and physical integrity of a historic building; and
- foster visitation by obtaining local and national recognition.

Achieve Community Acceptance

Because of the increased traffic and commotion that a newly established museum can generate, it can many times be an unwanted nuisance in the neighborhood. To me it seemed imperative that the neighbors accept and take pride in the newly renovated museum facility that was to be situated in their midst, for if they did not, vandalism, graffiti, and resentment could become major problems.

Bearing in mind the above concerns, I spent a morning touring and photographing the community that surrounded the firehouse museum. The neighborhood was mostly composed of late nineteenth- and early twentieth-century row houses, some nicely maintained, others vacant and boarded up, and there were several empty lots. I became convinced that powerful and exciting exhibits could become the vehicles for winning over and connecting the museum with the local residents and serve as a positive factor in the community.

Did the neighbors ultimately enjoy and take pride in the museum? Yes. Now every day when the children get off the school bus, before going home, they knock on the door of the museum and the director always lets them in so that they can say, "Hello" to Bert and Charley, the two horse replicas. When I saw this happen, I was delighted. Vandalism is almost nonexistent; the neighbors are proud of their museum.

Figure 2.44. Horses readying for a fire, the Pennsylvania National Fire Museum. Photograph by Rich LeBlanc, AIA, Crabtree, Rohrbaugh and Associates Architects.

Promote Donations of Artifacts

Generally a museum's lifeblood is in its collection, yet acquiring items for small institutions, especially those just starting up, is an ongoing problem. Donors do not want to turn over their precious possessions unless they are confident that the institution will have longevity and maintain them properly. At the beginning, PNFM desperately needed artifacts, so I felt it was critical to create an environment that would convey to donors that the museum was a vital entity and that their treasures would be properly displayed and protected. Shortly after the museum opened, artifacts just seemed to fly in, and today it has a sizable collection.

Protect the Visual and Physical Integrity of a Historic Building

Many times a historic building is the main reason for attracting first-time visitors. Viewing a beautifully restored structure and gaining a sense of its original ambiance may be a more important experience for the visitor than studying the exhibits. At the PNFM, the building's walls were purposely left free of displays, and all exhibits were placed in the centers of the rooms.

Foster Visitation by Obtaining Local and National Recognition

High visibility is critical for small museums, visitor centers, and historic sites, especially when they are not part of the normal tourist venue. This is especially true for start-up museums; they desperately need to have instant recognition, so that they can attract visitors, engender return visitation, acquire funding, and ultimately survive. In Harrisburg, the solution was to design a major iconic exhibit that addressed all of these concerns. Accordingly, I proposed a sound-and-light show that depicted the controlled panic that occurs when, in the late nineteenth century, men and horses prepared to respond to a fire. Did this exhibit create a national reputation for the PNFM? Yes, it did. Representatives from other fire museums who were planning exhibits came from all over the United States to visit it, and a few even came from Europe.

Numbering System

Similar to a Social Security Number that identifies each citizen, a number is used to identify every item that is part of an exhibition or even a simple exhibit.

Project exhibit numbers must be assigned to all exhibit components including artifacts, structures, exhibits, displays, and areas. These numbers are critical when managing, recording, and controlling a project, for they inform all participants about an item's location and its relationship to the others in an exhibition.

A numbering system is truly a lifesaver, especially when many of the participants working on a project are widely dispersed. Once, when planning/designing exhibits for a visitor center located in Nevada, my office was in Pennsylvania, the researcher/writer lived in Washington State, and the construction firm was in Utah. Thanks to a very good identification numbering system, the job progressed smoothly.

Numbering System Phases: Special Considerations

Schematic and Preliminary Phases
- Display items are given temporary or acquisition numbers.
- Exhibition numbers are not assigned during these phases.

Intermediate Phase
- Prepare the final exhibition numbering system.
- Produce an "exhibition inventory form."
- Commence to exhibition number, and document the display items.

Final Phase
- Complete the numbering of each item.

Documentation and Construction Phases
- Incorporate exhibition numbers into all documentation.

Installation Phase
- Use numbers to position and locate items and structures.

Post-Opening Phase
- The numbering system should be maintained and used for inventorying and coordinating future refurbishing and maintenance.

Once an exhibit number is assigned to an object it should never be changed for the duration of the exhibition. For that reason, the system that you devise has to be logical and flexible and easy to comprehend and update.

What Do You Number?

When you stand at the entrance to an exhibition and view the various exhibit areas with the thousands of items that each contains, just remember that everything you see, no matter how large or small, important or insignificant, had to have an exhibition number. These include all exhibit and display areas, artifacts and display items, exhibit structures, and graphic panels.

When Do You Assign an Exhibition Number to an Item?

During the schematic and preliminary phases the exhibit is in its formative stage, and many structures and items are being relocated, added, or eliminated. Throughout these stages, I use only titles to identify the various objects or areas and feel that it is best to wait until the intermediate phase when each exhibit element has been assigned a permanent location before applying a number to it.

Who Uses the Numbering System?

Everybody involved in the project including the museum, exhibit, and construction team members, bidders, and installers refer to the exhibition numbering system. These numbers also become part of any upgrading and maintenance programs and are included in the exhibition's archival records.

How Do You Design a System?

It is important when considering a numbering system that it be geared to those workers who will have the shortest length of time to learn how it works. For that reason I always start by designing the system with the installers in mind. Except for the construction firm's foreman and a few carpenters, the installers could be local carpenters and laborers, and although lacking previous knowledge of the project, they must hit the ground running during installation.

Since installers have to comprehend the numbering system quickly and instantly understand where all the pieces go, it's only logical that the same system would be easy to comprehend by the design, institution, and construction team members, who have far more time to study it in a relaxed and less hectic workplace.

Each exhibition is unique, and the numbering system that you devise has to address its specific needs. Figure 2.45 is a chart that details the hierarchical system that I usually employ.

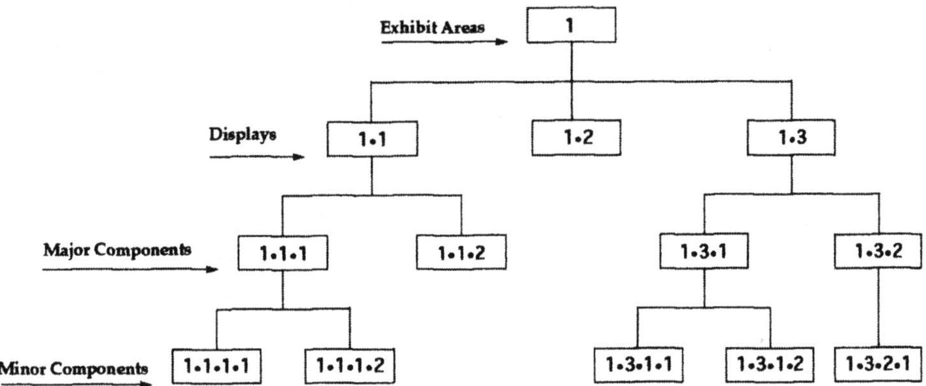

Figure 2.45. Exhibition numbering system.

When applying an exhibit number to a particular type of display item, an identification letter can be added:

A = artifact or specimen, for example, (1–A1), (1•1–A1), (1•1•1–A1), (1•1•1•1–A1)
S = special display, for example, (1–S1), (1•1–S1), (1•1•1–S1), (1•1•1•1–S1)
G = graphic panel or label, for example, (1–G1), (1•1–G1), (1•1•1–G1)

CASE HISTORY: "NEVER CHANGE EXHIBIT NUMBERS"

I once planned/designed an exhibition for the National Air and Space Administration (NASA), and since it was a major exhibit, each NASA center demanded that its equipment be displayed. Realizing that objects would be coming from all over the United States, I foresaw that installation could be a major problem. So I devised an artifact numbering system that keyed every display item to its exact location in the exhibit area. I then sent all NASA space centers, as well as the construction and installation firms, a list of the artifacts, their inventory numbers, and a floor plan that located each item. Everything seemed to be running smoothly, except at the last moment, when my contact at NASA called and casually informed me that he had changed every artifact's ID number. Since everything was now in transit to the exhibition site, the numbers could not be changed, and no longer were they keyed to the floor plan. Installation, which is always hectic, became a pure disaster.

Presentation Materials

Presentation materials are used to sum up, present, and inform the personnel involved in the project about the work that has occurred during a particular phase. They should be in a clear, concise, comprehendible format. At the start of each plan/design phase, the presentation materials are selected and laid out, and during these phases they develop and mature. At the culmination of each phase, copies of the presentation documents plus any additional information that would aid the museum team should be submitted to them for their review.

Presentation Materials Phases: Items to Be Prepared

Schematic Phase (for each concept presented)
- Floor Plan(s)
- Circulation Diagram
- Sketches

Preliminary Phase
- Floor Plan(s)
- Elevations
- Circulation Diagram
- Sketches

Intermediate Phase
- Floor Plan(s)
- Circulation Diagram
- Presentation Model
- Sketches
- Technical Drawings
- Colors and Materials Board

Final Phase
- Technical Drawings

Planning for the Presentation Meeting

Preparation starts at the beginning of the schematic, preliminary, and intermediate phases, with the selection of the types of materials, such as sketches, models, and floor plans, that are to be presented. During these phases, the materials are constantly being worked on, and only a few days are needed prior to the meeting for copying and assembling. Many times, however, information and details are still evolving, and some technical drawings may not have been completed by presentation time. It is always wise to prepare for this likelihood by advancing all the sheets so they appear to have the same density of information and drawing, and none will appear to be empty or unfinished.

Number of Attendees

I have discovered that the smaller and more remote the area where the institution is located, the larger the audience will be. Once, I found out that everyone in a tiny town knew about the upcoming presentation meeting and that most of them planned to attend. Needless to say, this developed into a major event, and I had to quickly prepare a PowerPoint presentation and secure the needed equipment.

The number of attendees at a presentation meeting will impact the selection of the techniques to be used and the visuals to be shown. Over the years I have developed a formula that is based on the anticipated size of the audience. Although I feel that presenting sketches and drawings seems to add a casual, friendly quality to the meeting, a PowerPoint presentation can be substituted.

Small-Size Group

For ten people or less, an informal type of meeting seems to work nicely; everyone sits around a conference table, the sketches are presented, and the exhibit program can be discussed in detail.

Medium-Size Group

Consisting of no more than thirty people, a stand-up easel presentation with enlarged drawings and sketches seems to work nicely. Because of the size of the audience, discussion is usually restricted to highlights of the design and a few major sections of the exhibition program.

Large-Size Group

When attendance exceeds thirty, a PowerPoint slideshow should be considered, and it is best to restrict discussion to a question-and-answer session.

Viewing Distance

It is important that everyone in the room is able to see your presentation materials, but of course there will always be someone who likes to sit in the last row. So when selecting presentation materials, distance will influence the materials that you choose to show.

Presentation Costs

The labor and material costs needed to produce and reproduce the presentation materials can be surprisingly expensive and should be calculated before selecting the materials and methods to be employed. Additional costs can also be incurred when the presentation materials are used for fund-raising and brochures, since they usually require upgrading the quality of the sketches and drawings involved.

It is useless to produce sketches for exhibits that are overbudget and will never be built. So before commencing with the presentation sketches, cost estimates should be prepared. Inevitably, I have had to adjust my designs to conform to the estimator's calculations, and frankly, it has unfailingly been difficult to eliminate displays to which I am committed and ones that I feel have real potential.

Presentation Drawings

Since the presentation floor plans and elevations will be advanced and developed throughout all the exhibit phases, and eventually will become the bidding documents, it is important that they be precise. A basic presentation floor plan should indicate the size, location, and footprint of the exhibit areas, displays, major objects, aisles, and public spaces.

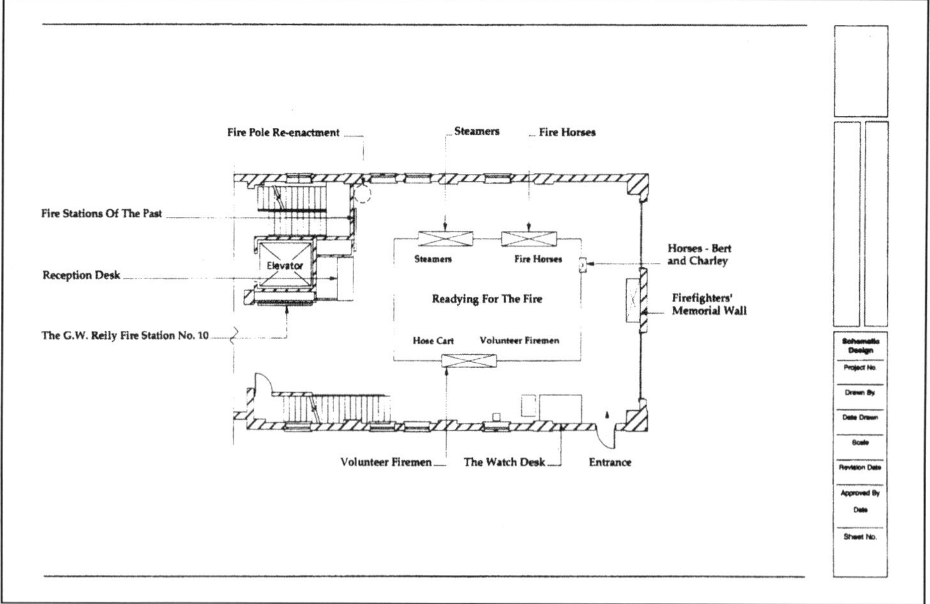

Figure 2.46. Floor plan: Schematic design.

Circulation Diagrams

Also called a "flow diagram," the circulation diagram indicates how the visitor will or ought to proceed through an exhibition space. When possible, it should be tied to the scheme's walk-through, which is part of the exhibition program.

Even though, as in the case of the plan shown in figure 2.47, the exhibit room may be small, and the path that a visitor would take is obvious, it is always advantageous to prepare this diagram for the presentation meeting. By introducing the circulation diagram last, after the floor plan and sketches have been shown, the presenter has the opportunity to review the important features and to sum up the advantages inherent in the design.

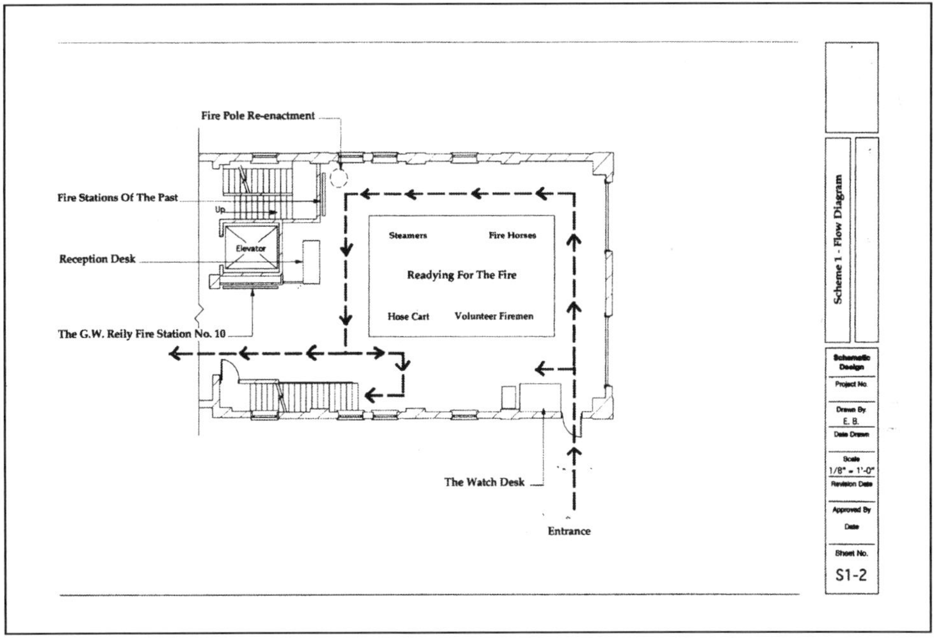

Figure 2.47. Circulation diagram: Schematic design.

Presentation Models

People seem to respond favorably to models and to comprehend the design concept faster and easier than when viewing floor plans and drawings. While a sketch can easily exaggerate and glamorize a design, a scale model is an accurate representation of the exhibit and can serve several purposes: to present and explain the exhibit to the museum personnel, to assist planners/designers when evaluating and studying the design, and for fund-raising and promotional endeavors. A model can be started at the beginning of the planning/designing phase since its dimensions and the building's interior structures are known. Today, many models are computer generated with minute details carved from acrylic or similar materials.

Detail Model

A detail model is a three-dimensional, scaled representation of the exhibition, and it shows details and represents the actual materials and colors that will be used for the proposed exhibition environment. It details the size, volume, color, and location of the exhibits, displays, structures, and the like. See figure 2.21, the *Traveling the Silk Road* exhibition model.

Massing Model

Also called a white model, study model, or volume study, a massing model depicts the exhibition's space, exhibits, displays, and the building structure. This type of model is an excellent way to convey the overall design concept and is usually presented during the preliminary phase.

However, a massing model can be very deceptive since it is usually finished in only one color, and lacking in fine details, it can visually unify even the most disjointed exhibit areas and structures. This type of model can be economically crafted from white paper and hardboard, with many of its details, walls, floors, displays, and so on, easily suggested by applying computer-generated drawings to its flat surfaces. A massing model is less expensive to construct than a detail model.

Figure 2.48. Presentation: Massing model. Photography by Shaeffer and Madama, Inc.

Contour Model

A contour model is an excellent way to present complicated forms and changes in levels. The white contour model, shown in figure 2.49, rcpresents a proposed thirty-by-eight-foot rock formation replica. It served as a study model and was also used during construction to establish the height and the shape of each level for a thirty-five-foot-long replica of a rock formation.

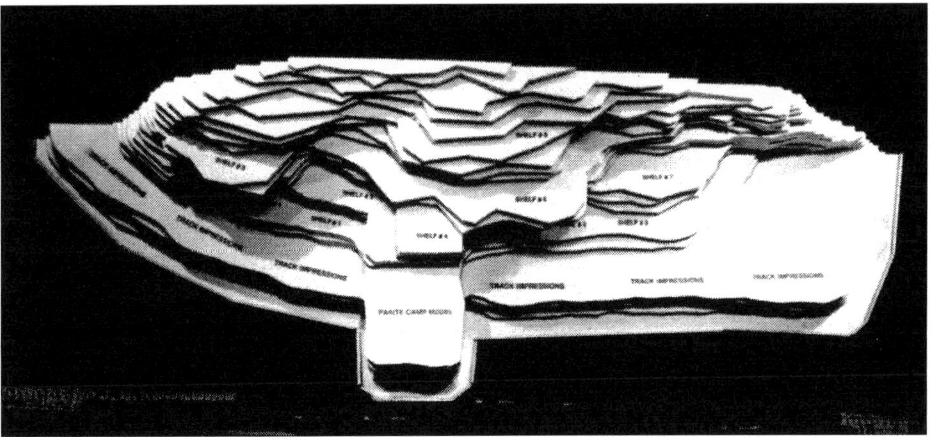

Figure 2.49. Presentation: Contour model.

Sketches

Used to illustrate concepts, sketches are done rather quickly. Loose and layered with ideas, they are "sketchy" and lack specific details. This type of drawing should never be dense with details or create the feeling that the design is carved in stone and could never be revised. Since this technique seems to lack permanence, it invites modifications, and people are more apt to suggest design changes than if they were shown finished renderings.

I prefer presenting sketches because they can become the vehicle that stimulates input and generates suggestions. This exchange of ideas usually improves the exhibit and can be most helpful, especially during the schematic and preliminary phases. However, keeping control of the exhibit concepts during these discussions can become problematic, since even a very good suggestion may sometimes not be compatible with the design. During these dialogues it is the planner/designer's responsibility to maintain the integrity of the design and to keep it on track.

There is a wide range of loose techniques that can be used to successfully present a design. During the schematic phase, even pencil or ink drawings presented on yellow tracing paper or white paper are acceptable. I usually prefer to present a colored sketch.

The sketch shown in figure 2.50 was part of a funded proposal for an exhibition called *Flags of the Civil War* to be located in a historically certified bank building circa 1859. This design was for the "Stars and Symbols" exhibit room that contained computer-generated and simple hands-on displays. Exhibits such as "Smells of War," "Make a Star," and "Symbols of the Flag" were just a few of the concepts that were part of this exhibit.

Figure 2.50. Presentation sketch.

When You Can't Sketch

What if you can't sketch? Planners/designers should never impose restrictions on their work because of their own technical limitations. Several times when I taught "Museum Exhibition Planning and Design," a few students would limit their exhibits to square structures in an effort to hide the fact that they were not computer savvy and could not delineate rounded or free-form shapes. There are always ways to present your concepts; sometimes one or a combination of the following techniques can be used in lieu of a sketch.

Presentation: Research Materials

When explaining a particular ambiance, concept, or color palette, the illustrations compiled during the research phase can be presented and discussed.

Presentation: Technical Drawings

Presenting elevations, floor plans, three-view drawings, and isometric drawings can be very effective. They are more accurate and precise than sketches and are wonderful tools for locating and explaining the exact size and shape of the exhibit areas and structures. Refer to the "Technical Drawings" section in this chapter.

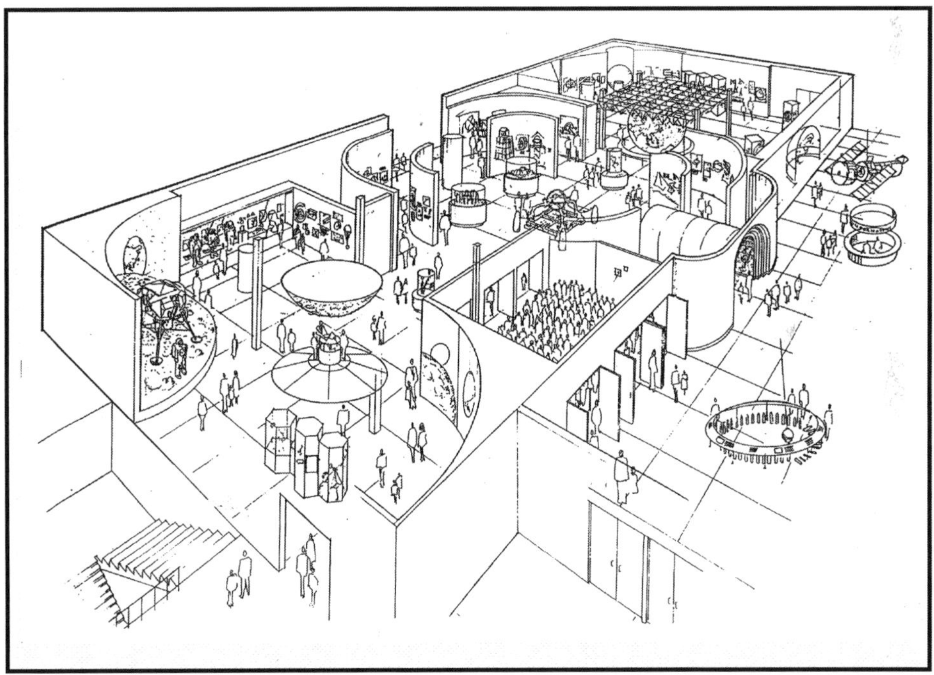

Figure 2.51. Isometric drawing: Taipei Astronomical Museum. Courtesy of J. F. Barnwell Jr., Design and Production Incorporated.

Presentation: Written Descriptions

Used in lieu of or in conjunction with a sketch or a model, a written description can explain the many issues that cannot be covered in a drawing, such as visitor's learning experiences and special exhibit techniques. Many times an exhibition description is in the form of a walk-through statement.

CASE HISTORY: "WHEN YOU CAN'T DRAW HORSES"

When preparing to present the design for the Pennsylvania National Fire Museum, I was faced with several problems: frankly, I can't draw horses, especially those showing a great deal of action; the budget did not provide for an illustrator; and, with the presentation scheduled in three weeks, time was not available to search for an alternative solution. Lacking horse-sketching ability, money, and time, I decided to present the concept by employing a floor plan, research materials, and a written description.

The floor plan shown in figure 2.46 aided everyone in understanding the dioramas and their relationship within the exhibition space. Throughout the presentation, this plan was placed on an easel so that the viewers could refer to it.

During the research period, many illustrations were compiled. The drawings in figures 2.52 and 2.53 were presented to explain the types of figures, action, and ambiance that would serve as the source for the "Hose Cart and Volunteer Firemen" and the "Fire Horses and Steamer" dioramas.

Figure 2.52. Fireman and hose cart. Courtesy of the Library of Congress.

(*continued*)

CASE HISTORY: "WHEN YOU CAN'T DRAW HORSES" (*continued*)

Figure 2.53. Fire horses and steamer. Courtesy of the Library of Congress.

Written Description

To explain what the visitors would experience, the following written description in the form of a walk-through was also presented:

> As the visitors open the door, a gong sounds announcing that a fire has just been reported. Suddenly they realize that they are part of a frantic scene as firemen and horses prepare to leave for the fire. A mélange of sounds becomes overwhelming: voices hollering, horses whinnying, hoof and foot sounds reverberating around the room, and the space is filled with flashing, moving lights. The atmosphere is chaotic, and yet, somehow controlled. Horses and men seem to know exactly what they have to do. The doors are about to open, and four men are straining to pull the hose cart forward. The horses are in place, one is already harnessed to the steam engine, the other positioned split seconds before his harness drops from the ceiling. Suddenly a voice shouts, "Get out." The room becomes silent; the visitors realize that the firemen and the horses have "left for the fire" and that the diorama experience is finished. They now observe that there are other exhibits in the room and proceed to view them.

Colors and Materials Board

A board with chips and swatches glued on is the traditional method used to present exhibit materials, paint finishes, and graphic colors. Sometimes to assist the reviewer to locate the colors and materials in the exhibits, a sketch or floor plan of the exhibit area is added to the board.

Although helpful, there are drawbacks to the traditional colors and materials board (C&M) board. In an exhibition, bright accent colors and materials are used minimally, while neutral ones are employed in large quantities. Yet, a typical C&M presentation is composed mainly of tiny colors and materials chips, all the same size, and lined up like little soldiers. In addition, even when white is not part of the color scheme, the samples usually are mounted on a white board that visually overpowers the chips and swatches. Some planners/designers have tried to overcome this defect by scaling the size of the samples to the size of the exhibit areas that they propose covering and applying these samples to a board that represents the color selected for the walls of the exhibit area.

A C&M board can also be generated via a computer printout. However, the traditional, and still the best way, is to present swatches of the actual materials. In so doing, everyone is given an opportunity to touch and feel the selected textures. Digitally scanning the color and materials board so that copies can be made and used for reference is always a good idea.

Where do you get the chips and swatches? At times this can become a problem. However, there are many sources that you can call on: manufactures, suppliers, and installers of walls, partitions, window and floor coverings, plastic laminates, and paints always seem glad to provide samples. Web pages can also be a helpful source. For graphic colors, the chips from the Pantone Color Specifier are an excellent and traditional source.

Generally, the colors shown on a C&M board are a basic palette and are only meant as a guide to control and harmonize those that will actually be used. They are not meant to limit the variety of colors. Depending on an exhibition's size, and the quantity and the variety of its structures, graphics, illustrations, and so forth, each color presented on a C&M board can be tinted, shaded, and toned as needed.

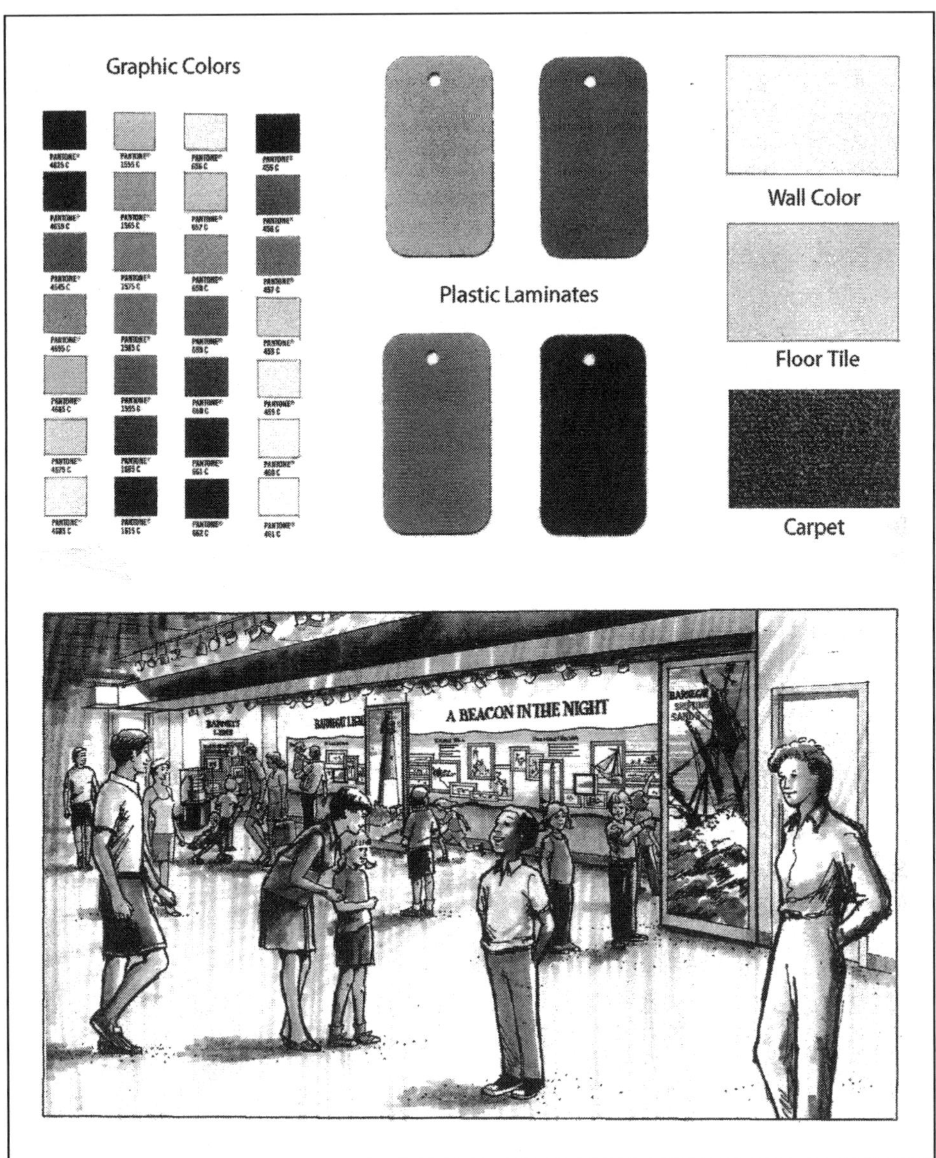

Figure 2.54. Colors and materials board.

Project Archival File

At the beginning of the post-opening phase, members of the museum team should assemble a reference file that will be used as a source for maintenance and refurbishing. For future generations it can become a wonderful historic document. Contained in it should be the following:

- Bid package (refer to the "Bid Package" section in this chapter)
- Close-out package (refer to the "Close-Out Package" section in this chapter)
- Project history

Project History

The project history statement is usually prepared by the planner/designer and discusses the philosophies that were the core for the exhibition design. It contains many of the items that are not addressed in the bid package or close-out package such as the following:

- Plan/design report (for details, refer to the "Design Preservation" section in this chapter)
- Names and addresses of contractor, subcontractors, and suppliers
- Copies of the presentation materials and the exhibition program
- Exhibition inventory forms
- Related information and documentation

Project Management

In order to bring about the successful completion of a project, every phase must have a designated project manager (PM) assigned to oversee the work. During the development and construction of an exhibition, the following three project managers are normally involved.

Museum Staff's Project Manager

The museum's PM represents the institution, is usually referred to as the director or the project director, and is responsible for the totality of the project, including the following:

- Planning/designing, bidding, and post-opening phases
- Installing the artifacts
- Reviewing construction
- Initiating and managing the planning/designing and construction contracts

Exhibit Team's Project Manager

This PM heads the exhibit team, is responsible for every aspect of the planning/designing process, and works closely with the museum and construction project managers. A few of the exhibit team PM's duties follow:

- Assign tasks and oversee the exhibit team.
- Supervise all design office procedures.
- Oversee development of the planning/designing process.
- Assist with selecting the artifacts.
- Coordinate the exhibit content and display objects.
- Maintain the plan/design and construction budget and time schedule.
- Ensure that all documentation is complete and accurate.
- Keep all designated participants fully informed.
- Schedule, organize, and conduct all planning/designing meetings, critiques, and reviews.

Construction Firm's Project Manager

This manager represents the construction firm and is responsible for the fabrication and installation of the exhibits. The construction firm PM is responsibility for the following:

- Overseeing and expediting every aspect of construction and installation
- Scheduling construction-related meetings
- Coordinating the project with the museum and the design personnel

Research

The information and the visuals assembled during the research period can influence every aspect of the exhibit design and contribute greatly to its creativity and uniqueness.

Research Phases: Special Considerations

Feasibility and Schematic Phases
  Locate the images and documentation needed to develop these phases
Preliminary and Intermediate Phases
  Assemble all the images and documentation
  Check accuracy for the text and visuals
Final Phase
  Check accuracy for the text and visuals

Research: A Valuable Design Tool

Research provides the necessary information to do the following:

- Prepare the exhibition program
- Develop the exhibit theme, ambiance, and design
- Select display objects, photographs, and illustrations
- Find methods to indicate the exhibition's time and place
- Develop the color scheme and text
- Design the graphics and select the typography

Research Procedures

The research process can vary greatly from project to project and depends on several factors, including personnel available, location of the research materials, and size of the exhibition. The following professionals are usually involved in obtaining the information and visuals needed to plan/design an exhibition.

Specialists

When a white paper about a particular subject is needed to develop an exhibition, experts are retained by the institution to research and write it. This report is then turned over to the planner/designer and becomes the basis for developing the exhibition.

CASE HISTORY: "WHITE PAPERS"

In preparation for a new exhibition at the Valley of Fire Visitor Center in Nevada, the director retained specialists to research and produce reports that focused on the natural resources of the Valley and its history. In this case, an archeologist, a geologist, a naturalist, and a historian were the experts hired. Based on their papers and on my visit to the site, I felt that I had the information needed to plan/design the exhibition. In retrospect, this method proved to be the perfect solution since the state park service did not have the staff to do the research, the visitor center was in a remote location and covered a highly diversified area, and each subject to be addressed required in-depth knowledge.

The Lone Researcher

Many times, when a project is very small and lacks an assigned staff, one person may be designated to perform all the research. Although at times this is the only solution available, I feel that the results can be problematic

CASE HISTORY: "THE PHONE THAT DIDN'T ANSWER"

Once when I was planning/designing an exhibit, the museum assigned one of its most highly placed, prestigious members of the institution to work with me. From the beginning it became obvious that this person was only interested in advancing his scientific career and not the exhibition. He would never answer my telephone calls, meet with me, or review my concepts. Unfortunately, the exhibits pertained to a very esoteric subject, and I lacked the in-depth knowledge that was needed. By default, I was forced to do all the research, develop the content, and write the text, and honestly, I struggled during the planning/designing of this exhibition. In retrospect, I felt that the exhibits lacked depth and could have been so much better if only this scientist had been willing to review the designs and to give me the input that I so desperately needed.

because, when a single individual is responsible for all the research, there is always a strong possibility that the project could develop tunnel vision.

Research Team

This occurs when several members of the exhibit team undertake the research process and, most times, when the project is large and the research is extensive. Even when an exhibition is quite small, however, such a team approach is always beneficial. Having several people involved, each with specialties and interests, adds diversification to the research and contributes to a wider variety of ideas.

On large projects the researcher and the curator play a major role in obtaining the needed information; however, it is always critical for the planner/designer to be involved. Frankly, I am usually reluctant to start the exhibit planning/designing process until I have had the opportunity to participate in the research. This involvement has invariably provided me with an amazing trove of pertinent information, design ideas, and visuals that have generally influenced and contributed to the exhibit design. It has also given me the opportunity to work with the researchers and curators, and to exchange design ideas and hear stories about a particular artifact.

Research Organization

In preparation for the numerous pieces of information and the visuals that will be obtained during the research period, it is important to develop a file system that will organize the materials and have it in place before the research begins. Procrastination will only lead to a sea of disorganized material that can become time consuming to organize and difficult to retrieve.

Yet devising a filing system for the research materials when the exhibit has not yet been developed can be challenging. So at the get-go, a quick and easy method is to file the materials according to the contents of a book dealing with the same subject. After the exhibit outline is firm, the research can then be reorganized to be compatible with the outline. However, there can be a disadvantage to using a book's contents for the start of the research process, since it can easily impact and influence the exhibit planning/designing and hinder originality and creativity.

Review Periods

The main purpose of review periods is to allow the exhibition committee the time needed to review the work prepared to date. These periods occur at the end of each planning/design phase and the documentation phase. It is also a valuable respite for the exhibit staff for it allows them the time to do the following:

- Clean up all loose ends and details.
- Prepare for the next phase.
- Copy and archive the pertinent documents that were prepared in that phase, including presentation materials, technical drawings, and minutes of meetings. During the course of a project, these archives can be valuable reference materials and are later used when preparing the job history.

Shape, Form, and Space

Each shape, form, and space that is part of an exhibition has its own distinctive body language. Whether display items, exhibits, or building structures, they interrelate with each other and must be carefully considered when preparing a design so that the result is a harmonious, cohesive exhibition.

Refer to chapter 4, "Shape, Form, and Space," for information about this subject.

Shipping

Usually the scope of work, as outlined in the specifications, requires that the construction firm wrap, secure, and protect the exhibit materials from adverse weather conditions and accidents during shipping and that all materials be transported in padded vans. It is always wise for the museum staff to check with the builder to make sure that they have the necessary insurance to cover any loss and damage that might occur to the exhibit materials during this period.

Site Survey

All museum facilities and related spaces involved in an exhibition must be surveyed or inspected early in the design phases to ascertain that they are able to accommodate comfortably and safely the heavy burden of an exhibition and its increased visitation. And during the planning/designing process, there are many inspections of the exhibition site performed by members of the exhibit team.

Site Survey Phases: Special Considerations

Feasibility Study
- Familiarization walk-through inspection; survey measurements are rarely taken at this time

Schematic Phase
- Walk-through inspection
- Photographs and measurements taken for developing the schemes and the floor plans

Preliminary Phase
- Major site inspection required
- Take additional photographs and dimensions of all areas and structures that will impact the exhibition design.

Intermediate Phase
- Revisit site to ensure that the exhibit design is compatible with it.

Bidding and Construction Phase
- Construction firms usually perform the following inspections:
  - Examine exhibit site
  - Check the unloading dock conditions at the site
  - Photograph and measure all factors pertaining to construction and installation
  - Review all pertinent conditions

Site Inspection

In order to determine if the site is adequate for the exhibition, the exhibit team members should visit and inspect it, and if required, engineers must check the floor loadings, utilities, and so on. The following are a few issues to be evaluated:

- Will the spaces, hallways, eating facilities, washrooms, lecture halls, and so forth, be adequate and provide the necessary accommodations?
- Are the dimensions of the exhibition spaces, for example, size, shape, height, location, and floor loadings, compatible with the needs of the exhibit?
- Is there ample parking and, if needed, public transportation?
- Can the artifacts and exhibit materials be protected and displayed successfully?
- Will accessibility requirements for the handicapped be met?
- Can a safe and secure environment for unloading and installing the exhibit materials be provided?

It is important to inspect and measure every condition that will impinge on the design and to be accurate when documenting the exhibit site, since these measurements will be used throughout all design phases. Take plenty of photographs; it's amazing how many times you will be referring to them when designing. Be careful, though; we have all heard about the man who built a boat in his cellar and, when completed, could not get it out the door. Don't laugh; it could happen to you. It would be humiliating to discover that your exhibits had to be left on the loading dock because it couldn't fit through a door opening, or that it was necessary to force a construction firm to revise your design of a display structure because it was too large for the moving van.

Most times, one site inspection is never enough. During the design development phases, it is important to revisit the site regularly to ascertain that the exhibits and the display items are compatible with the space and its infrastructure and that the existing lighting is adequate and will not adversely affect the proposed color scheme.

Having the latest architectural and engineering drawings of the building during these inspections is also extremely helpful. However, since renovations and changes may have occurred after the documents were initially issued (as-built drawings), they should always be checked for accuracy.

Building Conditions

Normally, the building's systems and its structures cannot be repositioned or revised and the exhibit has to be adjusted to accommodate them. The systems to be investigated include lighting, heating, ventilating, air-conditioning, fire suppression, security, and elements such as windows, doors, and columns. All must all be considered and recorded during your inspection.

Hazardous Situations

Every planner/designer should try to provide all visitors, especially the physically and visually challenged, with a safe and hazard-free environment. During inspection, it is necessary to evaluate everything that could prove to be dangerous: abrupt changes in floor levels, low overhead obstacles, inadequate door widths, dimly lighted areas, and unmarked steps and ramps are a few examples of the conditions to be considered.

Floor Loading Capacity

The total weight of the display objects, exhibit structures, visitors, and so forth, must be considered so that they do not exceed the floor loading capacity of the spaces involved. If this information is not readily available, a structural engineer may have to be consulted.

For example, the Betsy Ross House, located in Philadelphia, was built in 1773 as a single-family dwelling. Today, however, it has an annual visitation of over 325,000 people. So with this house, as with many other buildings, the safe floor loading (per square foot) plus the impact from constant visitation have to be major considerations for the planner/designer.

Ancillary Areas

To verify that a proposed exhibit structure or display object can be easily moved to the exhibition site, it is critical for an exhibit team to measure and inspect the loading dock, hallways, elevators, and door openings. A consideration, sometimes overlooked, is that the size and the weight of an item increase when it is enclosed in a crate or a protective wrapping or moved on a forklift or dolly.

Ceiling Heights

How does a planner/designer determine the floor-to-ceiling dimension when a ladder or a laser tape is not available? Well, it really is easy when you think back to your old high school plane geometry lesson: you know, the one where, by placing a ruler at an angle, you can divide a rectangle into equal segments. Here are the steps:

1. Photograph a wall, straight on, so that you get an elevation and not a perspective view; make sure that both the ceiling line and the floor line are included.
2. Select an easy-to-measure object that is part of the wall, such as a light switch or a doorknob, and measure its distance to the floor line. In figure 2.55, that object is 5'0" from the floor.
3. Place a ruler (scale) on the photograph, at an angle, so that it touches the floor line at zero inches and the object at the five-foot-zero-inch line.
4. The dimension on the ruler that touches the ceiling line will tell you the floor-to-ceiling height.

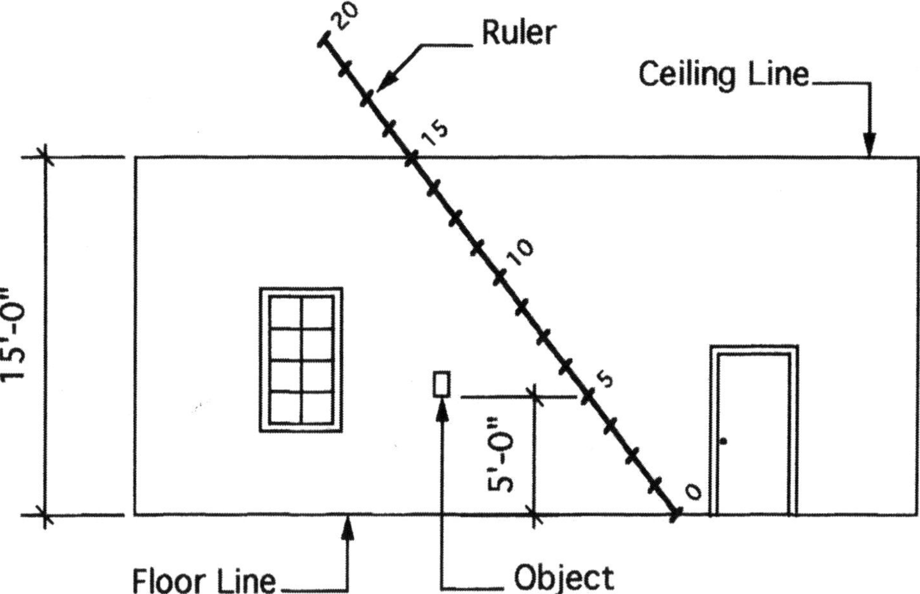

Figure 2.55. Ceiling heights: Floor-to-ceiling determination.

Specifications

Prepared by the planner/designer or specification writer, this document is an accurate, written description of the materials and hardware to be used in the project. Sometimes the manufacturer's written account of its product is included in whole or in part. Specifications are used during bidding to establish construction costs and serve as a reference "bible" when preparing the shop drawings and carrying out the work.

Always remember that contractors do not engage in mental telepathy; planners/designers have to provide them with all the information that they need to estimate, construct, and install the exhibits.

Specifications Phases: Special Considerations

Intermediate Phase
  Prepare a file system to organize product information.
  Start to assemble manufacturer's literature needed to prepare the specifications.
Final Phase
  Continue to assemble product information.
  As materials are included in the design, write the specifications.
Documentation Phase
  Complete all specifications.

Construction Specifications

The construction specifications (CS) is a written document that includes the information needed to define the materials, hardware, electrical fixtures, finishes, and the like, to be used in an exhibition.

Written Description in Lieu of a Technical Drawing

The CS and the bidding drawings are companion pieces that precisely inform the construction firm of the results that are to be expected. When feasible, and in lieu of technical drawings, a designer can elect to write a description or a specification of a particular item and include it in the CS.

Specifying a Particular Item

When specifying a particular item, it is important to be exact and to give as much information about it as is available. If possible, include the name of the item, model number, finish, and the manufacturer's name, address, and phone number. If you don't specify the quality, or the manufacturer of a particular item, it is almost certain that the contractor will substitute the cheapest similar item available. Public projects usually require several names, or an "or equal" phrase to be included when specifying a product.

When specifying an item for which you are not willing to accept a substitute, the material's upper- and lowercase trademark signature must be used. For example, Plexiglas with a capital *P* means that the contractor must provide Plexiglas, while plexiglas with a lowercase *p* could give the builder the right to substitute a generic product.

When to Start a Specification

As soon as a product, finish, or procedure has been agreed upon and selected, its specification can be written. Although starting this document in the early design stages may seem a bit premature, it has always been a lifesaver for me. Years ago, I always waited until the documentation phase before starting to write the specifications, until I finally noticed that I was wasting vast amounts of time looking for important bits of product information that seemed to have disappeared.

Graphic Specifications

Graphic layouts and written specifications (GS) are normally required when estimating and reproducing graphics.

Computer Generated

An electronic file containing all graphic layouts should be included in the GS. This enables the construction firms bidding on the project to determine if their equipment and that of the graphic designer are compatible. For quality control purposes, hard (paper) copies of typical graphic layouts can also be included in the GS. These copies can be scaled down.

Manually Produced

When graphic layouts are manually prepared, specifications and hard copies should be included in the GS.

Estimating in Lieu of Graphics Layouts

> Best-laid plans of mice and men oft(en) go astray.
>
> —Adapted from "To a Mouse," by Robert Burns

Why do graphic layouts always seem to be behind schedule, and why are they still being worked on during the bidding and construction phases? Honestly, I believe that it's because the text and the visuals are so important to the success of the exhibition that the time needed to check every bit of information and to locate all the visuals is an overwhelming task. Yet, even if the graphic layouts are not completed when the project is being bid, an accurate estimate can be obtained by providing the bidders with a list of the quantities and sizes of the graphic panels to be completed. Of course, it is up to the successful contractor to establish a drop-dead date for the delivery of any missing layouts, and if that date is not met, overtime costs will definitely be incurred.

Technical Drawings

These drawings are developed during all the design phases and are the accurate representations of the exhibition's areas and the structures that the planner/designer desires to have built. Without them it would be almost impossible to bid and construct an exhibit or even a simple display. Every piece of information on a drawing or in the written specification informs and guides the builder and must be accurate and complete.

Technical Drawings Phases: Special Considerations

Schematic Phase
- Design the project's basic drawing sheet including title block and grid.
- Lay out the floor plans.

Preliminary Phase
- Advance the floor plan
- Lay out elevations and circulation diagram.
- Begin to develop the technical drawings.

Intermediate and Final Phases
- Advance existing drawings.
- Develop additional drawings as required.
- Prepare reflected ceiling lighting plan.

Documentation Phase
- Complete all drawings.

Drawing Sheet Components

At the beginning of the planning/designing process, a sheet layout that will serve as the basis for all the technical drawings should be prepared. Since this master sheet will be used throughout every design and documentation phase, it must be easy to upgrade and revise.

Sheet Size

The size of the drawing that will be commonly used for the project should be the first consideration when laying out a master sheet. Standard sizes are 11 × 17, 17 × 22, 22 × 34, and 34 × 44 inch. Whenever possible, I prefer an 11 × 17–inch format, for it is easier to handle, file, copy, and bind than the larger sizes. The 8.5 × 11–inch size is just too small. However, if the exhibition area or project is large, the 34 × 44 inch is normally used.

Title Block

The title block is an essential part of any sheet, for it contains valuable information that is needed to identify, organize, and track a particular technical drawing. A title block informs the reader as to

- what the drawing contains;
- the organization responsible for the drawing;
- who made the drawing and who approved it;
- the dates when the drawing was issued and its latest revision; and
- the sheet identification number.

Title blocks not only assist in organizing and tracking a project but also are used to settle disputes. For example, additional compensation might be awarded to a construction firm if the revised date on a drawing indicated that upgrades to the project had been made to the documents after the contractor had submitted its bid, or an "extra" might be incurred when a sheet was not completed on time, causing construction and installation delays and mishaps.

Additionally, a title block could be construed as an art form. It should contain the information needed and express the image of the organization or institution.

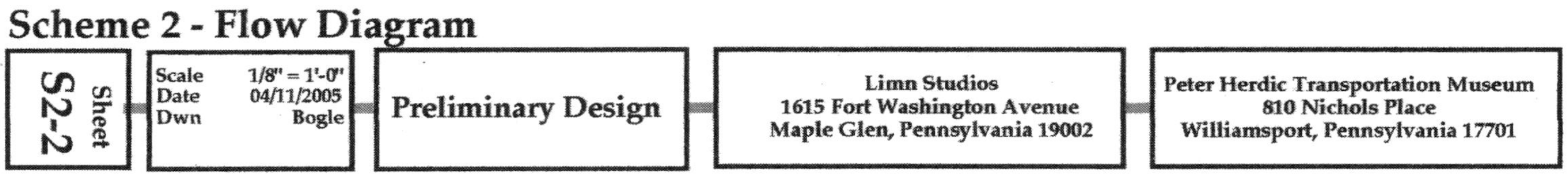

Scheme 2 - Flow Diagram

Sheet S2-2

Scale 1/8" = 1'-0"
Date 04/11/2005
Dwn Bogle

Preliminary Design

Limn Studios
1615 Fort Washington Avenue
Maple Glen, Pennsylvania 19002

Peter Herdic Transportation Museum
810 Nichols Place
Williamsport, Pennsylvania 17701

Figure 2.56. *Title block: Limn Studios.*

No.	Date	Revision
1	5.1.09	Issued for Bid

The Silk Road

American Museum of Natural History

Exhibit Design Drawings

TITLE
Silk Road
Exhibit Plan

SCALE 1/8" = 1'-0"
DRAWN BY
DATE 9.29.09
DRAWING NO 1.0.0
SHEET NO

Figure 2.57. *Title block: American Museum of Natural History. Courtesy American Museum of Natural History.*

ARTGUILD MUSEUM SERVICES
300 WOLF DRIVE
WEST DEPTFORD, NJ 08086
© 2012 856.853.7500

JOB NO.: 82639
PAGE NO.: XX_0000

PROJECT: JOB NAME
GALLERY: AREA OF MUSEUM
CLIENT: PROJECT NAME DESIGNER: DESIGN FIRM LOCATION: --
EXHIBIT TITLE: DRAWING NAME
DRAWN BY: DRS PM: -- CREATED: 00-00-0000 SCALE: AS NOTED
DESIGN DWG #: AGI FILE: DRAWING2.DWG PRINTED: 5/9/2012 9:50 AM

REVISION NO.: 0
REV. DATE: -- REV. BY: --
ISSUED FOR: APPROVAL
APPROVAL STATUS
YES AS NOTED NO RESUBMIT BY: DATE:

REVISION DETAILS:
1) XXXXX
2) XXXXX
3) XXXXX
4) XXXXX
5)
6)
7)
8)
9)
10)

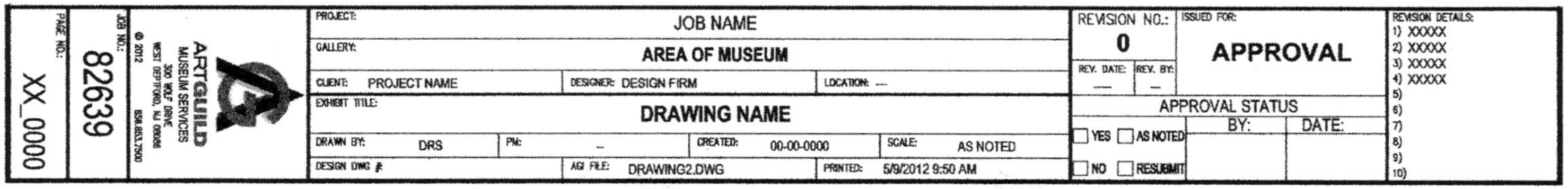

Figure 2.58. *Title block: Art Guild. Courtesy Art Guild, Inc., West Deptford, New Jersey.*

Format

After the title block has been designed, it's time to develop a format that will serve as the layout for all the technical drawings. It should do the following:

- Create a uniform, "family" look.
- Produce drawings that are organized, professional, and visually pleasing.
- Establish continuity throughout all the drawings.

When preparing a drawing sheet, I always include a border at the top and bottom. These lines visually help to frame and contain the drawings and text. For complete details, refer to the "Graphic Grid" subsection under the "Graphic Design" section in this chapter.

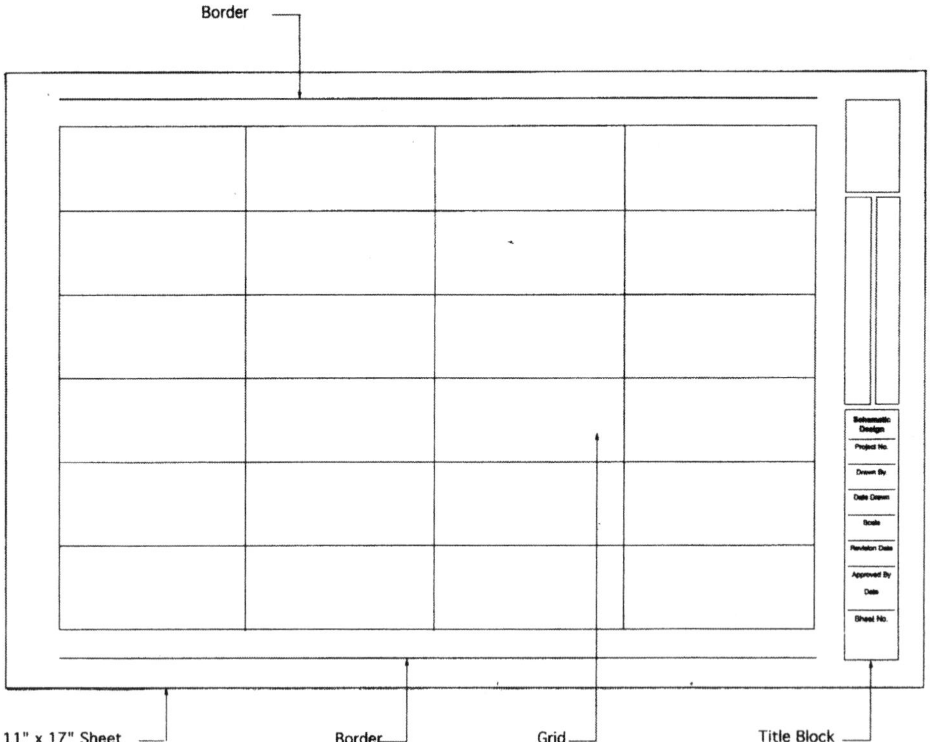

Figure 2.59. Drawing sheet: Layout.

Drawing Sheet Numbering System

Each drawing sheet has to have its own number, which is used as a reference throughout the project. Sheets should be numbered logically and consecutively with the floor plan usually being first, then the circulation plan, elevations, exhibit areas, and details.

Floor Plans

A typical floor plan is a bird's-eye view that shows the building, as it would appear from four feet above the floor. By using this height, windows that are usually positioned about three feet above the floor line can be indicated. As the exhibit areas and structures are developed, more information will be added to the plan, and it is advanced throughout all the design phases.

Scale

The scale that you select for your drawings will depend on the size of the exhibition area, the quantity of information needed, and the space available on the sheet. Floor plans and elevations are usually drawn at ⅛" = 1'0", or ¼" = 1'0". A larger scale requires more detail in order to give a drawing its integrity.

Orientation

How to orient the building and exhibit areas on your drawing is always a debatable issue. Architects traditionally place their buildings so that the north arrow faces upward. That makes sense to them, since they frequently design structures that have to be precisely located on empty fields or sites. However, museum buildings exist; therefore, I feel that placing the exhibit areas on the sheet to accommodate the north arrow may become confusing and disorienting. I usually position the floor plan according to how the visitor enters the building or the exhibition area.

Nevertheless, when the project involves architects and since I know that their plans will relate to a north arrow facing the top of the sheet, I always follow suit. It is for that reason that the floor plans presented in figures 2.60 to 2.63 are oriented to the north, and the arrow indicates that direction.

General Rules

There are a few rules that are generally followed when producing a technical drawing:

- Anything above the four-foot line is indicated with a dashed line (– – – – – –).
- Anything on or below the four-foot line is indicated with a solid line (————).
- The building structure (walls, columns, etc.) is indicated by a heavy line (————).
- Floor plans locate and indicate the size and shape of the windows, doors, exhibit structures, and so forth.

Basic Floor Plan

The basic floor plan is the first plan to be drawn and contains the basic exhibit space. It provides overall dimensions only.

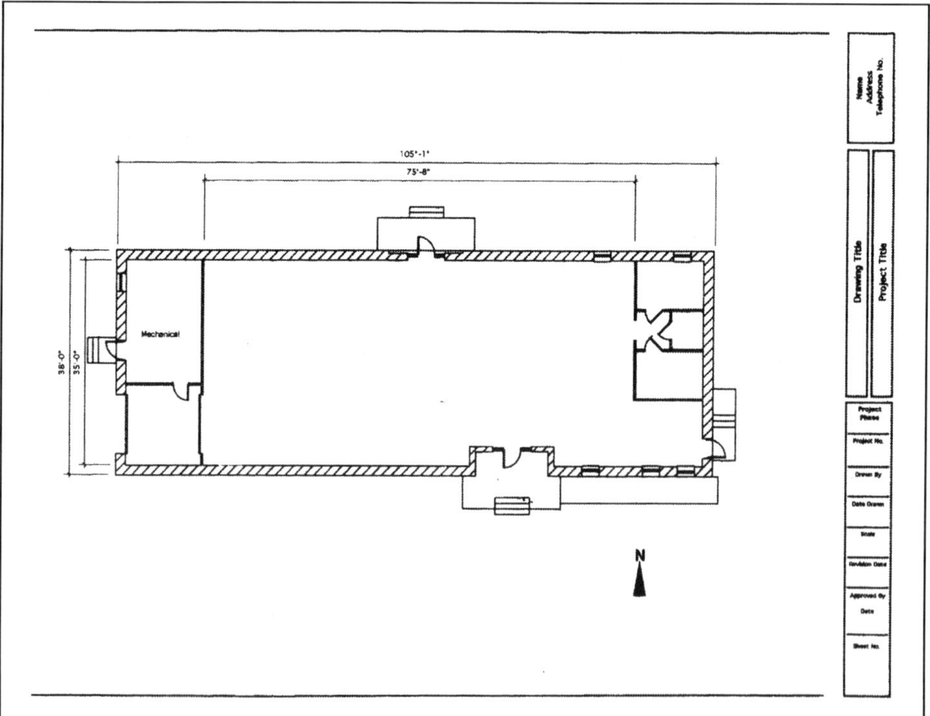

Figure 2.60. Technical drawing: Basic floor plan.

Advanced Floor Plan

The advanced floor plan is a bird's-eye view that indicates and locates the exhibit structures, furniture, and major artifacts in more precise detail.

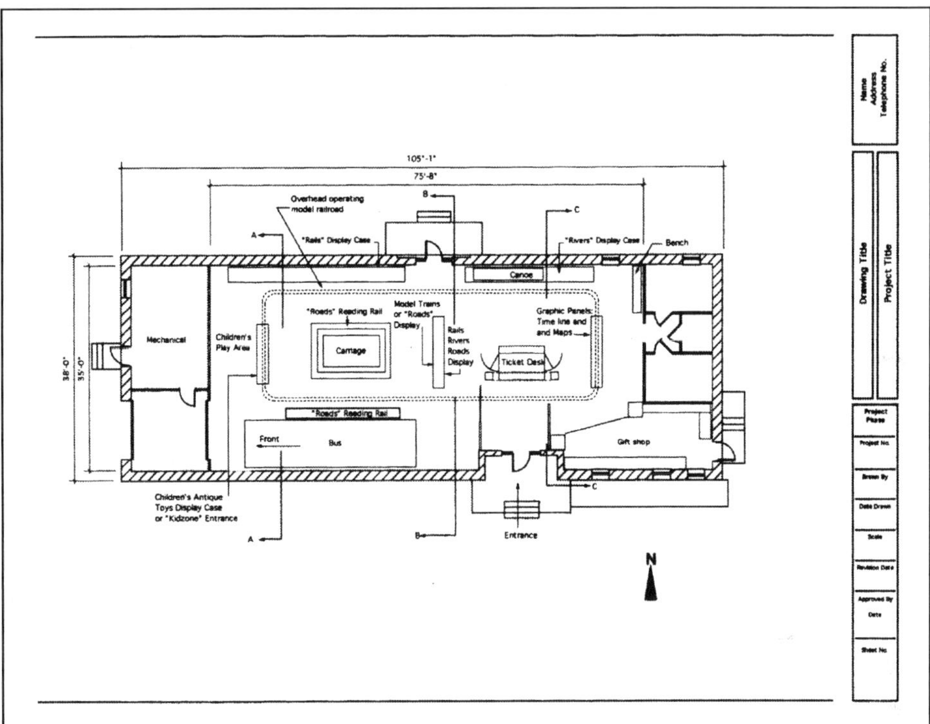

Figure 2.61. Technical drawing: Advanced floor plan.

Reflected Ceiling Plan

The reflected ceiling plan is a mirror image of the basic floor plan and indicates and locates all items that are mounted in the ceiling, for example, light fixtures, diffusers, sprinkler heads, and any graphic panels and exhibits. To make it easy to orient the reader, I always indicate the doors and windows.

Elevations

Elevations are drawings showing the vertical surfaces of a wall, architectural elements, and exhibit structures. An elevation drawing indicates the location of the windows, doors, building and exhibit structures, and so on. It does not indicate depth, and it is not a perspective drawing.

Figure 2.62. Technical drawing: Elevation.

Three-View Drawings

A three-view drawing is a combination of the front, top, and side views of a structure and is especially helpful in detailing display cases, bases, graphic panels, and so forth. Traditionally, there is an order for positioning a structure on a drawing: the top view is positioned directly over the front view, and the side view is lined up with the front view. Many times, this type of drawing can be used as a presentation drawing in lieu of a sketch. See figures 2.36 to 2.39.

Cross Section

A cross section is a drawing that shows a vertical slice through a structure. To indicate on a plan or elevation exactly where the cross sections occur, arrows are generally used.

See figures 2.36 to 2.39.

Inches and Metrics

Many construction materials and equipment used in exhibits are produced overseas and are built and specified using the metric system.

Converting metrics to inches is not that difficult to do. However, when designing an exhibit structure that combines some materials and items that were manufactured with metrics and others with inches can become critical and challenging for the planner/designer.

In 1958, the United States and the Commonwealth of Nations defined the length of the international inch (in) to be exactly 25.4 millimeters (mm). Therefore, when converting inches to millimeters, as a general rule, you multiply inches by 25.4. Figure 2.63 is an inches-to-metric conversion chart.

Text

Writing can be exacting and time consuming; it is an art form and one that is best left to professionals. As soon as fact-checked information becomes available, the text can be written and made part of the graphic layouts.

Text Phases: Special Considerations

Schematic Phase
  Prepare graphic schedule that addresses the topics and the content to be developed.
Preliminary Phase
  As the information about the subject becomes available, commence writing the text.
Intermediate Phase
  Continue writing text.
  Add approved text to graphic layouts.
Final Phase
  Complete the text, and make it part of the graphic layouts.

Unfortunately, on small projects, and sometimes by default, the curator, researcher, or planner/designer is often assigned the writing task. So, if you are forced to become the "Hemingway," here are a few considerations that I have found to be helpful.

Types of Readers

The information on a graphic layout should be directly related to the visitors and the length of reading time that they are willing to commit. There are three basic classifications of readers to be considered—scanners, samplers, and specialists—and the text should be compatible with all three.

INCHES		METRIC
Fractional	Decimal	mm
1/64	0.015	0.396
1/32	0.031	0.793
1/16	0.062	1.587
1/8	0.125	3.175
3/16	0.187	4.762
1/4	0.250	6.350
5/16	0.312	7.937
11/32	0.343	8.731
3/8	0.375	9.525
7/16	0.437	11.112
15/32	0.468	11.906
1/2	0.500	12.700
19/32	0.593	15.081
5/8	0.625	15.875
23/32	0.718	18.256
3/4	0.750	19.050
7/8	0.875	22.225
1	1.000	25.400
1 1/8	1.125	28.575
1 1/4	1.250	31.750
1 1/2	1.500	38.100
1 3/4	1.750	44.450
2 1/4	2.250	57.150
2 1/2	2.500	63.500
2 3/4	2.750	69.850
3	3.000	76.200
3 1/2	3.500	88.900
4	4.000	101.600
4 1/2	4.500	114.300
5	5.000	127.000
6	6.000	152.400
7	7.000	152.400
8	8.000	203.200
9	9.000	228.600
10	10.000	254.000
20	20.000	508.000
24	24.000	609.600
30	30.000	762.000
36	36.000	914.400
40	40.000	1016.000
48	48.000	1219.200
60	60.000	1524.000
80	80.000	2032.000
96	96.000	2438.400
100	100.000	2540.000

Figure 2.63. Inches-to-metric conversion chart. Source: The Engineering Toolbox.

Scanners quickly check out the headlines and only desire a basic understanding of the subject.

Samplers scrutinize the panel and select the text with which they are most interested.

Specialists are intensely interested, read every word, and usually know a great deal about the subject.

Writing Style

Some visitors will pore over every word on a graphic panel, while others will just move along quickly. For that reason, the inverted-pyramid style of writing seems to satisfy all types of readers. When reading a graphic panel or a text block, this top-loaded method allows the readers to stop at any place and still receive the information that they desire.

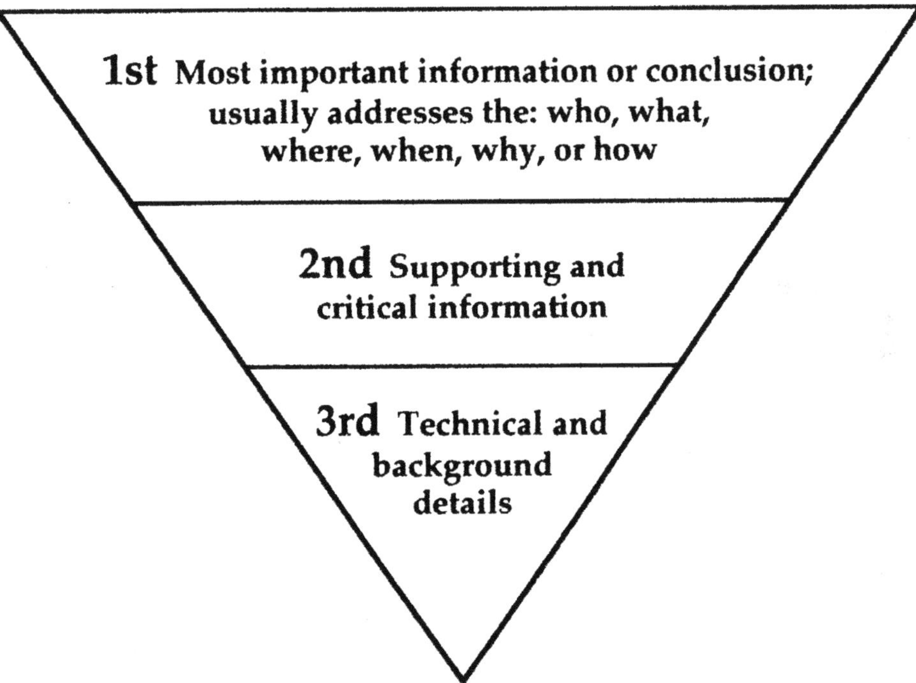
1st Most important information or conclusion; usually addresses the: who, what, where, when, why, or how
2nd Supporting and critical information
3rd Technical and background details

Figure 2.64. Text: Writing style.

Written Voice

Sometimes referred to as "tone," "mood," or "style," a voice gives the text its unique personality, and is the nonverbal vehicle used to convey information to the visitor. Normally via the exhibit text, it "speaks" directly to the visitor and enables the message to come alive. Usually active and friendly, voice should be easy for the visitors to identify with and touch their imagination. Sometimes a voice will take on the mantle of a person, an animal, or a force.

A single voice is normally used throughout the entire text of an exhibition and assists in uniting it. However, when an exhibition is large or contains a variety of subjects, several "voices" can be employed.

Density of Information

This is one of those cases where one size does not fit all. The number of words in a panel and the amount of information that you want to communicate can depend on the location of the institution and the visitor's commitment to the subject being shown.

Consider using text that is brief and to the point when an institution is located in close proximity to other competing museums and historic sites, or when the exhibit is housed in a megamuseum brimming with displays all bidding for attention. In both of these cases there is competition for attention, and visitors in their desire to see everything always seem pressed for time.

However, text can be dense when an institution or an exhibit, because of its subject matter or location, does not compete with other venues. Environmental centers, historic sites, and special exhibitions are just a few that can fall within this category. Generally, the visitors are very interested in the subject matter and are willing to drive some distance to get to a particular venue. When they arrive, they are committed to their visit and are willing to spend quality time reading the text. They are usually interested in and well informed about the subject.

Guidelines

There are many rules that can help when writing the text; here are just a few:

- Write for your target audience; assume that they do not know the subject.
- Target the eighth-grade level of comprehension.
- Keep it clear, simple, interesting, positive, and direct.
- Be brief and focused, and maintain a single, main idea.
- Avoid slang, jargon, colloquialisms, acronyms, and abbreviations.
- Produce short sentences, paragraphs, and text blocks.

Bilingual Text

Having a text in two or more languages can be costly, can be time consuming to write, and will increase the amount of space required. French and Spanish texts take about 30 percent more space than English. So, before adding bilingual texts to your panels, make sure that it is really needed. Frequently, other means of addressing this situation such as handouts and audio devices can be considered.

Theme

An exhibit theme is a recurring subject, principle, event, and so forth, that unites all the elements of the exhibition and is compatible with its mission and aims. A theme must be obvious enough to be easily recognized and comprehended and should be supported by the exhibit's color, form, milieu, motif, and the like.

Theme Phases: Special Considerations

Feasibility, Schematic, or Preliminary Phase
Theme is developed and approved.
Intermediate and Final Phases
Design should be reviewed to ensure that theme has been maintained.

CASE HISTORY: "THE PAST CAN BE DULL"

The National Archives and Records Administration's (NARA) regional office is located in the historic area of Philadelphia, a section of the city that regularly attracts many tourists who are excited to visit the Liberty Bell, Independence Hall, Carpenter's Hall, and the Betsy Ross House. NARA's collection by contrast consists of regional eighteenth- and nineteenth-century documents, which although interesting to most adults, can be unbearably boring for their children.

Even though NARA had many fascinating documents, their collection was quite esoteric, and I found myself designing one visually boring exhibit after another. That was, until I hit upon a theme that elicited the upbeat patriotic feeling we all experience during a Fourth of July celebration. Although it was far from subtle, drums, flags, and star motifs with a red, white, and blue color scheme created the right visual impact and the desperately needed excitement. The designs shown in figures 2.65 and 2.66 are two of the several submitted to NARA.

(*continued*)

CASE HISTORY: "THE PAST CAN BE DULL" (*continued*)

Figure 2.65. Temporary exhibit.

Figure 2.66. Interactive displays.

Time Schedule

Every exhibition must be ready for opening day, and it is the time schedule included in the work plan that guides a project from its concept to its opening. At the beginning of each phase, the team in charge prepares a schedule that lists each task and indicates the amount of time it requires. For additional information, refer to the schedules in chapter 1 showing the work plans.

CASE HISTORY: "KNOW WHEN TO SAY, 'NO'!"

Every exhibit planner/designer has things they regret having done, and I am not immune to that malaise. Several times I have been involved with government officials who had the power of the purse and who dictated the opening date of an exhibition. Of course, such dates are always politically based and usually have absolutely nothing to do with the real time required to prepare and construct an exhibit. Now that I am older and probably wiser, I always prepare from the get-go a very detailed time schedule to show these officials that the opening date they insist upon is impossible to meet, and I have learned over the years to have the courage to say, "No" if they persist.

Typography

Selecting the proper typeface is indispensable to the success of an exhibition, for it can foster ambiance, reinforce the theme, and suggest the who, what, when, where, and why of an exhibition. Fortunately, we are blessed with a wide variety of typefaces to choose from. Yet, coupled with all the variations that each typeface possesses, selecting and specifying one can be an overwhelming task.

The two guiding lights in determining a particular typeface and its size are legibility and readability. Legibility refers to design and the degree to which it influences word recognition. Readability is the measure of ease with which a text can be read, and it is a combination of the typeface's size and color, its background color, line spacing, and the length of text line. Even though legibility and readability are the main factors to consider when selecting a typeface, lighting, viewing distance, and the needs of the visually and physically challenged are additional important factors.

Typography Phases: Special Considerations

Preliminary Phase
  Select the typeface.
Intermediate Phase
  Confirm that the color scheme and typography are compatible.
  Check typography for readability.

Typeface and Backgrounds

Font color and its background color and pattern are major concerns when optimum readability is desired. There should be at least a 70 percent contrast between the typeface and its surround, and if at all possible, patterned backgrounds ought to be avoided or muted. The needs of the color-blind and the visually impaired visitor should be major considerations when deciding on background colors and patterns. Before selecting a color, see chapter 3, "Color and Light."

Figure 2.67. Typefaces and backgrounds.

Letter Case

Using both upper- and lowercase letters can add interest to a graphic layout and assist in avoiding monotony. An uppercase or capital letter stops the eye, can be seen from a distance, and attracts attention, while lowercase letters group themselves together and are easier to read. This is why sentences traditionally start with an uppercase letter and then continue with lowercase. With this is mind, whenever possible, it seems best to use uppercase letters for titles and brief introductions and lowercase letters for the body of the text.

Letter Spacing

Since we recognize a grouping of letters as a word, the space between each letter is important and should be carefully studied. Which word in the line of words in figure 2.68 do you feel can be most easily read?

Design is the organization of elements into a unified whole.

Design is the organization of elements into a unified whole.

Design is the organization of elements into a unified

Design is the organization of elements into a

D e s i g n i s t h e o r g a n i z a t i o n o f e l e m e n t s

D e s i g n   i s   t h e   o r g a n i z a t i o n   o f

Figure 2.68. Letter spacing.

Letter Style

Each font is designed to have a distinctive shape, identifiable outline, particular purpose, and unique personality. It is during the research phase that typefaces that would convey a particular message and be appropriate for the exhibit theme and design are collected.

Traditional	**TRADITIONAL**
Theatrical	**THEATRICAL**
School Days	**SCHOOL DAYS**
Whimsical	**WHIMSICAL**

Figure 2.69. Letter style.

Letter Weight

The boldness of a typeface, determined by the thickness of its stroke, is referred to as weight. Thanks to the computer, a wide variety of letter weights for most typefaces is now available, and we are no longer limited

Condensed
Light
Regular
Bold
Italic
Outline

Figure 2.70. Letter weight.

to just the few shown in figure 2.70. Yet with such diversity, it is so easy to fall into the trap of employing too many different weights when designing a graphic layout. It is always wise to limit the letter weight of a typeface to a few variations.

Line Length

The general rule for the length of a line of text seems to be about fifty to sixty letters and spaces. This length allows the eye to flow easily from line to line. However, as the typeface gets larger, as in an introduction, the number of words and spaces per line should decrease. Wheelchair-bound visitors ought to be able to read a complete line of text comfortably from a single vantage point.

The "Smithsonian Guidelines for Accessible Exhibition Design" recommends forty-five to fifty characters per line with a "not-to-exceed" limit of fifty-five characters. These numbers do not include spaces.

Line Spacing

The space between lines of letters is called "leading." This term stems from printers who traditionally inserted thin strips of lead between the text lines when adding more space.

Line spacing is measured from letter baseline to letter baseline and should be at least 20 percent larger than type size, for example, a ten-point

- Leading: 11 points
Graphic design is the arrangement and selection of elements for a graphic format. It is essentially a two-dimensional art form.

- Leading: 15 points
Graphic design is the arrangement and selection of elements for a graphic format. It is essentially a two-dimensional art form.

- Leading: 22 points
Graphic design is the arrangement and selection of elements for a graphic format. It is essentially a two-dimensional art form.

Figure 2.71. Line spacing (leading).

typeface would require a twelve-point line space. For legibility, more leading is required when the line length is long, illumination is low, and the contrast between the letter and its background is minimum. Which leading in figure 2.71 do you find the most comfortable to read?

Paragraph Alignment

When deciding on the alignment of a text block, there are four basic types to be considered.

Justified Left, Ragged Right

This setting is the easiest to read and is used when laying out a text block that is dense or when there are many blocks in a layout. Since the starting point of each line is always located next to the left-hand margin, readers can quickly find the beginning, and their eyes can flow effortlessly from one line to the next.

Justified Right, Ragged Left

This alignment can be difficult to read. It forces the reader to hunt for the start of each line, and for that reason, this type of justification is best confined to titles and to text blocks with large typeface or with few words.

Centered, Ragged Right and Left

Excellent for titles, this type of justification can add interest when laying out small paragraphs. Since it can be difficult to read, though, it should never be used extensively for large text blocks.

Centered, Justified Right and Left

Common to newspaper layouts, this arrangement is good provided that the text block or column is narrow. However, it can produce uneven letter spacing that could reduce legibility and be difficult to read.

Serif versus Sans Serif

A serif is that fine decorative line that is added to the stroke of a letter at its beginning and its end. A serif typeface is usually preferred for the text since all the letters in a word seem to be visually connected and grouped together.

Sans means "without" and indicates that the serif has been deleted. Sans serif typefaces are generally preferred for titles and brief introductory statements. It is generally believed that sans serif is more readable when viewed on a computer screen.

Care should always be taken when selecting a serif or a sans serif letter, because they can indicate a particular time frame and location.

Typeface Variations

Carl Sagan was famous for saying, "There are billions and billions of stars in the universe." I often think of that statement when selecting a font and having to choose from its endless varieties.

Usually limiting your layout to one or two typefaces with a few variations will produce an interesting and unified graphic.

Widows

This is a real no-no! At the end of a paragraph, never leave the last word on a line all by itself. Many times you may have to rewrite the sentence, so that a lonely "widow" will not occur.

Justified Left – Ragged Right

We are surrounded by color, and in a casual manner we accept it as part of our lives, yet color can deeply affect us physically, psychologically and spiritually. Color is one of our most appealing and important design tools, for it can create a mood and a depth of experience that cannot be achieved in any other way. Without text or visuals, color can convey significant information about a particular exhibition; it can reinforce the exhibit's aims, create ambience, foster a special feeling, and convey a particular time period, location, or social status. Lacking signs and arrows, color can direct and pace us through an exhibition. It can create a sense of nearness and distance, and even make objects seem larger or smaller.

Justified Right – Ragged Left

We are surrounded by color, and in a casual manner we accept it as part of our lives, yet color can deeply affect us physically, psychologically and spiritually. Color is one of our most appealing and important design tools, for it can create a mood and a depth of experience that cannot be achieved in any other way. Without text or visuals, color can convey significant information about a particular exhibition; it can reinforce the exhibit's aims, create ambience foster a special feeling, and convey a particular time period, location, or social status. Lacking signs and arrows, color can direct and pace us through an exhibition. It can create a sense of nearness and distance, and even make objects seem larger or smaller.

Centered – Ragged Right and Left

We are surrounded by color, and in a casual manner we accept it as part of our lives, yet color can deeply affect us physically, psychologically and spiritually. Color is one of our most appealing and important design tools, for it can create a mood and a depth of experience that cannot be achieved in any other way. Without text or visuals, color can convey information about a particular exhibition; it can reinforce the exhibit's aims, create an ambience, foster a special feeling, and convey a particular time period, location, or social status. Lacking signs and arrows, color can direct and pace us through an exhibition. It can create a sense of nearness and distance, and even make objects seem larger or smaller.

Centered – Justified Right and Left

We are surrounded by color, and in a casual manner we accept it as part of our lives, yet color can deeply affect us physically, psychologically and spiritually. Color is one of our most appealing and important design tools, for it can create a mood and a depth of experience that cannot be achieved in any other way. Without text or visuals, color can convey significant information about a particular exhibition; it can reinforce the exhibit's aims, create ambience, foster a special feeling, and convey a particular time period, location, or social status. Lacking signs and arrows, color can direct and pace us through an exhibition. It can create a sense of nearness and distance, and even make objects seem larger or smaller.

Figure 2.72. Paragraph alignment.

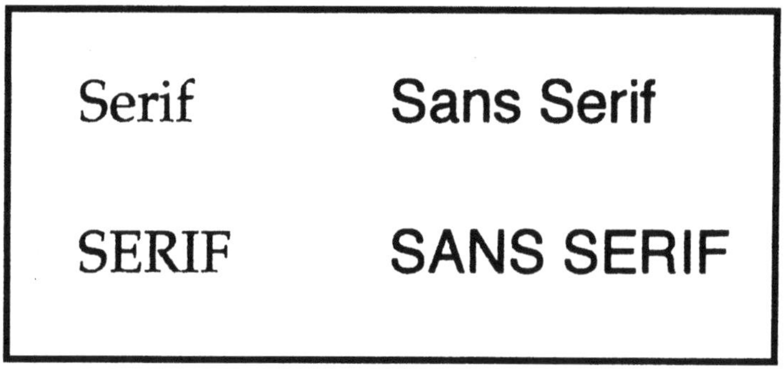

Serif	Sans Serif
SERIF	SANS SERIF

Figure 2.73. Serif versus sans serif.

Figure 2.74. Typeface variations.

Visitors

Never, never, forget them! During all the phases involved in an exhibition, visitors become those little birds on our shoulders that constantly remind us that it is their intellectual, physical, and psychological needs that should and must be addressed. Visitors are our guests; we have invited them into our "home," and their comfort and needs must always be considered. Once we allow those "little birds" to fly out the window, we have lost our

Paragraph with a "Widow"

The urge to collect is, for the most part, not based on age, gender, or the value of an item. It is just something we like to do, and thanks to this basic urge our institutions have received many an exceptional collection.

Paragraph without a "Widow"

The urge to collect is, for the most part, not based on age, gender, or the value of an item. It is just something we like to do, and thanks to this basic urge our historic societies, and science and art museums have received many an exceptional collection.

Figure 2.75. Widows.

audience, and our design has lost its focus and its purpose. The following are just a few words of caution.

Do we really care about our visitors? As planners/designers we all believe we do. Yet, there are times during the planning/designing of an exhibition when the pressures imposed upon us become so overwhelming that we spend our time "putting out fires" and the visitor becomes the first casualty. When this happens, we should stop, take a deep breath, and refocus on what they want and why they come.

Is the exhibition more important than the visitor? When an exhibit is preceded by a lot of hype, and fails to live up to the expectations that the advanced publicity alluded to, visitors become resentful and hesitate to return when the institution promotes another extravaganza. And when a blockbuster exhibition treats the visitors as if they were cattle being herded through a chute, they know that nobody really cared about them.

Many times a well-designed, low-budget exhibit can result in a successful visitor experience. Indeed, some of my best and most enjoyable times were spent in museums that seemed to have a small exhibit budget but provided a quiet, secluded spot where I could study and enjoy the simple objects that were sensitively and beautifully displayed.

Visitors want to spend their time and money wisely, and if an exhibition is boring or trivializing and has very little substance, they will feel cheated. We should never forget that visitors are critical to the success of a museum and that they should always be respected and their needs met. This book is really about them and how to make their visit a positive experience.

The exhibit planning/designing process is a marriage of the artistic, the intellectual, and the practical. Ultimately, the success of an exhibition depends on how well everyone who is participating understands and executes the tasks and issues involved and is aware of the numerous aspects and factors that are fundamental to a successful design.

3

Color and Light

> In the architectural opus, light generates space: without light, space does not exist. Natural light brings plastic forms to life, shapes the surfaces of materials, controls and balances geometric lines.
>
> —Mario Botta, *Light and Gravity*

If a planner/designer were ever assigned a muse, the muse would devote most of her energies to color and light. For they are our most powerful and important design tools, and for better or worse, color and light will always have a major impact on any exhibition design.

Color Phases: Special Considerations

Schematic and Preliminary Phases
- Colors are presented at this stage only to enhance the sketches and are not usually meant to suggest the final color scheme.

Intermediate Phase
- Select a color scheme for the exhibition and graphics.
- Produce a colors and materials board.
- Check proposed color scheme's swatches at the site with its lighting conditions.

Final and Documentation Phases
- Select, specify, and locate all colors.

Construction and Installation Phases
- Check to make sure that the colors are accurately reproduced.

Given that everything in an exhibition has a color and that it is a product of its lighting, it is necessary for planners/designers to understand how these two factors interact with each other and how they work together to convey a significant amount of information. Color and light aid in the following:

- Reinforcing the exhibit's aims and fostering a special impression
- Creating a particular mood and ambiance
- Conveying a definite time period, location, and social status
- Making us feel warm or cool, active or passive, and relaxed or tense
- Attracting and focusing attention
- Helping to direct and pace visitors and contributing to a safe museum experience
- Providing a sense of near and far and making objects seem larger or smaller

Effects and Interpretations

How a particular color affects a visitor is always a major concern for the designer during the color selection process. Unfortunately, there is never enough time in the short span of a museum visit to retrain and change a visitor's deeply ingrained color impressions, so colors must be selected that will instantly convey the desired messages. This section will discuss the following colors or groups of colors and their impact on the visitor.

Warm and Cool Colors

Visitors respond to color both emotionally and physically, and it is important that exhibit colors evoke the correct response and convey the proper messages.

Warm colors stimulate the visitor and should be used in areas of heightened activity. Yellow, yellow-orange, orange, red-orange, red, and red-violet are in this group. Neutrals and base colors such as tan and brown are considered to have warm attributes.

Cool colors relax the visitors and aid in their concentration. They produce a passive, calming, peaceful, and tranquil effect and slow down the perception of time. Yellow-green, green, green-blue, blue, blue-violet, and violet are referred to as cool colors. Gray and silver also have cool attributes.

Contrasts

Depending on the exhibit's needs, warm and cool colors can be used to express many conditions. Figure 3.1 provides a sampling of contrasting warm/cool impressions.

WARM COLORS	COOL COLORS
Heavy	Light
Opaque	Transparent
Stimulant	Sedative
Earthy	Airy
Near	Far
Dense	Rare
Sun	Shadow

Figure 3.1. Warm and cool colors.

Red

"Red with rage" "Red-carpet treatment" "Red herring" "Caught red-handed"

Strong, emotional, and compelling, red is probably our most dominant and dynamic color. It demands our attention and can even order us to stop. Red has high visibility, which is why stop signs, stoplights, and fire equipment have been traditionally painted red. In heraldry, red is used to indicate courage, and for that reason, it is a color found in many national flags. An opaque color, it leaves a strong afterimage.

"Seeing red" is a very meaningful statement. When people see the color red, their pituitary gland starts to work, their chemistry is altered, and their blood pressure, respiration rate, metabolism, and heart rate increase. They become more restless and nervous, and their motor activity increases.

Modified forms of red, such as rose, maroon, and pink are beautiful, expressive, generally appealing, and deeply emotional.

Attributes

Appearance: Brilliant, intense, dry, heat, hot, welcoming
Good impressions: Love, unity, brave, courageous, passion, desire, strength, energy, sexuality, danger, stop, blood, fire, revolution, excitement
Good or bad impressions: Passionate, active, eager, zealous, powerful
Bad impressions: Greedy, grasping, fierceness, hatred, aggression, cruelty, blood, war, fire, danger, anger

Design Considerations

Red can be detrimental to certain mental activities, such as problem solving and decision making. It is best used in exhibits and areas that are conducive to social interaction and conversation. Designers should avoid using red in study areas.

This color is excellent for active, upbeat, participatory areas. It attracts attention; brings text, titles, and images to the foreground; and is perfect for "Click Here" buttons on computer screens and interactive displays.

Red is an accent color and, unless modified, should never be used in large areas.

Orange

Bright, luminous, and glowing, orange combines the happiness of yellow and the energy and the passion of red; it has a warming, invigorating effect on people. Since orange is mellower and less primitive than red, it has a more livable charm.

Orange is said to increase the craving for food. It is used as a safety standard for acute hazards such as cut, crush, and burn. It is also a color that seems to energize and stimulate people and, for that reason, can be effectively used in museums that have blockbuster exhibitions and need to move visitors from one exhibit to another.

It is generally not preferred in its pure form but is very desirable in tints such as peach, salmon, and shades of brown.

Attributes

Appearance: Bright, luminous, glowing, appetizing, brave
Good impressions: Warmth, exuberance, joy, lively, energetic, hilarity, satiety, forceful, enthusiastic
Bad impressions: Cheap, inexpensive, forceful
Associations: Joy, autumn, tropics, sunshine, acute hazards, Halloween, Thanksgiving

Design Consideration

Orange can have a cheap and inexpensive connotation; for that reason, pure orange is rarely used in upscale establishments or in museums when displaying valuable objects. Clear orange and light blue used together denote cleanliness and is a perfect color combination for medium-priced family restaurants, displays of relatively inexpensive objects, and settings that focus on people of average income.

Yellow

"Yellow coward"   "Yellow belly"

Yellow is next to white in brightness and suggests light of a lesser purity than white. It is associated with both great intelligence and mental deficiency.

Yellow has a favorable effect upon human metabolism. It can sharply focus the eye, has the highest visibility of any color, and can be readily seen from a distance. Because of these qualities, yellow is used in dimly lighted areas, can be seen under most lighting conditions, and is often used for safety purposes.

Attributes

Appearance: Sunny, cheerful, incandescent, radiant
Good impressions: Cheerful, inspiring, celestial, high spirited, happy, healthy, intellectual, energetic, joyful
Bad impressions: With a greenish cast it can appear to be treasonous, deceitful, cowardly, mean
Associations: Caution, sunlight, sun, summer, God, gold, high intelligence, richness, glory, divine love, enlightening, understanding

Design Considerations

Yellow is an excellent choice for cutout letters and objects that have to be seen from a distance. In learning situations, yellow can be a problem color; studies have indicated that more mistakes are made when a person uses yellow paper or a yellow pencil rather than white paper or pencils of another color.

Green

"Green with envy"   "Greenhorn"   "Green-eyed monster"

Green absorbs the happiness of yellow and the tranquility of blue. In nature, it is our most prominent color; for that reason, it is closely associated with the environment. Even though a yellow-green is considered a cool color, its coolness depends on the percentage of yellow that is in the mix. Green tends to reduce nervousness and muscular tension. It is a quiet color that can provide an atmosphere conducive to concentration and is ideal for sedentary tasks. A brilliant green is one of the standard identifications for first aid equipment.

Attributes

Appearance: Clear, moist
Good impressions: Youth, growth, health, harmony, freshness, clear, moist, meditative, life, hope
Bad impressions: Nastiness, envy, greed, jealousy, depression, ghastliness, disease, terror, guilt, decay; it can also denote a lack of experience, for example, a "greenhorn" is a novice.
Associations: Cool, nature, life, hope, St. Patrick's Day, spring, fertility, safety, vegetation, ecology

Design Consideration

A green light or a green surface that reflects onto a person's face can make that face seem evil, near death, and repulsive.

Blue

"Feeling blue"	"True blue"	"The bluebook"	"Blueblood"
"Out of the blue"	"Blue Stocking"	"Blue-plate special"	

Blue is an outstandingly favorite color throughout the world. It stands for responsibility, caring, knowledge, and trustworthiness and is one of the reasons that most policemen and policewomen in many countries wear dark blue uniforms. A vivid blue is the standard for an industrial caution symbol and accessibility signs.

Blue is sharply reflected by the lens of the eye and can cause a nearsighted condition that disturbs some people. It is a difficult color for the eye to focus on, has low attention value, and can be objectionable as a light source. However it can be restful and calming; a deep blue can even seem quieting. Pale blue seems to bother human eyes and tends to give a blurred appearance to adjacent objects. Due to the filtering caused by their aging eyes, elderly people usually prefer blue.

Attributes

Appearance: Transparent, wet
Good impressions: Understanding, truth, constancy, loyalty, trustworthiness, caring, peaceful, unity, stability
Bad impressions: Fearful, secretive, shy, thief-like, melancholic, despondent, depressed, mysterious, conservative
Pale blue: Cold, sky, sea, water, ice, bleak, spirituality, divine eternity, human immortality, wisdom, intelligence, logical attitude

Dark blue: Depending on the design of the exhibit, dark blue can display many of the good or bad qualities mentioned above.

Design Considerations

Bright blue is desirable for decorative accents; however, unless there is a special ambiance that you wish to create, large areas of this color should be avoided, for they tend to seem cold and bleak.

Very pale blue can be considered for large areas, and a soft gray-blue is an excellent color to use in study and rest areas.

Violet

Represents the highest quality a person can possess. It is a soft color, has a feminine nature, and is associated with elderly, frail women.

Attributes

Appearance: Cooling, magnetic, antiseptic
Good impressions: Noble, spiritual, cool, mystical grace, faith, purification, honor, spirituality, self-esteem
Bad impressions: Mystical, wistful, mournful, loneliness, desperation, grief (but not as recent or deep as black would indicate)
Associations: Connected with religious ceremonies, spirituality, mist, darkness, shadow, mourning

Design Consideration

This is an excellent color to use when exhibiting historic royalty or elderly, dignified people.

Purple

"To the purple born" "Purple heart"

Purple is the hue between violet and red. It combines the stability of blue, the energy of red, and the royal aspects of violet. Deep or bright purple suggests wealth and is associated with imperial sovereignty. It is the principal color in Queen Elizabeth's crown.

Dark purple can convey gloom, sadness, and repentance. Lighter purples seem to be romantic and delicate, and elicit a nostalgic feeling.

Attributes

Appearance: Deep, soft, atmospheric
Good impressions: Dignity, wisdom, spirituality, nobility, royalty, independence, creativity
Bad impressions: Pompous
Associations: Power, nobility, mystery, magic, Easter, mystic, wistful

Design Consideration

Purple is dynamic, alive, and energetic, and is an excellent color to use when exhibiting living or young royal members. Because purple disturbs the focus of the eye, it is not suitable for large areas.

Violet versus Purple

When studying color, violet and purple tend to be sometimes treated as being the same, and each can be assigned red as its complement. Violet has a high percentage of blue; purple contains a high percentage of red.

Violet and purple are not interchangeable; they are separate colors, and each elicits its own distinct psychological message and reactions. It is interesting to note that, while violet has its own wavelength, purple does not. Purple is created by mixing red and violet.

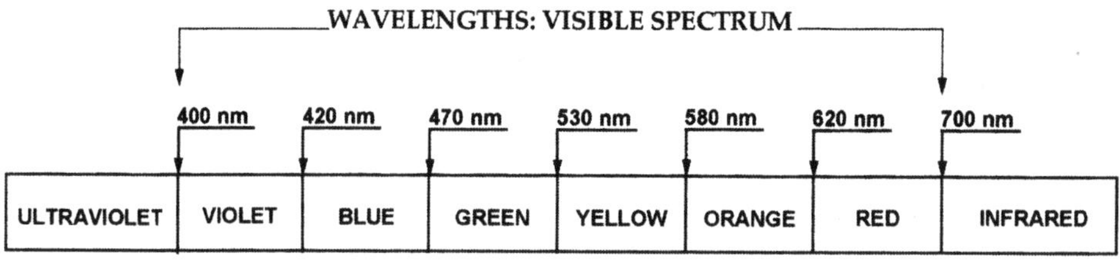

Figure 3.2. Wavelengths: Visible spectrum.

White

"White knight" "As white as snow" "White elephant" "White lies"

Reflecting all the colored light waves, it is the emblem of supreme divine power and is considered to be the color of perfection and simplicity. White, or its tints such as beige, ivory, or cream, is mostly used as neutral background colors and is a very important part of any color palette.

Attributes

Appearance: Pure light, brilliant
Associations: Cleanliness, cool, snow, hospitals, sanitary, sterile
Good impressions: Purity, innocence, peace, lightness, cleanliness, frankness, youthful, brightness of spirit, aseptic, normality, delicacy, refinement, chastity
Bad impressions: Blankness, ghostly, cold, clinical, vulnerability, pallor, sterility
Symbolism: Light, triumph, joy, surrender; in Western countries, it is the bridal color.

Design Considerations

Bright colors such as reds, blues, and greens when placed against a white or off-white background will appear to be brighter and more prominent. This is especially helpful when there is a need for a colored title or for an object to stand out.

The eye invariably goes to white or a pale color before seeing a dark color. To ensure that the visitor is first attracted to an artifact, care should be taken when placing a dark-colored artifact on or near a white or light-colored area. However a visitor's attention can be drawn to a dark or medium-shaded artifact or a painting if surrounded with a recessive color.

Black

"The Black sheep of the family"
"Black as ink"
"It's a black hole"
"Blacklisted"
"Black as night"
"Black-hearted person"
"Blackmail"

Black absorbs all of the colored light waves and is the opposite of white in its appearance, association, and impressions. It is a mysterious yet elegant color. Interestingly, the first black inks were made from dead bodies.

Attributes

Appearance: Spatial, dark, empty
Good impressions: Strength, dignity, sophisticated, refinement, authority, elegance, formality, prestige
Bad impressions: Deep mourning, death, defilement, funereal, ominous, fear, depression, mourning, negativity of spirit
Associations: Deep, restful, quiet, neutral, night, emptiness, unknown

Design Consideration

Since this is a very intense color, designers, when specifying black or when a black typeface is twenty-four points or higher, usually prefer that it be slightly softened by adding a small amount of white to it, thus making it a dark gray.

Gray

"It's a gray area."

Gray is a combination of black and white. It is a cool, conservative, passive color that seldom evokes strong emotion. Gray comes in many tints, from an almost white to a near black, and the message that it conveys depends on its black-white ratio. Light gray seems to be pure and angelic, while dark gray appears strong and mysterious. Grays when modified with tints of other colors can be cool, warm, or neutral.

Attributes

Appearance: Cloudy, metallic, mechanical
Good impression: Intellectual
Bad impressions: Dull, dingy, dirty
Associations: Elderly

Design Considerations

It is prudent to use light gray rather than white, and dark gray rather than black when selecting a background color for a graphic panel, a vast expanse of wall area, or a huge display structure. Used in large areas, gray can seem to be cool and lack emotion. However, by adding brown or another warm color, gray will appear warmer.

Brown

Brown is a combination of orange and blue and is the warmest of the neutral colors. Brown is associated with the earth and the material side of life, yet it seems to blend comfortably into all environments, social structures, and time frames.

Attributes

Appearance: Warm and earthy
Good impressions: Honest, wholesome, earthy, steadfast, simple, friendly, dependable, healthy, solid
Bad impressions: Repressed personality, lazy, dull
Associations: Earth, wood, stone, autumn

Design Consideration

Dark brown is a good replacement for black when a warmer palette is needed.

Modified Colors

"Seeing the world through rose-colored glasses"

Modified colors are combinations of two or more colors. Since there is a myriad of modified colors each sending out its own message, planners/designers will have to use their intuition in interpreting the thoughts that they convey. A few well-known modified colors and their messages are as follows:

Pink: Female, cute, love, joy, happiness, kindness, gentleness. This color is very popular with little girls.
Gold: Wealth, good health, divine love, wisdom, high ideals, enhancement
Silver: Wealth, sleek, elegant, graceful aging
Magenta: Passion
Indigo: Wisdom
Rose: Love, compassion
Peach: Mellow, livable, charm, appetizing, modesty, sincerity
Coral: Desire

Design Consideration

There are times when it is necessary to have the main theme of an exhibition connect subliminally to a secondary theme, and it is the degree to which you modify the colors that increases or decreases the impact of the subliminal message.

**CASE HISTORY: "PENNSYLVANIA LOST—
PENNSYLVANIA FOUND"**

The mission for this exhibit was to preserve Pennsylvania's old, historic buildings and to inform the public about grants and seed money available to save these wonderful structures. During the planning/designing phases, it was felt that a small touch of patriotism could help spur visitors into taking action. Yet knowing that a color scheme of bright red, white, and blue based on our flag might be too obvious, a palette of light blue, brick red, and cream was developed. I hoped these subliminal colors would suggest our wonderful heritage to the visitor.

Physiological and Psychological Aspects

Visitors react instantly and intuitively to a particular color so those selected for an exhibition must support the exhibit theme and not send conflicting and confusing messages.

Visitors' preference for a specific color is influenced by many factors, including not only their age but also their cultural, ethnic, social, and economic backgrounds and regional attitudes. For many, a special experience in which a particular color played a prominent part can be a strong influence when choosing or rejecting a color.

Age Preference

Age certainly influences how we interpret color. Children between two and three years old relate to the primary colors: red, blue, and yellow. In this age group, yellow can cause restlessness. At about six years of age, they start to favor bright red over all other colors, followed by orange, yellow, blue, purple, and green in their purest forms. Of course, most little girls just love pink, fuchsia, and lilac.

As we mature, our color preferences change. We generally start to prefer tints and shades, and gradually lose interest in intense colors. This change can be partially attributed to cultural and ethnic influences, but there are also physical factors involved. As we grow older, our eyes deteriorate, and the yellowing of our eye fluids gradually increases, thus changing our color perception. Statistically there is a drop from 85 percent acuity for blue at age 18 to about 10 percent acuity at age 69–80.

AGE	COLOR PREFERENCE
	High — Medium — Low
Birth to age 6	Red, Orange, Yellow, Green, Blue, Violet
Age 6 to 60	Blue, Red, Green, Violet, Orange, Yellow
Age 60 to 90	Blue, Green, Violet, Red, Yellow, Orange

Figure 3.3. Age preferences.

Design Consideration

It is important when selecting a color palette to know the visitor's age and the museum type. Are visitors elderly retirees or schoolchildren? Is it a traditional museum with a high rate of adult attendees, or is it a children's museum? The answer to these questions will definitely have an impact on the color scheme.

Color-blindness

With approximately thirty million people in the United States having some form of color-blindness, this physical deficiency *must* be considered when preparing a color palette.

Unfortunately, when selecting colors, planners/designers usually assume that the visitors are not color-blind, but this is not always the case. It is possible that not only visitors are color compromised but also the clients, coworkers, or even the planners/designers themselves.

Many people are unaware that they have a color deficiency. Even among the non-color-blind population, each person will have a slightly different interpretation of color. This is due to the structure of people's eyes and the variations in their rods and cones. Therefore, it is always counterproductive to agonize over a scheme that is being hotly debated and simply far better to adjust the exhibit colors so that most of the team members will be in agreement.

Color-blindness occurs when one or more groups of cones in the eye are damaged or have never developed. Fortunately, most color-blind people are only marginally damaged and can still accurately recognize some or even most colors. In the United States, about 7 percent of men and 4 percent of women have some form of this condition.

There are numerous types and degrees of color-blindness. People that are totally color-blind see only white, gray, and black, but this is an extremely rare condition. Many with a color deficiency have difficulty in perceiving certain colors, but they still do have normal brain activity and experience normal physiological responses.

Design Considerations

Color-blind people can perceive the difference between light and dark. For that reason it is important to use contrasting colors when designing graphics and preparing a color scheme.

When planning/designing an exhibit or graphics, color should never be the primary vehicle for conveying information. Color-coded elements such as directional signage, legends, and weather and geological maps should be designed with enough color value contrast that the profoundly color-blind person can interpret them as being white, gray, and black hues. Icons, shapes, symbols, and the like, should be used in conjunction with color.

Displays that rely heavily on color have a particular problem when providing information to the color-blind. For example, exhibits that interpret chemical reactions, identify materials by the color of their flame, interpret chemical testing strips, or rely on colored LEDs all require special consideration.

Color Combinations

There are a few colors that, when used together, make strong and precise statements, and even when modified their meaning can still be clearly understood. When using colors together, it is prudent to ensure that they express the desired intent. A few commonly used combinations are as follows:

Christmas: red and green
Halloween: black and orange
Patriotism: red, white, and blue
Easter: yellow and violet
Royalty: purple and gold

Design Consideration

The physical distance separating colors is also important: the closer the colors are to each other, the stronger the mental connection will be. For example, red and green placed next to each other will convey Christmas; however, as the distance between these two colors increases, the Christmas connotation will decrease until it completely disappears.

Cultural Associations

When selecting colors that are culturally based, it is important for the planner/designer to research and develop a palette that is compatible with the audience or the exhibit theme.

	Britain	China	Egypt	Iran	Japan	Ukraine
Courage	R	R		R	Y	
Death, mourning	BL	W	B	BL	W	BL
Good fortune		R	Y	R		
Happiness, joy	Y & O	R	Y	G	R/W	Y
Love	R				O	R
Nobility and/or status	P	Y	W		P	
Strength	R		G			O

Figure 3.4. Cultural associations. Key: R = Red, O = Orange, Y = Yellow, G = Green, B = Blue, P = Purple, W = White, BL = Black.

It is not unusual for a particular color to have several conflicting meanings or for several colors to have the same meaning. Countries such as India, Mexico, China, and Iran were formed from many remote communities, and during centuries of isolation, each village developed its own color associations.

Fatigue

Our bodies and especially our eyes function best when they experience a rhythm of work and rest. Under prolonged, intense stimulation, we become fatigued. If there are too many accent colors (bright reds, yellows, and blues), or even just one that covers a large area, we will rapidly tire and lose concentration. As the eye fatigues, intense colors will appear to change, lose their quality, and become darker.

Design Consideration

In most cases when covering a large area, it is preferable to use neutral colors and to limit the accent colors to the small areas where you want to attract attention.

Gender Preference

Women seem to know and to be quite familiar with hues such as burnt orange, moss, rattan, mauve, and claret; most men do not, and they are usually not really interested in the names and subtleties of color. Even so, gender does not seem to make a dramatic difference in the colors that are preferred by either sex. However, it is felt that females prefer warm shades and tints, and men cooler ones. One winner for both sexes that can't be overlooked is blue. Everyone seems to prefer blue by a wide margin. In order of preference:

Men prefer: Blue, red, green, violet, orange, yellow
Women prefer: Blue, red, green, violet, yellow, orange

Mood

As visitors move from one exhibit area to another, there are times when it is necessary for them to be relaxed and at other times to be stimulated. So when preparing a palette for an exhibit area, a major consideration is that the colors promote the desired visitor's mood and that they be compatible with its theme and aims. A good rule to remember is that warm colors stimulate and cool colors relax.

Warm, intense colors are best employed when visitors need to be upbeat and active, as in participatory areas. Conversely, cool, grayish colors can calm and relax the visitors and are a good choice for study areas and introspective exhibits.

Blues, greens, and violets will have a quieting effect, but to what extent will depend upon the degree to which these colors have been toned down. Green is a combination of yellow and blue; its calming effect will depend on the amount of yellow in the mix. A high percentage of yellow will increase the visitor's level of activity, while blue will decrease it. This is also true of violet that depends on the amount of red and blue for its serene look.

Small areas with bright, contrasting colors could cause visitors to be overly active, and they may have difficulty focusing on the details of an exhibit and its text. Conversely, a large, bland area can be boring and uninteresting.

Design Consideration

The larger the exhibit or the exhibition area, the more important it is for the planner/designer to anticipate the mood of the visitor. At times, it could be prudent to divide large areas into smaller sections, with some areas having a color scheme that produces a stimulating, active environment, while others are quiet and retrospective.

Nonpersonal Associations

Colors can also have meanings not associated with personal attributes. American Cherokees associate colors with personality traits, situations, and directions, and the Chinese link the color blue not only with immortality but also with the sky and clouds. The following, in order of preference, is a sampling of a few nonpersonal color associations:

Blue: North, cold, defeat, and trouble
White: South, warmth, peace, and happiness
Red: East, sacred fire, blood, and success
Black: West, problems, death

Design Consideration

If the majority of your visitors are from a particular cultural background, and your exhibit or graphics pertain to a different culture, then when deemed necessary, the visitor should be informed about the traditional color meanings. For example, when viewing a picture of African and Middle Eastern women wearing black, visitors should be told that many married women in these societies wear black as proud symbols of their social status and that they are not in mourning.

Physical Temperatures

Normally, it is impossible for a planner/designer to actually control the temperature of a room, yet with the proper choice of color, a visitor can feel cooler when viewing an arctic display and warmer when entering a tropical habitat. Warm colors make you feel warm or hot, and cool colors make you feel cool or cold.

Johannes Itten, when discussing temperature and its relationship to colors in his book *The Elements of Color*, stated,

> It may be strange to identify a sensation of temperature with the visual realm of color sensation. However, experiments have demonstrated a difference of five to seven degrees in the subjective feeling of heat or cold between a workroom painted in blue-green and one in red-orange. That is, in the blue-green room the occupants felt that 59° F. was cold, whereas in the red-orange room they did not feel cold until the temperature fell to 52–54° F. Objectively, this means that blue-green slows down the circulation and red-orange stimulates it.

Size and Distance

Colors can change the appearance of the size and distance to or from an object or a structure:

- Warm, strong, and bright colors will make an object appear closer and larger. Whites, reds, oranges, and yellows are included in this group.

- Cool colors such as blues, greens, violets, or grays and black will make an object seem farther away and smaller. Colors that are light in value and grayish will also have this effect.
- Colors will also seem softer at a distance where the items are outside the primary visual range of the visitor, such as with ceilings, corridors, and large exhibition spaces.

Taste

Studies have also shown that our perception of sweetness is driven by color: brown and pink candies were judged to be quite sweet, while green and blue candy seemed to be more tart. Some studies have shown that our taste buds engage better when we see red, orange, or yellow.

Time

Color can change a person's concept of time. Cool colors tend to slow down a visitor, and people seem to be more willing to take the time to study an exhibit. For warm colors, the exact opposite is the case.

Restaurateurs are masters of time-color concepts. Cheap eateries that thrive on a fast turnover, and want their customers to eat and run, tend to use orange in their color schemes. On the other hand, expensive restaurants desiring their guests to stay, relax, and spend a lot of money prefer maroons and browns.

Design Consideration

When anticipating an overwhelming visitation, a warm color scheme consisting of bright red and orange could assist in moving the visitors through the exhibition.

Trendy Colors

The old adage "here today, gone tomorrow" can apply to colors that are in vogue one day and out the next. It is wise for planners/designers to be alert to color trends, because they do convey important messages and can pinpoint a time period, social status, and sometimes even a location.

Design Considerations

Trendy colors that were popular during a historic period can be used successfully to indicate a particular time frame. For example, a Victorian palette would consist of dark, warm colors that reflect the era known as the "Brown Decades." A typical combination of shades of brown, black, and a subdued red-orange would be perfect for this time period. While colors such as robin's-egg blue, candy red, flamingo pink, mint green, black, and white could easily denote the 1950s.

When preparing a permanent installation, the use of current, trendy colors should be avoided. Although these colors will seem exciting on opening day, they will date the exhibit and could in part be responsible for its quick obsolescence.

Design Issues

When designing a color scheme, there are some basic considerations pertaining to the visitors' needs and the exhibition's requirements. Unless otherwise intended, visitors should never be confused, conflicted, or endangered by the colors that you have selected. And a good color palette must not only support the aims and ambiance of the exhibition but also pace and direct the visitors through the exhibition areas. In most cases, particularly in historically based exhibitions, the colors should inform the visitor about the who, when, and where of the exhibition's theme.

Color can be an important factor in establishing the proper ambiance and in immersing the visitor in a particular time frame, location, or social and economic environment. It can also be used to create a charged atmosphere or a quiet study area.

Display Items

Whether a display item is wall hung, freestanding, or in a case, visitors should first see the artifact before they become aware of the color that surrounds it. A general rule is that a light-colored display item will stand out if its background color is either darker than the artifact or a muted or recessive color such as gray, deep tan, brown, or greenish and bluish gray. However, when the artifact is dark or brightly colored, it is best to accent it by surrounding it with colors such as cream, beige, or gray.

The size and appearance of an artifact also influence the color selection. The larger and more attractive a display item is, the more it will draw attention and stand out. Conversely, the smaller and duller an artifact appears, the easier it can be overlooked. Yet, an item that might otherwise be ignored can easily be made to attract attention by spotlighting it, isolating it from other artifacts, placing it on a brightly colored base, or surrounding it with muted colors.

When selecting a background color to highlight an artifact or a display, it is helpful if the color, artifact, and illumination are observed together so that the background color can be critiqued.

Design Consideration

There are times, however, when an artifact should not stand out, which is when it is part of a historical, ecological, or archeological exhibit and the setting surrounding the item is of equal importance.

Pacing and Guiding

The larger the exhibition, the more need there is to guide the visitors. Like stepping stones along a path, bright colors can attract the visitors' attention and lead them systematically through an exhibition or a graphic panel. Accent colors can also be used to focus attention on an important area or a starting point.

Site Orientation

Most color schemes should be site oriented. An exhibit whose focus is the Antarctic should reflect the colors of that area and be different from an exhibition that deals with a rain forest or colonial Boston.

Types of Exhibits

Although most color palettes reflect the theme and the story line, they should also suggest and foster the following:

- The who, when, and where of historic exhibits
- The type of habitat for environmental and nature exhibits
- The atmosphere for scientific and technical exhibits

Weight and Balance

Color can easily affect the visual weight and the perceived stability of a display structure and the balance of exhibit graphics. The term "weight of color" depends on the color value and the size of the area that it occupies.

According to its position on the value scale, a color will appear to be either light or heavy. A color that is high on the value scale, such as a white or a yellow, will seem to be lighter in visual weight than black or dark blue that are of a lower value (see figures 3.13 and 3.14).

When striving for the proper color weight and balance for an exhibit case, base, graphics, or display items, the following are helpful considerations. In the illustrations in figure 3.5, figure A indicates a good exhibit structure order with the dark, stable color at the bottom (base), working up to the medium (artifact and vitrine) and light (header) colors. Figure B is a good typographical order with attention being put at the top (title) and working down to the medium color that contains the prime text and visuals, to the light area that is usually reserved for secondary information. Figures C and D seem to be haphazard, and care will be needed to give them the proper balance and stability.

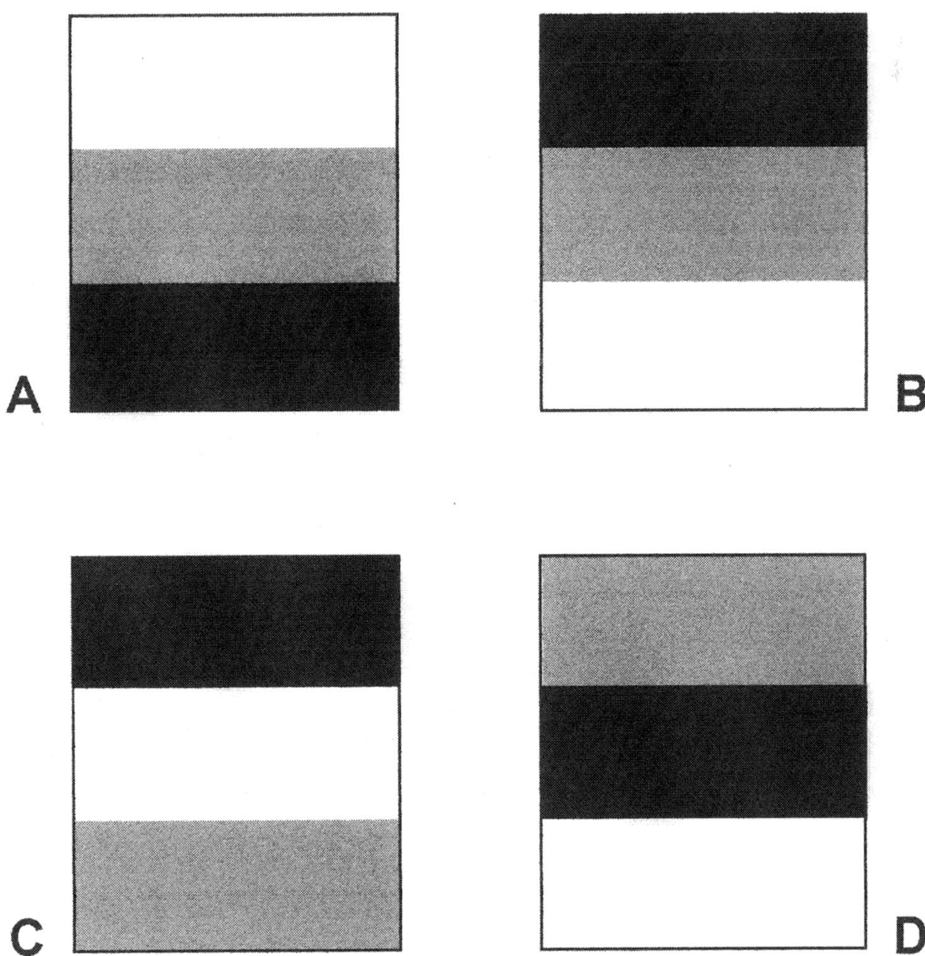

Figure 3.5. Weight and balance. Source: "Principles of Design" by Faber Birren.

Design Considerations

When visually balancing an exhibit area, the size of the space can be a major concern. If it is a large area with light-colored walls containing few exhibit bases and cases, a good solution is to increase the perceived weight of the display structures by finishing them in dark gray, black, or brown. Conversely, if it is a small room with light-colored walls and numerous exhibit structures, finishing them in white, light gray, or tan can visually unify and balance the space and lessen the cluttered look.

A display case containing a base, vitrine, and header can lack stability if these units are of different sizes, shapes, materials, and colors. No matter how diverse its parts, a display structure should be designed so that it appears to be well balanced and stable.

Color Harmony

Harmony is where all colors work together to create a sense of order. It is achieved by designing a color scheme that is attractive, well balanced, visually interesting, and pleasing to the eye. Color harmony should also be compatible with all aspects of a project, including the subjects, display techniques, logos, signs, graphics, advertising, and fund-raising materials.

When lecturing on "Color Harmony: Theories and Principles," I could always "read" the minds of the exhibition design students. For no matter what I said, or how I said it, I knew that they felt this subject was unimportant and fervently wished the lecture would end so they could return to their design projects. I always understood how they felt, since I remember that when I was a student the lectures on color harmony seemed to be totally boring and filled with information that I would never use. Wrong! The color theories and principles that I learned as an undergrad have become one of my most important design tools and have always been the basis for developing my color schemes and selecting the color palette for every exhibit.

Primary and Secondary Colors

Also called basic colors, primary and secondary colors are the foundation for the color wheel that Johannes Itten developed in the mid-1900s. His classification system consists of the colors that occur when a light wave is broken up by a prism and produces red, orange, yellow, green, blue, and violet color rays sequentially.

Primary Colors

As you know, red, yellow, and blue are the primary colors. These are pure hues and cannot be created by combining other colored pigments, dyes, inks, and so forth. Since they are not a combination of other colors, each has its own persona and sends out a strong and distinct message.

Secondary Colors

Orange, green, and violet are the secondary colors. They are made by mixing two primary colors together, and for that reason, their persona is a combination of the traits of the colors that produced them. For example, orange has the attributes of both yellow and red, but like a child who resembles one parent more than the other, the message that a particular orange conveys will depend on the percentage of red or yellow that it contains.

Twelve-Part Color Wheel

The twelve-part color wheel is a wonderful tool for planners/designers to use when developing a color scheme for an exhibition or even a graphic. Any palette based on this wheel will almost certainly be harmonious, pleasing, and well balanced, and it will prevent a scheme from becoming disorganized and confusing.

The twelve-part color wheel illustrated in figure 3.6 establishes a fixed relationship between two or more colors and determines color relationships. This wheel is based on the hue, saturation, and lightness (HSL).

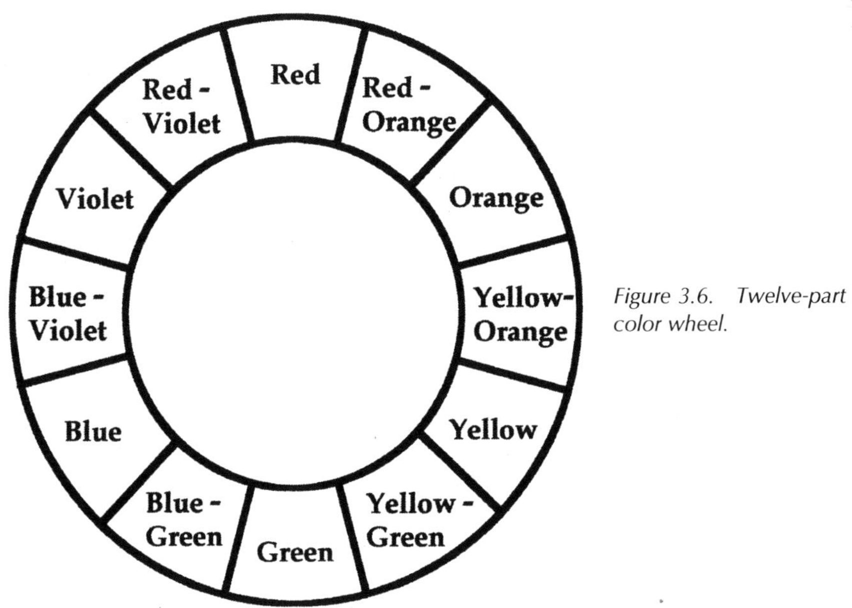

Figure 3.6. Twelve-part color wheel.

Color Harmonies

Working with a particular wheel does not mean that the color scheme has to be restricted to a few intense colors. On the contrary, incorporating the variety of tints and shades inherent in a color enables a designer to produce a palette that will have all the variations that the project requires while still maintaining a harmonious color scheme. The number of colors selected, of course, will depend on the size and complexity of the project. Although there are many color harmonies, the following are used frequently, and all are based on the twelve-part wheel.

Complementary

Complementary harmony consists of two colors: a warm one and its opposite, a cool one. Being opposites, a complementary color scheme is visually powerful and exciting, has the strongest contrast, and draws maximum attention.

Design Consideration A warm color that is used as an accent color such as red, orange, or yellow will create more attention if its complementary color is grayed down.

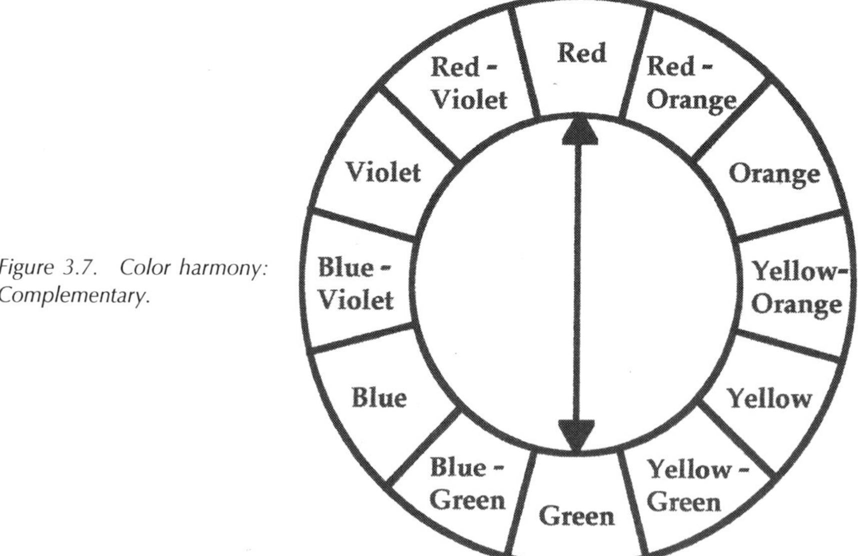

Figure 3.7. Color harmony: Complementary.

Split Complementary

The split complementary color scheme consists of a hue and the two adjacent hues that are next to its complement. It provides high contrast without the strong tension that is imposed by a complementary harmony, and it also offers more variations than a complementary scheme.

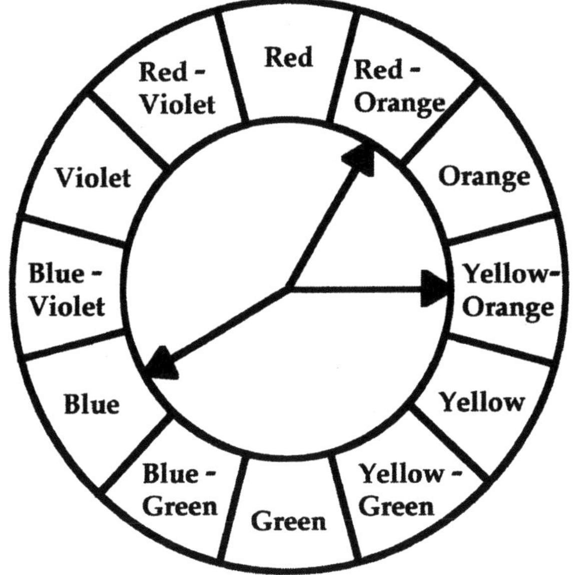

Figure 3.8. Color harmony: Split complementary.

Double Complementary

Consisting of two pairs of complementary colors, double complementary is the richest scheme and offers more variety than any other. This combination is excellent when designing a palette for a large exhibition or one having four equal exhibit areas.

Design Consideration A double complementary scheme is the hardest scheme to work with, since it requires balancing all four colors. If all are used in equal amounts, it is best to choose one to be dominant and to tone down the others. Avoid using pure colors in equal amounts.

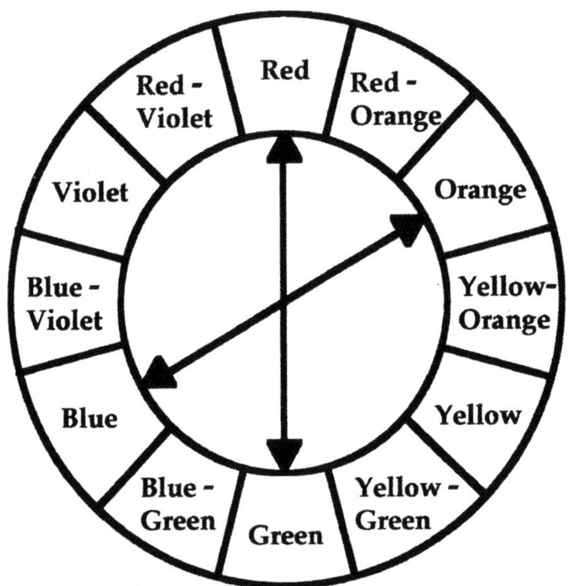

Figure 3.9. Color harmony: Double complementary.

Tetrad Double Complementary

When double complementary colors are evenly spaced on a twelve-part color wheel, it is referred to as a tetrad scheme.

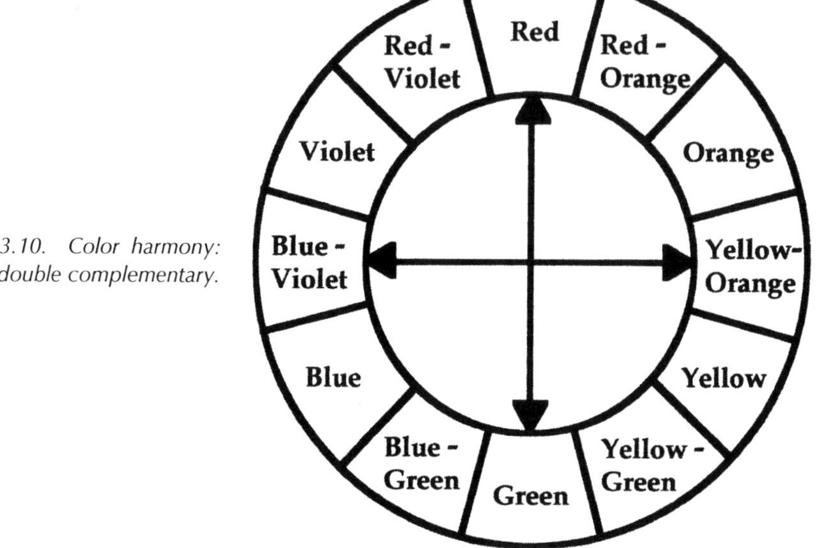

Figure 3.10. Color harmony: Tetrad double complementary.

Monochromatic

Monochromatic color harmony is a combination composed of one hue and a variety of its tints or shades and a variety of its tints or shades (see figures 3.13 and 3.14). Because it has a clean, simple, elegant look, it is an easy scheme to manage and always appears to be balanced and visually appealing. In the cool color range, this harmony is soothing and easy on the eyes. Unlike the complementary schemes, it lacks strong contrast, which can make it difficult to draw attention to a particular item or text. If used in large exhibit areas, it can be boring.

Analogous

The analogous color scheme combines three adjacent colors such as blue-green, blue, and blue-violet. Usually one color is dominant and the other two are subordinate. This scheme is as easy to create as the monochromatic, but it appears richer.

Design Consideration Analogous lacks color contrast. If warm colors are selected, the palette could be too bright and intense, but if cool colors are used, the scheme might become boring and uninteresting.

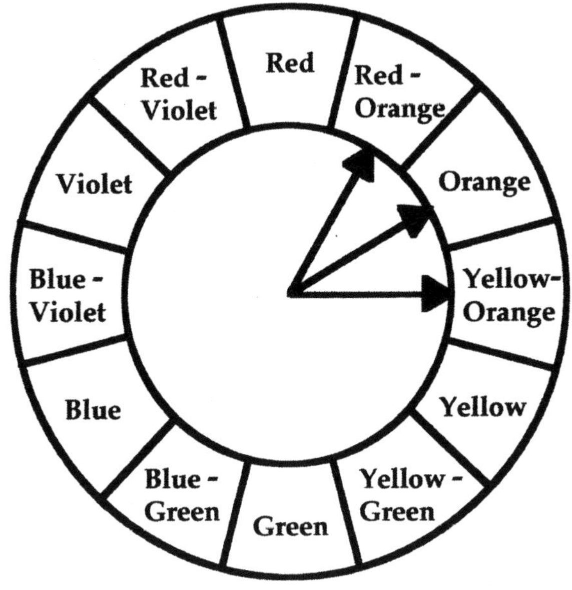

Figure 3.11. Color harmony: Analogous complementary.

Triadic

Consisting of three colors that are evenly spaced on the wheel, the triadic color scheme offers strong, high-visual contrast, while retaining harmony, balance, and richness.

Design Consideration One color should be chosen to be dominant and used as the accent color or in larger amounts. If the three selected colors appear too bright and gaudy together, choose one to be prominent and tint or shade the others.

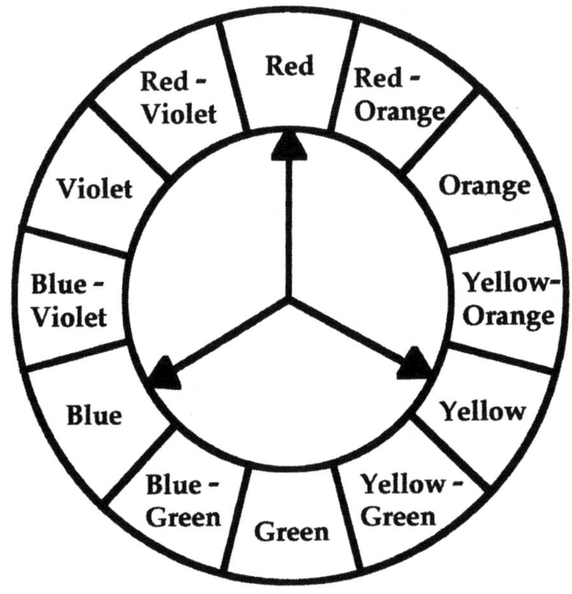

Figure 3.12. Color harmony: Triadic complemntary.

Color Contrasts

Contrasting colors are diametrically opposed to each other and are used to produce maximum contrast while creating a pleasing effect. Designers often use color-contrasting schemes when they need to have a typeface or a display object stand out and be easily perceived. Even though technically they are classified as noncolors, black and white are also considered part of this group. There are various color contrasts.

Complementary Contrast

By their opposing positions on the color wheel, a complementary contrast of two hues will create maximum contrast and when placed next to each other will appear brighter. Red/green, yellow/violet, and blue-green/red-orange are perfect examples of this type of contrast.

Design Consideration

Complementary contrast attracts maximum attention and is excellent for logos, symbols, and accent colors; it should never be used to cover a large area.

Hue Contrast

Hue contrast is a combination of pure, intense, undiluted colors. Some combinations are yellow/blue, red/blue/green, blue/yellow/violet, yellow/green/violet/red, and violet/green/blue/orange/black.

Design Consideration

The number of hues employed will depend on the theme and the size of the project. For example, an exhibit on folk art could employ many contrasting colors, and a palette consisting of four or even five contrasting colors might be used.

Intensity or Saturation Contrast

An intensity or saturation contrast addresses the degree of a color's intensity or saturation. High intensity means that a hue appears bright and is at its purest or unsaturated state. Low intensity refers to a color that has been dulled down and saturated by adding gray, black, or its complement.

Light and Dark Contrast

A light and dark color contrast is the difference between a hue's lightness and darkness. Some examples of this type of contrast are light blue to navy blue, pink to dark red, and white to black.

Design Consideration

This is an excellent combination to use when selecting hues for text and its background.

Color Modification

Colors can change their meaning if they are shaded, tinted, or toned. A red/orange will convey a different impression than red/blue, and of course baby blue and royal blue have two completely different meanings.

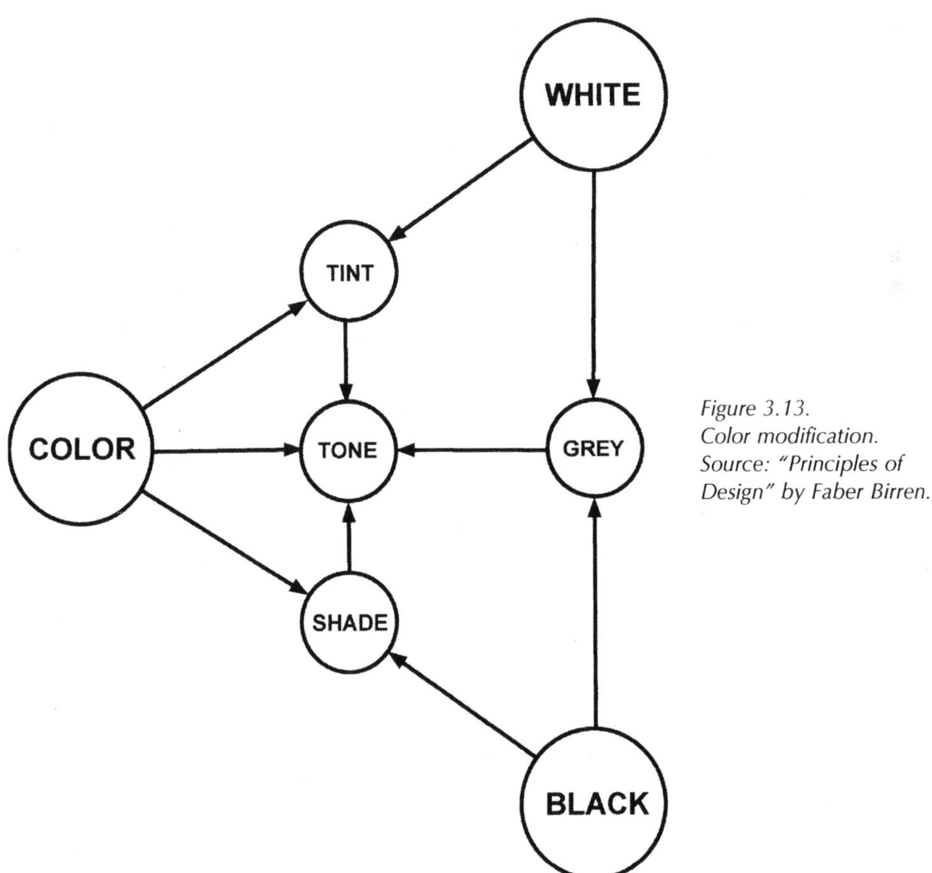

Figure 3.13. Color modification. Source: "Principles of Design" by Faber Birren.

Tint

Tint refers to the lightness of a hue. The degree of lightness depends on how much white has been added to the hue. A few examples of tints are follows:

Lemon is a tint of pure yellow.
Baby blue is a tint of pure blue.
Pink is a tint of pure red.

Shade

Hue + black = shade

Shade refers to the darkness of a color. It occurs when a hue is darkened by adding either black or its dark complementary color. A few examples of shades are as follows:

Burgundy is a shade of pure red.
Rust is a shade of orange.
Forest green is a shade of green.
Navy blue is a shade of pure blue.

Design Consideration

Shading is an easy method to establish an overall mood. It can be used successfully in small exhibit areas, but in large areas it might become boring.

Tone

Hue + complementary color = tone

Tone is a hue that becomes softer by mixing it with its complementary color or gray. Blue-gray, greenish-gray, and rose are all colors that have been toned down.

Value Scale

In most cases, professionals involved in exhibit design and construction rely heavily on the commonly used Munsell eleven-step color value scale. This scale starts with number 0 white and ends at number 10 black. Over the years, many different value scales have been developed, and it is prudent when discussing color value to make sure that all parties are referring to the Munsell scale. In Munsell's eleven-step value scale, each

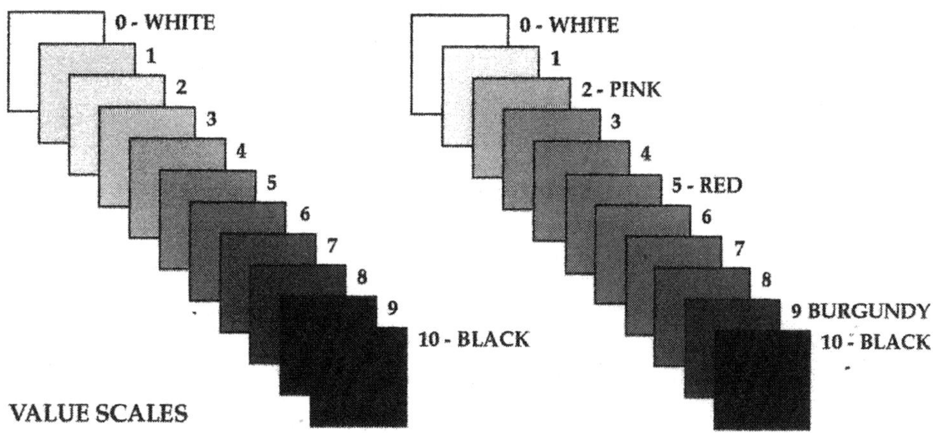

Figure 3.14. Value scales.

pure color is assigned a numbered place, but depending on the intensity of the color its place on the scale varies. For example, pure red and blue have values of five, while a pure yellow is placed at two.

Interaction

A color is never an island unto itself. Whether it is a letter on a sign, an artifact on a base, or a painting on a wall, every item that you design or place is affected by the colors that are in close proximity to it. Therefore, it is the size of the area that a hue covers and its intensity, position, and relationship with surrounding hues that are important design considerations.

Assimilation

Assimilation occurs when colors take the hue of those colors that surround it. For example, a white square on a red background will take on a reddish cast, while the same white square on a blue background will appear bluish.

Modulation

Colors that are not complementary or of the same intensity can modulate and soften each other, as in the following examples:

- Red can become dimmer and softer when it is next to violet or orange.
- A light or a pale color will seem lighter or paler if it is next to or surrounded by a dark color.

- Deep or bright colors can cancel the impact of a paler one and make the pale color seem even weaker.
- A bright color can appear weaker if it is close to or surrounded by a brighter one.

Design Consideration

Backgrounds and surrounding colors will affect the color of an object. A beautiful pale blue vase shown against a bright blue background could make the vase seem paler, washed out, and less attractive; a soft gray-blue or an off-white background would probably be a better solution.

Intensity

When placed side by side, complementary and bright colors will enhance and intensify each other. For example, a red square placed next to a green square of the same size will make both colors more brilliant than if they had been viewed separately.

Color Models

There are so many colors available that giving each a name would be an overwhelming task. For that reason, models have been developed that identify each color and relate it to all the others.

Color models are systems used to identify a wide range of colors based on the primary colors. Choosing which model to use generally depends on whether you are involved with painted surfaces, graphic inks, or lighting effects. Most times exhibition projects require the use of one or all of the following systems.

HSL Color Model

The HSL color model is an acronym for hue, saturation, and lightness. Traditionally a favorite of artists, exhibition designers, and exhibit builders, this model is one of the oldest systems in use and is based on the absorption and reflection of three pure pigments: red, yellow, and blue. It is also referred to as RYB, meaning red, yellow, and blue. This model is divided into twelve colors in three categories:

- Primary colors: red, yellow, and blue
- Secondary colors: orange, green, and violet

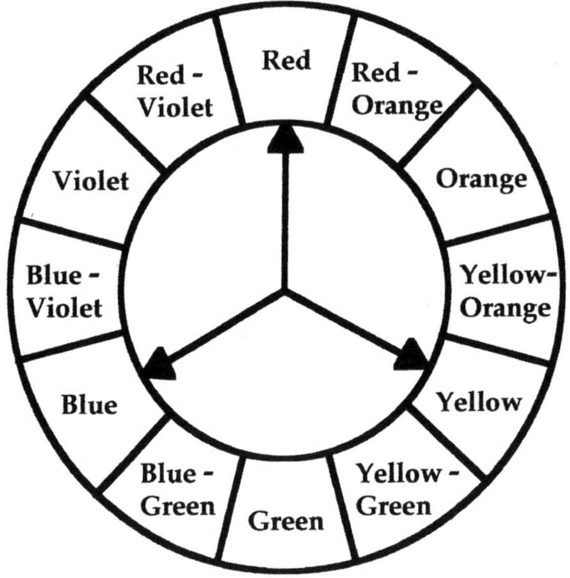

Figure 3.15. Color model: HSL.

- Tertiary colors: red-orange, red-violet, yellow-green, yellow-orange, blue-green, and blue-violet

CMYK Color Model

Based on printing processes and printers' inks, the CMYK color model is an acronym for cyan, magenta, yellow, and black. Black was added to

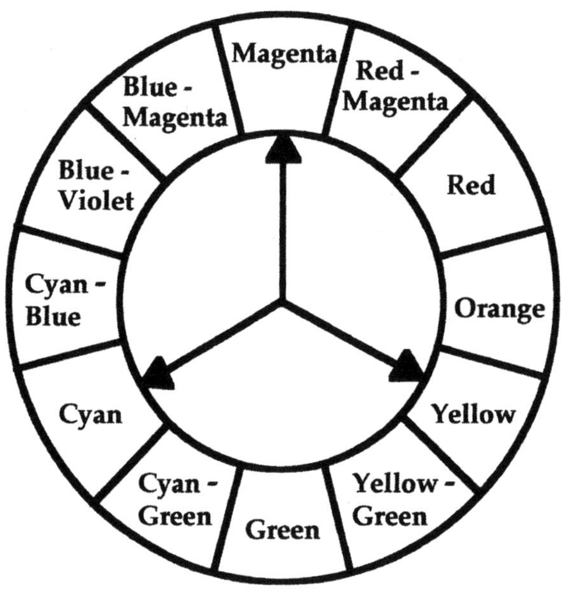

Figure 3.16. Color model: CMYK.

the model since these colors do not combine to make it. The letter *K* is derived from the German *kohl,* meaning black.

CMYK is based on the theory that when white light strikes a printed page, some of the color waves are absorbed or subtracted by the ink. The color that you see, therefore, comes only from the reflected waves. Many computer printers and traditional "four-color" printing presses use this model. Also referred to as the scientific color model or the subtractive color model, CMYK consists of the following:

- Primary colors: cyan, magenta, and yellow, plus black
- Secondary colors: red, blue-violet, and green
- Tertiary colors: red-magenta, orange, yellow-green, cyan-green, cyan-blue, blue- magenta

RGB Color Model

The RGB color model is an acronym for red, green, and blue. Based on mixing light, rather than on mixing inks or pigments, this system is used mainly when designing a lighting system or computer-generated graphics. RGB is also referred to as the additive color model.

In theory, if you take three flashlights, one with a red lens, one with a green lens, and one with a blue lens, and shine them all on a black wall at the same time, the three colors would form white when mixed in equal amounts. Light-based color-reproduction equipment such as video, film,

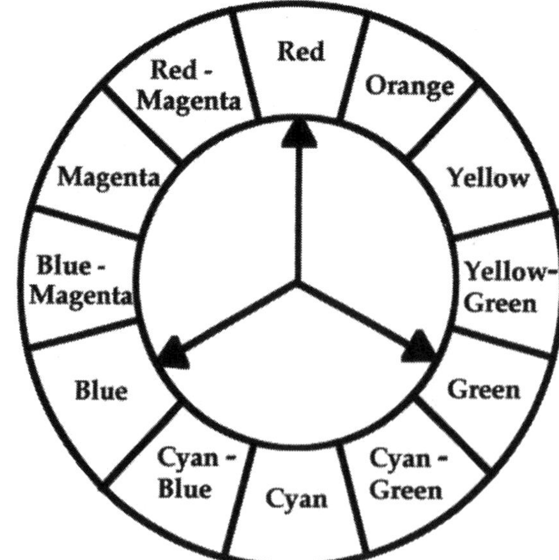

Figure 3.17. Color model: RGB.

monitor displays, color scanners, digital cameras, television, and theatrical lighting use the RGB color model:

- Primary colors: red, green, and blue
- Secondary colors: magenta, yellow, cyan
- Tertiary colors: red-magenta, orange, yellow-green, cyan-green, cyan-blue, blue- magenta

Additive and Subtractive

When studying color, the words "additive" and "subtractive" appear, and it is important to know how they relate to the above color models.

Additive

An additive color method is based on focusing and mixing colored and white light beams on a black background. The RGB color model (light) is an additive color system. Additive color mixing begins with a black background, and by overlapping colored light beams the mixture will become almost white.

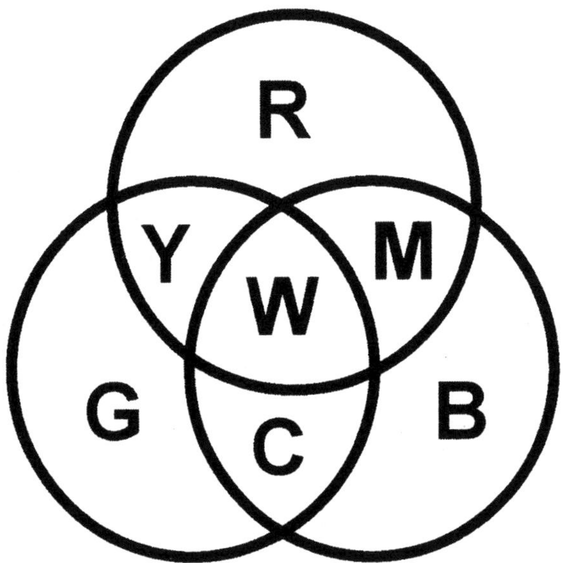

Figure 3.18. Additive color model.

Subtractive

Also called reflective, the subtractive color method is based on the absorption and the reflection of light rays on a white background, employing either pigment or ink. Both color models HSL (pigment) and CMYK (ink)

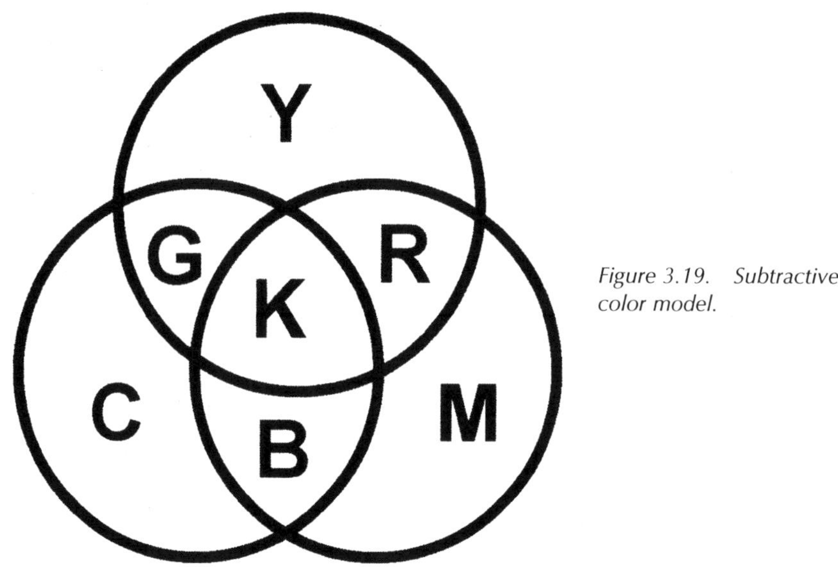

Figure 3.19. Subtractive color model.

are subtractive colors. Subtractive mixing means that one begins with a white background, and by adding colors, the mixture becomes darker until it reaches black.

PMS Color System

The PMS color system is an acronym for Pantone Matching System. The Pantone Matching System is the standardized international system used by planners/designers when specifying colors and by exhibit construction firms when finishing their exhibits. It is compatible with both the HSL and the CMYK color models.

Perception

We are encapsulated in a world of whites, blacks, and grays. Sunflowers that we see as having beautiful yellow petals, deep brown centers, and rich green leaves are actually shades of gray, and it is the light source and our eyes and brain working together that change our boring gray world into a smorgasbord of wonderful colors.

Our eyes and our brain create the colors that we experience. For that reason, each museum visitor is physiologically unique and interprets the same hue somewhat differently. When preparing a palette, planners/designers must understand our metamorphic, colored world and know certain truths:

- How we see color and understand its origin
- Why each person interprets the same color differently
- How, when, and why an object will change its color
- Why sharp details at times appear fuzzy
- Why we can't see color in the dark
- Why there is such a variety of colors

Light Waves

Light is transmitted in the form of vibrating waves, and it is these waves that allow us to perceive an object's color. Sunlight and most forms of artificial illumination are composed of light waves that appear to be colorless until they are broken up by a prism and become a spectrum of pure colors that we can see.

When referring to light, the terms "light beam," "pencil," "light ray," and "light waves" are commonly used. The following are simple definitions meant to explain a very complicated process:

- Light beam: A large volume of light that is composed of an infinite number of light rays divided into pencils.
- Pencil: A narrow beam of light that is divided into light rays.
- Light ray: The narrowest and smallest portion of a pencil; contains vibrating, colorless light waves. The infinite variation in the percent-

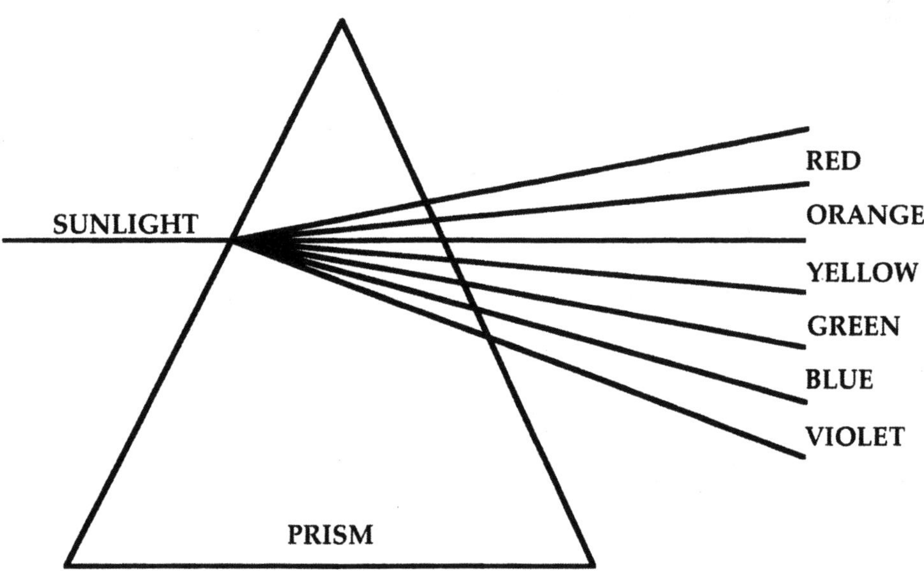

Figure 3.20. Perception light waves.

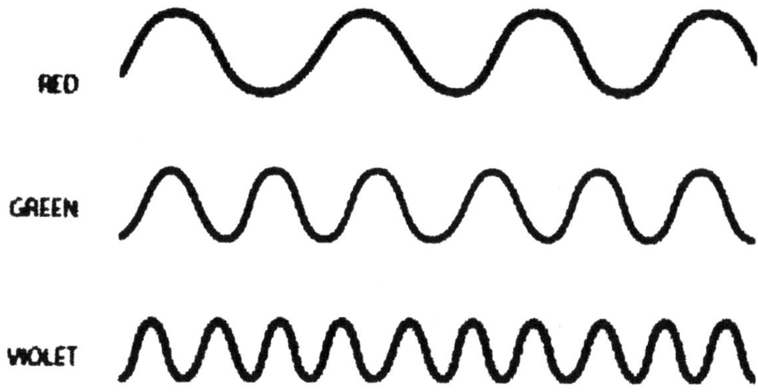

Figure 3.21. Perception wavelength. Source: NASA.

age of light rays entering our eyes at any one time is responsible for our seeing an immense array of colors.

- Light waves: Light is transmitted in the form of vibrating waves.

From Light to Color

As has been noted above, it is amazing that the colorful flowers and trees that we see are in reality just gray objects, and it is because of the way that our eyes and our brain function and the bright sunlight surrounding us that they are magically transformed into an array of beautiful colors. Yet as the sunlight diminishes, their colors gradually fade, until they become just dark silhouettes with soft, fuzzy outlines, devoid of details. Due to this phenomenon, the type and intensity of the exhibit lighting that is chosen will have a major impact on the objects and the colors that we view. The journey from our gray world to our colored one is an amazing trip that starts when the following occurs:

1. A light beam is emitted from a light source.
2. The rays from a light beam hit an object, and some rays are absorbed, while others are reflected and enter the eye through the pupil.
3. The pupil focuses these light waves onto the back of the retina.
4. The rods and cones, part of the basic structure of the eye, located at the back of the retina, are stimulated by the various vibrating light waves and interpret each wave to be a particular color.
5. Via the optical nerve these color impulses travel to the brain.
6. The brain then analyzes these impulses and tells us about a particular object's color, form, and details.

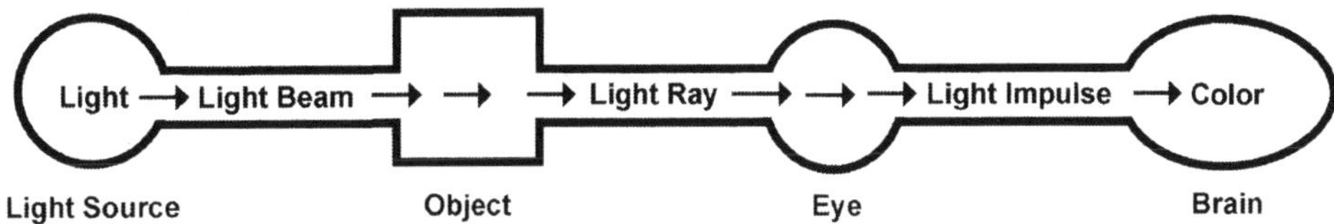

Figure 3.22. From light to color.

Eye

The eye is like a camera: both have black interiors through which light waves are directed to the back of the retina or to the film. Blackness prevents the waves from reflecting and bouncing around. Obviously, the eye plays a major role in how we interpret color and form, and is an important consideration when selecting colors and specifying illumination.

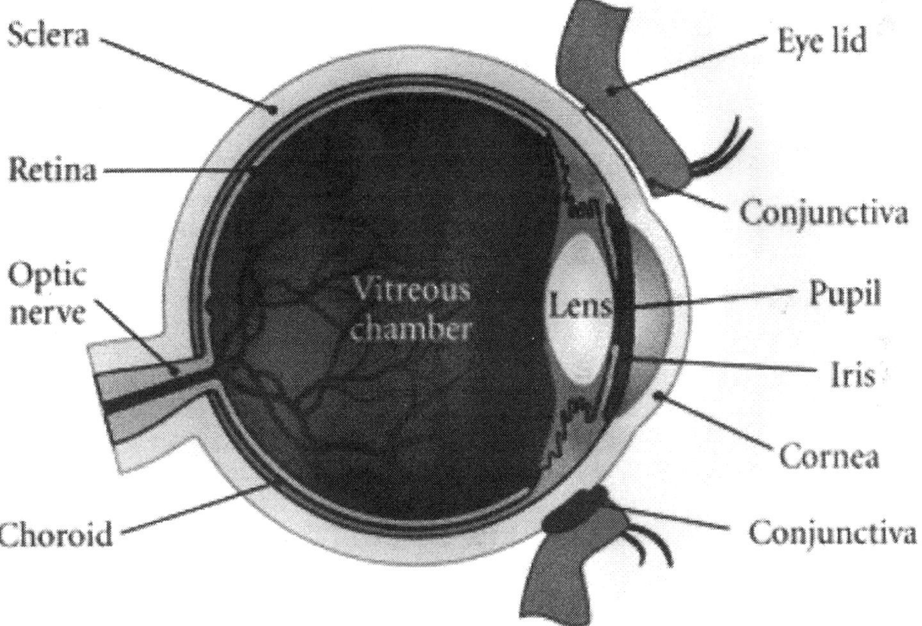

Figure 3.23. The eye. Courtesy of the National Institutes of Health, National Eye Institute.

Iris and Pupil

The iris is a shutter similar to that in a camera, and the pupil is the round, black opening in the center of the iris that allows light waves to enter. Thanks to the ability of the iris to open and close, and the pupil's ability to expand and contract, the amount of light entering the eye is controlled. This has the advantage of enabling us to adjust to a dimly or a brightly lit environment.

A person needs approximately twenty to thirty minutes to adapt fully from bright sunlight to complete darkness, and five minutes from darkness to bright light. When planning/designing exhibits and graphics, the time needed for a visitor to comfortably and safely adapt to light changes should be carefully considered. Needless to say, sudden changes in light levels are to be avoided since they can be dangerous.

Design Consideration

When graphics or exhibits are near the entrance to a museum they should be adjusted to the local light level. For example, visitors at a sunny seashore when entering a darkened museum need time for their eye levels to adjust. In this case, the displays should have high color (black and white) contrast, large images and typeface, and a minimum amount of text. Flooring and wall colors should also be light colored.

Lens

The lenses in our eyes are amazing, for they allow us to see at great distances, focus on a pinpoint, and make changes quickly, effortlessly, and without much thought. Located behind the iris and the pupil, the lens has two main purposes:

1. To focus light waves onto the retina.
2. To adjust to near or distant vision; this is called accommodation.

Unfortunately, as people age, their lenses turn yellow, they usually become sensitive to glare, and they experience a decrease in depth perception and color discrimination.

Retina

Our ability to see occurs in the retina that lines the interior of the eye. The back of the retina contains photoreceptors called rods and cones. Rods interpret forms, whites, grays, and black, and the cones interpret colors. Both photoreceptors send their impulses to the brain. The brain then interprets each impulse to be a particular color or detail. In figure 3.24, the rod is shown on the left and the cone is to the right.

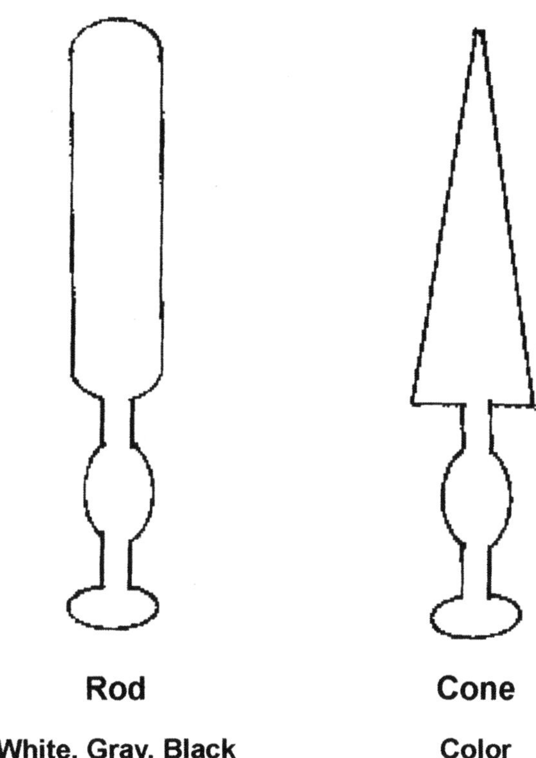

Figure 3.24. Rod and cone. Source: National Eye Institute and Washington University School of Medicine.

Rods

Rods interpret forms, shapes, and textures and allow us to see white, gray, and black. Several rods are connected to a single nerve, and when our cones are inactive, our rods remain active, thus enabling us to see even in very dim light. At that time, objects are devoid of sharp details, blend together, and lack color. Each eye contains about 120 million rods.

Cones

Cones are responsible for our seeing a wonderful array of colors, finely detailed objects, and precise images. They are light sensitive, analyze and interpret each light ray that enters our eyes, and identify it as a specific color. Each cone is connected to a single optical nerve.

There are three types of cones: some sensitive to red, some to yellow, and some to blue. All are active and used extensively during daylight or in highly illuminated areas. However, as the light dims, they gradually become dormant; red cones are the first to become inactive, next yellow, and finally blue. Some sources refer to yellow cones as yellowish-green or green cones. Each eye contains about six million cones.

Fovea

Located at the back of the retina, the fovea is in a direct path behind the center of the eye. It is the region of highest visual sharpness and where most of our cones are situated. For additional information, see the section "Frontal and Peripheral Vision" below.

Afterimages

These are optical illusions that appear once the original color is removed, and we then "see" its complementary color. When we stare at a color image for about twenty to sixty seconds, and quickly look away to a blank space, we will observe the same form but often in its complementary color. An afterimage is also called a "ghost image."

This phenomenon is attributed to eye fatigue that occurs when a color image is large and intense, such as a brightly colored display case or typeface. In such cases, the small movements of the eye that usually rest cannot relax, and the eye becomes tired.

Age and Distance

How rapidly and easily a visitors' eyes can react to abrupt changes in viewing distance usually depends on their age. Most young people can easily make this adjustment, since their lenses are more flexible than the elderly's. As noted above, with aging, our lenses gradually harden, and our ability to shift from near to far is impaired. For the elderly, abrupt change in viewing distance can be inconvenient, tiring, disorienting, and even dangerous.

Color and Distance

The visibility of an object depends on its color and its distance from the viewer. Each group of cones in the eye reacts differently to distance. Yellow cones allow us to see yellow objects at the greatest viewing distance, next are red, and last are blue.

Design Consideration

Yellow is mainly the color of choice for displaying objects, structures, cutout letters, text, and the like, that must be seen from a distance. Orange followed by red can also be used for this purpose, but those colors are not as effective as yellow. Because they need to be seen at a distance, yellow has always been a popular choice for life preservers.

Frontal and Peripheral Vision

When facing an object directly, we see its colors and details more clearly than if we viewed the same object using our peripheral vision. This phenomenon occurs because our frontal vision relies mainly on our cones, while our peripheral or side vision employs mostly our rods.

When desiring a clear visual image, it is still location, location, location. Cones produce our sharpest vision because they are positioned in the back of the eye, where our vision is most acute. Rods, on the other hand, are located on the back and sides of the retina, which produces a blurry image with softer colors. See figure 3.24.

Design Consideration

For visitors to appreciate a colorful, well-detailed item, it should be placed directly in front of them, thus employing their frontal vision. However, when a display item is used for ambiance, such as a rock, a plant, or an architectural element, and is not meant for study purposes, placing the object so that the visitor only views it peripherally is acceptable.

Optical Blending and Layering

Why do some objects vibrate and shimmer and others do not? This is because one has optically blended paints and the other a layered finish. The following blending and layering techniques are based on the finishes used for exhibit structures.

Optical Blending

Optical blending occurs when various colored light rays strike the retina at the same time; our eyes blend these rays together, and we see only one color. When red and yellow are blended or mixed together, they send an orange impression to the brain. Whether it is a red-orange or a yellow-orange will depend on the percentage of blended color rays. Blending is also referred to as glazing.

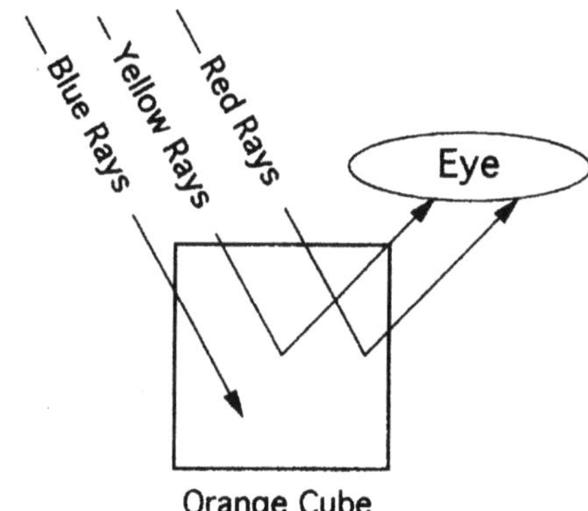

Figure 3.25. Perception: Optical blending.

Optical Layering

Layering occurs when one color is placed over another, thus allowing each color wave to enter the eye a nanosecond apart. In this situation, the viewer will see each color separately, and the object will seem to vibrate and shimmer. For example, by applying red paint over a yellow surface, each color will be reflected separately. The viewer will see red followed by yellow, and the object will appear to be alive and fiery.

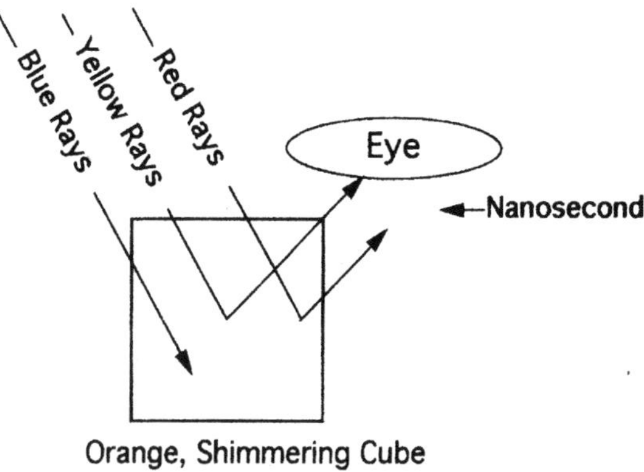

Figure 3.26. Perception: Optical layering, shimmering.

Monet was a master at employing the optical layering technique. He created cool, green landscapes that actually seemed to vibrate and radiate. Even though the viewers felt that they were looking at a wonderful green landscape, they were unaware that below the surface lay purples, blues, yellows, and even reds ready to bombard their eyes and make his green vegetation seem to be alive and shimmering.

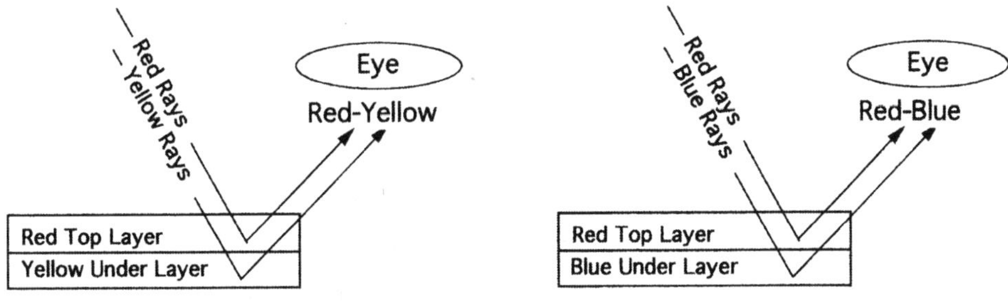

Figure 3.27. Perception: Optical layering.

> **CASE HISTORY: "SUBSTRATES CAN BLEED THROUGH"**
>
> As long as the subsurface color is not removed, it will always reflect or "bleed through." I once knew of a situation where new white panels were being combined with existing red ones. Each time the old panels were painted white, the red undercolor reflected and produced a pinkish cast. After seven frustrating attempts at repainting, the panels were discarded, and new white ones were ordered.

Design Consideration

When reusing exhibit materials, be very careful. If an existing display panel is yellow and another blue, and you wish to refinish both panels in red, the repainted yellow panel will become reddish yellow, while the blue panel will appear to be reddish blue. For that reason, when reusing exhibit materials, it is advantageous to sand and to paint them with the same undercoat, so that they will be identical.

Light

> Light is existential for all of us. As well as its biological effects, it shows us reality in constantly changing ways, thus offering a number of visual impressions that affect our perception emotionally. Light is with us night and day and makes life possible.
>
> —Max Keller, *Light Fantastic*

Illumination is essential to the success of any museum exhibit design, and it should never be overlooked or undervalued. Depending on the type of lighting system employed it can affect the visitor both physiologically and psychologically, modify the colors of a display item or area, and alter the exhibition's ambiance.

Light Design Phases: Special Considerations

Preliminary and Intermediate Phases
  Research illumination techniques.
  Commence selecting light fixtures.
Final and Documentation Phases
  Select, specify, and locate all light fixtures.
  Lay out illumination reflected ceiling plan.
Construction Phase
  Verify that the lighting fixtures are as specified.
Installation Phase
  Inspect the lighting system to ensure that it is as specified and that the fixtures are properly located and installed.

Absorption and Reflection

Why is it that objects, like the cubes illustrated in figure 3.28, all of the same size, material, and finish, are identical in almost every way except that one appears red, another blue, and the other yellow? The answer is found in the fact that each object has a surface finish that allows it to selectively absorb and reflect different vibrating light waves. It is these reflected waves that enter the eye and tell us the color of that particular object.

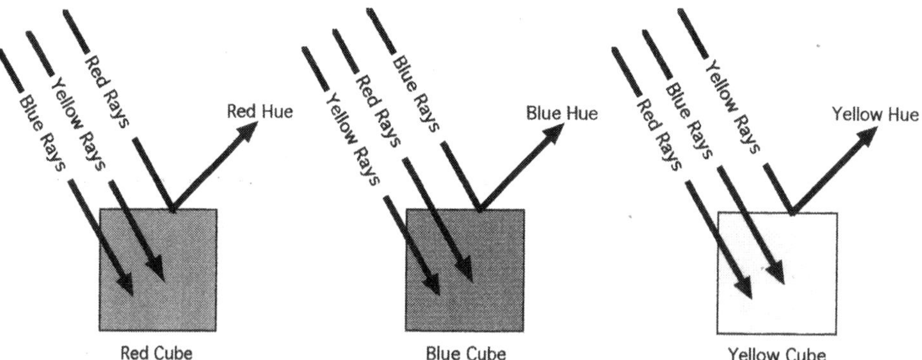

Figure 3.28. Absorption and reflection: Colored objects.

A white object will reflect all color rays and absorb none, while a black one will absorb all color waves and reflect none. Gray forms absorb and reflect both white and black waves.

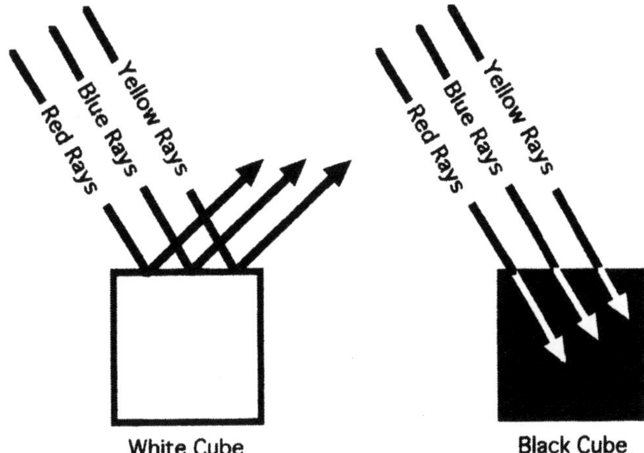

Figure 3.29. Absorption and reflection: Black-and-white objects.

Design Considerations

Why did the beautiful white exhibit structure turn pink when placed next to a red one? This was caused by the red rays reflecting from the structure onto the white one.

Rays from existing building features, such as floor covering, ceiling tile, and wall finish, with strong or deep-colored finishes (e.g., red, browns, or purples) can adversely reflect on a display structure. If this condition exists, it might be prudent to avoid placing white or light-colored exhibits nearby.

What is outside a building can be readily reflected inside, and these reflections can change the colors of your displays. Windows, especially the huge ones often found in many environmental and visitor centers, can

CASE HISTORY: "WHY DID THE YELLOW TURN GREEN?"

Once a colleague telephoned me in distress. She had specified that the walls of a room be a beautiful clear yellow, only to discover that when painted they became a bilious, greenish yellow. Two more times the room was painted, and each time the same strong greenish tint appeared.

What had happened? Well, the room had large windows overlooking a dense grove of trees just outdoors. The green from the trees was reflecting on the yellow walls inside giving them a greenish cast.

What could be done to rectify the situation? Cover the windows or change the color of the walls? After testing a warm beige at the site, she concluded that the green rays did not adversely affect her new choice, and the room was painted beige.

prove to be major problems. The light rays from those gorgeous green trees outside the windows can transmit a greenish cast and adversely affect the exhibit colors that you have selected.

Activity

Humans cannot respond to fixed stimuli for an extended period of time. Therefore, it is important to pace visitors at an exhibition and to balance the active and the tranquil areas. A color scheme should also be compatible with the type of visitor activity that a particular learning experience requires. A charged atmosphere is ideal for active and participatory displays, and in this instance warm colors would be a good choice. However, for study areas and exhibits that need concentration and time, cool colors ought to be considered.

Advancing and Receding

When two identical blocks, one red, the other blue, are next to each other, the red block will appear to come forward and seem larger, while the blue block will seem to recede and appear to be smaller.

Warm colors (red, yellow, and orange) are advancing colors; cool colors (green, blue, and violet) are receding ones. Even though green is classified as a receding color, since it is composed partially of yellow, a green item will actually appear to advance and come closer than a blue one.

Why Does This Happen?

Each type of cone in the eye differs in its ability to cause objects to appear to advance or recede. When light hits our red cones, a red object will seem to come forward and stand out; conversely, light hitting our blue cones will make a blue object appear to recede and become less prominent.

Design Consideration

Sometimes the need to bring an artifact forward visually when it is in a group of similar items can create a dilemma. A good solution is to place that artifact near a warm advancing color and surround the remaining items with cool receding colors.

Conservation

Often the decision to display an artifact can hinge on whether the intensity of its light source might destroy it. This concern is especially important when an item relies on fine detailing and gorgeous colors to be fully appreciated and when its beauty and visual impact would be lost if it was displayed in a dimly lit environment in order to conserve it.

Light Direction

The way an object is illuminated and the direction of the light affect not only its color but also its apparent size. For example, a cube will appear smaller when light hits it directly; the illuminated side will appear to be bright, while the unlighted sides will have darker shades. Conversely, a base that is illuminated equally on all surfaces will seem larger.

Figure 3.30 illustrates how a light source, either natural or artificial, can change the visual size of an object. The cube on the left has a strong light source, while the cube on the right doesn't.

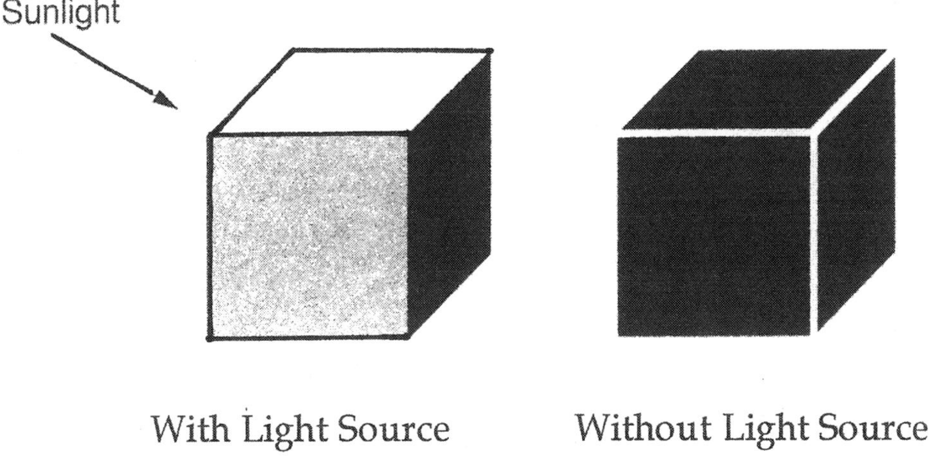

Figure 3.30. Light directions.

Design Considerations

Display bases or cases that are visually too large can be made to appear smaller if the light source is directed so that only one side is illuminated and the others are in shadow.

A large structure can appear smaller if its surfaces are painted different colors, for instance, front and back, tan; and the sides, brown.

Improper lighting can flatten out an artifact, make it seem dull, and produce shadows so that its intricate detailing becomes unrecognizable.

Down lighting can also create the "Frankenstein look" and transform a bust of an admired historic figure into a sinister one.

Figure 3.31. Illumination: Frankenstein look. © Chris Harvey.

Light Levels

Illumination can affect visitors and have an impact on what they see and experience. Many of us have been in museums after hours when the light levels are very low. At these times, the exhibit rooms are dark and gloomy, the artifacts always seem to be devoid of detail and color, and the experience can be depressing.

Light levels can also affect our mood. A brightly lighted area can stimulate us, and usually we become upbeat and happy. Conversely, in a dimly lighted area, we seem to be more relaxed, calm, and sometimes even pensive. Also, as the lighting gradually changes from bright to dim, our ability to see fine details deteriorates. As it continues to fade, a beautiful vase with fine detailing will slowly become a dark, blurry object.

As previously discussed, light levels can also affect our ability to interpret color. In bright light we experience an array of beautiful colors from brilliant reds and yellows to deep blues. As the light dims, however, colors change, and that bright red vase gradually becomes a deep burgundy and finally appears to be black. As the light fades, colors do not diminish at the same rate. Red is the first color that we cannot recognize, then yellow, and finally in very dim light only blue can be perceived. Just before the light is extinguished, everything will appear to be a deep gray or black.

Natural light is constantly changing and can become a planner / designer's nightmare. As noted above, this is especially critical when the exhibit space contains windows or is located outside. Weather (foggy, rainy, and sunny), seasons (spring, summer, fall, and winter), site location (Alaska, New York, or Texas), and time of day (11:00 a.m., noon, or 5:00 p.m.) all contribute to color change. For example, on a bright sunny day a red display case will appear to be red-yellow, which, if it is cloudy and overcast, could become blue-red. And you can also rest assured that a bright red color selected at an East Coast design office will appear to be a significantly different red when it is installed at the exhibit site in the South.

Design Considerations

It is best to select and test a color scheme at the actual exhibition site and under the same lighting conditions that will prevail during exhibition hours.

Lighting has many applications and can be used for aesthetic, practical, and safety purposes. Designing a lighting system is a complicated subject best left to professionals. Having said that, most times, because of budget restrictions, the exhibit planner / designer has to design and specify the lighting systems.

One reason that we go to museums is to connect with the people of past civilizations. To a great degree, this link can be established by observing an object's true colors, and by duplicating, as closely as possible, its original lighting conditions.

CASE HISTORY: "COLOR ACCURACY IS IMPORTANT"

When viewing an exhibition containing stone carvings from the Mexican archeological site at Mitla, I felt totally cheated of a wonderful experience. The planners/designers totally ignored the rich sunlight that originally bathed those beautiful Zapotec carvings with their warm, red pigment detailing. What were they thinking when they illuminated those striking artifacts with a blue-white light and in so doing flattened the images and changed that warm, red color to a blue-red? If that wasn't enough, they downlit many of the carved heads and created a Frankenstein effect. Having happily driven a hundred miles to see that exhibition, I returned home in a rage.

Professional Consultants

When it comes to designing the lighting system for an exhibition, and specifying the proper fixtures and filters, it is always advisable to retain a professional lighting consultant. These engineers always seem to be able to specify a system that will be compatible with the exhibit design, they are a wonderful source of information, and many times their input improves the design considerably.

However, when the design budget is meager, and the designer has to select the light fixtures and lamps, consulting with lighting manufacturers is a viable option. These suppliers seem to know all the latest techniques and are always willing to work with you to achieve the colors and the ambiance that you desire.

Color Rendering

Most conventional lamps can and do change the colors of exhibit structures and objects and, in so doing, heighten or adversely affect the ambiance and the visitor's experience. Incandescent and halogen lighting can make a color seem warmer, and enhance red, orange, and yellow, but they can give cool colors a slight reddish tint. Fluorescent fixtures, conversely, usually produce a cool light that enhances blues and greens, yet could give the warm colors a slightly bluish appearance.

The color-rendering index (CRI) is a measure of a light source's ability to faithfully reproduce the color of an object. A CRI 100 rating indicates that the lamp renders all colors as correct to the eye. Most lamps are given a CRI rating and a CRI of 70 or above is usually acceptable for general environments. For a museum's displays, the color-rendering demands are usually much higher, and an 89 to 100 range should be considered where color accuracy is required.

COLOR RENDERING INDEX

SOURCE	CRI
Incandescent Filament Lamp	100
Tungsten Halogen Lamp	100
Incandescent/ Halogen Lamp	100
Xenon	95
Deluxe Cool White Fluorescent	89
Metal Halide	65 - 80
Daylight Fluorescent	79
Deluxe Warm White Fluorescent	73
High Pressure Sodium	22 - 75
Cool White Fluorescent	66
White Fluorescent	60
Mercury Lamp	15 - 55
Warm White Fluorescent	52
Low Pressure Sodium	0

Figure 3.32. Color rendering index.

CASE HISTORY: "RED BECOMES ORANGE"

I once designed a traveling exhibit, oversaw its construction, and was responsible for its installation. Obviously, if anything went wrong I was to blame. The exhibit's accent color was a bright red, and it was used extensively throughout the graphic panels and the promotional literature. During installation at the first and most important venue, the bright red accent color became red-orange because of the display room's existing overhead lighting system. When the client saw that color, she exploded in rage. That was until I took her and a graphic panel outside in the sunlight and magically the orange color immediately became bright red again. As a result she had to accept the fact that depending on the site illumination her bright red color would again change. I also learned an important lesson: when you design a traveling exhibition, the colors you select will probably deviate from venue to venue.

Shadows

I have a little shadow that goes in and out with me,
And what can be the use of him is more than I can see. . . .
The funniest thing about him is the way he likes to grow—
Not at all like proper children, which is always very slow;
For he sometimes shoots up taller like an india-rubber ball,
And he sometimes gets so little that there's none of him at all.

—Robert Louis Stevenson, "My Shadow"

Shadows can be a good design tool. Although most times they seem to have a sinister connotation, they can contribute to an upbeat, lighthearted display.

Painted Shadows

A painted "shadow" can be extremely effective and is a simple method for imparting additional information and reinforcing a theme. For example, caricaturist J. I. I. G. Grandville, circa 1830, depicted members of the French cabinet with their shadows revealing their true natures: a drunkard, a devil, a pig, and a dupe (a turkey).

Figure 3.33. Members of the French cabinet with their shadows, by J. I. I. G. Grandville, circa 1830.

Projected Shadows

This technique involves a light source and usually a projector that focuses on an object. Movement can be made to occur either by having the projector scanning an exhibit or by projecting on the visitors as they move through the display. For example, shadows of visitors projected onto a historic diorama, such as the storming of the Bastille during the French Revolution, could subliminally connect them to it and make them feel part of that historic event.

Texture

Light direction also affects the way we perceive a textured surface and its color. When light waves encounter a texture, some of its parts will be brightly lit while others will be in shade, thus creating color variation. If the light moves, or its intensity changes, the textured surface will also appear to change.

A texture can appear flat if lit from above, while if lit from an angle, the light and dark surfaces that are created will define and enhance the texture.

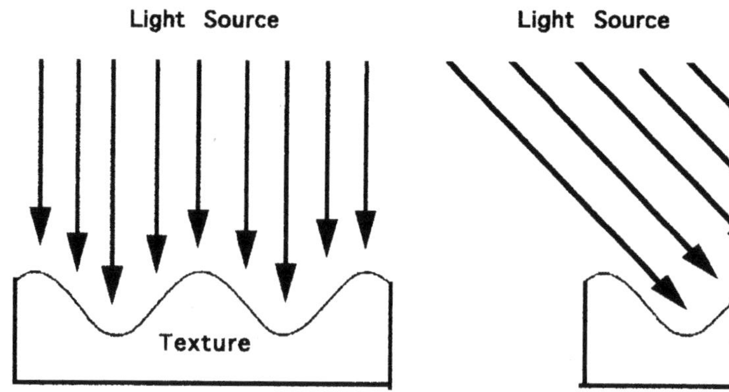

Figure 3.34. Illumination: Texture.

Design Considerations

The direction of the light source can become a major consideration when texture is a significant factor in the design. For example, during the colonial era, many American streets were paved with cobblestones. When preparing a display and text for that era, it would be necessary to emphasize the importance of the roughly textured streets and to stress the fact that the heavily burdened horses' feet had to grip the stones to prevent them from slipping, especially on a steep, wet incline. In an exhibit of this nature, proper lighting techniques to accent the irregular quality of the stones would be needed. If the stones were lit from an angle, their roughness would be accented; lit from above, however, they could be visually "flattened," and their importance easily overlooked.

Color and light are responsible for the wonderful world that we experience, and for all the beautiful things that we see and take for granted. As a mixture of both artistic and scientific aspects, they interact with each other and in so doing determine how and what we see.

It is due to color and light that our exhibits are perceived and enjoyed. Together they can reinforce an exhibit's theme, highlight its display objects, and create the desire ambiance. Depending on their intensity, they can also affect visitors both physically and psychologically. Color and light can cause them to become tense or relaxed, active or quiet, and can attract and focus their attention, create mood swings, direct and pace them, and cause have them to imagine temperature changes.

However, like chameleons, colors can and do change. While those lizards depend on cells for their color changes, we depend on light for our color variations. When lighting conditions are altered, colors do change, and in so doing the visitors' perception of a particular exhibit can be either positively or adversely affected. Color and light coexist and should be considered one of our most compelling and important design tools.

Figure 3.35. Color and light: Chameleon.

4

Shape, Form, and Space

> Don't watch the building, watch the faces of the people coming to the building.
>
> —uttered when two world-famous Italian artists, Federico Fellini, the film director, and Renzo Piano, the architect, were discussing how to judge the success of a design

Shapes, forms, and spaces are surrogate storytellers that can inform visitors about an exhibit's theme, time, place, mission, and aims. They are powerful design tools, and when used properly they can emphasize the ambiance, visually unite all its elements, and assist in producing a harmonious, cohesive result.

Every shape, form, and space must be planned/designed so that the exhibition will be harmonious and cohesive. Whether they are artifacts, structures, or areas, their configuration and placement should be compatible with each other and support the ambiance, aims, and story line. Each shape, form, or space conveys a particular message about the exhibition or display, and if modified even slightly, its meaning and importance can be changed and diluted.

Exhibits are art forms, and whether it is part of an exhibition or a display, they should always be a well-designed, artistic endeavor. Likened to a fine painting, sculpture, or building, an exhibit's shapes, forms, lines, and spaces should be balanced and harmonious, appear to be orderly and stable, and possess rhythm, emphasis, unity, and variety.

Every one involved in conceptualizing an exhibit must be able to produce a visually pleasing outcome. In the final analysis much of the success of an exhibit will depend on the planner/designer's sensitivity, artistic abilities, and knowledge of basic design principles. In this chapter, the major subjects that can influence the outcome and impact of an exhibition will be addressed in the following order.

Shape, Form, and Space Phases: Special Considerations

Schematic Phase
Lay out and position the major exhibit elements.
Preliminary and Intermediate Phases
Locate and indicate the exact size and shape of the major elements.
Final Phase
Refine and finalize the work prepared in the earlier phases.
Documentation Phase
Document, locate, and specify all the areas, structures, and spaces.
Construction Phase
Check that the exhibit structures are accurately reproduced.
Installation Phase
Confirm that the areas, structures, and spaces are properly installed.

Shape and Form

Everything that we see in an exhibition has either a shape or a form. It is how successfully these artifacts, structures, or graphics are designed, articulated, and positioned, and how well they blend together, that will impact the visitor's impression and ultimately determine the success of an exhibition.

Basic Shapes

Flat and two-dimensional, basic shapes are the circle, square, and triangle. Having only length and height, such shapes are relatively easy to comprehend and design. Artists and designers employ basic shapes to develop their layouts and to balance their designs.

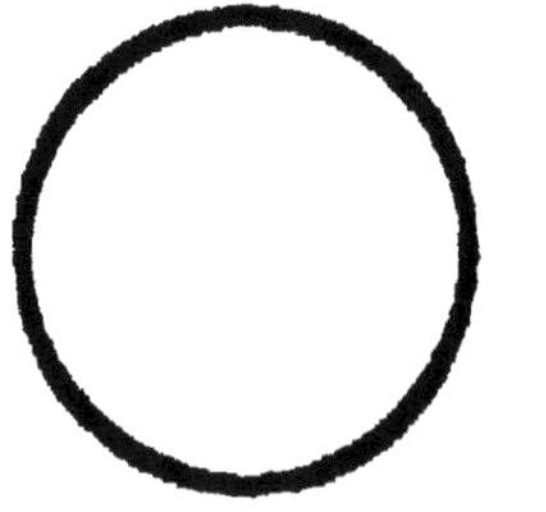

Figure 4.1. Basic shapes.

Basic Forms

Basic forms are three-dimensional forms that have length, width, and height. Thus, all sides of a form need to be carefully studied. Display cases, artifacts, and so forth, are classified as forms.

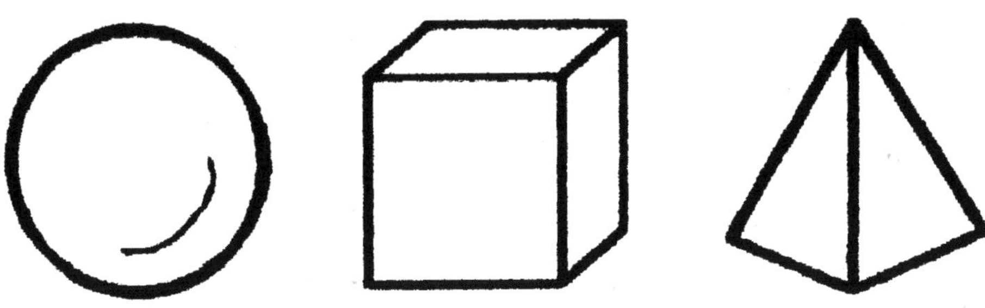

Figure 4.2. Basic forms.

Mental Images

Each shape or form possesses its own unique message and must be compatible with the goals of the exhibit. Solid, average, beautiful, or elegant are just a few of the mental images that a shape or form can relay to the visitor, and the taller and thinner a shape or form becomes, the more elegant it will appear. The diagram in figure 4.3 illustrates the various perceptions that can be conveyed.

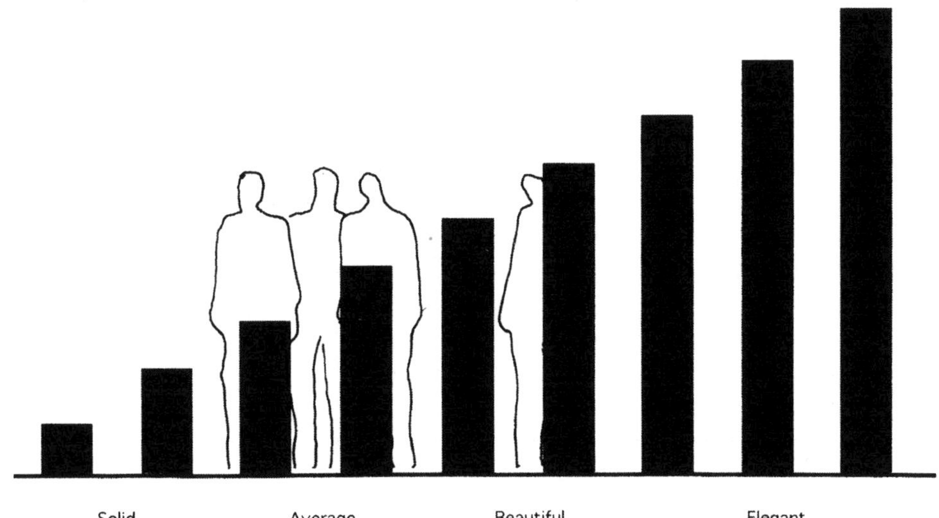

Figure 4.3. Perceptions from shapes and forms.

The height of an object or of a person creates a particular impression. Tall people seem to convey an aura of leadership and authority, and for that reason, artists and designers rely on height to denote those qualities, or when they desire that one person stand out from the crowd. It is interesting to note that of the last ten presidents of the United States most have been over six feet tall, with the exceptions of Richard Nixon who was five foot eleven and a half and Jimmy Carter at five foot nine and a half.

Line

A line is basically a very thin continuous shape that has two ends. In a three-dimensional design, a line can be a form that conveys width and depth.

We doodle, draw lines in the sand, and turn our signatures into our personal symbols. Our forebears drew lines on cave walls that today are considered works of art. The line is probably the most basic design element and usually the first art form that young children use.

Figure 4.4. Grandma, drawn by Amelia Larkin, age 4.

Figure 4.5. *Granddad, drawn by Amelia Larkin, age 4.*

Characterized by their length and direction, lines are an important part of most exhibits or graphic designs. They can be used to create shapes and forms, support ambiance, convey a specific feeling or action, indicate perspective, and point to important features. Lines can also lead a visitor visually, intellectually, and physically from one section of an exhibition or an object to another. The direction, contour, and quality of a line all have to be studied when placing it in a composition, and depending on their configuration, lines can convey a meaning, create a mood, imply motion, impart stability, indicate direction and action, and create forms, shapes, or spaces.

Rounded or bent, curved lines are aesthetically pleasing and usually suggest a sense of movement. A soft, curved line mainly implies a calm, quiet, and sensual feeling, while a curved line that changes its direction quickly can be very dynamic and impart a particular piece of information about a person, an object, an event, or a time. Lines can support an exhibit theme, create ambiance, and even add visual interest to an exhibit or a graphic that might otherwise be boring. They can also convey an overall mood and a sense of continuity.

Directional Lines

Lines can focus the visitors' attention and direct them through a composition or an exhibition. The notes on a musical score that lead a musician systematically through a composition or a road line on a map that guides drivers from one point to the next until they arrive at their destination are examples of directional lines.

Figure 4.6. Musical score.

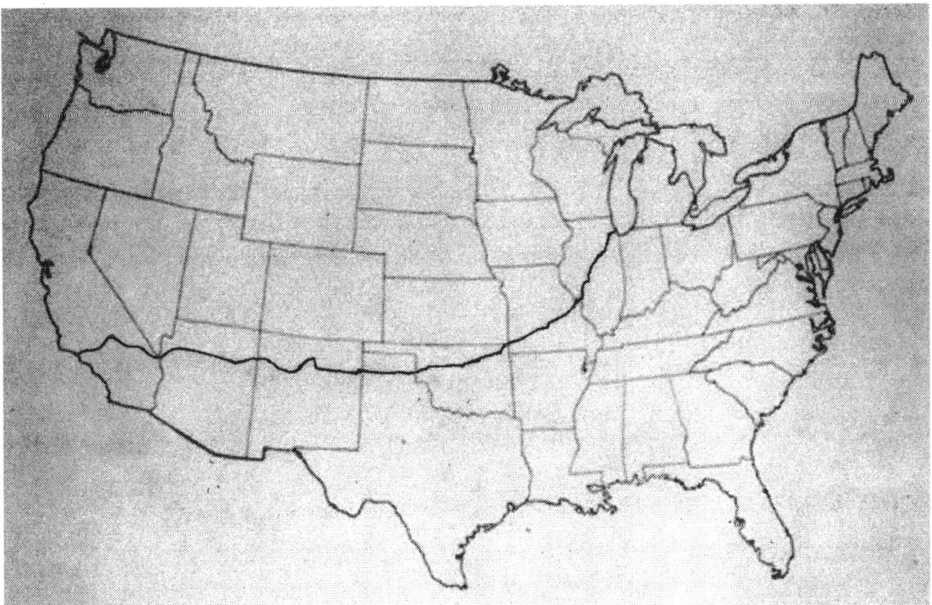

Figure 4.7. Road map: Route 66. Courtesy of the Library of Congress.

Implied Lines

Implied or invisible lines occur when two or more objects or shapes are lined up in close proximity to each other so that the viewer links them together mentally. Implied lines usually arrange objects in a straight or zigzag configuration and can be a valuable tool when placing display items; they can organize a variety of objects and suggest a commonality among them. When displaying just a few artifacts, placing them in a straight line (see figure 4.37) is usually employed; however, if there are many objects, such an arrangement could become boring, and an implied zigzag pattern should be considered.

Surrogate Lines

Exhibit and stage set designers have found it inexpensive and practical to use surrogate lines as a substitute for the real thing, or when there is a need to represent light, shadows, textures, patterns, shapes, and forms.

Lines may be used to represent a particular texture or pattern and suggest a special time or place. Applying lines to an exhibit structure to represent a faux finish can be a perfect design solution, especially if the exhibit is temporary, the floor loads can't support a heavy weight, and the construction budget is limited. Lines that represent a brick pattern are a perfect example.

Lines and Structures

Buildings and exhibit structures that have strong lines can create a feeling of depth and distance even though most exhibit planners/designers will rarely have the opportunity to work with such huge spaces and structures. However, even in relatively small spaces, employing lines to create a feeling of depth and movement can still be achieved. For that reason, we should all examine the architect Santiago Calatrava's work at the Milwaukee Art Museum and study the magnificent way he uses lines in the architectural forms he designs to achieve a wondrous feeling of depth.

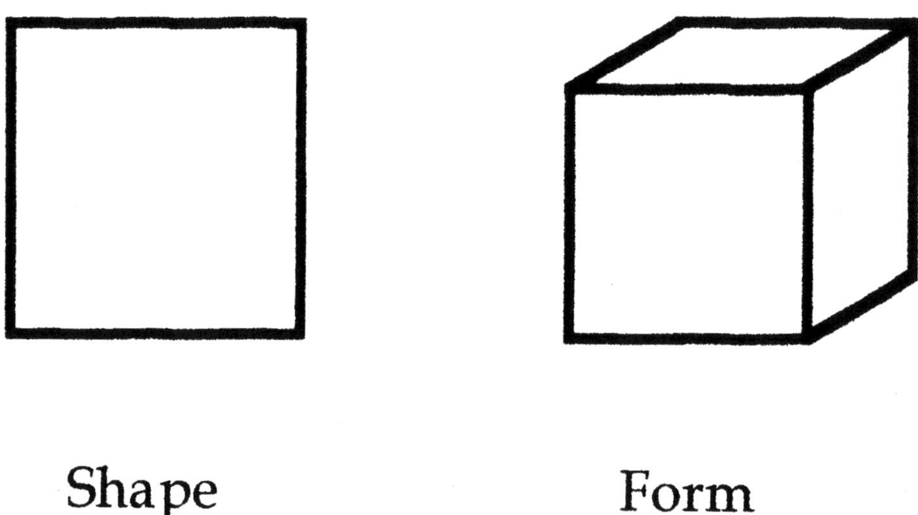

Figure 4.8. Surrogate lines: Shape and form.

Distance

Planners/designers can also use perspective lines to create a feeling of distance and can adjust them to fit the needs and the space requirements of a particular graphic or display.

The "railroad tracks" shown in figure 4.11 demonstrates the importance of lines to create a feeling of distance and illustrate how the lines can be refigured to accommodate different exhibit or graphic areas while still maintaining the feeling of depth and space.

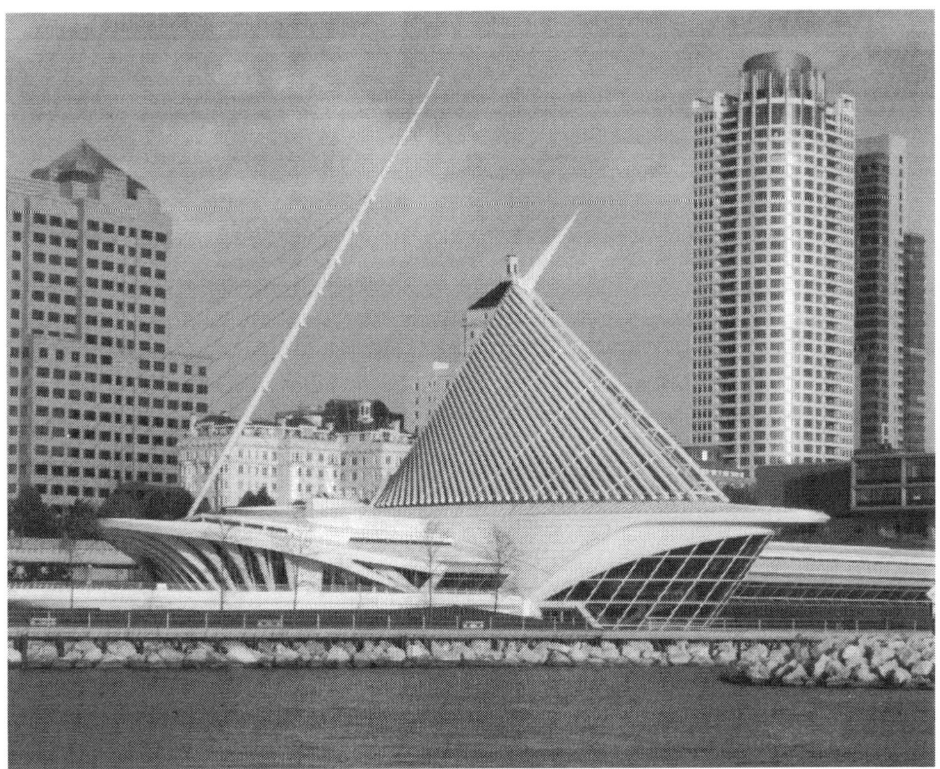

Figure 4.9. Milwaukee Art Museum. Designed by Santiago Calatrava.

Figure 4.10. Milwaukee Art Museum Baumgartner Galleria. Designed by Santiago Calatrava. Photo by Jyoti Srivastra.

Figure 4.11. Distance: Railroad tracks. Photograph by William Vann/ Epudic.net.

Space

Planners/designers must lay out, design, and manage the size and shape of every area and space that is part of an exhibition.

Sometimes referred to as volume, space is the invisible air that surrounds the artifacts, structures, and visitors. Often, because it is thought of as an empty area, space is overlooked and undervalued as a design element. Yet its size and shape can have a major impact on the success of a design; thus, each space should be studied so that it conveys the correct impression.

The size of the space will inform the visitor about the item that it surrounds. An artifact surrounded by a large space will seem to be more important and special than if it were displayed in a small, tight area.

Empty display and graphic spaces can be a haven for visitors. They allow the viewer's eyes and mind to rest, and even if only for a second, an area devoid of objects can serve as a welcome respite, especially after viewing a dense display.

Spaces must be designed so that they support the exhibition program, enhance the ambiance, and showcase the artifacts and displays. The following section will address many of the issues that the planner/designer faces when molding space to meet the requirements imposed by the exhibition.

Visitors and Spaces

The maximum number of anticipated visitors should be considered when determining the size of an exhibit space and the width of an aisle. Over the years, I have observed that the fewer the people in a space, the more profound the impact and the learning experience will be; conversely, the more people in an enclosure, the less powerful the experience seems to be.

Museum visitors are affected by not only an exhibit space but also what that space represents. It can be an awesome experience for a person to just be in the very room where John Adams, Benjamin Franklin, and Thomas Jefferson signed the Declaration of Independence. It doesn't seem to matter that little actually remains of that room in Independence Hall in Philadelphia where this event took place. Its wood paneling was sold and removed, the British used the furniture for firewood, and a major refurbishing left little of what our forefathers saw and touched. It is simply the act of being in the actual space where they stood that can make a lasting and memorable impression on a visitor.

Unfortunately, the number of people in a space can also have an impact on the visitor-space experience: when the room is empty, the feeling of history is awesome, but as the visitors increase in number, the experience can decrease proportionally.

Objects in Space

Space relates not only to the size, shape, and height of its enclosure but also to its contents. Whether it is an artifact, a graphic panel, a display case, or an exhibit structure, planners/designers have to place the objects in a space that will be satisfying and effective, and create the correct visitor response.

Space between Objects

Frequently it is the size and shape of the area around an object that affects how the visitor will perceive the displayed item.

Visitors should never be confused or in doubt about the relationship that exists between objects; items that are meant to relate to each other should be grouped together. However, when an object is to be viewed separately, there should be enough space around it so that it can be seen alone.

As the size of the space between display items increases, the objects become more isolated. A general rule is that the smaller the space between items, the more they relate to each other.

Height is also important; tall items, even though there may be a sizable space between them, can still be visually connected. Conversely, small items that need to relate to each other require a minimum amount of space.

Figure 4.12 is an illustration showing the position and relationship of artifacts. The tight space between the items on the left indicates that there is a commonality between them and they should be studied as a group. The huge space surrounding the artifact shown on the right indicates that this artifact should be examined separately.

Figure 4.12. Position and relationship of artifacts.

Objects and Enclosed Space

There are times when the area in a display case and the objects it contains are not visually or intellectually compatible. Using figure 4.13, the following discusses this objects-space relationship and suggests a few design solutions:

Left figure: The volume surrounding the small urn is huge, and the artifact seems lost and insignificant. If at all possible, place the item on a display base and add other relevant items, graphics, and the like.

Center figure: In this illustration, the space around the urn seems to be well designed and the object-space relationship is a comfortable fit.

Right figure: Here the artifact is too large for the case. If there is no other alternative, and a huge display item has to be installed in a case that is too small, it is best to leave plenty of space around the case or position it near a white or a light-colored wall.

Figure 4.13. Objects-space relationship.

Space and Object Rank

The size and shape of a space elicits a special meaning. A large space that surrounds an object or display will convey a sense of its elegance and power; emphasize its rank, value, and importance; create attention; and attract the visitor. Tight areas will convey the opposite.

A perfect example of an excellent space-object design is the famous Hope Diamond display at the Smithsonian in Washington, D.C. This exhibit is certainly worth discussing. Notice in figure 4.14 how the huge area that surrounds the case focuses the visitor's attention on the display and emphasizes its importance. And the space surrounding the diamond in the display case itself is enormous when compared to the jewel's size. The surrounding exhibit structure composed of fiberglass columns and a circular dome also focuses the visitor's attention on the diamond.

Yes, you can suggest that such a large space is needed to accommodate the vast number of visitors that come to see the Hope Diamond, and this is true. However, just observe how successful the planners/designers were in drawing the attention of the visitors to what is in reality an extremely tiny artifact. Observe how successfully all the design elements were handled, including the diamond being positioned in the center of the room,

Figure 4.14. Hope Diamond display area. Smithsonian Museum of Natural History. Courtesy of Fiberglass Technologies, Inc.

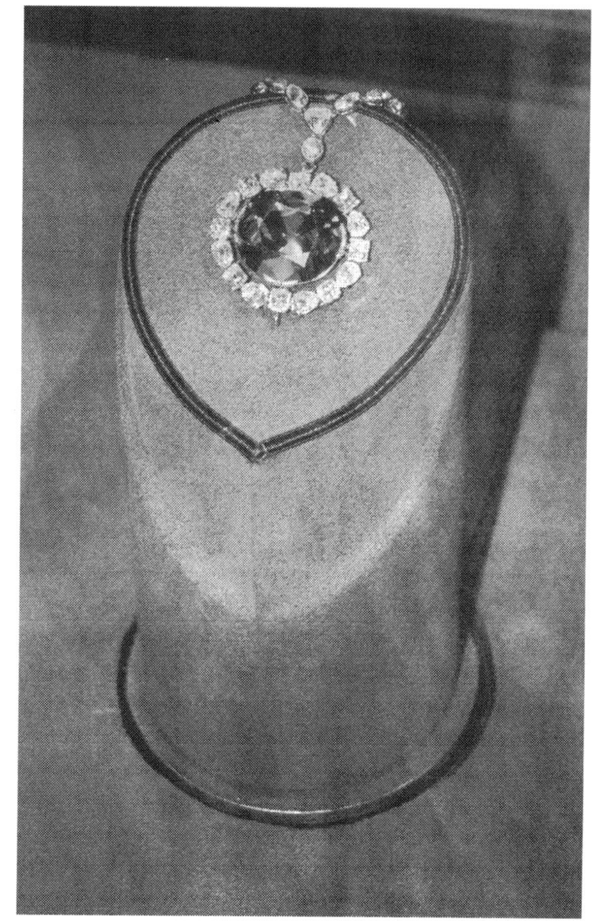

Figure 4.15. Hope Diamond display, Smithsonian Museum of Natural History. Photograph by David Bjorgen.

the vast space that surrounds it, the dark walls that frame it, the high-intensity lighting that spotlights it, and the beautifully designed display stand. This is a well-designed exhibit that should be carefully studied for its many valuable lessons.

Positive and Negative Spaces

A positive space is the area that is occupied by a shape or a form, and a negative space is the surrounding "empty" area. When designing or critiquing two- or three-dimensional art forms, their positive or negative spaces are of major concern.

Whether they are the shapes and spaces that make up a graphic panel, the forms and arrangements of the artifacts in a display case, or the size and placement of the exhibit structures in an exhibition area, it is how well the planner/designer balances these positive and negative spaces that determines the success of the design.

Usually, it is desirable to balance both spaces equally. However, the space-object ratio can vary according to the quantity and the sizes of the items on display. Most times, large or special items need additional space around them, while small or common items require less space.

A space should always be carefully considered, well designed, and, yes, even beautiful. Once I visited a museum where the spaces between the artifacts were so beautifully designed that I became enthralled and spent almost my whole visit looking at the negative spaces that surrounded the antique Chinese porcelains. Only after leaving the building did I realize that I had neglected to really study even one piece of porcelain. Did I waste my time? No! The spaces were beautiful, and I thoroughly enjoyed the time I spent at the exhibition (so much for being an exhibit planner/designer).

Exhibit Spaces

No matter how large or small a space may be, it must be well designed, pleasing, and comfortable, and it should never seem to enclose or confine the visitor, nor create an overwhelming, oppressive, or uncomfortable experience.

Spaces are defined by their walls, ceiling, and floor areas. Unfortunately, exhibition spaces are usually preordained. Their shape and size can be far from ideal, and their windows and doors always seem to interrupt the continuity of the displays and the flow of the story line.

Another space consideration is the area that exists between the ceiling and the top of a display item or an artifact. In figure 4.16, the structure on the left is visually too close to the ceiling and appears to be tight and uncomfortable, while in the one shown in the middle, the object-to-ceiling space is pleasant and comfortable. The structure on the right demonstrates that the space between the top of the structure and the ceiling is very generous and has a pleasing appearance.

There are times when planners/designers are forced to position structures that are too tall for the ceiling height of the room. This situation can result in creating display areas that are visually and psycho-

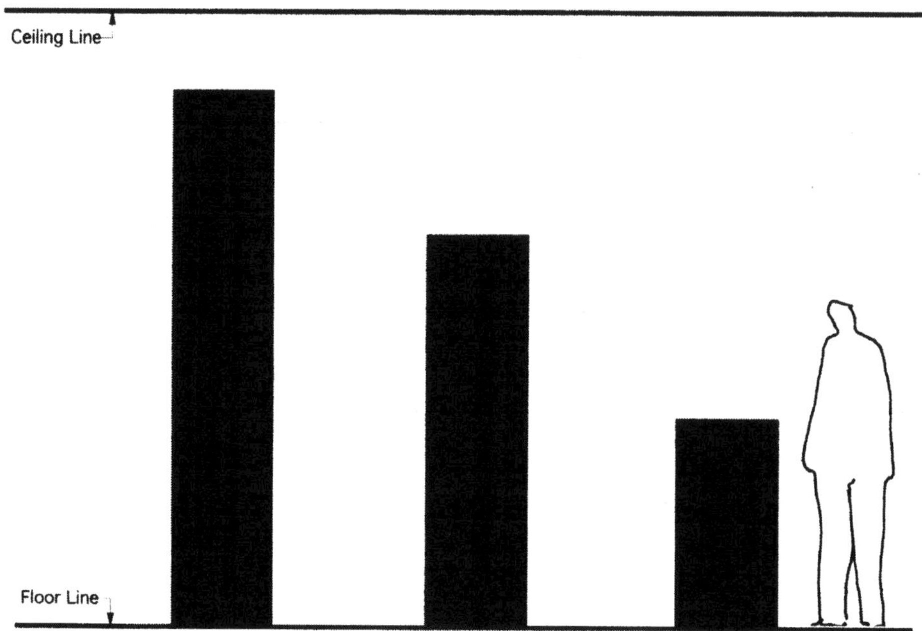

Figure 4.16. Object-to-ceiling space.

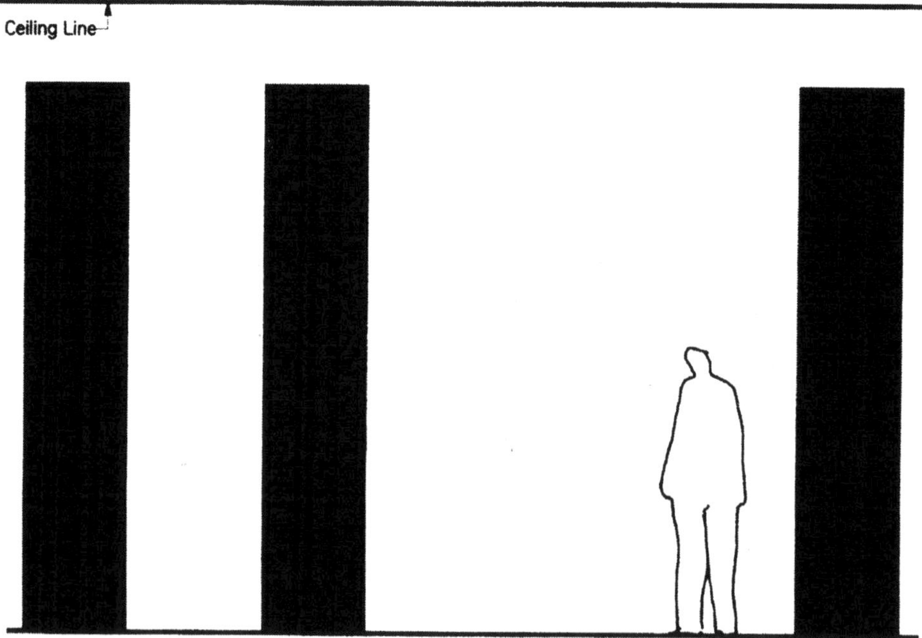

Figure 4.17. Positioning structures that are too tall for the ceiling height.

logically tight and uncomfortable. However, if the distance between the structures is widened, this situation will greatly improve. As illustrated in figure 4.17, the space between columns on the left seems to be very tight and can make the visitor feel restricted and confined, while the additional space on the right helps greatly to create a comfortable and pleasing viewing area.

Implied Spaces

Today, exhibit planners/designers employ the same techniques that have been used for centuries to create a sense of distance that in reality does not exist. Whether it is an illustration, mural, diorama, or historic setting, providing a feeling of depth can add a wonderful quality to a space that might otherwise appear flat and tight.

Implied space is based on how we perceive near and far distances. The illusion of nearness occurs when an object is large, colorful, and precisely detailed. However, when lacking these qualities, an object will appear to be distant from us. In the illustration shown in figure 4.18, notice how when going from near to far the following items gradually change: strong, bright colors become weak and muted, precise details diminish until they are nonexistent, and forms gradually decrease in size.

Trompe l'oeil

Considered a master of trompe l'oeil, architect Francesco Borromini created this three-dimensional architectural masterpiece shown in figures 4.18 to 4.20 for the arcaded courtyard at the Palazzo Spada in Rome. The diminishing rows of columns and a rising floor create an optical illusion of a grand, arcaded courtyard with a gallery that appears to be about 120 feet long (it is actually 26 feet), while the "life-sized" sculpture at the end of the arcade is only twenty-one inches high.

Most trompe l'oeil works are murals painted on flat surfaces. Today John Pugh is one of the leading artists who paints his murals on buildings and creates an incredibly realistic result that deludes the passersby into believing they are viewing an actual scene.

The trompe l'oeil mural, shown in figure 4.21, covered three sides of the Edison Brothers Building and depicts many of the major aspects of the St. Louis World's Fair.

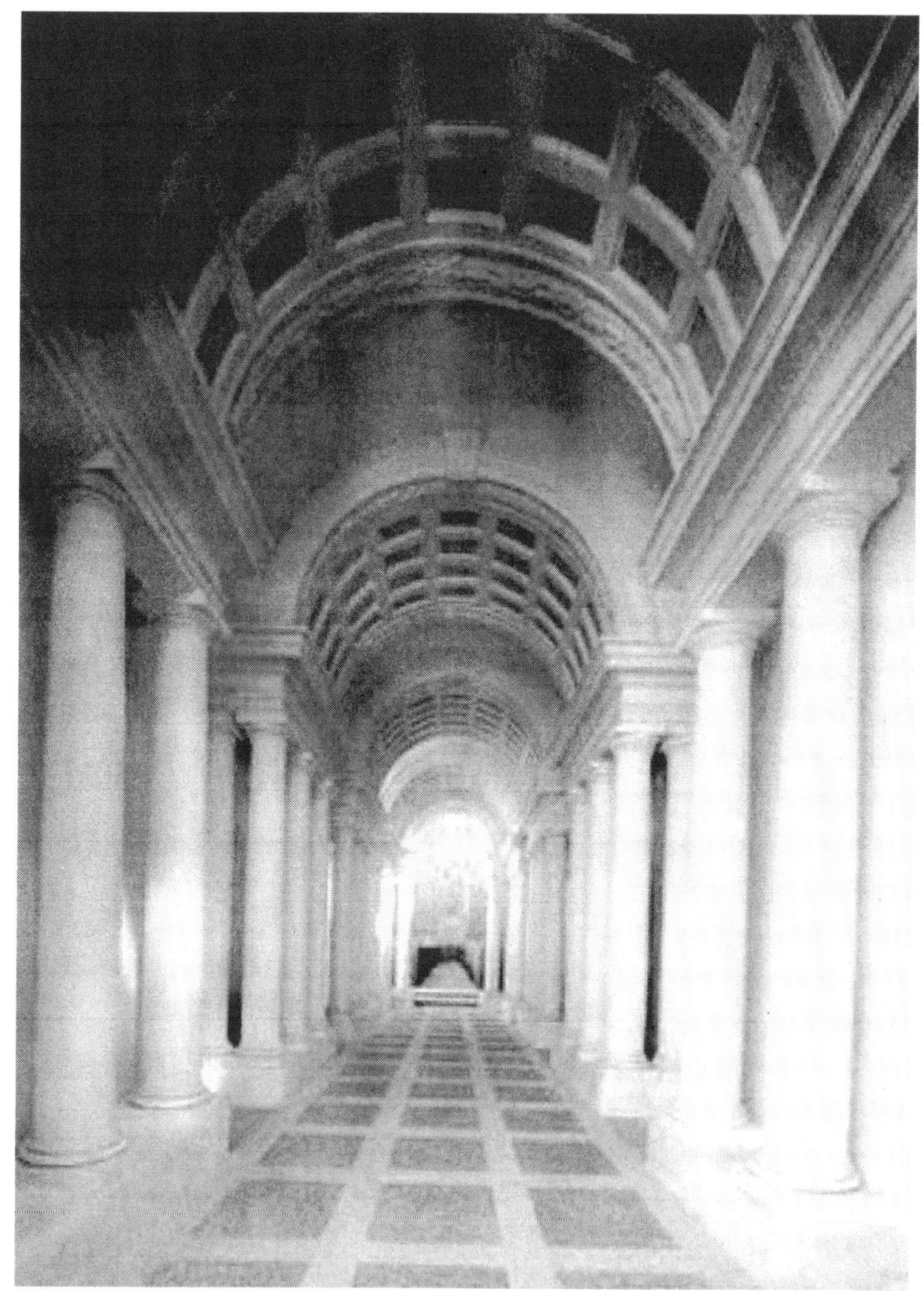

Figure 4.18. Arcaded Courtyard: Trompe-l'oeil. Courtesy of www.linkedin.com/in/apollospiliotis.

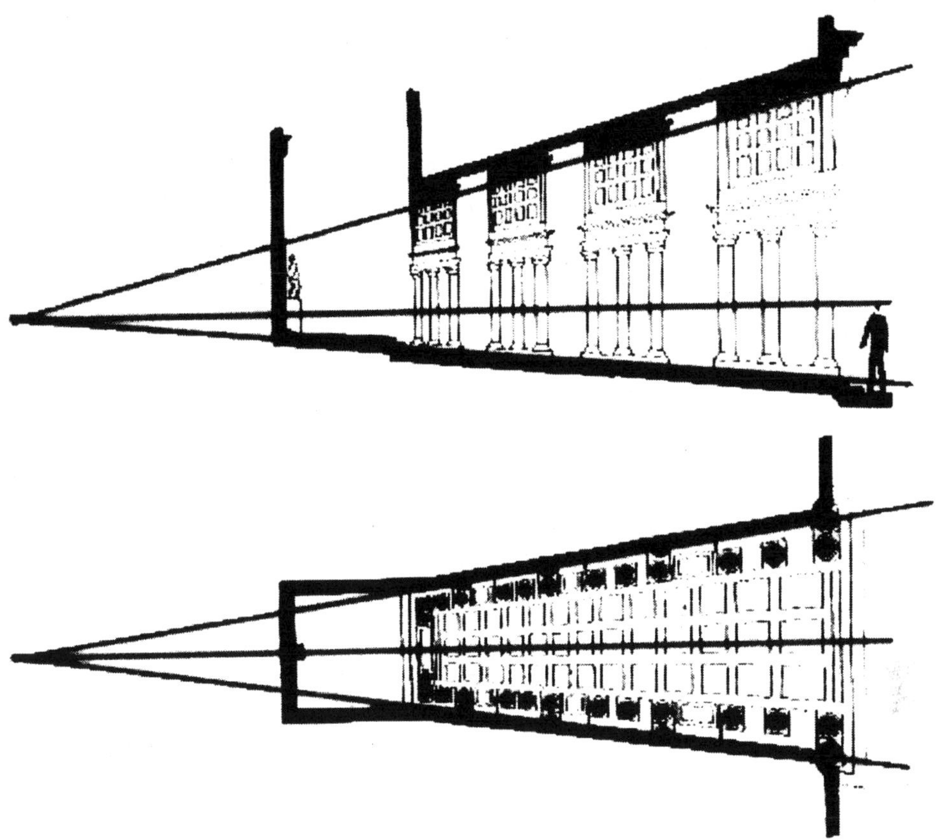

Figure 4.19. Arcaded courtyard: Trompe-l'oeil, plan and elevation. Courtesy of www.linkedin.com/in/apollospiliotis.

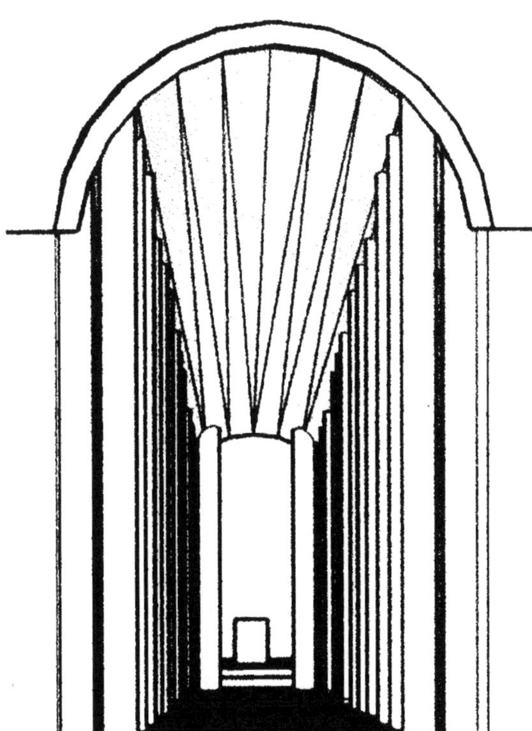

Figure 4.20. Arcaded courtyard, Trompe-l'oeil, one point perspective. Courtesy of www.linkedin.com/in/apollospiliotis.

Figure 4.21. A trompe l'oeil mural depicting the St. Louis World's Fair, Edison Brothers Building, St. Louis. Courtesy of the Library of Congress.

Balance

It is basic in our nature to strive for a well-balanced environment, and although the Leaning Tower of Pisa is beautiful and intriguing, it still made me feel uncomfortable, and I suspect I am not alone.

In exhibit design, balance is usually considered to be a harmonious or satisfying arrangement of shapes and spaces. Symmetry, asymmetry, and radial are considered to be the traditional methods of balance; however, color and value, density, form, shape, space, and texture should also be considered when balancing a design.

Symmetry

A symmetrical type of balance has a central axis, with one side the mirror image of the other. Also referred to as formal balance, it is rather easy

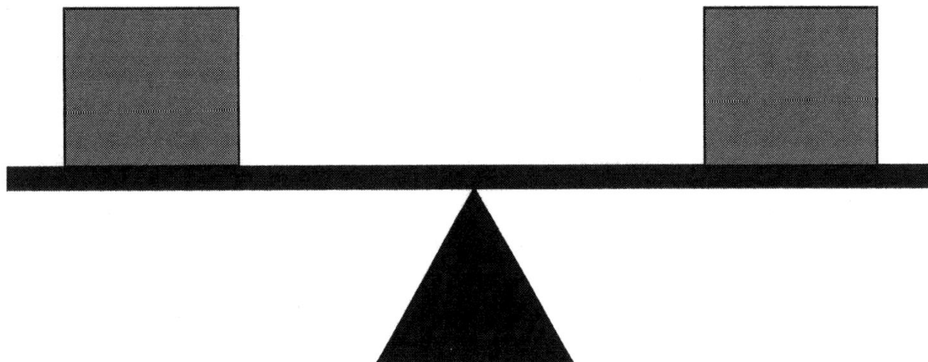

Figure 4.22. *A symmetrical design.*

to create and results in a stable, dignified, and calm effect. If overused, however, it can become boring.

A symmetrical design usually ensures that the right and left sides of the design will be well balanced. However, it does not guarantee that the top-to-bottom balance will be the same. Therefore, if the elements are top-heavy, an otherwise symmetrical design could lack stability and, if bottom-heavy, appear to be ungainly and graceless. Based on a symmetrical design balance there are several major variations to be considered:

Near Symmetry

A near symmetry type of balance occurs when the two halves vary slightly but the combination of objects has relatively the same visual weight. This design has a strong central axis and is symmetrically balanced.

Figure 4.23. *Near-symmetry design.*

CASE HISTORY: "A NEAR SYMMETRY DESIGN"

When I was planning/designing the displays for a transportation museum in a room with a seventy-five-foot-long wall divided in half by a door, a symmetrical design became the obvious solution.

That design consisted of two backwall display cases that would be companion pieces and contain the same density of artifacts and graphic materials. Both cases would be basically the same size and shape; however, since one exhibit was to address rail transportation and the other river traffic, each demanded a different look and its own unique, articulated motif.

Rail Transportation and Commerce Exhibit

The rail display, shown in figure 4.24, was designed to simulate the steel structural details prevalent in nineteenth-century train stations.

Figure 4.24. Rail transportation and commerce.

The details for the river display case, shown in figure 4.25, were taken from the elaborate designs used to embellish nineteenth-century paddlewheel boats.

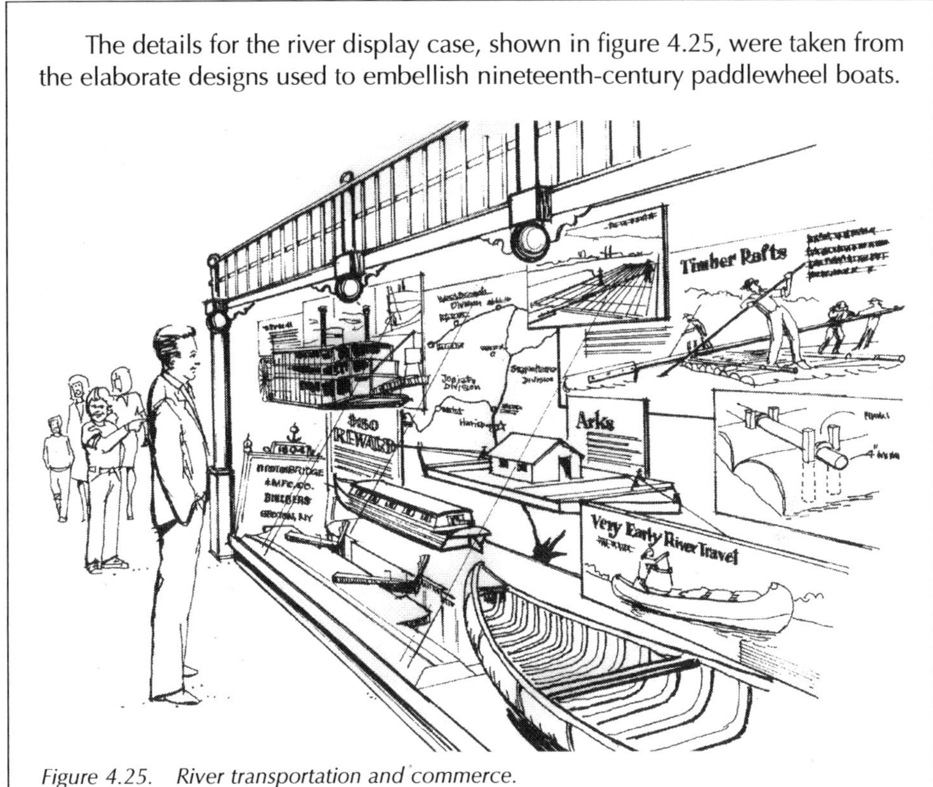

Figure 4.25. River transportation and commerce.

Inverted Symmetry

Inverted symmetry has a horizontal axis and two mirror images. Although rarely used in exhibit structures, it can be employed successfully in graphic design or as an icon design. Figure 4.27 is a king of hearts playing card showing an inverted symmetry type of design.

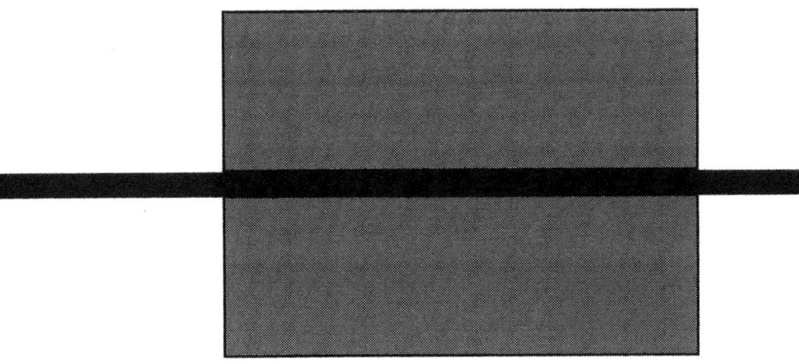

Figure 4.26. Inverted symmetry.

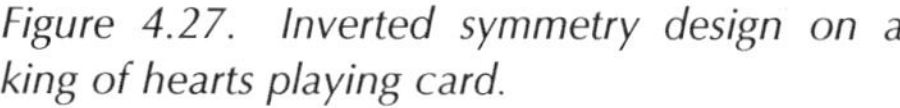

Figure 4.27. Inverted symmetry design on a king of hearts playing card.

Diagonal Symmetry

Diagonal symmetry is similar in every respect to the other types of symmetrical design, except that its axis is placed at an angle. Figure 4.29 is a jack of hearts playing card showing a diagonal balance.

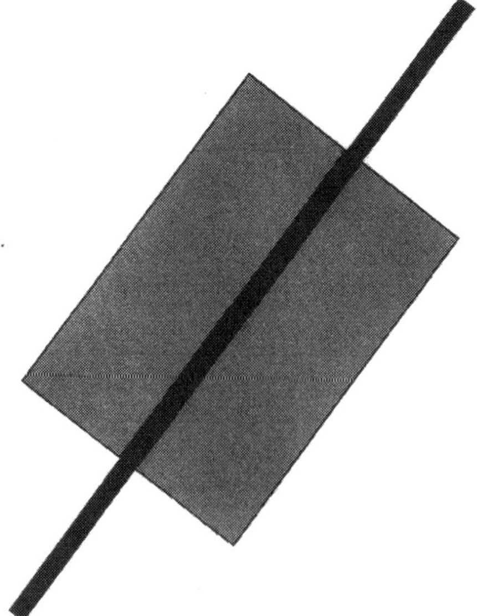

Figure 4.28. Diagonal symmetry.

Figure 4.29. Diagonal symmetry design on a jack of hearts playing card.

Asymmetry

Sometimes referred to as informal balance, asymmetry results when two halves of a composition's forms and spaces are not identical yet have equal visual weight. Because it can successfully include and visually unite a wide variety of display objects and graphics, this type of balance is commonly employed in exhibit and graphic designs. Since there are no set rules for balancing this approach, designers have to rely on their good judgment and creative sense.

CASE HISTORY: "CANAL BOAT" EXHIBIT

The exhibit shown in figure 4.30 was an audiovisual sound-and-light display and was filled to capacity with artifacts and props of varying shapes and sizes. Since density was a major factor in this exhibit, an asymmetrically balanced design was selected as the basis for the display.

This canal boat exhibit was balanced by placing huge replicas and artifacts, such as a canal lock door, barge hull, pilothouse and crane, gear, and anchor, on the right and left sides of the display. The center of the display contains smaller items, such as sacks, barrels, crates, anchors, and pylons. A projection screen covers the center backwall.

(*continued*)

CASE HISTORY: "CANAL BOAT" EXHIBIT (*continued*)

Figure 4.30. Asymmetrical balance.

Radial

Radial balance occurs when elements radiate outward from a central core at regular intervals. A perfect example of this type of design is the wheel or the carousel.

I usually prefer a radial-balanced design when there are numerous displays of equal importance assigned to a single exhibit. Although a radial balance can take up more space than the others, it usually has an open and inviting look, and it can create an exciting and fun type of environment that is appropriate for science museums and environmental venues.

CASE HISTORY: "WEB OF LIFE" EXHIBIT

The exhibit shown in figures 4.31 to 4.33 discussed how our survival here on Earth depends on the sun. A graphic-filled, backlighted "Sun" column was the hub of the exhibit and included eight displays that radiated like spokes from its center. Each was devoted to a particular subject: air, water, soil, plants, insects, reptiles, and so forth, and consisted of a backlighted graphic panel and a participatory display.

Figure 4.31. "Web of Life" presentation sketch.

Figure 4.32. "Web of Life" elevation sketch.

Figure 4.33. "Web of Life" exhibit floor plan sketch.

Odd Number Rule

The odd number design format occurs when a composition has an odd number of identical segments. A balance of this type is easy to work with and usually creates pleasing results. Figure 4.34 is an illustration of a Greek temple showing how its design was based on seven equal segments.

Figure 4.34. Odd number rule. Nicholas Revett.

Rule of Three

The rule of three balance is commonly used and is based on a composition that has one section twice as large as the other. Figure 4.35 is a graphic label that was designed using this type of balance, and in figure 4.36 is its layout in grid format.

Visual Influences

Employing the various forms of balance that are discussed above doesn't always ensure that a design will be stable and harmonious. Whether it involves graphics, display structures, or placement of artifacts, there are many other factors that can influence, for better or worse, the balance of a design. The following are a few major factors that can further impact the balance of a design.

Figure 4.35. *Graphic label using the rule of three balance.*

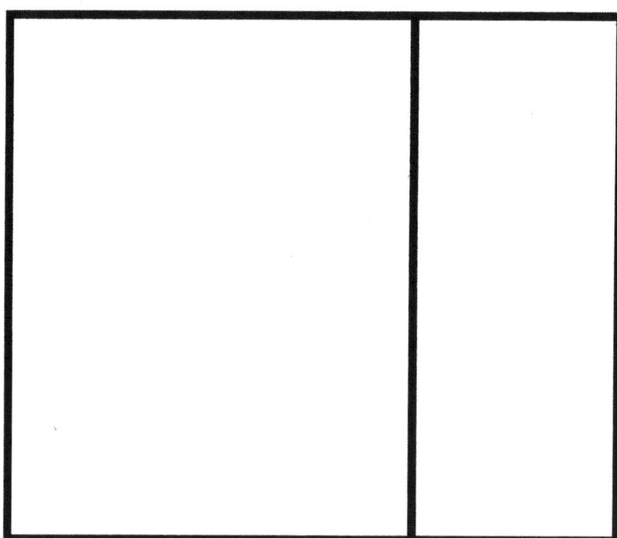

Figure 4.36. Graphic label layout in grid format using the rule of three balance.

Color and Value

Strong, bright, and dark colors are the ones with more visual weight and will stand out and overpower dull, weak, and light colors. A technique used when critiquing the color value of an exhibit or a graphic design is to squint, and with your eyes barely open check if all the colors blend together and that one color does not predominate. When a color or a group of colors is prominent, the composition is considered unbalanced, unless desired, and usually requires adjusting.

Density

A composition composed of dense and sparse areas can easily produce an unbalanced design. It is always wise to make sure that the visual weight of a composition is correctly distributed and, unless desired, that there are no gaping holes. A perfect example of a dense exhibit is the "Fibber McGee effect."

CASE HISTORY: THE "FIBBER MCGEE" EXHIBIT

A Fibber McGee display relies on a densely packed assortment of unrelated artifacts. The name stems from the "Fibber McGee and Molly" radio comedy show that started in 1939 and was one of the longest-running programs of its kind in the United States. The highlight of the program every week was when Fibber opened the door of his jam-packed closet and all of its contents tumbled out and crashed to the floor. In those days, this was considered uproarious.

Today, a "Fibber McGee" exhibit usually results when a museum elects to display its huge collection of stored and rarely seen artifacts. This treasure trove of unrelated objects is usually displayed on the floor in a cordoned-off area and relies for its success on the sheer density and diversity of unorganized or ungrouped artifacts. I really love this type of exhibit, for it allows me to find an artifact that just catches my eye, read its graphic label, and discover its significance.

Balance

To balance a composition, the forms, shapes, and spaces must be properly juxtaposed. The larger or more attention-getting a form or shape is, the more visual weight it will have. The size of the space surrounding an item will also influence its visual stability.

Texture

The surface of a three-dimensional object or painting is referred to as its texture. Usually, rough textures have more visual weight than smooth ones. Planners/designers usually balance these two opposites by increasing the size of the smooth areas and decreasing the size of the rough areas.

This balance also depends on the quantity and quality of the illumination. The lower the lighting level, the more likely it is that the rough surfaces will visually diminish and blend with the smooth textures.

Rhythm and Emphasis

Throughout the planning/designing process, the principles of rhythm and balance should be employed; this is especially critical when laying out spaces and graphics and when positioning artifacts and structures.

Rhythm and emphasis have to be used in the right proportions. When overused, they could be counterproductive to their intended purpose. Unfortunately, there are few rules that can assist planners/designers when employing these two tools. They must rely on their intuition and sensitivity, and develop an "eye" by observing and critiquing other designers' and their work.

Rhythm

Relying mainly on shape, color, line, form, or motif as its vehicle, rhythm is a timed movement, pacing, or beat that results in a regular pattern. In an exhibit or a graphic design, a particular rhythm can create predictability and assist in organizing items and information.

Rhythm can also aid the visitor in understanding quickly how to proceed visually, physically, or intellectually through complicated materials, information, and exhibit spaces. It is divided into the following three major categories.

Regular Rhythm

Regular rhythm, also know as repetitive rhythm, occurs when an object is repeated several times or when each segment of a pattern is similar. Normally, regular rhythms rely on size, shape, color, or texture to create a repetitive pattern. The layout of the stripes in the flag of the United States and the spacing of the Parthenon columns are excellent examples of this type of rhythm.

Regular rhythm is an excellent tool to use when there is a need for the visitors to understand quickly how to proceed when looking at a graphic layout, viewing a series of displays, or entering an exhibit area. If overused, however, regular rhythm can become visually boring and lose its effectiveness.

This type of rhythm is also very effective when it is desirable to suggest a commonality among display objects. When presenting Greek vases, shown in figure 4.37, a regular rhythm is established by using identical display bases that are spaced evenly apart.

Figure 4.38 is another example of regular rhythm. In this exhibit the display structures are exactly the same size, shape, color, and texture. Each case contains a diorama that illustrates the various flora and fauna that existed during a particular period in the Earth's early development.

Progressive Rhythm

Progressive rhythm occurs when, through a series of progressive steps, certain forms, shapes, or areas gradually change. Usually it is the size (small to large), the color (light to dark), or the illumination (dim to bright) that varies. Progressive rhythm is usually based on a hierarchical order where the displays proceed from the ordinary to the extraordinary.

Time-lapse photography is a perfect example of progressive rhythm where, for example, in a step-by-step process, each frame depicts the gradual development and growth of a flower. A staircase where the steps start at a low level and gradually proceed to a higher level is another example of this type of rhythm.

The "Birth and Death of a Star" display shown in figure 4.39 was based on a progressive rhythm format. This exhibit was composed of a series of rings that gradually changed in size and color. Each ring represented a particular time period in the life cycle of a star. Visitors were invited to journey through the display starting at the birth of the "star" and ending, when they exited into a "black hole" room, with its death.

CASE HISTORY: "KING TUT"

Over the years, I have seen several King Tut exhibits. One that I felt was very successful occurred when the designer used a progressive rhythm space to lay out the display structures and spaces. Size of the rooms, density of the display cases, and quality of the artifacts were the three factors used to generate this rhythm.

This exhibit was composed of three main areas. The first was small and crowded with cases containing artifacts of lesser Egyptian nobility. The next room displayed only King Tut's artifacts and was larger and provided ample space between display items and cases. Finally, just before exiting, the pièce de résistance, King Tut's gold throne, was displayed alone in a spacious room.

Figure 4.37. Display of vases showing regular rhythm.

Figure 4.38. Flora and fauna dioramas showing regular rhythm. Sketch by Mitch Gilbert.

Figure 4.39. "Birth and Death of a Star" exhibit, showing progressive rhythm. Sketch by Mitch Gilbert.

Flowing Rhythm

Lacking rigidity, flowing rhythm can vary in size and shape; yet, because of its strong flowing motion, it maintains a powerful pattern. This rhythm gives a sense of movement and seems more organic than the others. Tidal flow and ocean waves are wonderful examples.

A major concern is that since a flowing rhythm does not have the regular cadence or structure that other rhythms have, it can, at times, be difficult for a visitor to understand how to proceed through the exhibit areas or a display.

"The World of Dinosaurs" exhibit shown in figure 4.40 was based on a flowing circular pattern. The displays, graphics, and even the backwalls were laid out to emphasize this circular traffic flow and to indicate to the visitors how they should proceed through the exhibit.

Emphasis

Emphasis occurs when a particular exhibit, display, item, graphic, or text is designed to attract attention and become the focal point of the design. It is also referred to as an accent or a center of interest.

Emphasis is akin to a magnet, for it can be used to draw visitors to an area or an item and to hold and even refocus their attention. It can also make an item stand out from its surroundings and lead the viewer physically or visually through an exhibit, a display, or a graphic.

Figure 4.40. "The World of Dinosaurs" exhibit showing flowing rhythm. Sketch by Mitch Gilbert.

Although an exhibit or a graphic design can be well balanced and possess unity and variety, it can still be boring and lack direction. Emphasis can be used to counter this by accenting part or all of the design.

When selecting a particular item to highlight, the following design elements are a few of the factors that should be considered:

- Color: Apply an accent color that attracts attention.
- Size: Place an item in or on a large display case or base.
- Lighting: Spotlight an object.
- Space: Locate the item in a large or spacious area.
- Text: Make the font larger and brighter than surrounding fonts. Position the text at eye level and in the center of the layout.

Orderliness

The systematic and harmonious arrangement of shapes, spaces, and information is referred to as orderliness. When critiquing an exhibit design, verify that it has intellectual and visual unity and that it adheres to a logical and carefully planned succession of shapes, forms, and information that are compatible and balanced.

Orderliness is the opposite of chaotic. Museum visitors, and I am one of them, do not want to be assaulted by a confused and disorganized exhibition. We desire to have an orderly experience, both visually and physically, where the information, display objects, structures, and spaces have continuity and are compatible, and where there is an orderly arrangement of shapes, forms, colors, and spaces.

As the size and scope of an exhibit or exhibition grow, the need for orderliness increases proportionately, and planners/designers should constantly critique their work to ensure the following:

- Shapes and forms are compatible with each other
- Exhibit structures and graphic elements are logically placed so that visitors can quickly comprehend the layout

There are times, however, when a lack of orderliness is appropriate. This can occur when the exhibit theme deals with a chaotic situation, such as a war, earthquake, shipwreck, or holocaust. A disorganized layout can be very effective when artifacts are arranged in a scattered fashion as if they had just been discovered, for example, at an archaeological site. In this type of display, the story of the dig usually takes precedence over the artifacts being displayed.

Scale

This word "scale" is used when comparing one object to another that is perceived to be of average size. For example, when discussing the height of a person, we usually compare that individual to one of "normal" size and judge that person to be small, normal, or large in stature.

Although the items that we perceive as being of normal size are usually very comfortable to us, we do seem to be attracted to objects that are unexpectedly out of scale. Radically changing the scale of an object can be an excellent method to attract attention, highlight an object, and provide an immediate impact.

However, scale is in the eyes of the beholder. Gulliver felt that the Lilliputians were very small, and the Lilliputians felt that he was huge. Planners/designers must take heed of the requirements of the targeted visitor and adjust the scale that they use accordingly. Obviously the scale that would be used for a children's museum would be smaller than that for adults.

The word "proportion" is often used when discussing scale, yet it conveys a different meaning and cannot be used interchangeably. Proportion refers to the relative size of an object or a space within the context of its

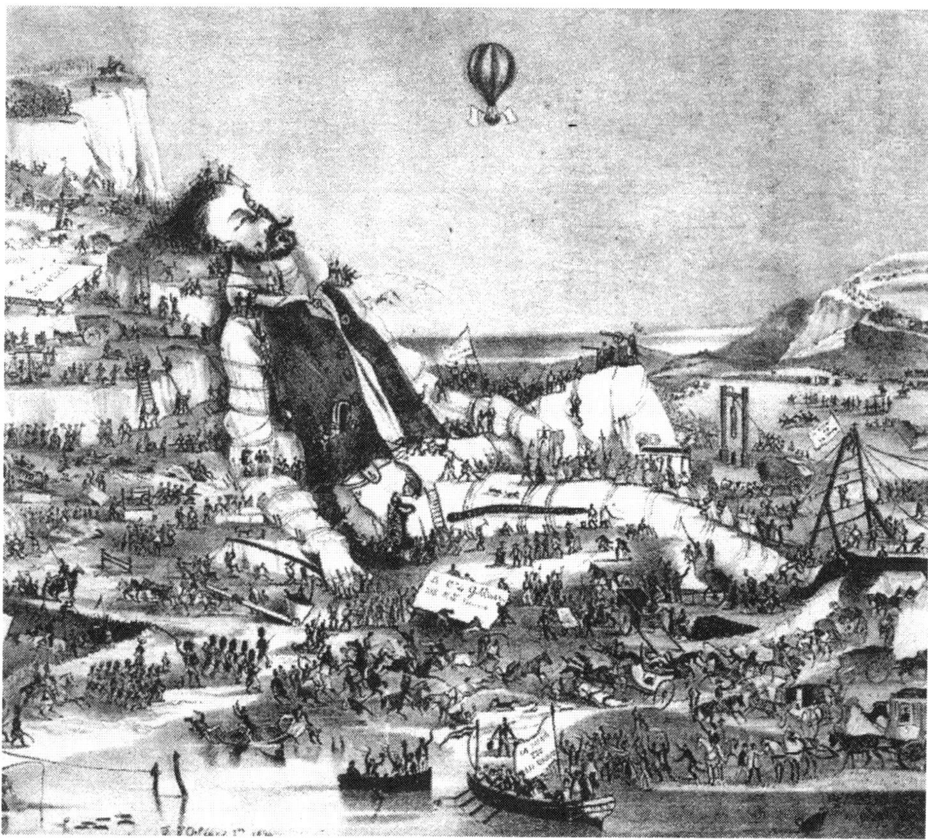

Figure 4.41. Gulliver's travels. Courtesy of the Library of Congress.

composition. When an item is "in proportion" or has the "right proportion," it means that it is in harmony with its surroundings. Conversely, when an item is referred to as being "out of proportion," it will be seen as too large or too small compared to its surroundings, and for the viewer this condition can be either an exciting experience or an unsettling one. Whether an item is purposely designed to be in or out of proportion, the planner/designer should be fully aware of the positive or negative effect a particular proportion will have on the visitor.

The word "size" refers to the physical dimensions of an object or of a space. However, when discussing an object, often the word size can be a comparative term.

Normal Scale

Also called "life size," normal scale refers to the actual size of an item. A normally scaled object or environment is what the visitor expects, and unlike up-scaled or down-scaled objects, a normal scale is easy to understand and usually does not need explaining.

Normal scale is just that: it is life size, and even though items designed in this scale usually lack drama and excitement, they are what we expect to experience when we are in a museum environment. Because normal-sized structures generally do not attract attention, planners/designers commonly employ this scale, since it allows the visitor to concentrate on the exhibit materials and to not be distracted by over- or underscaled displays.

Generally, visitors will interact with the museum environment based on their size, shape, capabilities, and limitations. Unless a compelling reason exists to do otherwise, all exhibit structures, walking distances, and sight lines should be planned to human scale and should be a comfortable fit for the average person.

Another compelling reason to use normal-sized figures is to make an instant physical and psychological connection between the viewer and a particular person, historic event, or specimen. The life-size figures in the photograph in figure 4.42 was designed to accomplish just that.

Figure 4.42. Volunteers readying for a fire. Photograph by Rich LeBlanc, AIA; Crabtree, Rohrbaugh and Associates Architects.

Undersize Scale

A scaled-down item or space is smaller than its actual size (see figures 4.43 and 4.44). For exhibit planners/designers, this can be a simple and effective means to attract the visitor's attention and to convey visual information about large and complex items and events.

Undersize-scaled objects invariably attract attention. Both children and adults always seem to be fascinated with a smaller-than-life object, and they appear to be willing to take the time to view and to study it in-depth. A perfect example of beloved undersize-scaled objects is the miniatures or dollhouses that seems to fascinate all ages, genders, and cultures.

Another reason for employing an undersize-scaled display is when the size and complexity of a subject are huge. Battlefields, building's interiors, and solar systems are just a few examples that can be explained by using undersize-scaled models.

However, when people are in an environment that is too small for them, they can feel clumsy, uncomfortable, and even overwhelmed. Adults can have this problem when they participate in exhibits and environments that were scaled down for children.

There are several design considerations involved when planning/designing scaled-down displays.

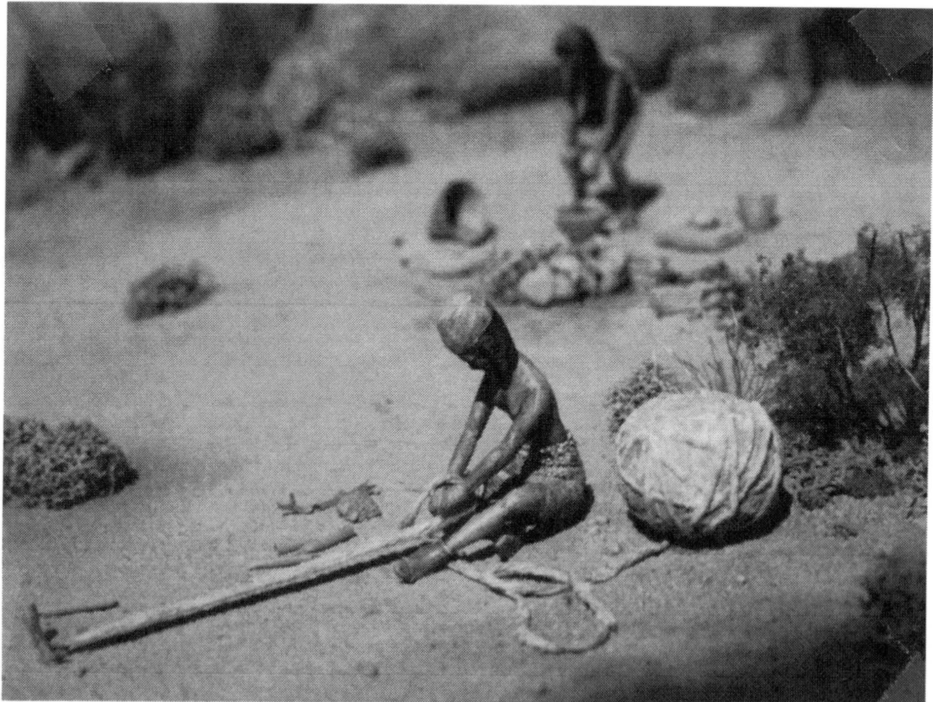

Figure 4.43. Scale model of an Anasazi camp.

Type of Detailing

To make it believable, attention to the type and the accuracy of the detailing is extremely important, and of course the larger the scale of an item is, the more detailing will be required.

Viewing Distance

Viewing distance is another consideration when conceiving an undersize-scaled model. Since most such models are very small and intricately detailed, visitors should be able to view and study them at close range. However, there are times when the model depicts a large area (e.g., the Acropolis, Yellowstone Park, or an automobile assembly line), and in this case, the viewer must stand back and adopt a bird's-eye view or be able to walk around the model.

Supplementary Information

A scale model can visually convey a great deal of information and reduce the amount of text that would be needed to tell a story. Yet many times it is advisable to supplement it with a visual or an audio text. The photo shown in figure 4.43 depicts an Anasazi camp, and with only a minimum amount of text this scaled-down model was able to convey a great deal of information about the various daily activities that took place there.

CASE HISTORY: "THE SECRET ANNEX"

"The Secret Annex" exhibit, shown in figure 4.44, was designed to tell the story of Anne Frank, her mother, father, sister, and three friends, and how they hid from the Nazis for over two years in an attic in Amsterdam during World War II. This story ended when they were discovered by the Gestapo and transported to concentration camps. Everyone that lived in the attic, except Otto Frank, Anne's father, died as a result of the internment.

During the planning/designing process for this museum, I thought about that long flight of stairs that took Anne from the street (freedom), to the attic (hiding), and back again to the street (death). I felt that those steps were so important and symbolic that they had to be represented. I also wondered, "What was Anne thinking and feeling when she went up the stairs knowing that she was leaving her home, friends, and school, and again two years later when she was captured and forced to walk down those same stairs knowing that she was going to a concentration camp and possibly to her death?"

(*continued*)

CASE HISTORY: "THE SECRET ANNEX" (*continued*)

I felt that the contrast of Anne's day and night activities was another compelling story. During the day, while the spice workers in the factory below were bustling and noisy, Anne and the other attic residents had to remain quiet and were even afraid to move. At night, the opposite occurred: the workers went home, and the family in the attic could walk around and talk.

For me these were powerful stories that had to be told, and I felt the best way to recount the drama of Anne's journey was with a scale model that included a narration and a synchronized lighting system. With this type of display, the viewer could see the attic and the stairs, peep into the spice factory below, and even observe the people who were free to walk the street outside.

Figure 4.44. "The Secret Annex" exhibit.

Oversize Scale

Defined as above average in size, this scale occurs when an object is larger than the one it represents. The following are just a few of the reasons to use an oversize scale and some of the considerations that are involved.

Enlarge a Small Object

An enlargement is a wonderful tool to use when explaining or studying an object that is so small or complicated that it or its components are difficult to see. Figures 4.45 and 4.46 show just a few enlarged replicas available that are easy to see and to understand.

Design Considerations

Sometimes an enlarged model can be just too big, so when considering the scale of an oversized display it is always wise to check the sight lines. "The Giant Heart" is a good example of the proper size; the viewers can see the aorta, arteries, and cava all positioned at the top of this model. However, I once experienced an oversized replica of Earth in a "Planet Earth" exhibit that was so tall that the top one-third of its synchronized LED light display could not be seen, which resulted in the visitor being deprived of its full educational value and unable to understand its purpose. Needless to say, this exhibit was an expensive failure.

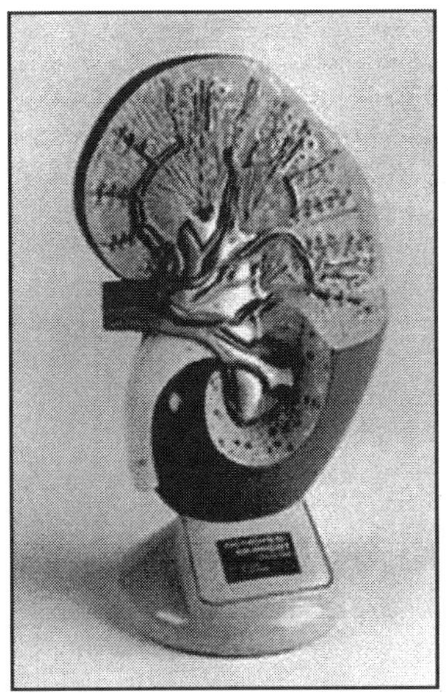

Figure 4.45. Human kidney model, 14" high. Courtesy of Carolina Biological Supply.

CASE HISTORY: "THE HEART"

This larger-than-life heart replica has for over fifty years been beloved by Philadelphians and is a must-visit designation at the Franklin Institute. This iconic exhibit is a perfect example of a wonderful teaching tool that has never lost its excitement or become boring.

Visitors are invited to walk the path that the blood takes as it passes through the interior of a human heart and to hear the blood's pumping sounds. I have always found this exhibit to be fascinating, and every visit to this science museum always includes my traditional walk-through of the heart.

Normally, oversize exhibits need supplementary display materials to contextualize them. "The Giant Heart" is just part of a larger display that includes blood, heart anatomy and physiology, health and wellness, and diagnostics and treatment. In addition, a monitor is available that re-creates a virtual experience for guests who cannot manage this display.

Figure 4.46. "The Giant Heart" exhibit, Franklin Institute, Philadelphia. Courtesy of The Franklin Institute, Philadelphia, PA.

Create a Monumental Effect

A monumental effect is highly advantageous when there is a need to create the impression that a person, place, or area is bigger than life, that it is not common or ordinary, and that it exceeds the norm. Some gigantic structures such as cathedrals, statues, memorials, and even some museum buildings are designed to produce this effect. A perfect example of a very successful monumental effect can be seen at the Franklin Institute in Philadelphia. A twenty-foot-high statue of Benjamin Franklin is a national memorial, and its size was meant to reflect the greatness of this man, the achievements that he accomplished, and the contribution that he made in forming this country. The statue had to be of an impressive scale so that it would not be dwarfed by the huge hall, where it is located.

However, there are times when a larger-than-life space or object can have an overpowering effect and be too overwhelming. The Grand Central Station ticket hall shown in figure 4.48 has this positive and negative effect. The space was conceived to be majestic and impressive, and its

Figure 4.47. Statue of Benjamin Franklin, Franklin Institute, Philadelphia. Courtesy of The Franklin Institute, Philadelphia, PA.

Figure 4.48. Grand Central Terminal ticket hall. Courtesy of the Library of Congress.

interior elements, such as the columns, windows, and cornices, are enormous, and their proportions reflect this grandiose concept. However, this space is way out of proportion to the people that it serves. It reduces them to "ant" size, and it could make them feel puny, uncomfortable, and even intimidated. Still, there is something deeply satisfying to the human spirit to experience a vast space.

Enhance the Viewing Distance

The size of the surrounding area is a major consideration when determining the scale of an artifact to be exhibited. Visitors need to be able to stand back and view an object in its totality, and whether large or small, anything placed in a crowded or congested area will lose its effectiveness. Normally, the larger the item, the more space there should be around it.

Both the "Red Cube," confined by tall buildings (figure 4.49), and the "Spoonbridge and Cherry" placed in an open field (figure 4.50) are good examples of oversize objects that are surrounded by spaces large enough to provide their viewers with a comfortable and ample viewing experience.

Another important consideration in the viewer-to-image distance is to slightly oversize a "people" image to compensate for the length of the viewing distance. Even a two-or three-foot space between the viewer and the person in the photo will cause that image to appear smaller and lessen its impact.

Figure 4.49. "Red Cube," New York City, by Isamu Noguchi. Photo by Chris Bradshaw.

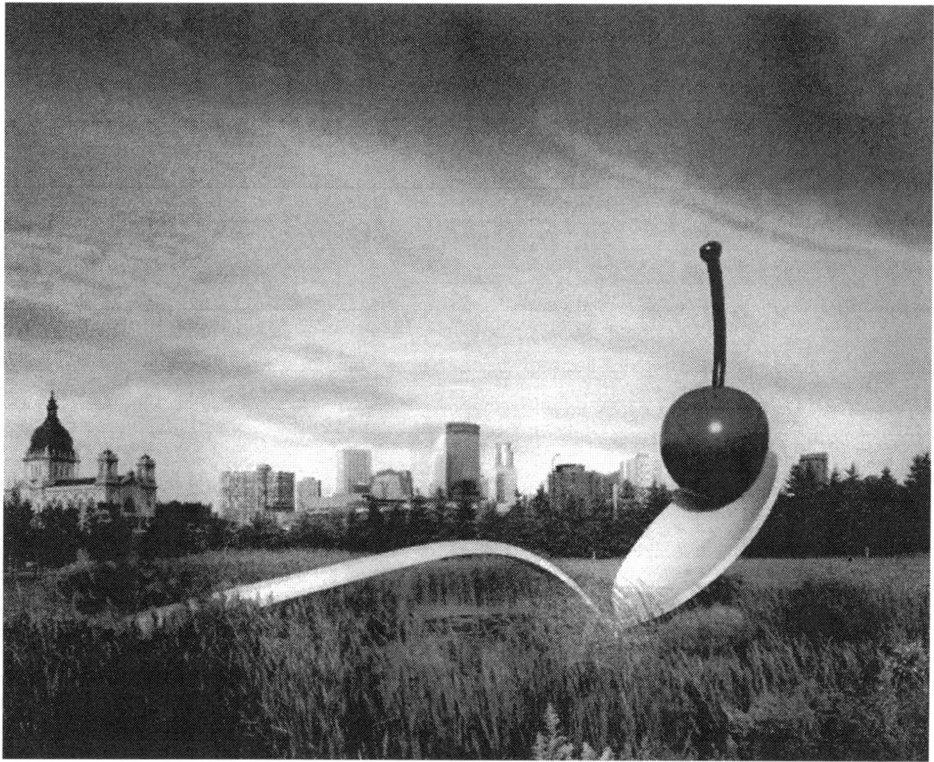

Figure 4.50. "Spoonbridge and Cherry" by Claes Oldenburg and Coosje van Bruggen.

Eye level is a further factor in trying to achieve a bond between the viewer and the person depicted in the image. When possible, it is beneficial to have both on the same eye-to-eye plane.

Provided that the proper viewer-to-image distance and eye level can be achieved, the Depression-era photograph shown in figure 4.51 is a good candidate for a display when making a viewer-subject connection.

Children and Scale

As with Gulliver and the Lilliputians, each had a different view of scale, and that is certainly true for children and adults. What is a normal scale for a child will be an undersize scale for an adult.

Scale is relative and depends on the user and the venue. No matter what type of museum it is, many adults come with children, and for that reason, attention should be given to a child's height and comfort. Usually, to meet the needs of their small visitors, children's museums will scale

Figure 4.51. Viewer to image distance. Courtesy of the Franklin D. Roosevelt Presidential Library and Museum, Hyde Park, New York.

down their displays, furniture, and environments. However, many adult-oriented museums do not make such provisions, and their display cases are designed for adults only and result in forcing children, when viewing the displays, to stand on their tiptoes. These museums should seriously consider peppering their exhibits with scaled-down and child-to-image eye-level displays to meet the needs and comfort of their small visitors.

When my grandchildren were stroller age, I selected and framed several prints and hung them just a few inches above the floor throughout my home. The criteria I used in choosing those prints was that the images had to relate to a child's scale and that the children had to be able to make eye-to-eye contact with the person in the painting. The children always loved those prints and certainly spent a lot of time looking at them. I felt it was a successful introduction to art, and in retrospect it was such a small thing to do. One of the selected prints was "Madame Henriot" by Pierre-Auguste Renoir, shown in figure 4.52.

Figure 4.52. "Madame Henriot," by Pierre-Auguste Renoir.

Motion and Stability

Although intellectually we know that most exhibit structures will not fall over, there are still occasions when some appear to be unstable. Granted, there are times when planners/designers desire to produce an exhibit that has the excitement of motion and activity, and an unstable look might be desirable, but this is the exception. Usually, as visitors we desire a comfortable museum experience and wish to be surrounded by structures and forms that seem to be stable and firmly anchored in place.

In this section, basic shapes and forms and the degree to which they convey motion or stability will be discussed. The following will address the techniques employed to achieve these conditions successfully.

Circle or Sphere

Lacking edges and corners and a beginning or an ending, circles or spheres seem to have a completeness within themselves, but since they rest on a small area, they appear to lack stability and to be easily rolled. Even when they are obviously secured in place, circles and spheres seem to be in motion.

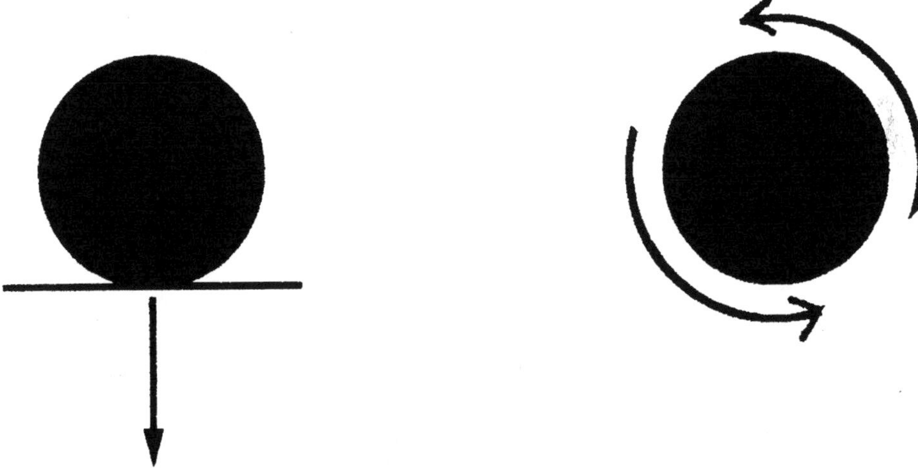

Figure 4.53. Circle and sphere.

A sphere's stability, both physically and visually, depends on its size and mounting. The larger the sphere, the more threatening it becomes. On the other hand, the smaller the sphere, the more we will be able to control it. When a sphere is placed on a flat surface and mounted on a substantial base, it will appear to be stable. However, when positioned on an inclined surface without a stand to rest on, it will appear unstable and easily rolled.

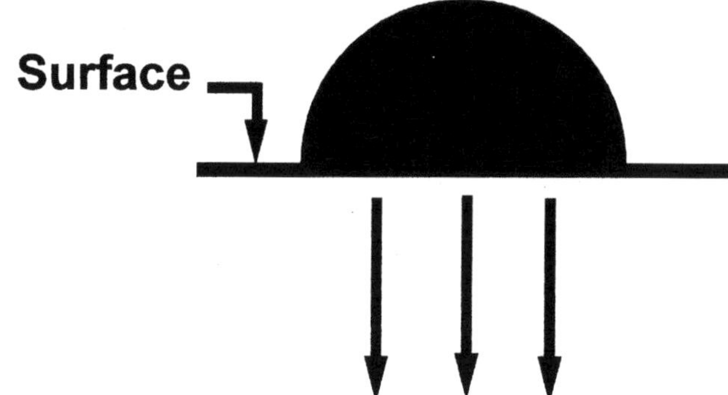

Figure 4.54. Hemisphere.

The hemisphere or dome is not a complete sphere; it has a flat base and is a very stable structure. Usually self-supporting and easy to install, it can be used when there is a need for a freestanding exhibit structure. Clear acrylic hemispheres are frequently used as protective display covers.

To represent a section of the Earth and its surrounding environment, hemispheres are normally used. Figure 4.55 shows an exhibit titled "Our Ecosphere." A suspended acrylic dome, painted to represent the atmosphere that surrounds our planet, and a circular display base, mounted on the floor, seemed a good and an economical way to tell the story of the Earth's lithosphere and hydrosphere.

There are times when it is the width and not the height of a structure that is critical to an exhibit design. In that case a flattened hemisphere can be employed to enclose a large area. "The Millennium Dome," shown in figure 4.56, is such a structure. Built to contain a major exhibition, its displays required a vast floor area but not the height of a hemisphere.

Square or Cube

Squares or cubes are very stable structures that appear to be totally compatible with gravity and indicate stability and immobility. When a square or a cube rests solidly on a flat surface, it will not seem to roll or slide. If placed on an inclined plane, however, it will appear to move downhill.

In figure 4.57, a square or cube (A) placed on a flat surface or floor and a square (B) placed on a blank panel or graphic both appear to be very stable. Squares and cubes also have a horizontal motion and a downward vertical thrust, and they can seem to expand visually and equally in those directions (C).

When placed at an angle, a cube will appear to be extremely unstable and defy the law of gravity. However, there are times when artists and designers desire to create such a dramatic effect. Noguchi's "Red Cube" (see

Figure 4.55. "Our Ecosphere" exhibit.

figure 4.49) is balanced precariously on one corner and, although anchored and stable, appears to be otherwise.

Triangle or Pyramid

Although these shapes and forms have an upward motion and energy, triangles and pyramids seem well rooted and depend on their downward thrust (see figure A in figure 4.58) for their visual stability.

When considering stability, the height-to-base ratio is an important concern. A triangle or a pyramid that has a wide base (see figure B in figure 4.58) compared to its height will appear to be stable. However, when the opposite occurs (see figure C), it could become or appear to be precarious.

Figure 4.56. The Millennium Dome. Photograph by George Doyle.

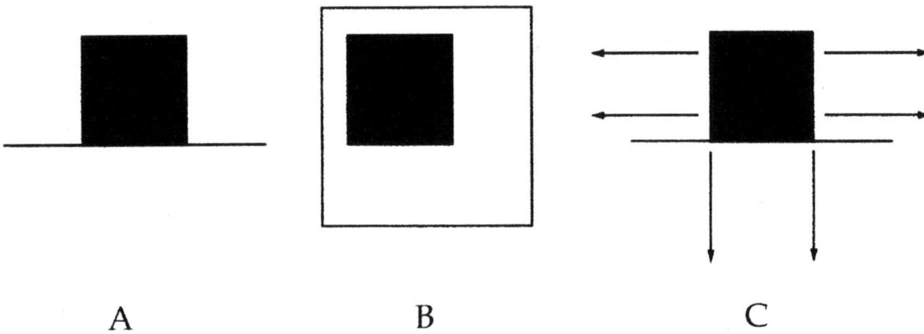

Figure 4.57. Square or cube.

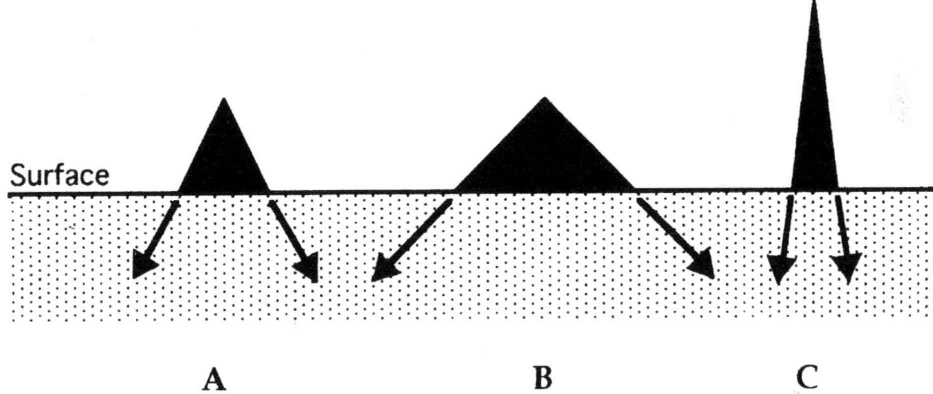

Figure 4.58. Triangle or pyramid.

Rectangle or Three-dimensional Rectangle (Rectangular Parallelepiped)

Rectangles depend on their height-to-width ratio for their stability. A low rectangle will appear very stable and cling to the ground (see A in figure 4.59). If, however, a rectangular form has a small footprint and is quite high, it will appear to be unstable and easily toppled (see B).

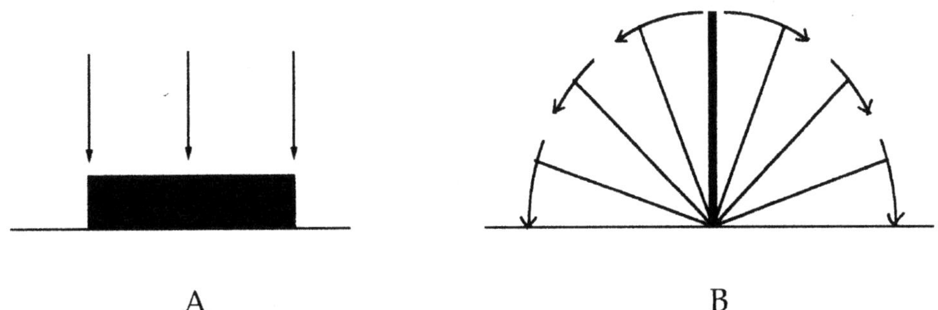

Figure 4.59. Rectangle or three-dimensional rectangle.

Perception of Stability

Everyone knows that trees generally have well-grounded roots and that skyscrapers have deep foundations, and for that reason viewers feel that they are stable and will not topple over. This is not true of exhibits, especially those that are constructed off site and placed on an exhibit floor. Designers need to make the visitors feel comfortable and to assure them that the exhibit structure is safely "rooted." Both the square and the triangular shapes shown in figure 4.60 have wide bases and for that reason seem to be stable.

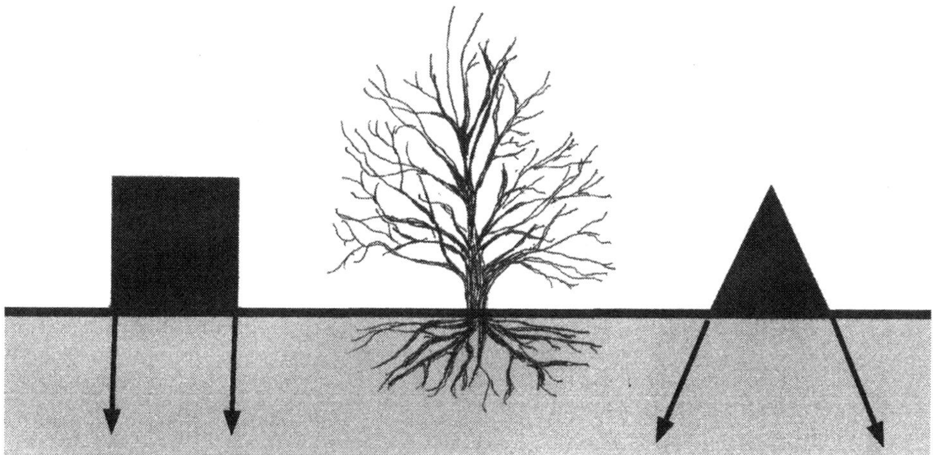

Figure 4.60. Square and triangular shapes that appear stable due to wide bases.

Certainly we all know that display structures can be engineered to be secure and, if necessary, bolted to the floor or weighted down with sandbags. Yet even though they are fixed in position and safe, they still have to appear to be stable.

When conveying stability, it is the relationship of the height of the visitor to the height of the structure that is important. The taller the structure, the more it will appear to be unstable. The reverse situation is also true: as a form decreases in height, it will appear to be more stable and less threatening. See figures 4.61 and 4.62.

A structure that is unbalanced can be disconcerting and, under normal circumstances, not suitable for an exhibit. However, when designing a piece of sculpture, such imbalance can be perfectly acceptable. Alexander Liberman's "The Way" shown in figure 4.63, was purposely designed to create a feeling of instability. However, the viewer does not feel physically threatened or endangered since there is ample space around the forms, the direction in which they would fall is predictable, and they are not too tall.

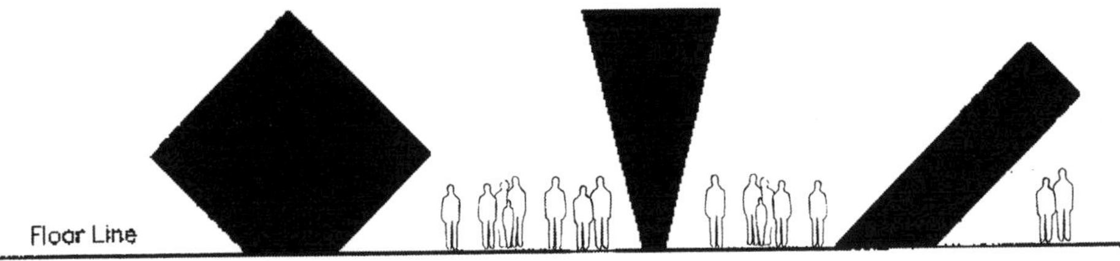

Figure 4.61. Stability: Tall structures.

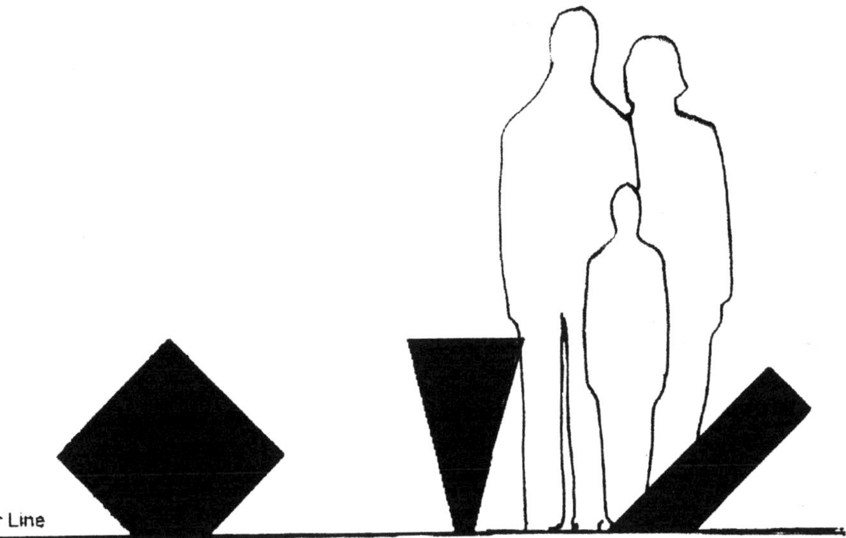

Figure 4.62. Stability: Small structures.

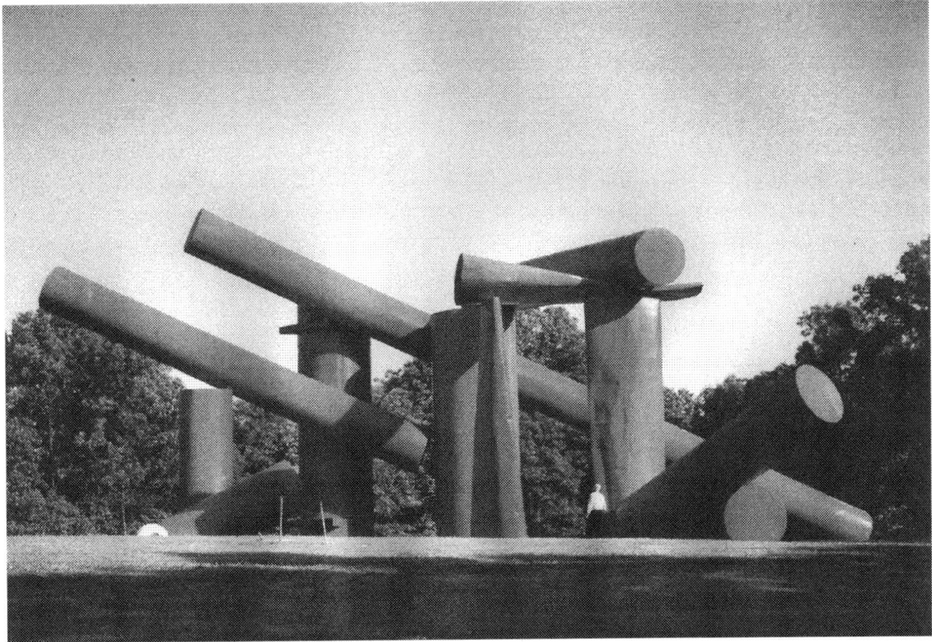

Figure 4.63. "The Way," by Alexander Liberman. Source: waymaking.com.

CASE HISTORY: "THE TILTED CRYSTALS"

Years ago when viewing a mineralogical exhibit, I found myself standing in a room filled with fifteen- to twenty-foot-high structures that resembled crystals. All were precariously tilted at about 30 degrees, and since the room was small, I was forced to stand under them. Even though each "crystal" was probably secured by a "big foot," which is a large, heavy metal baseplate attached to both the exhibit and the floor and concealed under the carpet, I still felt uncomfortable and threatened. Rather than concentrate on learning about crystals, I spent most of my time preparing to jump out of the way of a falling structure.

Symbolism

A symbol is a simplified image that stands for something and, in most cases, is a substitute for a complex idea or system. The Christian cross, the Star of David, the Statue of Liberty, and the Eiffel Towel are perfect examples of the vast variety of themes, and the sizes and shapes that they can embody. Symbols have a wide range of uses: they can indicate ideas, time frames, locations, subjects, or status, and even assist in establishing a particular ambiance.

There are times when the terminology "icon" and "logo" are substituted for the word "symbol." However, an icon is usually relatively small and represents a holy figure rather than a concept (see figure 4.64). A logo usually represents an institution, an association, or an organization. Most logos are based on a circular or a square format so they can be multitasked and easily adapted to letterheads, signage, brochure, and the like.

Symbols are a form of visual language that can convey a particular meaning or message, introduce a subject, and quickly communicate a great deal of complicated information.

They are a unique form of communication since their meaning is usually universal. Symbols are especially important when an exhibit is to be viewed by visitors who possess different language and educational skills, or who come from a variety of cultural backgrounds. With the rise in international travel, resulting in an increase in foreign visitation to museums, symbols are becoming an increasingly important means of communication.

Today many symbols have instant, universal recognition (see figure 4.65). The peace symbol is an example of a simple yet complex idea; it also demonstrates how a symbol can change its meaning. First designed for the British nuclear disarmament movement, and based on naval flag communications, its meaning evolved to become an internationally recognized symbol for peace.

Figure 4.64. Russian icon: The Lady of Kazan. Courtesy of the Library of Congress.

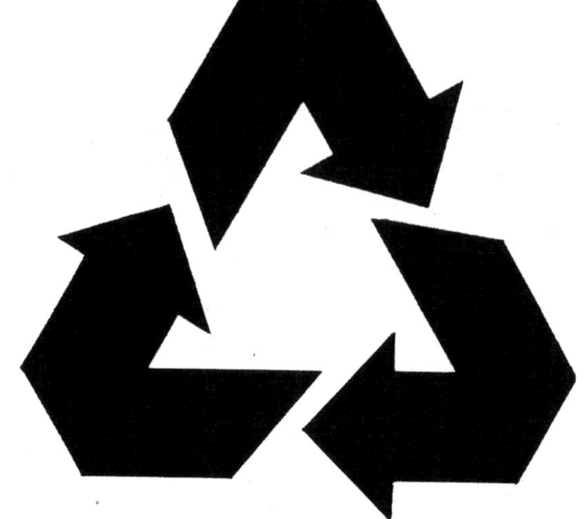

Figure 4.65. Recycle symbol.

Although most symbols are two-dimensional, three-dimensional symbols can also be important visual exhibit elements. Barber poles, fire hydrants, traffic lights, and costumed and historic figures are just a few that have been used successfully in displays.

Power of a Symbol

When a designer makes a powerful connection between the viewer and the subject being displayed, the exhibit seems more effective. For that reason, one of the most poignant and successful three-dimensional symbols, which every exhibit planner/designer should study, is the "Field of Empty Chairs" at the Oklahoma City National Memorial. Each of the 168 chairs installed in a grassy field represents an individual who died in the 1995 bombing of the Alfred P. Murrah Federal Building.

There are many reasons the chair is the perfect symbol for this monument. A chair is very personal object, and it is what we normally seek out when we need to be comfortable and rested. For that reason, it is not too broad a stretch to suggest that the person whose name is etched on that chair's glass base is also in a comfortable and restful place. When viewing each chair and reading the name, the viewer senses the tragedy caused by the loss of that individual and reflects on what that person might have accomplished. Especially poignant are the nineteen smaller chairs representing the children who tragically died in the bombing.

The arrangement of the chairs in the memorial should also be studied. They are not tightly grouped together as in an auditorium; rather, allotting a grassy space between chairs allows each to be slightly isolated, thus enhancing the victim's individuality.

Figure 4.66. "Field of Empty Chairs," Oklahoma City National Memorial. Courtesy of the Library of Congress.

The empty chair is a traditional symbol that for centuries has been used symbolically in paintings, monuments, theatrical productions, and recently in the heartbreaking song "Empty Chairs and Empty Tables," in the musical *Les Miserables*. And throughout history the chair has also been a symbol of status (see figures 4.67 and 4.68).

Categories

With such an overwhelming variety of categories represented by symbols that are easily recognized, designers can usually develop or employ an existing symbol to represent most of their exhibit themes or needs.

Concepts or conditions such as architectural, commercial, cosmic, directional, flora, fauna, handicapped, industrial, magical, military, patriotic, personal, professional, psychological, political, religious, status, surrogate, and traditional can all be portrayed by easily recognizable symbols. A few commonly employed by designers are as follows.

Figure 4.67. Abu Simbel, circa 1265 BCE, Egypt.

Architectural Symbols

Architectural symbols can create a particular ambiance, and whether they are in a two- or three-dimensional format, all can have universal recognition and quickly convey a specific location, time frame, and culture. Contemporary, Egyptian, Greek, Gothic, Middle Eastern, Megalith, Moorish, Oriental, Roman, and Tudor are a few of the more common, instantly recognizable architectural forms.

Personal Symbols

People tend to develop images to define themselves. For many, tattoos are currently becoming the latest and most obvious type of personal symbol. For Salvador Dali, a unique mustache (see figure 4.76) and a black cape were his.

Although maybe not as blatant as a mustache or a tattoo, personal signatures are symbols that are as unique as our fingerprints. They are icons that, for better or worse, can tell something about a person or a situation. When knowing that signing the Declaration of Independence was a treasonous act that could result in death, John Hancock had the courage to write his signature large and bold, and then said, "There, I guess King George will be able to read that." Today, a "John Hancock" has taken on

Figure 4.68. Virgin Mary and Child Christ, circa 1122 CE, Hagia Sophia, Istanbul, Turkey.

Figure 4.69. Architectural symbols: Asian, Gothic, and Roman arches.

CASE HISTORY: "AN ARCHITECTURAL SYMBOL"

The exhibit aims of the National Archives and Records Administration (NARA) were to inform visitors about the various genealogical records available to them. An exhibit entitled "We Discover Your Past" was selected to display and allow the visitor to peruse a sampling of immigration, naturalization, and ship's records housed in NARA's Philadelphia offices.

During the planning/designing of this exhibit, I studied the documents and felt that it was important to somehow personalize the people that they listed. And I wanted to prepare an exhibit that in spirit would connect the visitors with their forbears and hopefully raise the questions "How did they have the courage to leave the land where they were born, and why did they come here?"

Freedom, education, and prosperity seemed to me to be the basic reasons for their immigration to the United States, and I needed to create a single symbol to represent these three desires.

In this country during the nineteenth and twentieth centuries, the buildings that housed most of our banking, governmental, and educational institutions were traditionally built using the classical orders. Since these structures conveyed a feeling of stability, security, and intellectual achievement, the Ionic style was selected as the architectural symbol for the "We Discover Your Past" display structure.

To personalize the experience of our ancestors, silhouetted figures representing the various countries of origin and statements of their impressions upon arriving and living in this country were applied to the backwall. To add visual interest, the flutes of the columns were backlighted in red.

Figure 4.70. "We Discover Your Past" exhibit, National Archives and Records Administration.

a new meaning, and "put your John Hancock here" is a commonly used expression that applies to the act of writing a signature.

Surrogate Symbols

This type of symbol usually disguises a delicate subject and makes it palatable. Advertisers are masters of this technique. For example, when discussing bath tissue (formerly called toilet paper), observe how the manufacturers can take this sensitive issue and make it palatable and even enjoyable to watch by using fun-loving, dancing bear cartoon characters as surrogate symbols.

Exhibit planners/designers are faced with a similar problem. When preparing a display about an important yet sensitive subject, such as the digestive tract, they usually develop surrogate symbols and have found cartoon figures and abstract shapes or icons to be the perfect solution.

Patterns

A pattern is a repetitive design. Although usually they do not possess a complex meaning, they do serve to inform the visitor about a particular culture or a time period (see figures 4.73 and 4.74). Patterns can be a valuable tool, especially when there is a need to unite an area that is disjointed, or when it consists of an assortment of displays of various sizes and shapes.

Research: Symbols

The slightest change to a symbol can alter its meaning, origin, and time frame. For that reason, research is critical in understanding all the implications that are attached to a particular mark.

Over time a symbol can develop several conflicting messages. There are many in use today that were developed by various isolated cultures throughout history, and they now embody significantly different and contradictory meanings. The cross, five- and six-pointed stars, and the sun are good examples of symbols that possess many conflicting messages. If the symbol that you are displaying has several meanings, it is always prudent to explain its particular significance to visitors and to inform them how it relates to the displays being presented.

Developed over three thousand years ago by various remote groups of people, the swastika is a perfect example of a symbol that has numerous implications and embodies many shapes and forms. Unfortunately, during the Hitler era, the Nazis used it to symbolize their war efforts, and it is now seen by most people to represent the Holocaust and a horrible time in our

Figure 4.71. John Hancock's signature. Courtesy of the National Archives and Records Administration.

CASE HISTORY: "THE SIGNATURE THAT DISAPPEARED"

A signature is an indication of an act that in most cases a person actually performed and is an integral part of their being. I believe that is the reason visitors seem to attach a special interest to an autograph.

Accordingly, whenever possible, I always include the signature of the individual who is being featured, even though it was a lesson that I learned the hard way.

Early in my career I was assigned to plan/design the exhibits for the Thomas Edison Visitor Center in West Orange, New Jersey. Even though I had made sure that Edison's autograph was prominently displayed in the entrance area, for various reasons I failed to understand fully the power that visitors attached to his signature.

The visitor center was housed in Edison's old power plant, which over the years had become decrepit. I realized that visitors could easily trip on the crumbling terrazzo flooring, and on rainy days, as they tracked in water, the areas that were still intact could be very slippery. It was obviously a hazard, so when specifying the refurbishing that was needed, I had the floor patched and covered with a skid-resistant rubber tile. In so doing, I totally neglected to comprehend the importance of a bronzed, six-foot-long Edison signature embedded in the floor, and covered it over. Later, I learned how disappointed many of the visitors were when his autograph could no longer be seen. Apparently they really loved that signature, to the point that some would even get down on their knees so that they could trace that famous name with their fingers. If only I had realized its importance I could have easily left it exposed. My only consolation is that Edison's signature is still there, and when the flooring eventually gets replaced it can be revealed.

(*continued*)

CASE HISTORY: "THE SIGNATURE THAT DISAPPEARED" (*continued*)

Figure 4.72. Thomas Edison Visitor Center, West Orange, New Jersey.

Figure 4.73. Aztec pattern.

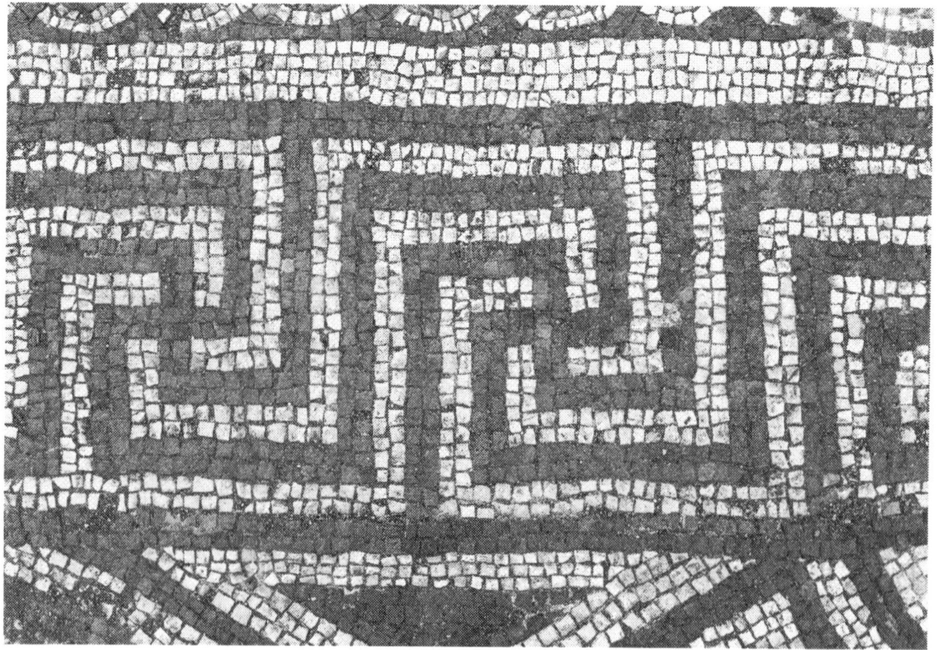

Figure 4.74. Ancient Italian floor mosaic.

Figure 4.75. Asian Buddhist swastika symbol.

history. Today, most visitors are unaware that this sign is a very old and sacred symbol found in the relics of just about every ancient community. Depending on its origin, the swastika can represent the cosmos, man, four directions of space, and even hope, good fortune, and blessing. It goes without saying that one swastika does not fit all conditions. The variety shown in figures 4.74 and 4.75 is a perfect example of the need for research and accuracy, and when used in a display, the need for explaining its meaning.

Symbolic Interaction

When laying out a diorama or an exhibit, or when selecting an image that involves more than one person, the interaction between people must convey the correct message.

People symbolically relate to each other and to their position in the group. A traditional wedding in this country is a perfect example of how, without scripts, everyone involved in the service performs symbolically. Before the ceremony begins, families are separated. The bride's family and her friends are seated on one side of the aisle, and the groom's on the other side. Prior to their marriage, the bride and groom enter the church separately, usually from two different locations. They meet at the altar and stand side by side for the wedding ceremony. After they have been married, they leave the church arm in arm symbolizing that they have been "joined" together. The families and friends are also mixed together as they leave, indicating that they too are now united.

Originality

Publishers of magazines and newspapers are masters at designing symbols to augment their articles. Likewise, exhibit planners/designers don't have to rely on existing symbols; they can invent new ones to fit the needs of a particular exhibition. However, when developing a symbol, there are two considerations: recognition and formats.

Recognition

If it doesn't have instant recognition, the visitor needs to be informed of its meaning. Ideally, this information should be at the beginning of the exhibit area where the symbol is first used.

Formats

An exhibit's signage, graphics, and brochures can all use a common symbol. Dali's mustache is a perfect example of a well-known personal symbol that could be adapted and used for many formats.

Figure 4.76. Symbol: Salvador Dali's mustache. Courtesy of the Library of Congress.

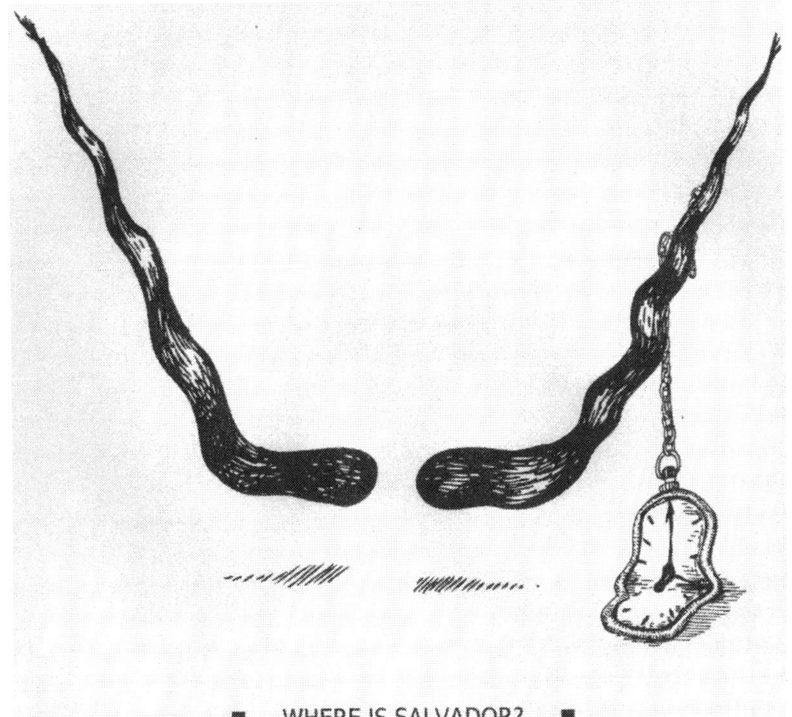

Figure 4.77. Salvador Dali graphic.

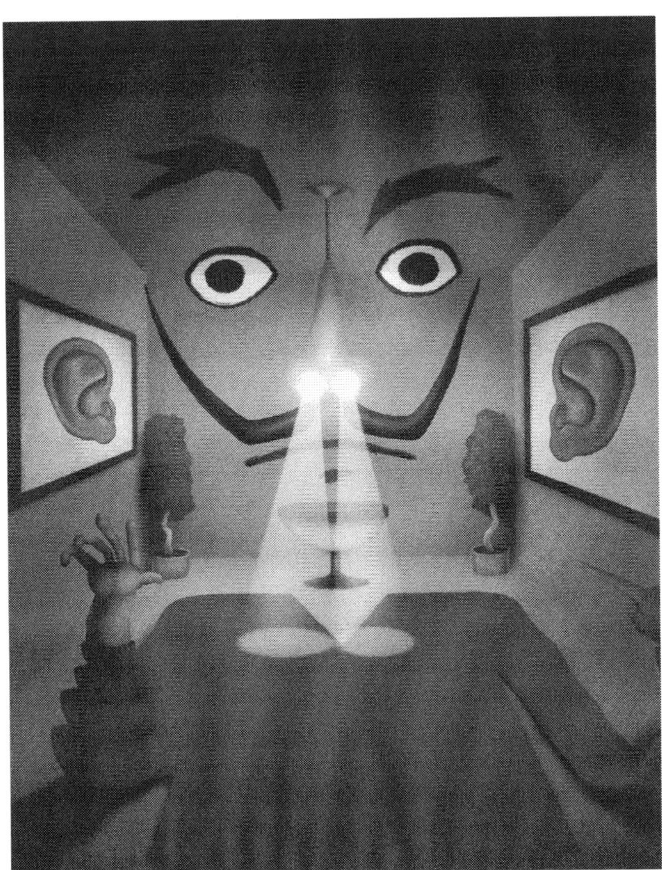

Figure 4.78. Salvador Dali art form.

Unity and Variety

> A composition devoid of any unifying element will nearly always seem haphazard and chaotic. A composition that is totally unified, without the relief of variety, will nearly always be boring. Those two overriding principles of design, unity and variety are like two sides of the same coin. Unity represents the control of variety, whereas variety provides the visual interest within unity.
>
> —Marjorie Elliott Bevlin, *Design through Discovery*

I love to visit small museums, yet so often I have found them to be visually dull and boring. Their display cases, colors, lighting, and materials all seem to have the same appearance and to blend together. Even though the information presented is usually well thought out and the artifacts of good quality, the experience generally leaves me slightly depressed, because I knew that with just a little variety those drab exhibits could have been made wonderful.

Unity

This condition occurs when all elements within a given area or composition combine to form a single, harmonious arrangement. Unity creates a feeling that everything is in its proper place, and it is usually achieved by correct balance and repetition.

Unfortunately, it is never easy to produce a unified exhibition when you are presented with an assortment of artifacts, a script with many subjects, and several poorly defined spaces. However, it can be achieved by

- selecting a few motifs, such as a particular shape, form, color, or material, and repeating them throughout the exhibit;
- grouping display items and structures so that they form a mass; and
- using a grid when positioning artifacts and preparing graphic layouts.

Producing a unified design where everything including the graphics, display items, exhibit structures, and architectural features and spaces is in harmony with each other can visually unite an exhibit and be highly advantageous. However, when an exhibit is too unified, it can lack surprise and excitement, and can quickly become dreary and boring.

Variety

Most exhibitions, even minor ones, require a "wow factor." They need something that will excite the visitor and be remembered. Variety or contrast, as it is sometimes referred to, can occur when a special artifact or display stands out, grabs attention, and creates excitement. It can also be made to happen by selecting forms, shapes, colors, textures, illumination, sounds, and so forth, that are different or contrasting from those commonly used.

Regrettably, many exhibit spaces have one unfavorable factor in common: they always seem to have neutral-colored walls, ceilings, and floors, which usually are permanent and cannot be changed. When such highly unified and very boring spaces occur, a good solution is to make the exhibits exciting and interesting by adding variety to the design.

Restraint is always needed when interjecting variety into a design, for too much can lead to visual overload, create a chaotic environment, and confuse and disorient the visitor. On the other hand, an exhibit that is devoid of variety can result in a mundane and boring museum experience.

Unity versus Variety

These two major design principles used together can contribute greatly to the visual success of a graphic or of an exhibit design. However, when planning/designing an exhibit or a graphic, one of the major concerns is how to juxtapose and successfully blend unity and variety together in the right proportion.

Unfortunately, there are no established guidelines to assist planners/designers when it comes to using these two design principles, so they have to rely on their creativity and judgment. Often, during the exhibit development phases, critiquing can be helpful, simply by questioning, "Will the visitor find a given exhibit or graphic to be visually and intellectually exciting and interesting?" If the answer is in the negative, then more variety is essential.

There are times when a boring display can seem to be an almost inevitable outcome. This usually occurs when a large collection of similar artifacts must be shown in its entirety. For example, when displaying numerous arrowheads together, the outcome could result in a very drab display unless the elements of interest, variety, and excitement are added. Just by varying the artifact mountings, adding graphics and accent colors, and dividing the collection into small groups, the exhibit can become upbeat and interesting and avoid a tedious viewing experience.

CASE HISTORY: "THE GLASS PYRAMID"

On a large scale, the architect I. M. Pei faced a similar problem when designing the new entrance structure for the Louvre Museum in Paris.

To be installed in a massive courtyard, and surrounded on three sides by unified, classical buildings that visually blend together into a gigantic mass, the museum entrance presented a major problem. Pei did not attempt to integrate it with the surrounding buildings. Instead, he elected to add variety and designed an exciting glass structure in the form of a strong, unadorned geometric shape. Although his glass pyramid is small compared to its enormous surroundings, it is light and airy, and instantly attracts and demands attention. As a result, it has turned what was previously a very dull courtyard and parking lot into an exciting space.

Figure 4.79. Pyramid entrance at the Louvre, Paris.

5

Materials

> Much of the impact of a design will depend upon the way the artist uses particular materials. Oil paints can be thinned with turpentine and laid on in transparent glazes; or they can be applied with a palette knife in a thick, plastic buildup known as impasto. Wood can be finished until it is almost as smooth as glass or left rough, in the manner of driftwood.
>
> —Marjorie Elliott Bevlin, *Design through Discovery*

When realizing their exhibits, most exhibit planners/designers use materials that have proven their ability to withstand the rigors of museum environments and are reliable, durable, available, workable, and easily obtainable. New, trendy materials will not be addressed here. It can be quite exciting to use the newest materials; however, until they can prove themselves to be of museum quality, it is usually wise to relegate them to temporary exhibits that have a short life span.

Materials Phases: Special Considerations

Materials are selected, researched, and specified during the following phases:

Preliminary Phase
- Suggest only the materials and hardware (M&H) that are important to the design concept.

Intermediate and Final Phases
- Perform product research and select all M&H.
- Commence assembling an M&H specifications file.
- Indicate and locate the M&H on the technical drawings.

Documentation Phase
Specify and locate all M&H.

Product Research

As planners/designers, we are entrusted with safeguarding the visitors, preserving and protecting the display objects, and employing exhibit materials and hardware that will withstand the ravages of time, environmental changes, and visitor abuse.

If you are not 100 percent certain that the selected products, finishes, and materials will meet the above criteria, you have to investigate to make sure that the materials you are choosing are appropriate for use and that their cost and availability meet the exhibit requirements.

The following is an unbelievable happening that occurred at one of the world's most prestigious museums. Tullio Lombardo's *Adam*, the most important Renaissance sculpture in the museum's collection and one of the most significant Italian sculptures outside of Italy, crashed to the ground and was seriously damaged when one section of the base of its reinforced plywood pedestal apparently buckled. Two years earlier, the original cherry wood pedestal on which *Adam* rested had been replaced with one made of medium-density overlay plywood, which was believed to be much sturdier and more durable. Needless to say, *Adam* will never be the same.

Based on newspaper accounts, the one-thousand-pound statue shattered into twenty-two major pieces and hundreds of smaller fragments after the museum had closed for the day and the visitors had left. No one even heard it crash, but it left a loud message: if you don't know what you are doing, get advice from someone who does. Although *Adam* will never be the same, and the emotional and financial losses are great, at least no one was hurt. Museum officials have stated that the restoration work will take ten years; it is now over ten years and counting.

Adam's message is very clear: even the most readily available, everyday material can fail if not used properly. The base supporting the statue collapsed because a highly reliable material was misused or the construction details were wrong. It is the designer's responsibility to make sure that every product specified can do the job and, if needed, to get technical advice. Frankly, we are to blame if our "*Adam*" falls. So with *Adam* in mind, let us consider the following.

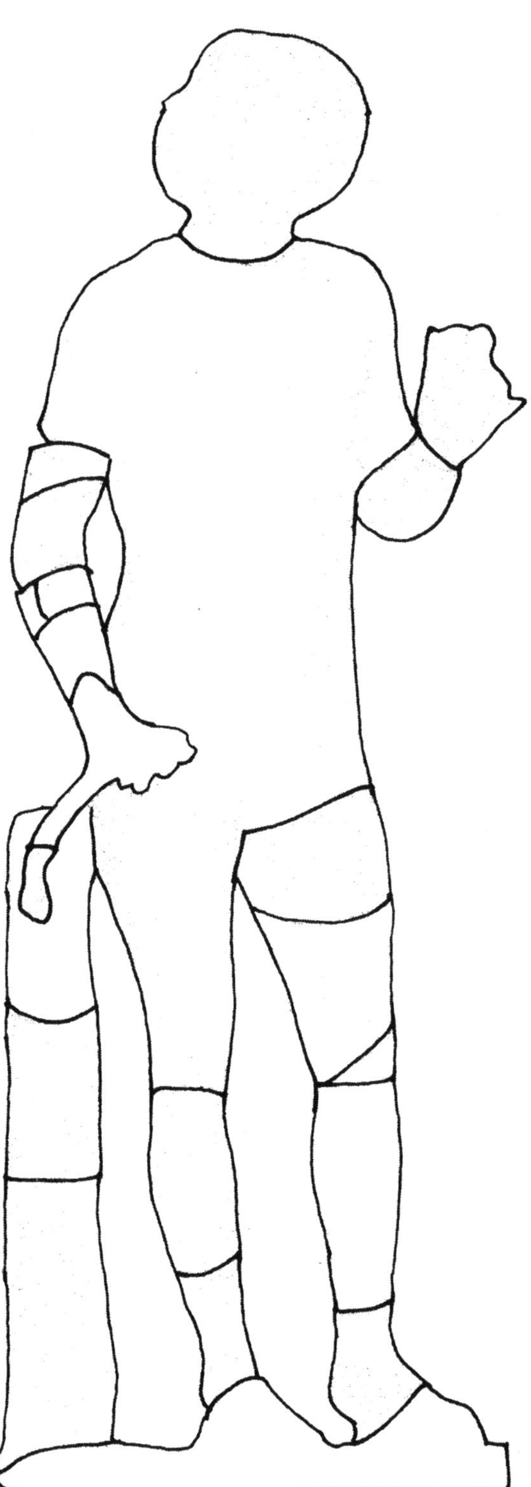

Figure 5.1.
Adam after the fall.

What Should You Consider?

In order for the visitors to be safe, structures to be stable, and display objects to be protected, planners/designers have to consider and question everything that is part of or can impact the exhibition. When selecting M&H, a laundry list of concerns is so extensive that it would go on for pages and still never cover all the items that need addressing. The following are just a few topics to be considered:

- Materials and finishes: longevity, stability, and toxicity
- Visitors' security and safety
- Structures and hardware: stability, longevity, and the ability to withstand visitor abuse

What Items Should You Research?

A good rule is to question everything and assume nothing. It is important to analyze construction details, materials, finishes, hardware, fixtures, furniture, and the like, and to make sure that they are compatible with the intended use, time frame, and budget.

CASE HISTORY: "DON'T DO WHAT I DID"

Early in my design career, I specified a special cast acrylic sheet material. During construction, I was informed that it required a six-month delivery time (the exhibition had to open in four months), it was extremely expensive (I had a tight budget), and to make matters worse, the manufacturer only sold the product in four-by-eight-foot sheets (I needed a two-by-two-foot sheet). Of course, I didn't get what I called for, and frankly, I should never have specified it.

Who Will Help You?

Usually you can research materials on the web and read the product's information sheets. Colleagues who may have used a particular product that you are interested in are also a wonderful source for providing first-hand, unvarnished information. And if you still have questions, then contacting the manufacturer and talking to either a product representative or a member of their research department is highly beneficial. These people always seem anxious to assist, they are willing to answer your questions, and often they will even send you samples.

Sheet Glass

Humankind has been making glass for at least five thousand years. The earliest known manmade glass is found in glazed ceramics circa 3000 BCE. The Egyptians and Mesopotamians had glass vessels 1,500 years later, and by 30 BCE glassmakers used blowpipes to shape it. In 50 CE, the first window glass was manufactured. In 1688, the process of casting plate glass was perfected, and by 1773 polished plate glass was being produced. James Hartley created rolled plate glass in 1847, and in the late 1950s float glass was developed.

Glass is a remarkable material that we take very much for granted. It is highly versatile, and during the manufacturing process, to fulfill a variety of end uses, it can be drawn, rolled, floated, molded, blown, spun, extruded, tempered, polished, laminated, coated, colored, tinted, patterned, etched, and ground.

Although flat and plate glass are rarely used today, it is still important to understand the evolution of sheet glass and the three processes that are used to make it. Flat glass is formed by drawing out molten glass; plate glass is produced by passing molten glass between rollers; and float glass is made by floating molten glass over molten tin. Today float glass makes up 90 percent of the world's production of sheet glass, and that includes almost all the sheet glass produced in North America. However, the term "plate glass" is still often used when referring to float glass.

Glass has unique characteristics that make it particularly suited for museum use. It can be drilled, cut, and bolted to form display cases or graphic panels of nearly any size. Copy applied to its surface can usually be wiped off and updated as needed. It shields and protects artifacts from dust, heat, and visitors and from most ultraviolet light rays. Clear glass is nearly invisible; resists scratching; allows viewers to see but not to touch; is inert; and will not offgas and damage artifacts.

Unfortunately, no material is perfect, and glass has some distinct disadvantages. It can cause reflections; it does not absorb moisture, and humidity can build up inside exhibits cases that could harm the artifacts; it is costly to ship and, depending on its size, could require special padding and crating; and, of course, it breaks, it breaks, it breaks!

Since exhibit planners/designers work mainly with sheet glass panels displayed indoors, outdoor variables such as heat expansion and contraction and weather are not considered here. Neither are blown or shaped glasses addressed. The following discussion pertains exclusively to float glass and its use in museums.

Having made the decision to choose glass over acrylic, the designer has to decide what type of glass to specify. Since glass comes in so many different varieties (Corning Glass alone has developed over one hundred thousand different kinds), the task can become overwhelming. Yet it need not be so, as long as you approach the choice logically, decide what you want the material to do, and determine if it will protect and conserve the artifacts. In addition to cost and construction requirements, there are various factors that should also be considered. First, though, here are a few relevant terms.

Glass Terms

double-glazed glass. Same as *insulating glass.*
insulating glass. Two single sheets of glass with a hermetically sealed air space between them.
laminated glass. Two or more sheets of glass that are held in place by a resin, typically of polyvinyl butyral (PVB).
monolithic glass. A simple, single sheet of glass.
safety glass. Same as *laminated glass.*

Breakage and Safety

Frequently, the designer's primary concern with glass is breakage. No museum wants a damaged artifact, an injured visitor, or a lawsuit. Designers need to factor glass location, activity level, and degree of visitor abuse into both exhibit design and glass choice. Since insurance rates can be influenced by glass selection, it is a good idea to have the museum check with its agent to determine if a savings in insurance premiums can be made by specifying a certain types of glass. Glass varies both in its degree of impact resistance and in its breakage pattern. (Thick or heavy float glass of any type is stronger than thinner glass of the same type.) The following are various types of glass and a few guidelines that should be considered when selecting a glass.

Tempered Glass

Tempered glass is a heat-treated monolithic glass that is also known as fully tempered glass. It is four or five times stronger and has a higher impact resistance than regular glass. Tempered glass is a safety glass, because when broken, it crumbles into small granular fragments like rock salt.

Regular or Annealed Glass

Found in simple windows, regular or annealed glass is a monolithic glass that has low-impact resistance and can fracture easily. It is also much more fragile than tempered glass and when damaged will break into large, sharp shards. It is an inexpensive glass, but because of its fragile and dangerous nature, it is rarely used in museums.

Heat-Strengthened Glass

Another monolithic glass, heat-strengthened glass is intermediate in strength between regular glass and tempered glass. It has twice the strength of regular glass, and when broken it fractures similarly to regular glass and is therefore not a safety glass.

Chemically Strengthened Glass

Chemically strengthened glass is created by treating regular glass in a heated chemical bath. The strength of such glass varies greatly depending on the length of time in the bath, the temperature of the bath, and the process used. It has a higher impact resistance than regular glass. When broken, it produces long, sharp-edged splinters. Unlike heat-treated glass, chemically strengthened glass has a thin surface-compressed layer that can be susceptible to scratching and can deteriorate over time.

Insulating Glass

Insulating glass consists of two or three monolithic glass sheets that are separated by an air- or gas-filled space. Its main purpose is to reduce heat transfer, and the degree of impact resistance and shatter pattern depends on the glass used. An insulating regular glass unit will bear 1.8 times as much weight as a regular monolithic sheet; an insulating heat-strengthened unit will bear 3.6 times as much; and an insulating, fully tempered unit will bear 7.2 times as much. Insulating glass products are used when the building's climate control systems are less than ideal or for live animal exhibits where chicks, reptiles, animals, and the like, are being displayed.

Laminated Glass

This glass is made from combinations of regular, heat-strengthened, fully tempered, and chemically strengthened glass sheets in conjunction with interlayers of different materials. When a glass laminate breaks, the splinters that are produced tend to adhere to the plastic interlayer. This type of glass is an obvious choice when safety is of paramount importance, as for example, in exhibits geared toward active children. It comes in a bewildering variety of combinations, and any laminated glass can be called a safety glass due to its interlayer. This glass is usually recommended for high-risk situations such as street-front displays, protection of extremely valuable artifacts, live animal displays, and where security is an issue. Security laminates are classified into different strengths such as burglar resistant, bullet resistant, attack resistant, and bomb resistant. Weights and thicknesses of laminates vary greatly. The strongest flat laminates can be over two inches thick, weigh more than twenty pounds per square foot, and will withstand pressures of fifty-seven pounds per square inch. Laminated glass is a good choice for slanted glass in exhibits.

Specialty Glasses

Specialty glass comes in a wide variety of types and fills a particular purpose.

Wire glass, glass with wire cast in, has half the impact resistance of regular monolithic glass. When broken, jagged splinters tend to remain in place with broken wires protruding. Wire glass is frequently found in fire doors and hallways because it is considered to be fire resistant.

Special laminates are used in aquariums to withstand enormous amounts of water pressure and have high-impact resistance.

Decorated and patterned glass's strength depends on the glass configurations, decorative materials (such as ceramic frits), and the processes (etching, laminating, etc.) employed.

Physical Properties

When designing with glass, careful attention must be paid to its placement and to the framing and mounting methods used. A few considerations are as follows.

Reflections

Antireflective glass coatings can reduce reflections from 1 to 8 percent, are available in monolithic and laminated products, and can also reduce lighting and heating costs. Reflections on glass can be reduced by manipulating the lighting and the placement of the glass.

Sound

When sound control is needed, glass laminates with an acoustical interlayer should be considered. Sound can be controlled to a limited degree by using glass panels to separate spaces such as an exhibition area and a hallway without reducing visibility.

Thickness

When determining the thickness of glass, temperature, impact conditions, framing methods, placement (horizontal, vertical, or slanted), length and width of the sheet, and the load it is designed to withstand are all factors to be considered. In general, the thicker the glass, the greater its load-bearing capacity will be.

Weight

Weight is a major consideration because it influences the glass frame size, mounting devices, and the shipping and installation methods that will be used. Figure 5.2 is a thickness-related-to-weight table issued by PPG Industries for clear sheet glass.

The total weight of a glass unit must also be factored into any design and will vary with framing systems, sheet thickness, sheet size, and configuration. Glass framed on two sides will support a lighter load than glass framed on four sides. Because its thickness and strength allow for greater spans, a heavy glass (of varying thicknesses) can be used for shelving and straight-sided aquariums.

Thickness		Per Square Foot
3/32"	=	1.16 LBS
1/8"	=	1.56 LBS
5/32"	=	1.98 LBS
3/16"	=	2.43 LBS
1/4"	=	2.89 LBS
5/16"	=	4.05 LBS
3/8"	=	4.90 LBS
1/2"	=	6.36 LBS

Figure 5.2. Thickness-related-to-weight table for clear sheet glass. Issued by PPG Industries.

Designer's Tools

Glass is an incredibly versatile tool for the exhibit designer. It can be transparent or opaque, clear or colored, impervious to the elements, strong enough to be walked on and to support artifacts, resistant to scratching, and fire and somewhat ultraviolet resistant. Display cases are probably the most common use for glass in museum design, but glass really comes alive when it is decorated, lighted, or screened. A few considerations are as follows.

Decorative, Patterned, and Custom Glasses

There are many, many decorative glasses to choose from, and manufacturers are constantly updating their product lines. Glass can be bonded with colored ceramic frits; etched or frosted with patterns; laminated with a decorated interlayer; coated or tinted in almost any hue; and produced in varying degrees of opacity. Graphics can be digitally etched on the surface or applied to a laminate interlayer.

Drilling, Cutting, Etching, and Sandblasting

Regular or annealed glass is the only glass that can be drilled, cut, bolted, etched, and sandblasted at the exhibit construction site, but it should always be sent out for tempering after any invasive procedure. Should the planner/designer choose to invade the surface after strengthening, cuts should be limited to no more than 10 percent of the glass surface. Any postfabrication processes will reduce its strength.

Mirrors

Mirrors can be positioned underneath an artifact to show details that would normally not be seen. Transparent mirrors (two way) often serve as an adjunct to security systems. A major concern, however, when washing copy from mirrors is ghosting and coating degradation.

Text

When a lacquer- or enamel-based text is applied to glass it can usually be removed from uncoated glass without ghosting. However, abrasives and chemical removers can damage glass, especially the coated ones. It is best to check the manufacturers' guidelines before applying text to a glass panel or removing it.

Transparency

All glass has some color, and many untinted glasses are greenish at the edges. Low-iron glass is very clear, transmits more light than ordinary glass, and has little green at its edges. When using tinted glass, keep in mind that the thicker the glass, the darker the color. A laminated interlayer can also affect transparency.

Artifact Protection and Conservation

Maintaining artifacts while on display is the exhibit team's responsibility, and properly selected glass can be a powerful weapon in the designer's artifact-protection arsenal. A few factors that need to be considered are the following.

Ultraviolet Radiation

Ultraviolet (UV) rays can wreak havoc with artifacts. Fabric and paper deteriorate rapidly from ultraviolet radiation, and almost any organic artifact will degrade to some degree under ultraviolet attack. Clear, regular glass will block approximately 29 percent of ultraviolet radiation, while laminated glass with polyvinyl butyral (PVB) interlayer(s) can block 99.5 percent. Monolithic glass with UV-resistant coatings is a further consideration.

Thermal Energy Transfer

Thermal energy transfer is another enemy of artifacts. Depending on the situation, artifacts may need protection from heat or cold, or may tolerate little temperature change. When thermal energy transfer is an issue, glass choices can include insulating glass, tinted monolithic glass, low-emissivity (low-E) glass treated with a thin, transparent energy-efficient coating, and solar-energy-resistant laminated glass. The degree of solar energy resistance varies greatly among products and is outlined in most manufacturers' literature.

Fire

Heat, smoke, fire, and water destroy artifacts. Heat-resistant glass products have been tested in furnaces between 1,000 and 1,638 degrees Fahrenheit and are rated accordingly. Fire-resistance ratings range from twenty minutes to three hours. When fire is the enemy, the resistance of the framing elements and surrounding structures must be included in decision making. Water impact is also an issue, and some fire-rated glass can withstand up to three hours of continuous high-impact spraying. Wire glass is primarily fire resistant, since the wire in it prevents shattering and breaking when exposed to high temperatures and acts as a barrier that prevents the fire from spreading.

Theft

When any artifact is on display, thievery is always a major consideration. Security laminates are the designer's choice here, and they are available in many different strengths. When necessary, exhibit structures containing glass can be wired into security systems.

Moisture Control

Unlike wood and textiles, glass and metal do not absorb moisture. This can become critical when you have a display case with large glass areas and metal framing. Under certain conditions moisture can build up inside the case, especially when it is located in direct sunlight near a window. High levels of humidity in and around a case should be monitored carefully.

Cost and Availability

The final factors in choosing glass are cost and availability. Obviously as the complexity of the glass product increases, so does its cost. When budgets are tight, even plywood occasionally wins out over glass. Handling, shipping, and crating of glass can also become pricey. Even with an unlimited budget, availability is a big issue. Most glass is produced for the building industry, and manufacturers are geared to large-quantity projects with plenty of lead time. Designers must check to see if the product of their choice is available when required in the quantity desired. Often, to avoid costly packing and shipping, construction/installation firms tend to buy the glass near the installation site. A good insurance policy is to contact a glass distributor near the site early in the design phase and to discuss the project's glass requirements with them.

Construction, Installation, and Maintenance

Although these three tasks are in the hands of others, planners/designers should still be aware of several factors when determining the type of glass to use:

- Glass is at its most vulnerable when carried horizontally. Door openings and hallways should, if at all possible, allow for glass to be carried vertically.
- Great care must be exercised during construction and installation, in order to avoid damage and breakage.
- Generally, no amount of preparation or attention to detail will eliminate all breakage. If possible, allot enough replacement time should breakage occur.

Make sure museum maintenance personnel understand how glass products are to be cleaned. Different types of glass, especially coated glass, require different cleaning agents. Again, check with the manufacturer.

CASE HISTORY: "THE GLASSY SNOW"

I still remember a glass disaster that occurred on one of my jobs. The construction firm had taken every possible precaution to protect a huge, thick, tinted glass panel that was a major part of the exhibition's signature exhibit. As the sheet was being put in place, it was lightly scratched by a worker's ring. Being heat-tempered glass, it disintegrated instantly into a pile of granules. I still have a picture showing the stunned worker standing in a glassy snowdrift. The nearest sheet of glass of that size, color, and type was three hundred miles away, and it had to be crated, be shipped, have graphics applied, and be installed for the grand opening two days later. Yes, it was ready when the first guests arrived. Truly, I am always amazed at how resourceful exhibit construction firms can be.

Acrylic Sheet

It is hard to believe that acrylic, which is a material that is used extensively every day throughout the world, is really a Johnny-come-lately. Virtually unknown before World War II, acrylic has had a meteoric rise in popularity since 1843 when methacrylic acid, a derivative of acrylic acid, was formulated. In 1877, German chemists Fittig and Paul discovered the polymerization process that turned methyl methacrylate into polymethyl methacrylate. Otto Rohm patented the product in 1933, registered it under the name of Plexiglas, and three years later introduced the acrylic sheet to the public. Today this material is used throughout the world and now ranks in popularity with glass, wood, and plywood as an indispensable material that all museum exhibit planners/designers rely on when designing their display structures. It is called acrylic sheet or acrylic glass because there are many products that are made from acrylic acid, including paints, rods, tubes, and powder.

This material is an alternative to glass. The most common type of acrylic sheet is polymethyl methacrylate (PMMA) sold under brand names as Plexiglas, Lucite, and Perspex. Since PMMA sheets are now being produced in India and Asia, it is best always to specify a brand name when an acrylic sheet is required.

Acrylic Terms

casting. A manufacturing process in which a liquid material is poured into a mold and allowed to solidify.
extrusion. The process that occurs when a semisoft material is forced through a shaped mold or nozzle.
forming. The process used to create or change the shape of an object or a material.
heat resistance. Ability of a material to maintain its physical, chemical, and electrical integrity.
light transmission. The degree to which light can travel through a material without being absorbed or scattered.
thermal. Pertains to heat.

Processing

Cell casting, continuous casting, and extruding are the three methods normally used to produce acrylic sheets. Not all acrylic is equal; it depends on how it was produced. The following are brief and simplified explanations of what are complicated processes.

Cell Casting

Heated acrylic material is poured (or sandwiched) into a mold that typically consists of two sheets of glass separated by a gasket the thickness of the acrylic sheet desired. The molds are cooled and disassembled, and the acrylic sheet is removed. Of all the materials, this cell casting acrylic sheet is the best for optical clarity. It also has greater surface hardness and machines more cleanly than the other products. This material comes in a wide variety of colors and thicknesses. However, the fact that it has more thickness variation than the following two methods could be a disadvantage when the thickness tolerance is critical to the design.

Continuous Casting

The continuous casting acrylic sheet is mass produced and formed when an acrylic monomer and its catalyst are poured between two stainless steel belts that are separated by the thickness of the acrylic sheet desired. These belts, ten feet wide by three hundred feet long, convey the material through a series of cooling and heating units that regulate the curing process. It is second best for clarity and is very good at maintaining uniform thickness. During thermoforming, it has less shrinkage than have extruded materials. However, this acrylic is not as hard as cell cast materials, will show scratches more readily, and does not machine as well. In addition, design choices are somewhat limited, since its sheets do not come in the varieties of colors and thicknesses that cell casting offers.

Extruding

Extruding combines a resin with an acrylic monomer and a catalyst. The resulting semimolten liquid is pushed through rollers and pressed into sheets of the desired thickness. This method produces good quality material and comes in a wide selection of colors, sizes, and thicknesses. Today it makes up the majority of the commercial market. Compared to the other two processes, extruded sheets are the least expensive. However, extruded acrylic sheets are the softest, contain more impurities, can scratch more readily, become gummy during fabrication, and are more prone to joint failure. Finally, this material may present difficulties during thermoforming, for it can shrink along the extruded direction and expand across the extruded direction.

Properties

Acrylic sheets have their own unique properties, and in many cases they are different from those found in glass. When detailing and specifying an acrylic sheet, a few of the main considerations are as follows: thermal expansion, heat resistance, electrical characteristics, chemical resistance, and light transmission.

Thermal Expansion

Although it is very stable, this material is not glass. For any application where the temperature differential is one hundred degrees Fahrenheit, a twenty-four-by-twenty-four-inch sheet will expand ⅛ inch in both directions. This means that a 48-inch-square sheet can become a 48¼-inch-square sheet if installed in an area where the temperature fluctuates greatly. If the sheets have no expansion space, they will start crazing. We have all seen outdoor signs where the acrylic covers become crazed because the frame that held the sign was not deep enough to accept the acrylic's dimensional changes. Yet when allowed to expand, acrylic is an excellent material to use outdoors for it is virtually unaffected by extreme environmental conditions, and it will not shrink, deteriorate, or turn yellow after long years of service.

Heat-Resistant Acrylic

Heat-resistant acrylic sheets can be used between negative thirty degrees and two hundred degrees Fahrenheit. Space should be provided between a hot element, such as a high-wattage lightbulb, and an acrylic sheet. Once I saw the top of an acrylic vitrine that had melted and deformed because someone, to illuminate the artifacts inside, had placed a photographers high-wattage lamp directly on its top.

Chemical Resistance

Most foods do not affect acrylic, and it has excellent resistance to many chemicals including ammonia and sulfuric acid. However, alcohols and lacquer thinners can affect and attack acrylics. If designing an exhibit where acrylics come into contact with chemicals and food, it is best to conduct research to make sure that it is appropriate for that use.

Light Transmission

Clear, colorless acrylic has a light transmission of 92 percent and is clearer than glass. Translucent white acrylic has excellent light-diffusing properties and is preferred for most types of lighting fixtures and signs.

Forming

Unlike glass or wood, acrylic can be formed into almost any desired shape. Cold forming and heat forming are the methods used to change the shape of an acrylic sheet.

Cold Forming

Cold forming is when a sheet is forced at normal temperature into a curved frame, where to keep its form, it is usually secured in place. Room temperature can affect the amount of bending that can be achieved, and crazing can occur during this process. Stress marks may also appear if the acrylic is too cool when forced into a shape. The following is a guide to the radius that can be accommodated in cold forming. These dimensions, however, can vary and will ultimately depend on the size and the temperature of the acrylic:

A sixteenth-inch-thick sheet can form an eleven-inch radius.
A quarter-inch-thick sheet can form a forty-five-inch radius.
A half-inch-thick sheet can form a ninety-inch radius.

Heat Forming

Acrylic is a thermoplastic that when heated can be bent, drawn, stretched, and draped. Heat is usually applied by placing the acrylic in an oven, next to an infrared lamp, or over a heated rod until it becomes soft and pliable. Acrylic can be heated to approximately 340 degrees and can be reheated and reformed many times. Stress marks can occur when the acrylic is forced into a shape while it is too cool. The are many methods to heat form acrylic sheets, but the most commonly used for exhibits are the following.

Strip Heating or Line Bending

Strip heating or line bending occurs when an acrylic sheet is placed on a hot rod and heated until it becomes soft and can be bent to assume the angle desired. When cooled, it will retain its newly formed shape. This method is used to form acrylic sheets into stands and supports for small signs, books, and artifacts.

Drape or Stretch Forming

Drape or stretch forming is used when a soft, pliable, heated, acrylic sheet is laid, draped, or stretched over a form usually made of wood. When the acrylic sheet cools, it will retain the shape of the form.

Vacuum or Free Forming

In vacuum or free forming, the soft, heated acrylic is clamped over a board or a flat surface that has a cutout shape. Air pressure is applied to the sheet and forces the acrylic through the hole, usually resulting in a dome shape. The air pressure determines the height of the dome. This method is used to make the dome-shaped covers for artifacts and models.

Machining and Joining

Thick acrylic sheets can be cut, cemented, drilled, fastened, routed, and turned, and employ the same methods used to machine wood. Dull drills and blades can cause the acrylic to chip or melt.

An acrylic-to-acrylic joint can be very strong and become almost invisible; it can be superior to wood or glass joints, which are quite obvious. A good acrylic joint relies on experienced craftsmen, good preparation, the right solvent, proper equipment, and a clean environment. The type of joint usually depends on the construction budget and the quality desired. A mitered joint is often preferred, because it is far less noticeable. However, it is more expensive than a butt joint that can be seen more readily. There are several types of solvents used to join acrylic sheets: solvent cement softens the acrylic's edges and melts them together, while a polymerizable cement holds the sheets together by forming new polymers in the joint.

Design Considerations

For the planner/designer, acrylics sheets offer a profusion of design choices that include patterns, tints, colors, solids, and textures. It can be mirrored, fluorescent, transparent, translucent, opaque, abrasive, or bullet resistant and can filter out ultraviolet rays. A few of the many design considerations that must be taken into account are rigidity, temperature, scratching, combustibility, and environmental conditions.

Acrylic is not as rigid as glass, and it can be bent. When an acrylic sheet is hit it could pop out of its frame, and a strong wind could cause it to sail out of its frame. These situations can be avoided if the frame or channel that holds the acrylic sheet is deep enough, and if the sheet itself is thick enough to withstand the impact. When detailing an exhibit case, it is especially critical to make sure that a thief cannot pop the acrylic sheet out of its frame during a "snatch and grab" operation.

Avoid installing an acrylic sheet on a slanted surface where visitors' rings and belt buckles could scratch it.

Acrylic is a combustible thermoplastic material, and the same fire precautions that you would use for wood and paper products must be observed.

Acrylic is weather resistant and is virtually unaffected by blazing sun, extreme cold, saltwater spray, and so forth. It will not turn yellow or become brittle. If taken care of, it can remain new looking for several decades.

A standard acrylic sheet size is four feet wide by eight feet high. Although sheet thicknesses usually include one-eighth, three-sixteenths, one-quarter, three-eighths, one-half, three-quarters, and one inch, thicker sheets are available.

When detailing it is important to know that the thickness of an acrylic sheet can vary by plus or minus 10 percent, and it can also vary throughout the sheet. Normally, plus or minus 5 percent or less occurs.

Acrylic is 50 percent lighter than glass. The chart in figure 5.3 is in pounds per square foot and is approximate.

Acrylic Sheet Weight

Thickness	Weight .
1/16"	0.365
1/8"	0. 694
1/4"	1.424
3/8"	2.136
1/2"	2.879
3/4"	4.322
1"	5.759

Figure 5.3. Acrylic sheet weight, pounds per square foot.

Standards

When investigating a particular use for an acrylic sheet it is best to consult a testing laboratory or information provided by ASTM International (American Standard for Testing and Materials). Their "Abstract" is a good overview of the information that is available.

Quality Control

Today most construction firms send their acrylic work out to plastic fabrication firms that have the latest equipment, facilities, and techniques. For that reason the quality of the work is usually excellent, the joints are precise and crystal clear, and the size of the item is accurate. But when the lowest bidder gets the job, it's best to know how you should judge their work. Being alert to and never accepting substandard work is critical.

Joints

A good acrylic joint should have the appearance of a single sheet, be air- and watertight, and be free of bubbles, imperfections, or chips. Edges should be sharp and precise. Never accept solvent drippings or chipped or nicked edges, which usually indicate that the cutting tool was dull. Melted edges means that the saw wobbled and the material was heated and melted.

Drill Holes

Only accept clear and smooth drill holes. A properly drilled hole has a smooth, semimatte finish that can be brought to a high polish. We have all seen drill holes where the back (or second surface) is chipped or fractured. This is due to the drill's not having a sixty-degree tip. Sometimes a wooden block is used to back up the acrylic. The drilling process should be done slowly.

Surfaces

Never accept crazed or scratched surfaces.

Maintenance

Acrylic is a strong product that resists breaking and will last for years. However, scratches will occur and can usually be removed by gentle sanding and buffing. Acrylic does attract dust, and the cleaner the environment the easier it is to maintain. To keep a crack from spreading, a small hole can be drilled at each end. Nicks can be filled with cement that has been thickened by adding acrylic chips to it.

Sheet Glass versus Acrylic Sheet

The first issue a designer must resolve is whether to use glass at all. Because there are no firm rules when choosing sheet glass or an acrylic sheet, it can at times be a difficult decision to make. The primary pull of glass is the aesthetic quality it brings to any project. Glass is class. The big advantage acrylic has over glass is that it doesn't break so readily, and from the visitor's standpoint, it is a safer material to use.

Although sheet size and thickness will affect the properties of both glass and acrylic, the facts presented below summarize the major differences between them:

- Glass is heavy; a one-eighth-inch square foot of glass weights 1.56 pounds. Acrylic is 50 percent lighter.
- Glass breaks. Acrylic has between six and seventeen times greater resistance to breakage.
- Glass does not flex. Acrylic can twist and withstand shocks and vibrations.
- Glass has a bluish or greenish cast that can affect an artifact's appearance. Acrylic is clear.
- Glass requires special handling during construction and installation. Acrylic is easier to work with.
- Glass shatters into small, sharp splinters. Acrylic breaks into large pieces.
- Glass is very stable. Acrylic expands and contracts.
- Glass cannot be heated and molded to many different shapes; acrylic can.
- Glass resists scratching. Acrylic scratches easily.
- Glass does not create static electricity; acrylic does.
- Glass is fire resistant. Acrylic is combustible.
- Glass is not as good an insulator as is acrylic.
- Glass requires special care and handling when shipping; acrylic does not.
- Glass cannot be readily cut to make many different shapes; acrylic can.
- Glass is rigid. Acrylic can be bent, be twisted, and withstand shocks and vibrations.
- Glass can rarely be machined and drilled on-site. Acrylic can and is easier to work.
- Glass is easy to clean and maintain. Acrylic surfaces attract electrostatic dust.

Wood

Wood is an ancient and reliable material, and woodworking tools have been found in Neanderthal sites. Our traditional woods can be elegant and plentiful, and they can adjust to many sizes, shapes, and forms. However, planners/designers should be aware that wood is an unforgiving, complex material. Unlike glass, acrylic, and even engineered woods whose properties are fairly consistent, wood can be a spoiler. It is never stable, and even after a tree has been cut down and seasoned, it is still "alive." Depending on the humidity it can swell or shrink after it has become an exhibit structure, and if not properly detailed, joints can fall apart and inset panels can become dry, crack, and fall out. To design with wood you have to know it, respect it, and understand its characteristics.

Wood is stronger along the grain and weaker across it. As a result, it expands at different rates, usually more in one direction than the other. And to make matters worse, its color, weight, and grain pattern vary from species to species, and even from board to board.

Yet why do exhibit planners/designers specify this problematic material? It is because a beautiful hardwood denotes elegance, wealth, and even sophistication. A particular wood and its finish can establish an exhibit's time frame and location. Wood can enhance a visitor's experience. It is a warm material that is pleasant to the touch and, with its endless variety of beautiful colors and grains, is pleasing to the eye.

Designing with a local wood provides a unique advantage over other exhibit construction materials, for it can connect the exhibit and its locale, visitors, community, and environment. For that reason, whenever I can, I always use local materials for the exhibit structures.

Wood consists of a variety of species, and care should be taken when selecting a particular wood to make sure that it

- is strong enough to do the job;
- can resist decay and sustain visitor use;
- is available and its cost is within the construction budget; and
- supports the exhibit's design, ambiance, time frame, and theme.

In order to answer the questions that the planner/designer should address when considering wood in an exhibition project, a knowledge of this material should include the following.

Wood Terms

board foot. A unit of measurement for the volume of lumber; a board is twelve inches long by twelve inches wide and one inch thick or its cubic equivalent.

crowning. Occurs when the center of the board strip is higher than its edges. Also called "convex" or "crowned" (opposite of *cupping*).

cupping. Occurs when the edges rise above the center. Also called "concave" or "dished" (opposite of *crowning*).
dimensional stability. The ability of wood to maintain its original dimensions when influenced by a foreign substance such as moisture.
distressed. An artificial texture that gives the wood a timeworn antique look.
end joint. When two pieces are joined together end to end.
figure. Inherent markings or configurations on the surface of the wood that vary from regular grain. Bird's eye, blister, burl, curl, dimple, and fiddleback are all considered figures.
filler. A substance used to fill holes and irregularities and to decrease the porosity of a surface before applying finish coatings.
knot. A flaw in the wood made by a branch.
moisture control. The amount of moisture in wood expressed as a percentage of the weight of the oven dry wood.
pin wormhole. A small, round insect hole about one-sixteenths inch in diameter.
relative humidity. The amount of moisture in the air compared to the amount of water the air can "hold" at that temperature.
unfinished. A product that will be finished after installation.
warping. Any distortion in a piece of wood.

Lumber Grades

Grading is usually based on the wood's appearance, strength, board width and length, position of knots and holes, and degree of bowing, warping, and twisting. Exhibit grades are usually FAS, FIF, and SEL. The following ranking starts with the highest lumber grade and is based on the standards established by the National Hardwood Lumber Association.

FAS

FAS (firsts and seconds) is the best classification of wood, and its grade is based on its poorer face. It is suitable for fine exhibit cabinets and structures, and is specified when the design calls for wide boards and when both sides will be viewed. This category contains the most expensive woods.

FIF

FIF (FAS one face) is the same as FAS, except the board is graded from its best face.

SEL

For an SEL (select) grade, the face side is FAS, and the back side is No. 1 Common (see below). This is normally used in paneling when only one side is exposed to view.

Common Grades

Starting with the best lumber, lesser wood grades are usually numbered as follows:

- No. 1 Common
- No. 2A Common
- No. 2B Common
- No. 3A Common
- No. 3B Common

Construction Methods

Wood is a very versatile material that can be sawed, joined, planed, drilled, bored, routed, glued, sanded, scraped, filed, and finished. Since it comes from trees, its width and length vary, and usually several wooden planks are joined together to form an exhibit structure or panel.

When a wood joint is a major design element, the designer must specify not only the type of joint but also how the pieces are blended together and color matched. When a joint is not a design feature, based on the planner/designer's control drawings and specifications, the construction firm usually decides on the methods that they will use to join the wood and to frame the structures.

When working with wood, the planners/designers must understand wood construction methods and the terms used. In addition, they must be able to comprehend and review shop drawings and to maintain quality control.

Wood Joints

A wood's strength, stability, appearance, use, and cost are major considerations when specifying a particular jointing method, and a good surface must be provided for adhesives to fasten the pieces together. The traditional methods used to join wood are wood joints themselves, adhesives, or mechanical devices. Yet, no matter what type of method is used, a joint must be able to

- support the load;
- have stability and the required longevity;

- withstand the exhibit site's fluctuations in temperature and humidity;
- allow the wood to expand and contract without cracking or breaking; and
- be compatible with its structure and environment.

There are hundreds of types of joints, and the planner/designer should understand the ones that are commonly used in exhibit construction. These include the dowel, butt, dado, rabbet, lap, dovetail, mortise and tenon, miter, spine, and tongue and groove as part of their repertoire. Selection of a particular wood joint depends on the exhibit theme, construction budget, and desired visibility. For example,

- mitered joints are more expensive but less noticed; and
- butt joints are cheaper and easier to make but are more readily seen.

Butt and dado joints are frequently used in exhibit construction. Depending on the stress, application, and visibility of a joint, it will be secured with either or both adhesives and staples. Screws and nails are sometimes used.

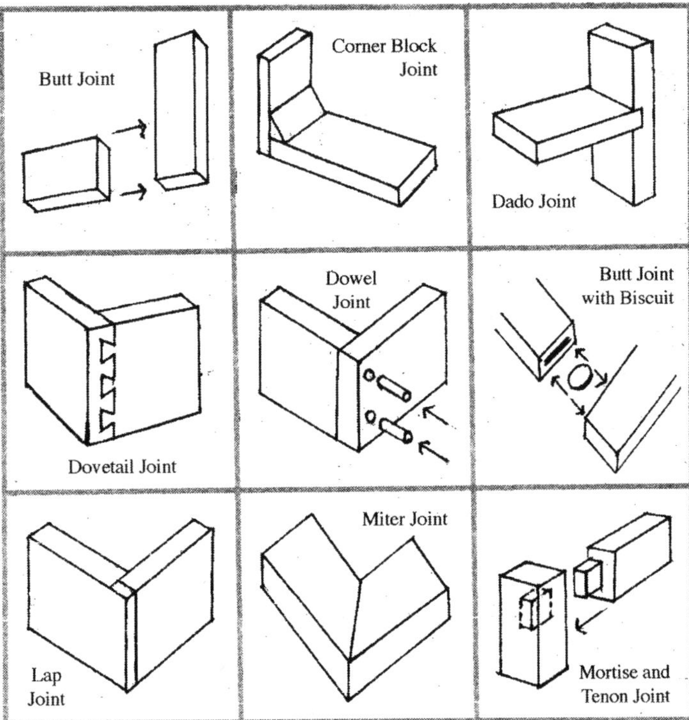

Figure 5.4. Wood joints.

Glued Joint

> Properly glued, the assembled parts of a project are stronger than if they were carved from a single piece of wood.
>
> —Nick Engler, *Woodworking Wisdom*

Glue is frequently used to attach wooden pieces together and to allow two boards to become one. Glue is a manufactured product and can be called cement, resin, epoxy, or mastic. If a problem develops with a glued joint, it is usually due to

- the type of wood or the adhesive used;
- the environmental conditions at the construction site; or
- the condition of the wood surfaces to which the adhesive was applied.

Mechanical Devices

Including the hinge that holds a door to its frame, there is a wide variety of mechanical devices that are meant to secure two pieces of wood together. Although staples are the main mechanical device used today, nails, brads, tacks, screws, bolts, and metal plates are all employed to join wood.

Physical Properties

Hardness, softness, strength, fragility, stiffness, stability, adaptability, fire rating, and resistance to decay are just a few of the factors that must be considered when selecting lumber for a particular use.

Hard and Soft Woods

There are soft woods that are harder than some hard woods. These terms are misnomers for they do not apply to a wood's strength but rather to its ability to resist water and to the type of tree that produced it. For example, balsa, which is very light and soft, is classified as a hardwood, while Douglas fir, a much harder wood, is designated as a softwood.

Hardwoods

Hardwoods come from deciduous, broad-leaf trees such as cherry, walnut, and oak. They are usually a luxury wood with beautiful grain and rich color, and are mostly specified for trimming exhibit structures and flooring. Hardwoods are usually graded FAS, FIF, or SEL and are more expensive than softwoods.

Softwoods

Softwoods are obtained from coniferous, thin, needle-leaf trees such as pine, Douglas fir, cedar, and hemlock. Generally they cannot withstand visitor abuse and are used mainly for framing an exhibit panel or a structure. Softwoods can be easily shaped and, because they are mostly lighter than hardwoods, can be used for constructing items that need to float or to fly. They are usually graded in the Common category.

Offgassing

Refer to chapter 2's "Conservation" section on "Offgassing."

Finishes

Most wooden exhibit structures are covered with a finish coat or a laminate. This is usually done to enhance their appearance and to protect the wood from the following:

- Abrasion or indentations
- Accumulating dirt, thus making the surface easier to clean
- Changes in color that are usually due to light or pollutants
- Fungi and insects
- Moisture, thus avoiding the consequences of dimensional change
- Wear and tear
- Weather conditions, if installed outside

Whether applied to a wooden or to a composite board surface, a finish coat or a laminate should have stability, satisfy local fire codes, and be compatible with the materials it is covering and the exhibit's location and use. The planner/designer when choosing a finish must also consider the use to which a structure will be subjected and its environmental conditions. There are three basic methods used to prepare a wooden surface.

Coating

Years ago the term "enamel" meant a durable, glossy, oil-based, protective finish. Today "enamel" is used to describe any coating designed as a durable finish. Most exhibit construction firms now rely on water-reducible enamels when finishing wooden structures, because they are durable and will not crack easily. These enamels can dry to a good hard surface within a half hour, if adequate airflow and low humidity are provided. This quick drying time allows for the usual three sublayers of base coats to be applied within one working day. However, water-reducible enamels do have a few disadvantages: their shelf life is relatively short, and after about two years their color will change, which can be a problem when there is a need to refurbish or to touch up a structure.

Penetrating

Oils, dyes, and stains soak into the wood and do not remain on the surface. They do not protect the wood, and for that reason, these products are rarely used to finish exhibit structures, especially in high-density visitor areas.

Veneering and Laminating

Lumber can be covered with a variety of veneers and laminates such as plastics, wood, metal, and even paper. Veneers are usually thin sheets of quality wood, glued to a wooden structure of lesser quality. They can enhance an inexpensive structure and be stained. Laminates are printed, colored, or textured plastic sheets that are glued to a structure or a board.

Specifications

The following clauses should be considered:

- When applying finishes it is important to specify that they must be applied in a dust-free environment.
- When specifying a wood product it is best to state that the material should be in the construction shop two weeks before construction begins. This will enable it to stabilize and to adjust to the local humidity before cutting and joining take place.
- When boards are joined, their wood grain, direction, and color must be matched so that they blend together visually and abrupt changes in appearance do not occur.

Engineered Wood

Engineered wood (EW), also called composite wood, manmade wood, and manufactured board, includes a wide range of manmade products produced from wood particles or fibers that are bonded together to form boards. Compared to traditional solid woods, EWs are more economical and stable, come in convenient sheet sizes, are easier to work with, and usually can be cut, drilled, jointed, glued, and fastened.

In the United States, these boards are engineered to precise design specifications and meet national and international specifications. Many types of EWs such as bending plywood offer more design options than wood. However, some products may burn quicker than solid lumber and their adhesives may be toxic. Some EWs may be more prone to warping than solid wood, and many are not appropriate for outdoor use. Nevertheless, most can be coated with a paint or a lacquered finish, or covered with wood veneers, plastic laminates, and decorative finishes. Engineered wood boards come in many forms.

Plywood

Plywood (PW) is flexible, inexpensive, workable, and reusable, and can be locally manufactured. It is made by bonding thin sheets of wood that are glued together at right angles to each other to form a larger and thicker board that is stronger and stiffer than the sum of its parts. Today it is one of the most widely used wood products and is a staple of the exhibit construction industry.

Plywood is often referred to as the original engineered wood and can trace its lineage back to the Egyptian pharaohs, where a form of laminated wood was found in their tombs. The Chinese, a thousand years ago, were known to have made furniture from shaved wood that was glued together. Today's plywood was invented by Immanuel Nobel, father of Alfred Nobel, when he realized that several thin layers of wood bonded together would be stronger than one single, thick layer. The first plywood patent was issued on December 26, 1865, to John K. Mayo of New York City. At roughly the same time, John Henry Belter, a furniture maker in New York, invented a method of layering veneers to form curved shapes.

Plywood versus Solid Wood

Plywood is less expensive than wood, yet when a wood veneer is applied to its outer surface it can almost appear to be as rich and as elegant as solid wood. Compared to wood, plywood is flexible, cheaper, and comes in convenient sizes that are easy to cut and work with. Because it is composed of layers, PW is stronger and stiffer than traditional wood. Plywood is resistant to cracking, shrinking, splitting, twisting, and warping; has dimensional stability; and is equally strong in all directions. Because of its crossbanding, plywood will hold a nail that is driven through the plies better than wood does, but it will not hold a nail driven into the edge of the board. PW is bonded from wood veneers and, for that reason, is harder to bend than wood, the exception being flexible plywood. Plywood edges (end grain) are unfinished and, if left exposed, need to be concealed by taping, framing, edging, or the like.

Types

Softwood plywood: Made of cedar, spruce, pine, or fir and is typically used in building construction.

Hardwood plywood: Both face and back surfaces are covered with hardwood veneers. It is widely available in birch and oak, and is also available in other species such as ash, maple, mahogany, rosewood, and teak.

Marine plywood: Made from durable tropical hardwood veneers and resists delamination and fungal attack. It is usually specified where a material is exposed to humid, moist, and wet conditions for an extended period of time. Marine plywood is regularly used in the construction of docks and boats.

Flexible plywood: Usually consists of a thinner central core and two thicker "tenderized" outer layers. Flexible plywood can adjust to a multitude of forms and will hold its shape once it is glued, laminated, or veneered. It can be used to wrap around columns and make free-form structures. It is also known as bendy plywood, flexi-ply, and flexi plywood.

In addition to the above there are more specialized types of plywood, including fire-retardant, moisture-resistant, sign-grade, and pressure-treated plywood.

Grades

There are many plywood grading systems in use today, and they can vary with the country and even between organizations. The Engineered Wood Association and American Society for Testing and Materials are just a few of the grading organizations that exist. The following is a brief summary of U.S. Plywood Standard (APA PS1-95 Construction and Industrial Plywood) grades:

Grade A: Surfaces should be firm, smoothly cut, and free from knots, pitch pockets, open splits, and other characteristics. When more than one piece is used, the pieces should be well joined. Minor defects are repaired with synthetic filler.

Grade B: Surface shall be solid, smooth, sanded, and free from open characteristics and broken grain. Slightly rough grain should be permitted. Minor sanding and patching characteristics, including sander skips, should not exceed 5 percent of panel area. This grade should have more repaired defects than grade A and can potentially have small knots up to one inch across.

Grade C: Sanding characteristics shall not impair the strength or serviceability of the panel. Knots shall be tight and not more than 1½ inches across the grain. Any number of knotholes up to one inch are permitted. Occasionally, a 1½-inch knot across the grain can be permitted. Splits should not exceed eight inches long and half an inch wide. Accepted are several minor defects that have been repaired, knots up to 1½ inches across, and discolorations and sanding defects. Surface may be stitched together from smaller veneers.

Grade D: Any number of plugs, patches, shims, wormholes, sanding effects, and other characteristics are permitted, provided they do not seriously impair the strength or serviceability of the panel. Knots and knotholes up to 2½ inches across are accepted. Sanding defects and discoloration are permitted, and a board may be stitched together from many pieces. This grade has limited exhibit use.

Plywood sheets can be purchased with face and back sides consisting of two different grades. Based on the U.S. Plywood Standard the following is a guideline for museum exhibit construction:

A-A grade: The face and back of plywood are both grade A. This grade is the most expensive and is used when both sides have to be finished or veneered, and will be seen by the visitor. Both surfaces can be painted and veneered.

A-B grade: Used when the face is laminated or veneered, and when the back is only seen occasionally. Good quality cabinets, panels, and tabletops are proper uses for A-B grade panels.

A-C grade: Suitable for applications where the face is visible or laminated, and the back is hidden and never or rarely seen. Using A-C grade is a good choice when cost savings are paramount.

B-B grade: A common grade for general usage where the face and back should be of decent quality but where it will be used in a darkened area, semiconcealed, or seen from a distance.

B-C grade: An economical and common grade. The grade B face can be seen, while the back is usually concealed.

C-C grade: An economical, common, and utility grade. Used where the face and back are not important but the panel should be strong. Rarely employed in exhibit construction; however, a carpet-covered platform would be a good use for this material.

C-D and D-D grades: Inferior grades of plywood; rarely used in exhibit construction.

Lamination

Imperfections in a plywood surface such as knots or plugs will eventually telegraph through a laminated surface, and their imprint will be seen. For that reason it is best to specify a grade A surface when applying a veneer for a panel that will be seen.

Sheet Size

Traditional sheet sizes are four by eight feet.

Thicknesses are as follows: one-eighth, one-quarter, three-eighths, one-half, five-eighths, three-quarters, and one inch, going up to three inches.

Masonite

Invented in 1924 by William H. Mason, by the 1930s Masonite was a commonly used construction material. Today it has many applications and fulfills a wide variety of exhibit construction needs including facing panels, cabinets, and bases.

Masonite is a smooth, burnished finish board that is formed when steamed wood chips are disintegrated and then pressed and heated to form a board. The chemicals in the original wood serve to bond the fibers together, thus eliminating adhesives and formaldehyde-based resins. It is considered to be environmentally friendly.

Because of its smooth surface, Masonite makes an excellent base for a spray paint or lacquer finish, and for that reason, it is used in making exhibit panels, cabinets, and bases. It is also used in dioramas, historic setting, and film sets.

Masonite's long fibers give this material a high bending strength, tensile strength, and density. However, Masonite can swell and rot when exposed over time to the elements. Because of its stability, excellent surface, and reusability, Masonite has proven to be a dependable material on which designers rely.

Fiberboard

Fiberboard (FB) is a generic term that describes a board that is manufactured from treated wood chips, shavings, sawdust, or other vegetable fibers held together with wax, wood lignin, and a synthetic resin or binder. Producing FBs can be an involved process that is governed by the materials used and the density and properties desired. Basically, FBs are formed by treating the fibers with pressure or steam and then pressing and extruding them into sheets. A bonding agent is usually added to increase a FB's strength and resistance to moisture, fire, or decay, and to improve its sound-deadening qualities.

Fiberboards were first produced in about 1898 when a hardboard type of material was invented by hot pressing waste paper together; by the 1900s, low-density fiberboards were being manufactured commercially. In about 1924, William Mason invented a product similar to hardboard, and in the 1960s, medium-density fiberboard was developed in the United States.

Generally, fiberboard is less expensive, denser, and more uniform than traditional solid wood or plywood. The normal size sheet is four by eight feet, although larger panels can be obtained. Depending on the material, the thickness can vary, but usually it is from 3/16 to 1 5/16 inches, with the most being one-half and three-quarter inches thick.

Because of the lack of linear grain and the small size of the particles in fiberboard compared to plywood, fiberboard is more likely to break, sag, or bend under a load. Fastening methods, including screws, nails, or staples, are more likely to fail when attached to fiberboard. Because of FB's softer interior, the joints are not as strong as in plywood's joints, and many traditional joints such as dado and rabbet are not practical to use in FB construction. Even though it is weaker, a butt joint is generally used when joining fiberboards together. Because of FB's smooth, flat, hard surface, it is an excellent material to paint, laminate, and veneer.

Although there are many different types of fiberboards being produced throughout the world today, the following three types are the mainstay of the exhibit construction industry in the Untied States.

Low-Density Fiberboard

Low-density fiberboard (LDF) is made from tiny pieces of wood, sawmill shavings, or sawdust glued together and pressed into sheets. LDF is cheaper and more uniform than wood and comes in various strengths and densities. The higher the density of LDF, the stronger it is, and its ability to retain screws and fasteners increases. Painting or applying a wood veneer to its surface can enhance its appearance considerably.

LDF is the cheapest and lightest of the fiberboards and can be bent into free-form shapes. Unless it is sealed or painted, it is rarely used outdoors or in high-moisture environments, since it can readily expand and discolor. However, when bonded with phenol formaldehyde resin, it can have external applications because of its increased water resistance.

Medium-Density Fiberboard

Medium-density fiberboard (MDF) is cheaper and denser than plywood, yet it has similar uses. Since urea-formaldehyde resins (UFR) are mainly used in the manufacturing process of MDFs, these resins are continually being released from the fiberboard, so care should be taken to ventilate the spaces where this product is installed. Studies also have shown that exposure to MDFs may cause cancer in humans and animals. Another resin used in making MDF is phenol-formaldehyde (PF), which is more durable and does not emit formaldehyde after it is cured. It is best when specifying MDF to state that it should be made with a PF resin.

High-Density Fiberboard

In the 1920s, improved methods of exploding tiny pieces of wood and compressing the pulp at high temperatures created a high-density fiberboard (HDF) that is the strongest and hardest of the fiberboards. Because it lacks grain or knots, it is a good substrate for plastic laminates, veneers, and vinyls, and is also a good surface for a paint finish. This board differs from particleboard in that it will not split or crack and does not need a binding agent, although sometimes a resin is added.

All fiberboards come with at least one side having a smooth finish. The sheets are marked S1 or S2 to designate if one or both sides are smooth. HDF comes in standard four-by-eight-foot panels and thicknesses that include one-sixteenth, one-eighth, and one-quarter inches.

Tempered hardboard is another form of HDF. This board is coated with a thin film of linseed oil and baked. It is more water and impact resistant and has more hardness, rigidity, and tensile strength than has HDF board.

Aluminum

Aluminum can trace its heritage back to the Persians around 5300 BCE. However, as we know it today, aluminum started to be produced about 1825 and because of its cost was regarded as a precious metal. When cost-saving production techniques were developed, aluminum became economically feasible for everyday use. Today more aluminum is being produced in this world than all the other nonferrous metals combined.

Properties

Aluminum has many advantages: it can be easily machined, cast, drawn, and extruded. It is also a soft, lightweight, durable, ductile, and malleable metal. It is nonmagnetic, does not ignite easily, and is a good thermal and electrical conductor. Aluminum can resist corrosion due to the thin surface layer of aluminum oxide that forms when exposed to air, and it has a lovely natural silver to gray color and a good reflective surface. It is about one-third as dense and stiff as steel.

It is the metal of choice for exhibit construction firms because they can easily cut, drill, and assemble aluminum structures in their shops. However, they do send extrusions to aluminum finishers for powder coating and anodizing.

Because aluminum is easy to extrude, there are now structural systems comprising aluminum shapes, connectors, and locks that can be easily assembled into an infinite number of exhibit display cases, bases, and structures. These can become permanent display structures or be disassembled and reconfigured into display cases and bases of various sizes and shapes.

Anodizing versus Coating

Anodizing is a simple, electrochemical process that forms a protective coating of aluminum oxide on the surface of the aluminum and gives it a deeper, richer metallic appearance. The lifetime of the finish is proportional to the thickness of the anodic coating applied. The advantage of anodizing is that the coating actually becomes part of the metal and cannot peel off. Because of its durability, anodized structures are used in high-traffic areas where the coating can withstand a great deal of physical abuse. However, like all materials, it can scratch. Therefore, so that the scratches will not be obvious, consider using a clear anodized finish in heavy-traffic areas. There are now about thirty colors to choose from including rich bronzes and even bright reds and greens.

Powder coating happens when a pigment is encapsulated in a powdered resin and then electrostatically sprayed on an aluminum structure or extrusion and cured in an oven. This curing process does not usually emit volatile organic compounds (VOCs). Powder coating can provide an immense variety of colors, yet for small projects, the choice of colors could be limited, so it is best to research the colors that are available before specifying.

Green Materials

> The first question many people ask is how to get started. Museums have adopted sustainability practices in numerous ways, but often it begins with the passion and commitment of at least one person who champions the ideas and gets others inspired.
>
> —Greenexhibits.org

The green movement that is evolving today is highly reminiscent of the accessibility movement that took place in the last half of the twentieth century and resulted in hallmark legislation such as the Rehabilitation Act of 1973 and the Americans with Disabilities Act (ADA) of 1990. Museums were in the vanguard of the accessibility movement, and they formed committees and held meetings and conferences to revise their facilities and exhibits, and to address the needs of the challenged. Children's museums were especially active and even went so far as to install exhibits that addressed the problems of the handicapped child. Today the accessibility movement is still ongoing, and we should never overlook the fact that all our lives have been made easier and better because of it.

Green Materials Terms

As with any new movement, a vocabulary soon starts to develop. The following terms are regularly being used:

ecosystem. A community of living organisms, such as plants, animals, and microbes, and their environment, consisting of the air, water, mineral soil, and so on, with which they interact.

environmental footprint. A standardized measure of human demand contrasted with the planet's ecological capacity to regenerate. For example, in 2007, the impact of humanity's total ecological footprint was estimated to be growing 1.5 times faster than the Earth could renew it.

green materials. Products that are environmentally nonthreatening. Green materials are composed of renewable resources that inflict minimal or no harm on humans and the environment. Also called environmentally friendly, eco-friendly, and nature friendly.

indoor air quality (IAQ). Products that have minimal emissions of volatile organic compounds (VOCs) and also maximize resource and energy efficiency while reducing chemical emissions.

life cycle assessment (LCA). An evaluation of the relative "greenness" of a material or product; addresses its impact throughout all of its life stages.

low or nontoxic. Materials that emit few or no carcinogens, reproductive toxicants, or irritants as demonstrated by the manufacturer through appropriate testing.

recycle. To process a material or item so that it can be reused.

stewardship. An ethic that embodies responsible planning and management of human life and ecosystems.

sustainability. The practice that relies on renewable/reusable materials and processes that are green or environmentally benign. It is our long-term commitment and responsibility to improving the quality of all human life and of all the ecosystems that exist throughout the world.

volatile organic compounds (VOCs). Organic chemicals that at room temperature can turn into a gas and pollute the air. For example, the formaldehyde in paint can become a gas at negative two degrees Fahrenheit, slowly exit the paint, and pollute the air.

The Green Movement

The green movement has spread throughout the world and has encompassed a huge population. Yet, it is still in its infancy. Again, it is the museums that are among the leaders of this effort, and today green museums and exhibits are regularly being built. The movement is here to stay, and planners/designers should support it, since it will make our lives and the rest of the world better just as the accessibility movement did.

Children's museums early on adopted exhibits materials that were green. It grew out of concern for the children who visited the museums, physically touched the carpet, and sometimes even mouthed the exhibit structures, participatory exhibits, furniture, structures, and instruments. The museums also realized that the materials and equipment they used in their exhibits sometimes produced toxic emissions and contributed to indoor air pollution. This toxic air could affect not only their visitors but also their staff members. This was a major concern, especially since many of the basic exhibit and graphic materials on which planners/designers relied were toxic or offgassed, including acrylics, woods, engineered woods, solvents, adhesives, paints, finishes, inks, fabrics, and wall and floor coverings.

Museums have the knowledge and the experience acquired during the accessibility movement and from their mandate to educate the public, so that they can lead the green movement by example. Sustainable materials and toxic-free air are now major considerations when designing an exhibition. Exhibits and lectures pertaining to this subject are common, and many museums have established a "green list" to aid their exhibit teams in evaluating and selecting green materials and procedures. Some of the items on these lists include the following:

- Design exhibit structures that can be recycled.
- Whenever possible, refurbish and reuse existing exhibit structures.
- Use modular exhibit structures that can be reconfigured and reused.
- Use low-VOC paints and adhesives.
- Use water-based paints.
- Avoid vinyl-based products, such as signs, fabrics, and wall coverings.

- Install timers and sensors to adjust lighting levels and improve their energy efficiency.
- Use materials that are certified to be sustainable.
- Select materials that are durable, have longevity, and are low in maintenance.
- Avoid materials, finishes, and adhesives that offgas or emit pollutants.
- Select products and systems that resist moisture or inhibit the growth of biological contaminants.
- Select materials that are made from renewable, recycled, salvaged, and local materials.
- Select materials that were made without employing dangerous substances.

Green Research Materials

Today there are numerous green products that reduce the environmental impact associated with extracting, transporting, processing, fabricating, installing, reusing, recycling, and disposing of exhibit construction materials. Researching and gathering the technical information is essential in deciding if a material is "green," and if it will fit your needs. Manufacturers' information is available and could include material safety data sheets (MSDS), indoor air quality (IAQ) test data, product warranties, source material characteristics, recycled content data, environmental statements, and durability information. Yet, be aware of manufacturers who exaggerate the sustainability of their products and always hoist a "red" flag when a material data sheet contains words like "danger," "poison," "warning," "caution," and a list of unpronounceable chemical names.

There can be no doubt that the sustainability movement and green materials are here to stay. Obviously this is only the beginning, and there is a lot of work to be done.

Museum Terms

absorb. The ability of an *object* to take up *light*, energy, and so forth, and not transmit it.

aim. The goal, objective, or purpose of an *exhibit* or a *display*; the desired results.

aisle. A walkway between *exhibits* and *displays.*

ambiance. The intellectual and physical atmosphere that surrounds us; the environment or atmosphere that envelops an *exhibition* or an *exhibit* area.

anatomy. The structure or organization of an *object* or a project.

ancillary. A subordinate or secondary part of a unit.

archive. A place devoted to the storage of special records and *objects.*

artifact. A manmade or a natural, two- or three-dimensional item having special value.

artwork. A two- or three-dimensional piece of original art.

as-built drawings. *Drawings* that have been marked up to reflect changes made during construction and installation. Also called record drawings.

aspect. A particular point of view.

attribute. A quality, property, or characteristic of somebody or something; an assigned value; to give credit.

balance. A state of equilibrium in which all elements work together to form a satisfying and harmonious whole.

bid package. The *document* containing all the information, specifications, and *drawings* that are required for construction firms to quote on building, *shipping,* and installing *exhibits.*

bidding drawings. The *technical drawings* that are included in the *bid package.*

bidding phase. A *phase* of the work dedicated to the bidding process.

bleed. When a *graphic* print stops at the edge of the paper or *graphic panel.*

boilerplate. A uniform language used normally in legal *documents.* Traditionally, a boilerplate is part of the *general conditions.*

bond. A written legal obligation usually stipulating a financial payment if a specific, agreed-upon act is not performed.

book. A term used to describe a *display,* an *exhibit,* or an *exhibition* that contains too many words.

brief. A concise statement or summary.

budget. The probable cost of a project.

buildings and grounds. The areas and structures that are part of an *institution.*

building-use plan. A report that records and details the condition of an institution's *buildings and grounds;* it may make recommendations for changes.

camera-ready art (CRA). An image or a digital *file* that is ready to be printed, and needs no further sizing or manipulating.

capacity. The measure of the amount that can be held, supported, or allowed.

change order. A written *document* describing the work and cost that were added to or deleted from the original *contract.*

clarification. A detailed explanation needed when something is unclear.

cleanup. The complete *exhibit* area including cases, *panels,* structures, and floors should be made clean, free of debris and finger marks.

close-out package. A *document* or *file* containing all the information, instructions, drawings, and *guarantees* needed to maintain an *exhibit* or an *exhibition* after it has been completed.

collection. A group of *objects* to be seen, studied, displayed, or kept together.

color. A particular quality of an *object* that is caused by reflected *light.*

color-blindness. Inability to clearly distinguish between different colors of the spectrum.

color model. A system used to identify and to group a wide range of colors numerically. The most common color models are RGB, CMYK, and HSB.

color wheel. A circular *diagram* designed to show the relationships among a particular group of *colors.*

column. A vertical *graphic* element; a building or an *exhibit* structural support.

community. The people who live in a particular area; a group of people having a common interest.

comprehensive evaluation. An assessment that investigates all aspects of a *museum* or an *institution;* usually performed during the master planning *phase.*

computer graphics. Images generated by a computer.
condition. A state of being.
cone. A receptor or cell in the retina of the eye that allow us to see *colors* and fine details.
conservation. The act of preserving or restoring an *object.*
construction. The act of assembling or fabricating an *object* or *structure.*
construction phase. The time *period* when the *exhibit* construction takes place.
contextual. The meaningful relationship established between all elements of an *exhibit* project.
contract. A binding legal agreement between two or more parties.
contrast. The placing of opposing elements such as *materials, display items, colors,* forms, or *lines* in close proximity to each other for the purpose of producing an intensified effect.
copying. The act of using information, designs, or *objects* that have been produced by others.
craftsperson. A skilled, trained individual who makes things by hand, such as a carpenter or a *model* maker.
creativity. The act of developing new ideas or relationships.
critique. An informal appraisal of an *exhibit design.*
cross section. A scaled *technical drawing* that represents a vertical or horizontal slice through an area, a *display,* an *exhibit,* or a *structure.*
curator. One who is in charge of a museum's *collection* and oversees and manages it.
deliver. The act of providing *materials* to a designated place.
deliverables. Copies or photographs of sketches, *drawings, models,* and other *documents* prepared during a particular *phase* and delivered to the exhibit committee for review.
dense. The state of being compacted, crowded, impenetrable, or thick.
description. A written or verbal explanation.
design description. A written *description* of an *exhibition,* an *exhibit,* or a *display.*
design process. A system used to create and produce a design.
diagram. A simple *drawing* showing basic *shapes* and placement of elements.
dimension. A symbolic language used to describe an *object*'s length, width, and height.
diorama. A three-dimensional scene that captures a moment in time.
display. A group of items having a commonality; part of an *exhibit.* Several displays can make up an exhibit.
display item. Any two- or three-dimensional *exhibit object,* such as an *artifact,* a painting, an illustration, or a specimen.
display object. Same as *display item.*

display panel. Imparts the information that is pertinent to a *display*.
dock. A platform connected to a building where trucks can unload.
document. A nonfictional, written record or an *object* that contains or stores information.
documentation phase. The *period* in which all the *technical drawings* and specifications required to bid and build an *exhibition* are produced.
drawing. An illustration usually consisting of *lines* sometimes with shading and *color*. It is more accurate and precise than a *sketch*.
educator. A person who develops and implements educational *programs*.
elevation. A flat representation of a wall; a scaled *technical drawing* that shows the height and length of a wall area and its displays and building structures.
entrance panel. Introduces the *visitor* to the *exhibition* and discusses its purpose and its *theme*.
ergonomics. The study of how an area, a *structure*, or a piece of equipment can be designed for comfort, safety, and efficiency.
estimate. Project cost based on the value of the labor and *materials* of an actual design.
evaluation. The act of examining and judging.
exhibit. A subdivision of an *exhibition* that has a common *theme* and usually contains several *displays*.
exhibit brief. A *document* that clarifies all the conditions and ramifications that will impact an *exhibition*. It is part of the *exhibit program*.
exhibit design. The act of planning/designing an *exhibition*, an *exhibit*, or a *display*.
exhibition. The total area devoted to presenting *exhibits* and *displays* that have a common *theme*.
exhibit panel. Imparts the information that is pertinent to a particular *exhibit*.
exhibit planner/designer. A person who plans and designs *displays*, *exhibits*, and *exhibitions*, and produces the construction *drawings* and specifications.
exhibit program. A *document* that contains the information needed to develop an *exhibition*.
exhibit team. A group of people involved in the development of an exhibition or exhibit.
exit panel. Sums up the *exhibition*.
face. See *typeface*.
feasibility study. An analysis to determine if a proposed *exhibit* or *exhibition* will be successful and if it should be developed.
file. Collection of *documents* and small items.

final phase. The *exhibit design period* where every element pertaining to an *exhibit* is resolved and made ready for documentation.
fire retardant. A chemical product or combination of chemicals used to reduce flammability or to retard the spread of fire over a surface.
flame spread rating. A measure of a *material*'s propensity to burn rapidly and spread flames.
floor plan. A type of *technical drawing* that is a "map" of a floor area showing the arrangement of spaces and structures.
form. Three-dimensional item having length, width, and height.
format. The *layout* and organization of a *document*, a *drawing*, or a *graphic*.
formative evaluation. An assessment that occurs during the developmental stages of an *exhibition* and is meant to test the effectiveness and appeal of the selected *displays*, *graphics*, *text*, and so forth. Many times a *mockup* of displays and graphics is used to assist with this type of *evaluation*.
front-end evaluation. This *evaluation* occurs during the outset of the *exhibit* planning/designing process. It explores what the *visitors* want to learn or experience in an exhibit or education *program* and assists in developing the *displays* and *text*.
general conditions. A *document* that is part of the written specifications that establishes the working relationship between the *institution* and the contractor. It also includes information that is not shown elsewhere in the *bid package*.
gestalt. A unified whole; the organization of *shapes* and forms into groups to provide a strong unit.
goal. See *aim*.
graphic. Flat art usually containing *text*, photographs, and illustrations.
graphic layout. A scaled or full-size *layout* of a proposed *graphic*.
graphic mockup. A reproduction of a proposed *graphic*.
graphic panel. A *structure* designed to display *graphics*.
grid. Used during the design *phases*, it is a network of *lines* that serves as a basis to lay out something and to organize *text*, *visuals*, or *objects*.
guarantee. An agreement between two or more parties that assures of a particular outcome.
hard copy. A paper printout or copy.
harmony. A pleasing combination of *objects*. A satisfying effect produced by an arrangement of *colors*, forms, *shapes*, and elements.
hazard. A dangerous item or element.
hierarchy. An arrangement in order of importance.
history. Recounting of past events, people, countries, and institutions; a record of an *exhibit* project.
humidity. Amount of water vapor in the air.

HVAC. Abbreviation for heating, ventilating, and air-conditioning.
illumination. The effect caused by a *light* source.
inspection. A careful and critical examination aimed at forming a judgment of flaws, quality, and correctness.
inspiration. A person or a concept that stimulates the human mind to a high level of creative thought or artistic endeavor.
install. To place in position, connect, and make ready for use; connecting *exhibits* to a power source.
installation phase. The time *period* required to *install* an *exhibition* or a *exhibit.*
institution. See *museum.*
intensity. A degree of strength, power, brightness, or *saturation.*
interaction. The result of two or more elements working together and affecting each other.
intermediate phase. The *exhibit design phase* where the preliminary design is advanced and made ready for the final design phase.
inventory. A detailed list of *objects.*
isometric drawing. A *technical drawing* that shows a three-dimensional, scaled *object,* using a horizontal thirty-degree *grid.* An axonometric drawing is similar to an *isometric drawing* except it is based on a forty-five-degree grid.
label. *Text* that identifies and explains a particular item or *artifact.* It is usually brief and could contain an illustration.
label panel. Identifies and briefly discusses a particular *object* or *artifact.*
layout. A *drawing* showing how the parts of a unit are positioned.
leading. Space between the lines of type; also know as line spacing.
letter spacing. Space between individual letters.
light. A source of *illumination* that makes vision possible.
light beam. A large volume of *light* that is composed of infinite number of *light rays* and is divided into pencils.
light level. The degree of *intensity* of *illumination* from dark to bright.
light pencil. A narrow beam of *light* that is divided into *light rays.*
light ray. The narrowest and smallest portion of a *light pencil* containing vibrating, colorless *light waves.*
light waves. Vibrating waves used to transmit *light.*
line. A continuous stroke connecting two points.
line art. Artwork limited to black and white areas and *lines.*
maintenance manual. A *document* that contains the information needed to maintain *exhibits.*
management. The act of organizing and controlling a project.
master plan. A comprehensive study that involves all aspects of an *institution.*

material. The substance used to make or construct things; also facts, notes, and *research* used in preparing an *exhibit design*.
meeting. A group of people assembled for a specific purpose.
migration. Movement of one or more elements from one place to another.
minutes. An official record of what was discussed during a *meeting*.
mission. A statement that addresses the overall purpose of an *exhibition* and defines the basic reasons for its existence.
mockup. A scaled or full-size, many times rough, reproduction of a design or part of a design used for study purposes. It does not have to be an exact representation of the item.
model. A three-dimensional, scaled representation of an *object* or a group of objects.
modify. To make a slight change.
mood. A state of mind that a person or a group of people experience at a particular time.
museum. A building open to the public with a mandate to collect, safeguard, store, and display *objects* of educational value.
museum quality. The highest construction quality possible.
object. A three-dimensional *form*.
objective. See *aim*.
offgas. The release of a toxic or noxious gas from a *material* into an indoor or confined space, such as a room or a display case, under normal conditions of *temperature* and pressure.
orientation. An adjustment or adaptation to a new environment or situation; the position or direction in which something lies.
orientation panel. Familiarizes the *visitor* with the *layout* of the *exhibition*; locates washrooms, exits, and so forth; and lists special events that will occur.
originality. The ability to think creatively and to present new ideas.
outgas. The gas that is emitted from an *object* into the environment or an outdoor space under normal conditions of *temperature* and pressure.
panel. A flat, usually rectangular, piece of *material* that is applied to or is part of an *exhibit structure*; a flat piece of material between two posts.
pattern. A regular or repetitive surface treatment or design.
perception. The process of using the senses to become aware of or to understand the surrounding environment or situation.
period. An interval of time taking place between two events.
phase. A particular stage of development.
physically challenged. A person who is unable to use or has difficulty using a particular body part including the eyes and the brain.
physiology. The science that addresses the body and relates to its mechanical, physical, and biochemical activities.

pivotal. A vitally important element that could determine the outcome, progress, or success of a project.

plan. A scaled *drawing* or a *diagram* that shows *layout,* arrangement, or *structure;* a method of doing something.

plan/design. The process that conceives and produces *displays, exhibits,* and *exhibitions.*

post-opening phase. The *period* between an *exhibition*'s opening and its closing.

preliminary phase. The *exhibit design period* where the selected schematic design is developed and advanced.

program. A plan of action for doing and achieving something, usually in the form of a written *document.*

project manager. A person who oversees, organizes, and is responsible for the work involved in a project or a segment of a project.

project manual. A *document* that contains all the written information required for a contractor to bid on a project; it is part of the *bid package.*

proportion. The relative *size* of an *object* or a *space* within the context of its composition.

proposal. An offer or bid to do a certain project in a prescribed manner; usually a written *document.*

prototype. A *mockup* of an item containing one or more systems that can be operated and tested.

provide. The act of purchasing, fabricating, delivering, and installing *exhibit materials,* structures, and equipment.

psychology. The science that deals with mental emotion and behavior as it applies to an individual or group of people.

punch list. A list of items that need to be completed or repaired; this list is compiled at the end of the *exhibition installation phase.*

purpose. See *aim.*

reflect. The ability of an *object* to redirect the *light,* energy, and so on, that strikes a surface.

relative humidity. A measure of the amount of water vapor in the air, at a specific *temperature,* compared to the maximum amount of water vapor that the air could hold at the same *temperature.*

replica. An exact copy or reproduction of an item, usually on a smaller *scale.*

request. A *document* asking for information.

research. A scholarly and methodical investigation of a subject; the act of locating and documenting images and items.

rhythm. A regular *pattern* or beat of sounds, words, *objects,* forms, *shapes,* or *colors.*

rod. A receptor or cell in the retina of the eye that interprets forms, *shapes,* and *textures;* it is responsible for our seeing white, gray, and black.

sans serif. Without *serifs*.
saturation. The degree or ability to *absorb*.
scale. The *proportion* used to represent the *size* or *intensity* of an item or *structure*; comparison of an *object* with one that is perceived to be of average size; also a measuring device.
schematic phase. The first *period* in the planning/designing of a project. Several *exhibit design* schemes are usually produced in this *phase*.
scriptwriter. A person who *researches* and writes *exhibit text*.
section. A subdivision, component, or part.
serif. A small decorative *line* added to the basic form of a letter.
shape. A flat, two-dimensional item having length and height.
shipping. The act of transporting something.
shop drawings. *Documents* prepared by a contractor showing exactly how an item will be built.
site. A location; an area, building, or plot of land where something is located.
size. The physical *dimensions* or *proportions* of an *object* or a *space*. When referring to an object's proportion and *scale* this can also be a comparative term.
sketch. A hastily executed *drawing* that lacks details.
source. Something or someone who supplies information or *materials*; one who creates a piece of artistic work.
space. A blank or empty two- or three-dimensional area.
specialist. One who is extremely knowledgeable in a particular branch of study.
specification. A detailed written *description* of a *material*, product, or process.
structure. A three-dimensional *object* that is made up of parts; the whole or a segment of a *display*, *exhibit*, or building. A system or organization made up of interrelated parts that function as a unit.
substrate. A solid base *material* on which another material or substance is adhered to its surface.
summative evaluation. The wrap-up *evaluation* performed after the *exhibit* has been installed. Also know as outcome evaluation.
survey. *Document* or action resulting from a careful *inspection* of a group of items or the measurement of an area.
symbol. Something that stands for or represents something else.
system. A combination of related elements organized to form a complex entity; a kit containing the pieces needed to assemble a *display*.
team. A group of people organized to work together.
technical drawings. Two-dimensional *drawings* that represent the *exhibit* areas and structures.
temperature. The hotness or coldness of an item measured on a particular *scale*.

terminology. Specific words related to a specialized activity or field of work.
text. A body of printed or written words.
texture. The feel and appearance of a surface.
theme. A distinct, recurring, unifying quality or idea.
title panel. Displays the title of the *exhibition*.
trendy. Relating to or exemplifying the latest fad or fashion.
tutorial. A brief instruction or lecture concerning a special topic that is given by a knowledgeable person.
typeface. A particular design or style of type. Same as the word "face."
typography. The arrangement and appearance of type.
unfinished. A product that will be completed after installation.
venue. The place where an *exhibition* or event is held.
viewing angle. The maximum angle that allows the *visitor* to view a *display* with acceptable visual performance.
visitor. A person who visits a place for a relatively brief time.
visual. Generic term used to represent a photograph or flat art; an item intended to be seen; the manner in which one conceptualizes something; pertaining to the sense of sight; a person's ability to see.
voice. The writing style that usually takes on the mantle of a person who "speaks" directly to the reader.
volume. A book; a collection of written or printed sheets bound together; a *space* or *shape* devoid of *objects*.
wavelength. The distance between one peak of a *light wave* and the next corresponding peak.
word spacing. Space between words.
work plan. A list containing each task involved in a project.
work schedule. A plan that includes the time involved in starting and completing each task listed in a *work plan*.
x-height. The height of a lowercase x, u, v, w, or z; also referred to as letter height.

Resources

Business

Orselli, Paul, ed. *RFP Issue, Exhibitionist* 26, no. 1 (Spring 2007): 8–90.

Color and Light

Albers, Josef. *Interaction of Color*. New Haven, CT: Yale University Press, 2009.

Birren, Faber. *Principles of Color: A Review of Past Traditions and Modern Theories of Color Harmony*. West Chester, PA: Schiffer, 1987.

Botta, Mario. *Light and Gravity: Architecture 1993–2003*. New York: Prestel, 2004.

Butterfield, Jan. *The Art of Light + Space*. New York: Abbeville, 1993.

Itten, Johannes, and Faber Birren, eds. *The Elements of Color*. New York: Van Nostrand Reinhold, 1970.

Keller, Max. *Light Fantastic: The Art and Design of Stage Lighting*. Munich: Prestel Verlag, 1999.

"Lighting, Lighting, Lighting." *Exhibit Builder Magazine*, September/October 2005, 12–33.

Conservation

Shelley, Marjorie. *The Care and Handling of Art Objects: Practices in the Metropolitan Museum of Art*. 3rd rev. ed. New York: Metropolitan Museum of Art, 1992.

Story, Keith O. "Approaches to Pest Management in Museums." Smithsonian Institution, 1998. http://www.si.edu/.

Thomson, Garry. *The Museum Environment*. 2nd ed. Oxford, UK: Butterworth-Heinemann, 1997.

Drawing Techniques

Ching, Frank D. K. *Architectural Graphics*. 5th ed. Hoboken, NJ: Wiley, 2009.
Oliver, Robert S. *The Complete Sketch*. New York: Van Nostrand Reinhold, 1989.
Spencer, Henry Cecil, and John Thomas Dygdon. *Basic Technical Drawings*. 2nd ed. New York: Macmillan, 1968. Reprint (8th ed.), New York: McGraw-Hill, 2004.

Ergonomics

American Association of Museums. *The Accessible Museum: Model Programs of Accessibility for Disabled and Older People*. Washington, DC: Author, 1992.
Axel, Elizabeth Salzhauer. *Art beyond Sight: A Resource Guide to Art, Creativity, and Visual Impairment*. New York: American Foundation for the Blind Press, 2002.
Majewski, Janice. *Part of Your General Public Is Disabled: A Handbook for Guides in Museums, Zoos, and Historic Houses*. 2nd ed. Washington, DC: Smithsonian Institution, 1993.
Sartwell, Marcia, ed. and interviewer. *The Accessible Museum: Model Programs of Accessibility for Disabled and Older People*. Washington, DC: American Association for Museums, 1992.
Ziebarth, Elizabeth K., and Zahava D. Doering. *Accessible Exhibitions: Testing the Reality*. Washington, DC: Smithsonian Institution, 1993.
———. *Equal Access: Smithsonian Publications and Events*. Washington, DC: Smithsonian Institution, 1994.

Evaluation

Hudec, Heather. "A Critical Step in Creating Effective Museum Exhibits." Master's thesis, 2004. http://mps.uchicago.edu/docs/2005/articles/hudec_thesis_short.pdf.
Taylor, Sam. *Try It! Improving Exhibits through Formative Evaluation*. Washington, DC: Association of Science Technology Center, 1991.

Exhibit Planning/Designing

Alexander, Edwards P. *Museums in Motion: An Introduction to the History and Function of Museums*. Nashville: American Association for State and Local History, 1979.
Bedno, Jane, ed. *The Senses* issue. *Exhibitionist* 23, no. 1 (Spring 2004): 5–33.
———. *Technology* issue. *Exhibitionist* 22, no. 2 (Fall 2003): 4–30.
Belcher, Michael. *Exhibitions in Museums*. Washington, DC: Smithsonian Institution, 1991.

Bevlin, Marjorie Elliott. *Design through Discovery*. 3rd ed. New York: Holt, Rinehart and Winston, 1977.

Bloom, Joel N., Earl A. Powell III, Ellen Cochran Hicks, and Mary Ellen Munley. *Museums for a New Century: A Report of the Commission on Museums for a New Century*. Washington, DC: American Alliance of Museums, 1984.

Exhibitionist. Semiannual journal. National Association for Museum Exhibition, Washington, DC.

Hall, Margaret. *On Display: A Design Grammar for Museum Exhibitions*. London: Lund Humphries, 1987.

Kennedy, Jeff. *User Friendly: Hands-On Exhibits That Work*. Washington, DC: Association of Science-Technology Centers, 1994.

Klein, Larry. *Exhibit: Planning and Design*. New York: Madison Square Press, 1986.

Lord, Barry, and Gail Dexter Lord, eds. *The Manual of Museum Exhibitions*. Walnut Creek, CA: AltaMira, 2002.

———, eds. *Planning Our Museums: National Museums of Canada*. Ottawa, Canada: Museums Assistance Programme, National Museums of Canada, 1983.

McLean, Kathleen. *Planning for People in Museum Exhibitions*. Ann Arbor, MI: Association of Science-Technology Centers, 1993.

Miles, R. S., M. B. Alt, D. C. Gosling, B. N. Lewis, and A. F. Tout. *The Design of Education Exhibits*. 2nd ed. London: Taylor and Francis, 1988.

Neal, Arminta. *Exhibits for the Small Museum: A Handbook*. Lanham, MD: AltaMira, 1996.

Simon, Neil. *Museum 2.0* (blog). http://museumtwo.blogspot.com/.

———. *The Participatory Museum*. Santa Cruz, CA: Museum 2.0, 2010.

Velarde, Giles. *Designing Exhibitions: The Principals and Process of Contemporary Show Space Design*. New York: Watson-Guptill, 1988.

Graphics and Typography

Hurlbut, Allen. *The Grid: A Modular System for the Design and Production of Newspapers, Magazines, and Books*. New York: Van Nostrand Reinhold, 1978.

———. *Layout: The Design of the Printed Page*. New York: Watson-Guptill, 1978.

Serrell, Beverly. *Exhibit Labels: An Interpretive Approach*. Walnut Creek, CA: AltaMira, 1996.

Spencer, Herbert, and Linda Reynolds. *Directional Signing and Labelling in Libraries and Museums: A Review of Current Theory and Practice*. London: Graphic Information Research Unit Royal College of Art, 1982.

Tufte, Edward Rolf. *The Visual Display of Quantitative Information*. Cheshire, CT: Graphic Press, 2001.

White, Jan V. *Graphic Design for the Electronic Age: The Manual for Traditional and Desktop Publishing*. New York: Watson-Guptill, 1988.

———. *Mastering Graphics: Design and Production Made Easy*. New York: R. R. Bowker, 1983.

Green Materials and Practices

Belew, Greg, Kathy Gustafson-Hilton, Sharon Handy, and Lyn Wood. "Splinters from Green Materials: Conversations About the Frictions of Green Exhibition Design." *Exhibitionist* 29, no. 1 (Spring 2010): 56–64.

Brophy, Sarah S., and Elizabeth Wylie. *The Green Museum: A Primer on Environmental Practice*. Lanham, MD: AltaMira, 2008.

Shapiro, Stephanie. "A Greener Tomorrow: Museum Take Steps toward Sustainability." *Museum* 91, no 4 (July–August 2012): 36–43.

Materials and Construction Techniques

Architectural Woodwork Institute (AWI). *Architectural Woodwork Standards*. Potomac Falls, VA: Author, AWMAC, and WI, 2009.

Bowman, Daria Price. *Presentations: Proven Techniques for Creating Presentations that Get Results*. Holbrook, MA: Adams Media, 1998.

Engler, Nick. *Woodworking Wisdom: The Ultimate Guide to Cabinetry and Furniture Making*. Emmaus, PA: Rodale, 1997.

Forest Products Laboratory. *Wood Engineering Handbook*. 2nd ed. Englewood Cliffs, NJ: Prentice Hall, 1990.

Hoadley, R. Bruce. *Understanding Wood: A Craftsman's Guide to Wood Technology*. Newtown, CT: Taunton, 2000.

Hosker, Jan. *Complete Woodfinishing*. Lewes, UK: Guild of Master Craftsman Publications, 1995.

Kirby, Ian J., and John Kelsey. *Mastering Woodworking: Making Joints; Techniques, Tips, and Problem-Solving Tricks*. Emmaus, PA: Rodale, 1996.

Self, Charles. *Woodworker's Guide to Selecting and Milling Wood*. Cincinnati: Betterway Books, 1994.

Relevant Publications

Aimone, Steven. *Design: A Lively Guide to Design Basics for Artists and Craftspeople*. New York: Sterling, 2004.

Clifton-Mogg, Caroline, and Piers Feetham. *Displaying Pictures and Photographs*. New York: Crown, 1988.

Cumming, Robert. *Annotated Art: The World's Greatest Paintings Explored and Explained*. New York: Dorling Kindersley, 1995.

Ellison, Nancy. *In Grand Style: The Glory of the Metropolitan Opera*. New York: Rizzoli, 2008.

Hanks, Kurt, Larry Belliston, and Dave Edwards. *Design Yourself!* Los Altos, CA: William Kaufmann, 1977.

Gombrich, E. H. *Shadows: The Depiction of Cast Shadows in Western Art*. London: National Gallery, 1995.

Lewis, Robert H. *Manual for Museums*. Honolulu: University Press of the Pacific, 2005.
MacGregor, Neil. *A History of the World in 100 Objects*. New York: Penguin, 2011.
Schwarzer, Marjorie. *Riches, Rivals, and Radicals: One Hundred Years of Museums in America*. Washington, DC: American Association of Museums, 1976.
Seckel, Al. *Masters of Deception: Escher, Dali, and the Artists of Optical Illusion*. New York: Sterling, 2004.
Sherman, Daniel J., and Irit Rogoff. *Museum Culture: Histories, Discourses, Spectacles*. Minneapolis: University of Minnesota Press, 1995.
Ultimate Visual Dictionary. London: Dorling Kindersley, 2011.

Visitors

Loomis, Ross J. *Museum Visitor Evaluation: New Tool for Management*. Nashville: American Association for State and Local History, 1987.
Screven, C. G., and Harris H. Shettel, eds. *ILVS Review: A Journal of Visitor Behavior*. Semiannual publication. International Laboratory for Visitors Studies, Milwaukee, 1988–1990.
Wilkening, Susie C. G., and James Chung. *Life Stages of the Museum Visitor: Building Engagements over a Lifetime*. Washington, DC: American Alliances of Museums, 2009.

Index

About the Author

Elizabeth Bogle is an exhibit planner/designer. She has been vice president of a museum exhibit construction firm and museum director of another. She was also an account executive for the largest exhibit construction firm in Paris and art director for the Consortium Oil Companies in Tehran. In 1971, she founded Limn Studios, a museum exhibition planning/design firm, and designed projects in the United States, Canada, and elsewhere abroad.

During the course of her extensive professional career, Bogle has been responsible for all phases of museum exhibit work from its concept to its installation. She has conducted research and selected artifacts, designed and laid out exhibits and graphics, prepared technical drawings and bidding documents, produced and checked shop drawings, purchased construction materials, and estimated and supervised construction of projects.

Bogle graduated from the University of the Arts in Philadelphia with a degree in industrial design and later returned to that institution as an adjunct associate professor in its graduate studies program. She taught "Museum Exhibition Planning and Design" for ten years and "Construction Materials and Fabrication Techniques" for several years.

For the Thomas Alva Edison Visitor Center, Bogle received an award from Print Casebooks 5 as "The Best in Exhibition Design," where the jurors responded to the "exhibit's simplicity and its careful, harmonious blend of color and texture." She also received a grant from the National Endowment for the Arts to conduct research to write a book on "Museum Exhibition Planning and Designing." She has published numerous articles in professional magazines.